学术英语写作技巧

刘进平 编著

中国林业出版社

内容简介

本书内容共分十单元。第一单元主要论述英语最具特色的造句技巧；第二单元主要论述不同句型及其修辞效果；第三单元主要论述在措词和句法上掌握简洁与清晰风格的技巧；第四单元主要论述强调修辞的句法技巧；第五单元概述段落展开方式及保持衔接与连贯的技巧；第六单元详细介绍各类过渡词的用法和句例；第七单元介绍最常用的学术英语修辞方法；第八单元介绍学术英语最易误用的标点符号的使用规范；第九单元介绍容易出错的句子；第十单元介绍英语科技论文的写作技巧。本书既可供研究生学术英语写作教学使用，也可供相关学者进行学术英语写作时参考。

图书在版编目(CIP)数据

学术英语写作技巧/刘进平编著. —北京：中国林业出版社，2021.5
ISBN 978-7-5219-0958-6

Ⅰ. ①学… Ⅱ. ①刘… Ⅲ. ①英语-写作-高等学校-教材 Ⅳ. ①H315

中国版本图书馆 CIP 数据核字(2020)第 259766 号

中国林业出版社教育分社

策划编辑： 高兴荣　范立鹏
责任编辑： 高兴荣　范立鹏
电　　话： (010)83143611

出版发行	中国林业出版社(100009　北京市西城区德内大街刘海胡同 7 号) E-mail：jiaocaipublic@163.com　电话：(010)83143500 http：//www.forestry.gov.cn/lycb.html
经　销	新华书店
印　刷	河北京平诚乾印刷有限公司
版　次	2021 年 5 月第 1 版
印　次	2021 年 5 月第 1 次印刷
开　本	787mm×1092mm　1/16
印　张	19.5
字　数	350 千字
定　价	48.00 元

未经许可，不得以任何方式复制或抄袭本书之部分或全部内容。

版权所有　侵权必究

前　言

英语在当今学术界交流作用举足轻重，通过英语写作论文和专著实现知识共享已成趋势。孔子曰："言之无文，行而不远"，也就是说，如果表达、写作不讲究文采修辞，就不能流传很远。因此，为了更好地交流学术成果，领会并掌握学术英语写作技巧就很有必要了。

本书试图从句法角度论述学术英语的写作技巧，具有以下几方面的特点：第一，句法是学术英语写作的核心，而中国人在学术英语写作时遇到的最大困难在于造句。因此，在兼顾词汇、段落和篇章的情况下，本书以句法的解读、梳理为重心，全面论述学术英语的写作技巧；第二，本书文理科均可适用。书中所指学术，既包含自然科学，也包含社会科学和人文历史。为了方便不同学科的读者使用，本书选取例句尽可能来自不同学科的论文和著作，尽可能配有名家或专家的精典译文（没有译文的例句由我翻译，供读者参考）。因此，读者不仅可学习例句的写作技巧，还可体会例句的翻译方法；第三，写作不仅是英语使用的一个主要方面，也是学习英语的一条重要途径。在听、说、读、写、译五种能力培养方面，写作也是重要一项。从写作的角度学习英语，能让读者从一个特别的视角领会英语的魅力，提升对英语学术作品的阅读和欣赏能力。本书假定读者已具备一定的英语语法基础，因此，重点是让读者体会各种句法技巧，而不进行详细的语法分析。

句法对于写作的重要性，怎么强调都不过分。作者下笔可供驱使的句法越多，行文就越自如，就越能收获良好的修辞效果；相反，如果作者腹笥中缺少句法或不讲究句法，文章就会显得单调、乏味，达不到良好的修辞效果，有时没有适当的句法，甚至根本无法达意。句法这么重要，但是传授句法却没有传授章法那么容易。

一般而言，写作始于模仿。所以本书中尽可能提供丰富的例句，使读者能够了解和把握对英语句法的基础上，通过体会和模仿掌握学术英语的造句技巧。另外需要指出的是，国内虽然引进出版了不少国外的权威学术英语写作论著，但是这些论著论述的重点多在偏重如何使句子清晰和简明方面，对于英语句子的基本造句技巧涉及得较少。另外，结合中国学生英语写作的重点和难点——如何排除汉语的干扰，构造地道的英语句子，因此，本书可以说是专门针对中国学生的薄弱环节进行考量，打造最适合培养中国学生学术英语写作能力的教材。

本书的出版受到海南大学教学名师工作室项目(hdms202012)和海南大学世界一流学科建设经费项目资助，另外，本书引用的句例绝大多数出自本书所列的参考文献与进一步阅读文献中，在此一并表示感谢。

本书既可作为本科生与研究生学术英语写作教材使用，也可供相关学者进行学术英语写作时参考。由于编者水平有限，编写时间紧迫，不足和错误之处在所难免，读者如有反馈和建议，请通过电子邮件(liu3305602@163.com)进行交流。

刘进平
2020 年 1 月

目 录

前 言

第一单元　造句技巧 …………………………………………………… 1

　一、定语从句 ……………………………………………………… 3
　　（一）定语从句分类和语法 …………………………………… 3
　　（二）限制性定语从句 ………………………………………… 4
　　（三）非限制性定语从句 ……………………………………… 8
　二、分词结构 ……………………………………………………… 16
　　（一）现在分词结构 …………………………………………… 16
　　（二）过去分词结构 …………………………………………… 25
　　（三）分词形式的独立主格结构 ……………………………… 28
　三、同位语结构 …………………………………………………… 30
　四、形容词结构 …………………………………………………… 33
　五、介词结构 ……………………………………………………… 34
　六、动词不定式 …………………………………………………… 45
　七、造句原则 ……………………………………………………… 46
　　（一）长句和复杂句造句原则 ………………………………… 46
　　（二）造句"尾重原则" ………………………………………… 48
　　（三）平衡与对称原则 ………………………………………… 51
　　（四）英语思维造句原则 ……………………………………… 54

第二单元　句型变化 …………………………………………………… 59

　一、长句与短句 …………………………………………………… 60
　二、松散句和尾重句 ……………………………………………… 62
　三、主动句与被动句 ……………………………………………… 66
　四、对称句与平行句 ……………………………………………… 71

第三单元　简洁清晰 …… 83
一、简洁 …… 84
(一)讲究措词 …… 84
(二)经营句法 …… 86
二、清晰 …… 97
(一)引导性成分不要太长，或直接以主语开头 …… 97
(二)避免主谓或谓宾之间插入成分 …… 102
(三)由旧信息向新信息顺序流动 …… 105
(四)避免抽象名词或较长的名词结构作主语 …… 107
(五)句首铺设主体架构 …… 113

第四单元　注重强调 …… 119
一、句尾是首选强调位置 …… 120
二、句首是重要强调位置 …… 129
(一)状语成分置于句首 …… 129
(二)从句中要强调的成分置于句首 …… 130
(三)实质信息置于句首 …… 131
三、标点符号突出强调 …… 132
四、通过重复加以强调 …… 133
五、通过拆句加以强调 …… 134
六、专门的强调句型 …… 135
(一)It is + 要强调的成分 + that/who/when/where 等引导的定语从句 …… 135
(二)not…, but / rather…句型 …… 139
(三)比较级结构与否定式比较级结构 …… 143

第五单元　衔接与连贯 …… 145
一、段落展开 …… 146
二、句子衔接统摄全局 …… 149
(一)使用连环结构 …… 149
(二)重复关键词 …… 152
(三)使用过渡词 …… 153

第六单元　过渡词用法 …… 159

一、相似关系

  (一)similarly ·········· 160
  (二)likewise ·········· 161
  (三)as ·········· 161

二、增补或递进关系

  (一)furthermore ·········· 163
  (二)moreover ·········· 164
  (三)besides ·········· 165
  (四)also, so, nor ·········· 166
  (五)in addition, in addition to ·········· 168

三、例证关系

  (一)for example, for instance, to illustrate ·········· 169
  (二)such as ·········· 170
  (三)like ·········· 171
  (四)including ·········· 171
  (五)namely ·········· 172

四、强调关系

  (一)in fact ·········· 172
  (二)indeed ·········· 172
  (三)certainly ·········· 173
  (四)of course ·········· 174
  (五)surely ·········· 174
  (六)especially ·········· 175
  (七)in particular ·········· 175

五、重复关系

  (一)or ·········· 176
  (二)in other words ·········· 176
  (三)put another way, to put it the other way round ·········· 177
  (四)that is, that is to say, i.e. ·········· 177
  (五)namely ·········· 178

六、转折或对比关系 ·········· 179

(一) however/but ·· 179
(二) although, though ·· 185
(三) whereas, while ·· 187
(四) by / in contrast, on the contrary ································· 190
(五) on the other hand ·· 191
(六) despite, in spite of ··· 192
(七) yet ·· 194
(八) conversely ·· 195
(九) rather, rather than ·· 195
(十) instead, instead of ·· 196
(十一) nevertheless ··· 197
(十二) otherwise ··· 198
(十三) even if, even though ··· 198
(十四) save, except, but that ··· 199
(十五) apart from ·· 200
(十六) far from ·· 201

七、时间关系 ·· 201
(一) when, while, as, meanwhile ······································· 201
(二) before, after, until, since ·· 203

八、顺序关系 ·· 204

九、目的关系 ·· 205
(一) so that, in order that ·· 205
(二) for this purpose ··· 206

十、结果关系 ·· 206
(一) therefore, thereby, thus, hence ·································· 206
(二) consequently, accordingly, so ···································· 210
(三) as a result, as a consequence ··································· 212
(四) then ··· 213

十一、原因关系 ·· 213
(一) because, as, since, for, insofar as ····························· 213
(二) because of, owing to, due to, on account of, thanks to ·········· 217

十二、结论关系 ………………………………………… 219
第七单元　常用的修辞 ………………………………………… 223
　　一、比喻 …………………………………………………… 224
　　　　(一)明喻 ……………………………………………… 224
　　　　(二)暗喻 ……………………………………………… 226
　　二、类比 …………………………………………………… 227
　　三、定义 …………………………………………………… 229
　　四、推理 …………………………………………………… 231
第八单元　标点的使用 ………………………………………… 237
　　一、逗号的用法 …………………………………………… 238
　　　　(一)引导性成分 ……………………………………… 238
　　　　(二)插入语和修饰成分 ……………………………… 242
　　　　(三)两个独立分句的连接 …………………………… 246
　　　　(四)排比成分 ………………………………………… 247
　　　　(五)句子中任何需要停顿的地方 …………………… 249
　　二、分号的用法 …………………………………………… 251
　　三、冒号的使用 …………………………………………… 252
　　四、破折号的使用 ………………………………………… 256
第九单元　易错的句子 ………………………………………… 263
　　一、单复数问题 …………………………………………… 264
　　　　(一)谓语动词的单复数与定语从句动词的单复数 … 264
　　　　(二)非 and 连接的名词或名词结构作主语 ………… 265
　　二、垂悬修饰语问题 ……………………………………… 269
　　三、平行结构错误 ………………………………………… 277
第十单元　论文的写法 ………………………………………… 283
　　一、论文选题与设计 ……………………………………… 284
　　二、论文构思 ……………………………………………… 285
　　三、论文写作 ……………………………………………… 286
　　　　(一)标题 ……………………………………………… 287
　　　　(二)摘要 ……………………………………………… 288
　　　　(三)前言 ……………………………………………… 288

(四)材料与方法 ……………………………………………………… 289
(五)结果 …………………………………………………………… 290
(六)讨论 …………………………………………………………… 291
(七)参考文献 ……………………………………………………… 292
四、论文修改与写作水平的提高 …………………………………… 293

参考文献 ……………………………………………………………… 295

第一单元

造句技巧

英语句子从语法结构上来讲，通常可分为简单句、并列句（或并列复合句）和复合句（或主从复合句）。简单句通常是指只有一个主语或几个并列主语及一个谓语动词或几个并列谓语的句子。并列句通常是指由并列连词（and, but, or 等）或分号把两个或两个以上的简单句连在一起而构成的句子。复合句即主从复合句，通常是指含有两个或更多主谓结构的句子，但以一个句子为主体（即主句），其他句子充当主句的成分（即从句），从句基本上可以分名词性从句、形容词性从句、副词性从句三类，而根据修饰的成分，从句又可作为定语从句、状语从句、主语从句和宾语从句等。复合句的从句中还可再嵌套下一级从句，形成多级或多层次的复合句。

与汉语相比，英语句法上最大的特点是其定语从句。中国近代启蒙思想家、翻译家，被康有为称赞为"精通西学第一人"的严复，在《天演论·译例言》中写道："西文句中名物字，多随举随释，如中文之旁支，后乃遥接前文，足意成句。故西文句法，少者二三字，多者数十百言。"学者沈国威评论道："严复认为中英两种语言在句子层面最显著的差别是从句，特别是定语从句（《英文汉诂》，1904 年）。对名物加以各种限定、修饰是西方科学著作的特点，而汉语的特点是句子短小，没有很长、很复杂的定语成分。"

实际上，除了定语从句外，具有相同的功能还有非谓语动词形式（现在分词或过去分词）、同位语结构、形容词结构、介词结构、不定式结构等。从结构上讲，英语句子往往在一个主谓结构或主谓宾结构或者（复合句中的）主句框架下，勾连各种从句和结构，形成一个复杂的树状或网状结构。造句时，通常将解释性的、补充性的事实信息或可以忽略的信息置于定语从句中，或者置于各种功能类似的结构中，而不是另起一个完整的句子。学术英语常将从句压缩为现在分词结构、过去分词结构、同位语结构、介词结构、不定式结构或形容词结构，使得句子结构紧凑、表达简练、随意灵活。

从学习造句角度而言，简单句、并列句是比较容易的；即使在复合句中，除定语从句之外的其他类型复合句也是相对容易的。这是因为其结构与现代汉语表达类似。例如：

例 1-1 <u>Whether or not fibrous proteins permeate the nucleus to create an equivalent structure to the cytoskeleton</u> has been controversial.（复合句，划线部分为主语从句）

译 纤维蛋白是否渗入细胞核以形成与细胞骨架同等的结构一直是有争

议的。

例 1-2 Energy is released from ATP <u>when the phosphate bonds are hydrolysed</u>. (复合句，划线部分为状语从句)

🔤 当磷酸键被水解时，ATP 释放能量。

因此，本单元主要介绍英语中功能强大的定语从句、现在分词结构、过去分词结构、同位语结构、形容词结构、介词结构、不定式结构。其功能强大除表现在修饰和限制作用外，还起到补充说明、交代细节和伴随状况、分层叙述等作用。这些结构能表达原因、结果、目的、条件、让步和转折等逻辑关系和语义内容。读者如能熟练掌握此类造句技巧，写作地道的英语就不是一件难事了。

一、定语从句

(一)定语从句分类和语法

定语从句也称关系从句或形容词性从句，就是位于名词或代词后，对其进行修饰或限定的句子，也就是具有定语功能的句子。与汉语的前置定语(位于所修饰的先行词或中心词之前)不同，英语中较复杂的修饰语通常采用后置的(位于所修饰的先行词或中心词之后)定语从句表示。定语从句结构通常为"先行词+关系词+从句"，关系词有 which, that, whose, whom, who, why, when, where 等。此外，定语从句内部还可以再包含或嵌套另一个定语从句，理论上可以向右无限扩展。

定语从句可分为限制性定语从句和非限制性定语从句两类。前者对所修饰的先行词意义起限定作用，这类从句不能省略，否则会使句意模糊不清或产生歧义；后者对先行词或前面的句意进行补充说明，可以省略非限制性定语从句，且并不影响先行词的所指意义。

限制性定语从句示例如下：

例 1-3 The difficulties <u>which we all have as intelligent amateurs in following modern literature and music and painting</u> are not unimportant.

🔤 我们作为现代文学、音乐、绘画的业余爱好者，大家都有悟性，而碰到的困难并非无关紧要。(杨自伍译)

非限制性定语从句示例如下：

例 1-4 The concept of citizenship of the Union was introduced in the Maastricht Treaty, <u>which provided that all nationals of the member states are also citi-</u>

zens of the Union.

[译]《马斯特里赫特条约》首次提出了欧盟公民权利的概念，规定所有成员国的公民同时即欧盟的公民。(戴炳然译)

从上述两例我们可看到，限制性定语从句与前面的修饰词之间无逗号隔开，从句不能省略，否则会影响句意，而非限制性定语从句与前面的修饰词或句子之间有逗号隔开，从句省略不影响句意。

另外，用限制性从句与非限制性从句表示会在句中产生不同的意义。如陶博(Preston M. Torbert)著、罗国强(Steel Rometius)编《法律英语：中英双语法律文书中的句法歧义》中有如下两个例句：

例 1-5 A whole new approach to water law had to be developed in the Western states that could not support agriculture without irrigation.

[译] 西部那些没有灌溉就无法支持农业的州必须制定一套全新的水(资源)法。

用限制性从句表示西部那些没有灌溉就无法支持农业的州，这意味着只是一部分西部的州，西部还存在不需要灌溉就能进行农业生产的州。

例 1-6 A whole new approach to water law had to be developed in the Western states, which could not support agriculture without irrigation.

[译] 西部所有州没有灌溉就无法支持农业，因此各州必须制定一套全新的水(资源)法。

非限制性从句表示西部所有州没有灌溉就无法发展农业。

限制性定语从句的引导词最常用的是 which/that, 当先行词为不定代词，如 all, each, some 等，或被序数词、形容词 only, no, very 或别的形容词最高级修饰的先行词，其定语从句的引导词只用 that 而不用 which. 非限制性定语从句最常用的引导词是 which. 如果先行词为人或人性化的事物，引导词可用 who/whom/whose/that. 此外，非限制性定语从句还可由 as 引导。

如果先行词在定语从句中作及物动词的宾语时，可省略先行词或关系词。如果先行词在从句中作介词的宾语，那么可在从句的引导词 which 前面加介词；关系副词 when/where/why 作先行词，相当于“介词+ which”结构，可互换使用。但这种情况在 way, reason, direction, distance, amount, time, number of times (units)后面的定语从句可省去“介词+ which”结构，或者用 that 引导。

(二)限制性定语从句

例 1-7 For instance, Freud does not consider the social context in which the failure of memory takes place, nor the possibility that names may be originally registered with different degrees of intensity according to circumstances.

译 例如，弗洛伊德没有考虑失掉记忆的社会情境，也没有考虑在最初记忆名字的时候，就有因情境不同而可能导致记忆强度的不同。（尹莉译）

例 1-8 Once we cease to feel that we must either prostrate ourselves before them or denigrate them, we are free to discover religions as repositories of a myriad ingenious concepts with which we can try to assuage a few of the most persistent and unattended ills of secular life.

译 一旦我们不再感到需要非此即彼地做出选择，即要么在宗教面前五体投地，要么对宗教进行诽谤诋毁，我们便能自由地发现，宗教实乃无数天才概念的宝库，借此或可舒缓世俗生活中某些最源远流长却又未予以有效关注的病苦。（梅俊杰译）

例 1-9 On the contrary, its diversity was the quality which Romantic artists and writers prized most highly as the expression of their individuality, and which has defeated every attempt to define it.

译 相反，它的多样化正是浪漫主义艺术家和作家最最珍视的品质，认为这是他们的个别性的表现，是无法一言以蔽之的。（董乐山译）

例 1-10 Focusing on work to the exclusion of almost everything else is a plausible enough strategy in a world which accepts workplace achievements as the main tokens with which we can secure not just the financial means to survive physically, but also the attention that we require to thrive psychologically. （梅俊杰译）

译 在这个世界，既然大家都把职场成功当作头号标记，借此不仅谋得安身立命的经济资源，而且赢得令自己心花怒放的羡慕目光，那么，埋首专注于职场工作，对其他一切都不闻不问，便是一条貌似充分合理的策略。

例 1-11 God may be dead, but the urgent issues which impelled us to make him up still stir and demand resolutions which do not go away when we have been nudged to perceive some scientific inaccuracies in the tale of the seven loaves and fishes.

译 上帝或许已死，然而，曾经促使我们祭起上帝的那些迫切问题依然困扰着我们，仍在要求我们拿出示解方案。哪怕经人提示后我们知道，耶稣拿五个饼两条鱼让众人饱餐的故事在科学上并不准确，但那些需要解决的问题还是挥之不去。（梅俊杰译）

例 1-12 One major organelle is the nucleus which contains DNA.

[译] 细胞的一个主要细胞器是含有 DNA 的细胞核。

例 1-13 The flow is controlled by nucleoporin proteins which project into the channel, sorting and propelling the various molecules in the correct direction.

[译] 这种流动是由核孔蛋白控制的，核孔蛋白在通道中突出，对流动方向正确的不同分子进行分检与推动。

例 1-14 Besides its role in protein synthesis, the ER is a versatile organelle which can both receive and transmit signals and act as a cellular store for calcium, and is also responsible for the synthesis of lipids.

[译] 除了在蛋白质合成中的作用外，内质网还是一种多功能的细胞器，既能接收和传输信号，又能作为钙的细胞储存处，还负责脂质合成。

例 1-15 Obesity is consequently a disorder of energy balance that results from the continued accumulation of lipid droplets within the adipocytes.

[译] 因此，肥胖是一种能量平衡紊乱，是脂肪细胞内脂质滴持续积聚的结果。

例 1-16 Because our skin is warm and moist, it provides an attractive surface that is constantly colonized by bacteria and fungi.

[译] 因为我们的皮肤温暖、湿润，它为细菌和真菌不断繁殖生长提供了一个有吸引力的表面。

例 1-17 The new mRNA is then tagged with proteins that will target it to a nuclear pore prior to passage into the cytoplasm, where it will combine with a ribosome to form the machinery for making a new protein.

[译] 然后新 mRNA 被蛋白质标记，使其靶向核孔，新 mRNA 进入细胞质后，在那里与核糖体结合，形成制造新蛋白质的机器。

例 1-18 Continental philosophy is a highly eclectic and disparate series of intellectual currents that could hardly be said to amount to a unified tradition.

[译] 欧陆哲学在很大程度上是一种兼收并蓄、互不关联的思想潮流，很难把它们说成是一个统一的传统。(江怡译)

例 1-19 Each protein cargo is 'tagged' by an amino acid sequence that acts like a luggage label to ensure that they finish on the correct side of the nuclear membrane.

[译] 每一种蛋白货物都被一个氨基酸序列(像一个行李标签)"标记"，以确

保它们最终到达核膜的正确一侧。

例 1-20　Enclosing the genetic blueprint of the cell within its own compartment has fostered the diversity we see in both unicellular and multicellular eukaryotic creatures.

译　把细胞的遗传蓝图封闭在它自己的小室内，形成了我们在单细胞和多细胞真核生物中看到的多样性。

例 1-21　Roosevelt, as a public personality, was a spontaneous, optimistic, pleasure-loving ruler who dismayed his assistants by the gay and apparently heedless abandon with which he seemed to delight in pursuing two or more totally incompatible policies, and astonished them even more by the swiftness and ease with which he managed to throw off the cares of office during the darkest and most dangerous moments.

译　罗斯福，作为社会名流来看，是一个率真、乐观、爱好快乐的统治者，他使得自己的助手们心神不安，因为他戏笑恣意大而化之，似乎喜欢推行两种或更多种完全不相容的政策，他使助手们更为惊讶的是，在最黑暗最危险的时刻，他敏捷轻松地设法抛开公务的烦恼。（杨自伍译）

例 1-22　Richard Rorty is one of the few English-speaking philosophers who has consistently and heroically attempted to blur the distinction between analytic and Continental philosophy by working with a foot in both camps.

译　理查德·罗蒂是少数几个这样用英文写作的哲学家之一，他们英勇无畏，坚持致力于消除分析哲学与欧陆哲学之间的差别，做法就是涉足于两个阵营当中。（江怡译）

例 1-23　The same explorers and traders who had returned to Europe with tales of the behaviour of primitive people also brought back descriptions and sometimes suitably preserved specimens of many exotic plants and animals.

译　探险队和贸易商带回了现代人在原始状态下的生活行为方式的种种故事，同时也带回了对许多植物和动物的描述以及一些保存良好的动植物标本。（冯兴元译）

例 1-24　And those English scientists who do not simply accept the *status quo* are frequently Communists, which means that, however intellectually scrupulous they may be in their own line of work, they are ready to be uncritical and even dishonest of certain subjects. (前者为限制性定语从句，后者为非限制性定

语从句)

[译] 那些不愿简单接受现状的英国科学家常常是社会主义者，也就是说，尽管在自己的工作中他们保持了理智上的谨慎，但在某些事情上他们是可以不加批判甚至于不尽诚实的。(吴简清译)

例 1-25 One is more likely to recall the name of a new acquaintance with whom one has spent an evening than that of a person to whom one has been briefly introduced at a party.

[译] 一个人更可能回忆起与之度过整晚的某位新交的人的名字，而不是那位在聚会上被简单介绍认识的人的名字。(尹莉译)

例 1-26 If I were to attempt to write down the names of all the poets and novelists for whose work I am really grateful because I know that if I had not read them my life would be poor, the list would take up pages.

[译] 我真是非常感激某些诗人和小说家的作品，因为要是我没有读过他们的作品，我的生活就要贫乏得多。不过，假如我要把他们的名字都写下来的话，那得写好多页纸。(朱树飏译)

例 1-27 Some proteins may need to pass through one or two membrane barriers before reaching the site where they fulfil their function.

[译] 一些蛋白质可能需要通过一层或两层膜屏障，才能到达发挥功能的部位。

(三)非限制性定语从句

例 1-28 His response is that when science becomes our passion, then there is a fragmentation and specialization of the various areas of knowledge, which leads to an atrophy of the metaphysical ground of scientific activity.

[译] 他对此的回应是，当科学成为我们的爱好，那么，各种知识领域就会有分化和专业化的过程，这些会导致科学活动的形而上学基础的衰落。(江怡译)

例 1-29 *The Appeal* was in part couched as an answer to James Mill's *Essay on Government*, well known at the time, which argued that women need no political rights as they are adequately represented by their fathers or husbands.

[译]《控诉》部分是为了回应詹姆斯·穆勒的《论政府》一书。该书当时非常有名，认为女人不需要政治权利，因为她们的父亲或丈夫足以代表她们。(朱刚和麻晓蓉译)

例 1-30　In 1869, John Stuart Mill published *The Subjection of Women*, which also argued that the subordination of women was both wrong and 'one of the chief hindrances to human improvement'.

译　1869 年，约翰·斯图尔特·穆勒出版了《论女性的从属地位》，书中也认为奴役女人是错误的，是"人类进步的主要障碍之一"。（朱刚和麻晓蓉译）

例 1-31　Such compensation usually has implications for the Community budget and looks like a zero-sum game, which can lead to conflict between those who pay and those who receive, even if the package of compensation and competition, taken together, benefits both parties.

译　这种补偿通常会对共同体预算产生影响，即便补偿与竞争综合起来对双方都有利，但看起来总像零和博弈，造成付出者与接受者之间的冲突。（戴炳然译）

例 1-32　Philosophy was an eminently practical activity, which is markedly different from the overwhelmingly theoretical enquiry it has become since the 17th century.

译　哲学最初就是一种实践活动，明显不同于 17 世纪之后占主导地位的理论探索。（江怡译）

例 1-33　The scientific conception of the world, which dates back to the early decades of the 17th century in England and France, dominates the way we see things and, perhaps even more importantly, the way we expect to see things.

译　这种科学的世界观可以追溯到 17 世纪早期的英国和法国，它支配着我们看待事物的方式，或许更为重要的是，支配着我们期望看待事物的方式。（江怡译）

例 1-34　So, all logical propositions are reducible to either tautologies or contradictions, which are either necessarily true or necessarily false, but all such propositions are verifiable and therefore meaningful.

译　所以，所有的逻辑命题都可以还原为重言式或矛盾式，它们或者必然为真，或者必然为假，但所有这些命题都是可以得到证实的，因而都是有意义的。（江怡译）

例 1-35　It stems to a degree from the American system of government, which, unlike the parliamentary structure in most of Europe, separates executive and legislative authority in order to prevent a single individual or group from wielding excessive power. (颜元叔译)

🔵译 它似乎可以以言代法溯源到某个程度的美国政府体制，而美国政府体制与欧洲大多数国家中的国会结构不同，是为了防止某一个人或单个团体行使过大的权力而将行政与立法权限分开。

例 1-36 What he means by this must be understood with reference to the deflationary effects of the Kantian critique of traditional metaphysics outlined above, which not only denied human beings cognitive access to the speculative objects of classical metaphysics (God, the soul), but also removes the possibility of knowing both things-in-themselves and what Kant described as the 'noumenal' ground of the self, having no phenomenal presence.

🔵译 要理解他这种说法的意义，就必须联系上述康德对于传统形而上学的批判的泄气效果，它不仅否定了人类可以认识到古典形而上学的思辨对象(上帝，灵魂)，而且消除了认识自在之物和康德所描述的自我之"本体"基础，即没有现象呈现的可能性。(江怡译)

例 1-37 The story of Fichte's dismissal is a rather seedy and sorry affair, which bears some comparison with Bertrand Russell's own atheist conflict in New York in 1940, where he was prevented from taking up his position at City College, New York on the basis of a campaign of character assassination waged against him for his professed atheism and liberal views on sexual morals.

🔵译 费希特被免职是一件相当令人不快和惋惜的事情，与伯特兰·罗素本人1940年在纽约遭遇的无神论冲突有相似之处，当时他由于宣传无神论和开明的性道德观点招致针对他的人格诋毁运动，因此被阻止担任纽约城市大学的教职。(江怡译)

例 1-38 The mother role is universally carried out by women, which is biologically based.

🔵译 母亲的职责普遍地由妇女付诸实施，这从生物学角度来看是有根据的。(谭卫国译)

例 1-39 Tinnitus is often triggered by exposure to loud noise, which destroys cells in the inner ear that transmit sound signals to the brain.

🔵译 耳鸣通常是由于暴露在巨大的噪声下而引起的，噪声会破坏内耳中传递声音信号给大脑的细胞。

例 1-40 Soon after he began donating, doctors discovered that he had the rare antibody that could prevent Rhesus disease, which is caused by an incompatibility between the mother and baby's blood types.

❸ 译 在他开始献血后不久，医生发现他有一种罕见的抗体可以预防由于母亲和婴儿的血型不相容造成的溶血性疾病。

例 1-41　The Hunt found a set of proteins called cyclins, which accumulate during specific stages of the cell cycle.

❸ 译 亨特发现了一组称为细胞周期蛋白的蛋白质，这些蛋白质在细胞周期的特定阶段积累。

例 1-42　In plants this is called the epidermal layer, which secretes a waxy coating or cuticle that helps the plant retain water.

❸ 译 在植物中，这被称为表皮层，它分泌一层蜡质涂层或角质层，帮助植物保持水分。

例 1-43　Blood is formed from a collection of various cell types, which are continuously produced from a small number of stem cells.

❸ 译 血液是由各种细胞类型的集合形成的，这些细胞类型是由少量干细胞不间断地产生的。

例 1-44　The is due to the intense packaging and fibrous nature of the nuclear contents, which make it virtually impossible to follow a length of chromatin over any distance in the thin sections required for transmission electron microscopy.

❸ 译 这是由于细胞核内容物具有的高强度包装和纤维性质，因而几乎不可能在透射电子显微镜所需的薄切片中跟踪染色质的纵长。

例 1-45　Most daughter cells are identical, and will have identical fates, which is to differentiate to perform a particular function, eventually die, and be replaced.

❸ 译 大多数子细胞是相同的，并且具有相同的命运，它们将会分化以执行特定的功能，最终死亡并被替换。

例 1-46　The first division separates one of each pair of chromosomes to two new daughter cells, which then divide directly producing four gametes which now have half the original DNA complement (haploid).

❸ 译 第一次分裂将每对染色体中的一条分裂成两个新的子细胞，然后直接分裂产生四个配子，现在这四个配子有一半的原始 DNA 补体（单倍体）。

例 1-47　All cells are enclosed by a boundary structure, the plasma membrane, which provides a barrier to other cells and the external environment.

🔵 所有的细胞都被一个边界结构(即质膜)所包围,它为其他细胞和外部环境提供了屏障。

例 1-48　The major internal membrane system in eukaryotic cells is the endoplasmic reticulum, which forms a network throughout the entire cell.

🔵 真核细胞的主要内膜系统是内质网,它在整个细胞中形成一个网络。

例 1-49　Both the nuclear membrane and the lamina below it are pierced by nuclear pore complexes, which control the flow of everything into and out of the nucleus, apart from very small molecules which can pass directly through the nuclear envelope.

🔵 核膜及其下面的薄层都被核孔复合物穿透,除能直接穿过核膜的非常小的分子以外,核孔复合物控制着所有物质进出细胞核。

例 1-50　Amid the coding sequences (exons) there are intervening non-coding sequences (introns), which need to be removed before use.

🔵 在编码序列(外显子)之间插入有非编码序列(内含子),使用前需要去除内含子。

例 1-51　These may be the remains of information accumulated over an evolutionary lifetime, which may be silent for millions of years, but can be reactivated and actively transcribed.

🔵 这些可能是在进化过程中累积信息的残留,它们可能沉默了数百万年,但可以重新被激活和主动转录。

例 1-52　Once in the cytoplasm, ribosomes bind to messenger RNA, which then acts as a template for the linking together of amino acids into proteins, a process called translation.

🔵 一旦进入细胞质,核糖体便与信使RNA结合,信使RNA随后作为氨基酸连接形成蛋白质的模板,这一过程称为翻译。

例 1-53　The first change occurs in the mitochondrial inner membrane, which becomes damaged by aberrant biochemical activity, leading to the formation of pores in the mitochondrial membrane.

🔵 变化首先发生在线粒体内膜,线粒体内膜因异常的生物化学活动而受损,导致线粒体膜上形成孔洞。

例 1-54　Labeling takes the form of short sequences of amino acids, known as topogenic signals, which then attach to receptor proteins to allow them through membrane barriers to reach the correct destination.

🔄 标记采用短序列氨基酸的形式，这种短序列氨基酸（称为拓扑信号）随后附着在受体蛋白上，使其通过膜屏障到达正确的目的地。

例 1-55 The actual passage through the pore requires attachment of 'chaperone' proteins called importins or exportins, which accompany the cargo through the pore but are then chopped off as the cargo exits the pore and reattached to more cargo.

🔄 通过核孔的实际通道，需要附着称为输入蛋白或输出蛋白的"伴侣"蛋白，这些蛋白质伴随货物通过核孔，但当货物通过核孔后就被切下来，重新附着到更多货物上。

例 1-56 Proteins called nesprins, which are anchored in the inner nuclear membrane, reach across the perinuclear space, pass through the outer nuclear membrane, and extend for some distance into the cytoplasm, where they attach to the cytoskeleton.

🔄 名为 nesprin 的蛋白质锚定在核内膜上，通过核周间隙，穿过核外膜，在细胞质中再前进一段距离，在那里附着在细胞骨架上。

例 1-57 There is another type of fat cell, termed brown fat cells, in which fat is broken down to generate heat by a process termed thermogenesis.

🔄 另一种类型的脂肪细胞称为棕色脂肪细胞，其中脂肪被分解产生热量，这一过程称为产热（作用）。

例 1-58 The next stage is anaphase, in which one chromatid from each chromosome is separated and moved to opposite ends of the mitotic spindle.

🔄 下一个阶段是后期，在这个阶段，每个染色体上的一个染色单体分开并移动到有丝分裂纺锤体的两端。

例 1-59 Having spent their short (but useful) life at the top of the villus, the enterocytes lose attachment to the basement membrane, at which point the detached cells get ejected by crowding of surrounding cells rather like grasping and squeezing a bar of soap until it shoots out of your hand.

🔄 在绒毛顶端度过短暂（但有用）的生命后，肠细胞失去了对基底膜的附着，此处分离的细胞会被周围细胞挤压而弹射出来，就像抓住并挤压一块肥皂，直到它从你的手中射出。

例 1-60 Nuclei are then rebuilt in each daughter cell, during which the rigid and rod-like chromosomes appear to lose their individual identity as they decondense and merge back into the overall structure of the daughter cell nuclei.

🔵译 然后在每个子细胞中重建细胞核，在此过程中，当被解聚并融合成子细胞核的整体结构中时，刚性的棒状染色体似乎失去了它们的独特外形。

例 1-61 Lord Russell was described by Joseph Goldstein, attorney for Mrs Jean Kay, who led the campaign against Russell, as 'lecherous, libidinous, lustful, venerous, erotomaniac, aphrodisiac, irreverent, narrow minded, untruthful, and bereft of moral fibre'.

🔵译 金凯太太领导了这场反对罗素的运动，她的律师约瑟夫·戈德茨坦把罗素描绘为"淫荡好色、贪婪纵欲、色情狂、傲慢狭隘、不诚实、道德伦丧"的人。（江怡译）

例 1-62 This prejudice has so subsumed the teaching of culture as to have more or less stamped out the ambitions of Mill and Arnold, as well as the magniloquent hopes of Rilke, who in the last line of his poem *Archaic Torso of Apollo* surmised that it was the ultimate wish of all great artists to admonish their audiences, '*Du must dein Lebren ändern*' ('You must change your life').

🔵译 如此这般的偏见早已浸透了文化教育，已使其基本上放弃了穆勒和阿诺德的宏大抱负，也毁灭了里尔克高调表述的希望。里尔克在诗篇《古老的阿波罗躯干雕像》的最后一行中推断，世上所有的伟大文艺家至高无上的希望就是告诫其受众："你必须改变自己的生活"。（梅俊杰译）

例 1-63 It becomes rather, in John Locke's formula at the beginning of *An Essay Concerning Human Understanding* in 1689, an under-labourer to science, whose job is to clear away the rubbish that lies in the way to knowledge and scientific progress.

🔵译 用约翰洛克1689年在《人类悟性论》开篇所说的话，它变成了科学的清道夫，其工作就是清除在知识和科学进程中的垃圾。（江怡译）

例 1-64 This recalls Nietzsche's definition of metaphysics, where the scientific conception of the world would recover the unity of experience enjoyed in mythic world-views.

🔵译 这让我们回想起尼采对形而上学的定义，即科学的世界观将会恢复神话的世界观中所得到的统一体验。（江怡译）

例 1-65　In 1784, Hamann wrote his *Metacritique of the Purism of Reason*, where he criticized Kant for formalism, namely for his overvaluation of the formal character of knowledge, and for the belief that reason could be separated from experience, the a priori could be divorced from the a posteriori.

❶译　哈曼在 1784 年的《理性纯粹主义的元批判》中批评了康德的形式主义，即他对知识的形式特征的过高评价，以及相信理性可以与经验相分离，先验的东西可以与后验的东西相分离。（江怡译）

例 1-66　Nihilism is the breakdown of the order of meaning, where all that was posited as a transcendent source of value in pre-Kantian metaphysics becomes null and void, where there are no cognitive skyhooks upon which to hang a meaning for life.

❶译　虚无主义就是意义次序的崩溃，一切在前康德形而上学中被作为价值超验来源的东西都变成了空无，不存在使生命意义得以依附的认识挂钩。（江怡译）

例 1-67　Proteins made on the ER enter the space (lumen) between the ER membranes, where they are folded into a final configuration before being passed on to other sites such as the Golgi bodies.

❶译　内质网上制造的蛋白质进入内质网膜之间的空间（空腔），在那里折叠成最终的构型，然后转移到别处（如高尔基体）。

例 1-68　The biggest problem with cancer is metastasis, where cells dissociate from the primary tumour, penetrate the surrounding tissue, and ultimately access the bloodstream, from which point they can generate secondary tumours virtually anywhere in the body.

❶译　癌症最大的问题是瘤转移，即细胞与原发肿瘤分离，穿透周围组织，最终进入血流，从而几乎可以在身体的任何地方产生继发肿瘤。

例 1-69　While skin provides a remarkably efficient watertight and mechanical barrier to the external environment, these parameters are exactly the opposite of the requirements of gut epithelium, where we need to optimize our uptake of nutrients, while at the same time inhibiting the uptake of anything potentially harmful.

❶译　虽然皮肤对外部环境提供了一个非常有效的防水和机械屏障，但这些参数与肠道上皮的要求正好相反，后者需要优化摄取营养物质，同时抑制摄取任何潜在的有害物质。

例 1-70 The system can function brilliantly, as it did during the Watergate investigation of Richard Nixon.

[译] 这种体制可以发挥极好的效用，在尼克松水门事件调查时便是如此。(颜元叔译)

例 1-71 The reason these matters are important in a computerized age is that there may be a tendency to mistake data for wisdom, just as there has always been a tendency to confuse logic with values, and intelligence with insight.

[译] 这些事之所以在计算机化时代重要之原因在于：可能会有误把资料数据当作智慧的趋向，正如向来都把逻辑与价值混淆，把智能与洞察力混淆的趋向。(颜元叔译)

例 1-72 The product of the artist is more revelatory of his personality than is that of the technician, just as the quality of a people is peculiarly expressed in its culture rather than in its civilization.

[译] 艺术家做出来的成品比技术师的成品更能流露其个性，正如一个民族的特质是在其文化中而不是文明之中特别表现出来的。(颜元叔译)

例 1-73 In literature, vulgarity is preferable to nullity, just as grocer's port is preferable to distilled water.

[译] 凡文学作品，庸俗比空洞无物还是要好些，就好比杂货铺里的葡萄酒总比蒸馏水强。(朱树飏译)

二、分词结构

英语句子一般只能有一个谓语动词(动词并列结构除外)，其余的动词结构要采取分词的形式，也就是非谓语动词形式。分词结构分为现在分词结构和过去分词结构两种。现在分词结构表达主动语态或正在进行的含义，过去分词结构则表达被动语态或过去动作的含义。如果分词结构前面无主语，则其逻辑主语自然为句子的主语。英语句子中大量使用分词结构，不仅结构简练，而且用法灵活，位置多变(可在句首、句中和句尾)。汉语一般多短句和小句，英语则可用分词结构表达。分词可用作定语、状语、表语、补语等成分，这里主要介绍其作状语和定语的情况。分词结构作状语时，表达原因、目的、条件、结果或伴随状况；作定语时，对主语等成分的补充说明。分词结构可看作从句(如状语从句或定语从句)的省略形式。

(一)现在分词结构

例 1-74 Lock's *Second Treatise on Civil Government* provided the intellectual justification of the English Revolution of 1688, setting out a contractual view of government as a trust which can be revoked if it fails to provide for the security and liberty of the subject's person and property.

译 洛克的《再论公民政府》为1688年的英国革命作出理论性辩解，提出了一种契约式的见解，认为政府是一种信托，如果政府不能为其人民提供人身和财产的安全和自由的保障，这种信托就可以撤回。（董乐山译）

例 1-75 The original British concerns, reflecting the interests of consumers, of taxpayers, and of international trade partners that provide essential export markets, have turned out to be the interests of the majority of EU citizens too.

译 英国最初的关切反映了消费者、纳税人和提供必要出口市场的国际贸易伙伴的利益，现在也变成了欧盟大多数公民的利益。（戴炳然译）

例 1-76 The temptation of the educator is to explain and describe, to organize a body of knowledge for the student, leaving the student with nothing to do.

译 执教的人总是想替学生解释、描述、组织一套知识，让学生落得无事可做。（颜元叔译）

例 1-77 The result was the EEC's customs union, abolishing tariff and quota barriers to their mutual trade, and creating a common external tariff.

译 因此建立了欧洲共同体的关税同盟，从而废除了相互贸易的关税与配额壁垒，并确立了共同的对外关税。（戴炳然译）

例 1-78 Some federalists, finding this an insufficient safeguard against over-centralization, have proposed that the treaty should list competences reserved to member states.

译 有些联邦主义者觉得这还不足以防范过度的中央集权，建议条约应列出那些保留给成员国的权限。（戴炳然译）

例 1-79 The programme was to be empirical, based upon observation, shunning metaphysical speculation and restraining 'the intemperate desire of searching into causes'.

译 要做的工作是经验性质的，以观察为基础，避免做形而上学的推测，抑制"要追究原因的强烈愿望"。（董乐山译）

例 1-80 Unfair competition can also take the form of subsidies given by a member state government to a firm or sector (in the EU jargon 'state aids'), enabling it to undercut efficient competitors and undermine their viability.

译 不公平竞争的另一种形式是成员国政府向某个公司或某个行业发放补贴(欧盟术语为"国家援助"),用以削弱主要竞争者的实力,动摇他们的优势地位。(戴炳然译)

例 1-81 Attempting to prove the non-existence of God can be an entertaining activity for atheists. Tough-minded critics of religion have found much pleasure in laying bare the idiocy of believers in remorseless detail, <u>finishing only when they felt they had shown up their enemies as thorough-going simpletons or maniacs</u>.

译 对无神论而言,试图证明上帝并不存在会是件欣喜愉快之事。宗教的铁杆批评者非常乐于把信教者的愚蠢低能一点一滴、毫不留情地暴露在光天化日下,不把敌手彻底笨蛋、十足疯子的面目揭露个够,他们是不会善罢甘休的。(梅俊杰译)

例 1-82 A major objection to these indirect taxes was that they bear hard on the poorer states and citizens, <u>making them pay a higher proportion of incomes than the richer</u>.

译 反对提取这些间接税的一个重要理由是:它们给较贫困国家和公民带来了沉重的负担,使之比富国和富人要支付其收入的更高比重。(戴炳然译)

例 1-83 The Commission has proposed a carbon and energy tax to discourage damaging emissions of carbon dioxide (CO_2). But this was opposed by industrial sectors that use a lot of energy, <u>arguing that it would make them uncompetitive unless other industrialized countries too adopted the tax</u>.

译 委员会曾提议征收一项碳与能源税,以减少二氧化碳的有害排放。但这遭到使用大量能源的工业部门的反对——他们认为,除非其他的工业化国家也征收此税,否则会使他们失去竞争力。(戴炳然译)

例 1-84 These progenitor cells divide many thousands of times, <u>progressively undergoing a process of differentiation that changes biochemistry, shape, and size until, finally, a mature blood cell is produced</u>.

译 这些祖细胞分裂数千次,渐进地经过在生物化学、形状和大小方面改变的分化过程,直到最终产生成熟的血细胞。

例 1-85 The treaty sets very general objectives for the Common Foreign and Security Policy (CFSP), <u>ranging from international co-operation to support for democracy, the rule of law, and human rights</u>.

  译 条约为共同外交与安全政策确定了非常宽泛的目标，从国际合作到支持民主、法治和人权都有涉及。（戴炳然译）

  例 1-86 Corporations have instead chosen to set up shop along the base of this pyramid (Maslow's famous pyramid of needs), making minor improvements to services and products designed to help us to sleep, eat, be safe or move while leaving unaddressed our desire to self-actualize, learn, love and inwardly grow.

  译 公司相反执意沿着金字塔（马斯洛著名的"需求金字塔"）的底部建立门店，只对方便我们衣食住行的现有服务和产品作点小修小补，却不去理会我们要自我实现、要学习、要关爱、要修身养性的需求。（梅俊杰译）

  例 1-87 He precipitated the crisis of 'the empty chair', forbidding his ministers to attend meetings of the Council throughout the second half of 1965 and evoking fears among the other states that he might be preparing to destroy the Community.

  译 他决然挑起"空椅危机"，在 1965 年下半年禁止其部长出席理事会会议达半年之久，引起了其他成员国对他可能准备毁灭共同体的担忧。（戴炳然译）

  例 1-88 Many in France went beyond this, envisaging a Europe that could challenge American dominance in the field of defence.

  译 许多法国人则看得更远，构想着一个可以在防务领域挑战美国优势的欧洲。（戴炳然译）

  例 1-89 Overall, respiratory syncytial virus (RSV) was the biggest culprit, accounting for nearly one-third of all cases.

  译 总的来说，呼吸道合胞病毒（RSV）是罪魁祸首，占所有病例的近三分之一。

  例 1-90 Pneumonia kills nearly 1 million children every year, but the lung infection's precise cause is often hard to diagnose, forcing doctors to rely on antibiotics without knowing whether bacteria are to blame.

  译 每年有近 100 万儿童死于肺炎，但肺部感染的确切原因往往很难诊断，这迫使医生在不知道细菌是否是罪魁祸首的情况下依赖抗生素。

  例 1-91 A new easy-to-use standardized method makes it possible for almost anyone to calibrate these cameras without any specialized equipment, helping amateurs, science students and professional scientists to acquire useful data with any consumer camera.

    译 一种新的易于使用的标准化方法使得几乎任何人都可以在没有任何专用设备的情况下校准这些相机，帮助业余爱好者、理科学生和专业科学家使用任何消费级相机获取有用的数据

例 1-92   Relationships tend to be impersonal and a pronounced division of labor exists, <u>leading to the establishment of many specialized professions</u>.

    译 人际关系趋于非个性化，劳动分工十分明显，从而确立了许多专业。（谭卫国译）

例 1-93   The number of latex-producing plants is over 20,000 and encompasses phylogenetically unrelated groups, <u>representing a good example of convergent evolution in plants</u>.

    译 产乳胶植物的数量超过 20,000 种，包含相互之间系统发育上无关的群体，这是植物趋同进化的一个很好例子。

例 1-94   Each of these partial theories describes and predicts a certain limited class of observations, <u>neglecting the effects of other quantities, or representing them by simple sets of numbers</u>.

    译 每一局部理论只描述并预言一定范围的有限的观测，而忽略其他量的效应，或仅以简单的一组一组的数值代指它们。（谭卫国译）

例 1-95   The British, <u>having espoused free trade in the nineteenth century</u>, were accustomed to cheap food, with large imports from the USA and the Commonwealth and with subsidies paid to British farmers to keep their prices down to world levels.

    译 但从 19 世纪就倡导自由贸易的英国人则习惯于低价食品，他们从美国和英联邦国家大量进口农产品，并对英国农民支付补贴，以将其农产品的价格维持在低于世界的水平。（戴炳然译）

例 1-96   Governments, <u>looking over their shoulders at domestic public opinion</u>, are naturally reluctant to renounce their privileged positions.

    译 各国政府都得顾忌本国的公众舆论，因此自然不肯轻易放弃特权。（戴炳然译）

例 1-97   Some Western women, <u>having fought for women's right to take jobs outside the home, and struggled to achieve their own 'liberation' from domestic drudgery</u>, look for not-too-expensive help with domestic work.

译 曾经为了妇女外出工作权，为了把从繁重家务中"解放"出来而积极斗争过的一些西方妇女，现在寻找廉价的家务帮手来。（朱刚和麻晓蓉译）

例 1-98 Rejecting Descartes' assertion that human ideas were innate, Lock argued that they were derived from our sense impressions, either directly, or else by the reflection of the mind on the evidence provided by them.

译 洛克反对笛卡尔的人类思想是天生的说法，认为它们来自我们的感官印象，不论是直接的，还是大脑对这些印象所提供的证据的反射。（董乐山译）

例 1-99 Accepting that man's instinctive aim was to increase pleasure or happiness and avoid pain or misery, he argued that this was not limited to him.

译 他承认人的本能目标是增进快乐和幸福，避免痛苦和不幸，他认为这不仅限于自己。（董乐山译）

例 1-100 Culture, being the immediate expression of the human spirit, can advance only if that spirit is capable of finer efforts, has itself something more to express.

译 文化既是人类精神的直接表现，唯有在这种精神能有卓越精美的努力成果，有更多它自己要表达的东西时，才能有进步。（颜元叔译）

例 1-101 The Soviet Union refused to accord the Community legal recognition, seeing it as strengthening the 'capitalist camp'; and the Community refused to negotiate with Comecon, the economic organization dominated by the Soviet Union. (前者为现在分词结构，后者为同位语结构)

译 苏联拒绝在法律上承认共同体，认为它强化了"资本主义阵营"；共同体则拒绝与受苏联控制的经济互助委员会进行谈判。（戴炳然译）

例 1-102 Following 1989, and the dissolution of the Soviet bloc, the Central and East European countries turned towards the Community, which they saw as a bastion of prosperity and democracy. (前者为现在分词结构，后者为非限制性定语从句)

译 1989 年后，随着苏联集团的解体，中东欧国家转向共同体，将之看作繁荣与民主的堡垒。（戴炳然译）

例 1-103 Here accumulation of lipids leads to formation of fatty plaques, resulting in atherosclerosis (hardening of arteries), which limits blood flow and thus can lead to heart attacks and strokes.

译 在这里脂质的积累导致脂肪斑块的形成,发生动脉粥样硬化(动脉硬化),限制血液流动,从而导致心脏病发作和中风。

例 1-104 Cyclins then start to build up again, <u>keeping a score of the progress at each point of the cycle, and only allowing progression to the next stage if the correct cyclin level has been reached.</u>

译 然后,细胞周期蛋白又开始累积,在细胞周期的每一个时间点上保持某种水平的累积,且细胞周期蛋白只有在达到正确的水平时才允许细胞周期进行到下一个阶段。

例 1-105 <u>Having spent their short (but useful) life at the top of the villus,</u> the enterocytes lose attachment to the basement membrane, at which point the detached cells get ejected by crowding of surrounding cells rather like grasping and squeezing a bar of soap until it shoots out of your hand.

译 在绒毛顶端度过短暂(但有用)的生命后,肠细胞失去了对基底膜的附着,此处分离的细胞会被周围细胞弹射出来,就像抓住并挤压一块肥皂,直到它从你的手中射出。

例 1-106 This demonstrates that the shape of cells follows the laws of physics, <u>ensuring the maximum surface coverage for the minimum use of material for each squame.</u>

译 这表明,细胞的形状遵循物理定律,确保单位面积内材料使用最少而表面覆盖最大。

例 1-107 Connective tissue is characterized by large amounts of extracellular matrix secreted by well-separated cells, <u>providing skeletal tissues such as bone, cartilage, tendons and ligaments that make up the structural framework of the body.</u>

译 结缔组织的特点是包含大量细胞外基质,它们由分离良好的细胞所分泌,提供诸如骨、软骨、肌腱和韧带等组织,构成身体结构框架。

例 1-108 Insects are different, <u>producing an exoskeleton made up of layers of chitin, a dense horny waterproof substance providing a protective cover which doubles up as their skeleton.</u>

译 昆虫有所不同,它产生由几丁质层构成的外骨骼——这是一种致密的角质防水物质,既作为一种保护性的覆盖物,又兼有骨骼的作用。

例 1-109 Several of these 'cell death' genes were those genes that were routinely mutated in many mammalian cancer cells, confirming that apoptosis was a mechanism to delete cells with damaged DNA.

🔵 译 若干"细胞死亡"基因是许多哺乳动物癌细胞中经常发生突变的基因，这证实了细胞凋亡是一种 DNA 受损细胞的去除机制。

例 1-110 Mutations in the cell death genes blocked apoptosis, allowing cells with damaged or mutated DNA to develop abnormally and generate tumours.

🔵 译 细胞死亡基因的突变阻止细胞凋亡，使 DNA 受损或突变的细胞异常发育并产生肿瘤。

例 1-111 Thus, the nuclear lamina protects the nuclear contents from mechanical stress, and also anchors the position of the nucleus in the cell, providing sites for attachment to the cytoskeleton in the cytoplasm.

🔵 译 因此，核膜层不仅保护核内容物不受机械应力的影响，也把细胞核固定在细胞中的某个位置，为细胞质中的细胞骨架提供附着部位。

例 1-112 They (peroxisomes) are important in the breakdown (oxidation) of substances such as fats, providing a major source of metabolic energy in animal, yeast, and plant cells.

🔵 译 它们(过氧化物酶体)在诸如脂肪等物质的分解(氧化过程)中很重要，为动物、酵母和植物细胞提供主要的代谢能量来源。

例 1-113 The job of ribosomes is to make (synthesize) proteins from amino acids, holding and joining the amino acids to make peptides, then polypeptides and complete proteins.

🔵 译 核糖体的作用是用氨基酸合成蛋白质，即将氨基酸固定并连接起来形成肽，然后形成多肽和完整的蛋白质。

例 1-114 However, the main barrier to the medical use of genomes is that diseases such as cancer, diabetes, or Alzheimer's are invariably caused by many DNA variations, making it difficult to identify clear targets for either drug intervention or diagnostic indicators, and consequently limiting the idea of personalized medicine based on an individual genome-at least for the time being.

🔵 译 然而，医学上使用基因组的主要障碍是诸如癌症、糖尿病或阿尔茨海默病等疾病总是由许多 DNA 变异引起，这使得很难确定药物干预或诊断指标的明确靶标，从而限制了基于个体基因组的个性化药物概念的落实，至少目前如此。

例 1-115　Lysosomes can also fuse with phagocytic vacuoles (phagocytes) containing engulfed material such as bacteria, <u>killing and digesting the invading organisms</u>.

译　溶酶体也可以与包含被吞噬物质（如细菌）的吞噬泡（吞噬细胞）融合，杀死和消化入侵的生物体。

例 1-116　Inside the nucleus, the sequence of nucleotide bases forming the code for a particular protein is first copied from the template DNA in the process called transcription, <u>producing a new molecule of messenger RNA (mRNA)</u>.

译　在细胞核内，首先从模板 DNA 复制编码形成特定蛋白质的核苷酸碱基序列，这个过程称为转录，产生一个新的信使 RNA(mRNA) 分子。

例 1-117　Messenger RNA then passes out of the nucleus, <u>undergoing modification (called splicing) along the way</u>.

译　信使 RNA 然后从细胞核中出来，在这一过程中进行修饰（称为剪接）。

例 1-118　Mitochondria are closely associated with the sites of lipid production, <u>providing the energy for fat formation</u>.

译　线粒体与脂质产生部位密切相关，为脂肪形成提供能量。

例 1-119　Protein misfolding is very detrimental, <u>leading to disorders such as cystic fibrosis and diabetes</u>.

译　蛋白质错误折叠是非常有害的，会导致囊性纤维化和糖尿病等疾病。

例 1-120　Excess consumption of alcohol can cause changes in the way that the liver breaks down and stores fats, <u>leading to more severe conditions such as cirrhosis</u>.

译　过量饮酒会改变肝脏分解和储存脂肪的方式，导致更严重的疾病，如肝硬化。

例 1-121　The genes themselves are complex structures, <u>having a starting code (promoter) built into the beginning of each gene and an exit code (terminator) at the end</u>.

译　基因本身是复杂的结构，在每个基因的开头都有一个启动码（启动子），在结尾有一个退出码（终止子）。

例 1-122　The longevity of bone is due to the deposition of minerals such as calcium phosphate into the bone matrix by cells called osteoblasts, <u>creating the structural rigidity</u>.

译 骨的持久性是由于矿物质(如磷酸钙)被成骨细胞沉积到骨基质中,形成结构刚性。

例 1-123 In primary biliary cirrhosis, proteins (autoimmune antibodies) are produced that attack nucleoporins, eventually leading to complete cirrhosis of the liver.

译 在原发性胆汁性肝硬化中,产生的蛋白质(自免疫抗体)攻击核孔蛋白,最终导致完全肝硬化。

例 1-124 Centrosomes act as a microtubule organizing centre, controlling the turnover and distribution of microtubules.

译 中心体作为微管组织中心,控制微管的周转和分布。

例 1-125 It is a short technical step from growing cells in plastic flasks to providing a suitable environment, allowing the flask to be placed on a microscope stage for living cells to be observed as they go about their business.

译 在塑料瓶中从培养细胞到提供合适的环境,这是一个不长的技术步骤,但却可以将塑料瓶放在显微镜台上,观察正在进行生命活动的活细胞。

例 1-126 The nuclear envelope separates the nuclear contents from the cytoplasm, also controlling a constant and massive molecular interchange between the two compartments.

译 核膜将核内容物从细胞质中分离出来,也控制着两个小室之间的分子交换。

例 1-127 Mitochondria were first isolated biochemically and analysed by Alfred Lehninger in 1949, confirming the presence of the enzymes required for energy generation by oxidative phosphorylation, a highly efficient process in which nutrients are oxidized to produce adenosine triphosphate (ATP). (前者为现在分词结构,后者为同位词结构)

译 1949 年,阿尔弗雷德·莱宁格首次利用生物化学方法分离出线粒体,并对其进行了分析,证实了其中存在通过氧化磷酸化产生能量所需的酶。氧化磷酸化是一种将营养物质氧化以产生三磷酸腺苷(ATP)的高效过程。

(二)过去分词结构

例 1-128 The average reader, initially puzzled by the undeniable eccentricties in Faulkner's style, and then infuriated by the apparent perversity in his ways of telling a story, very largely ignored him during the years when he was doing his best work.

🔤 一般读者，开始被福克纳写作风格中不可否认的怪癖性困惑，接着又被他说故事的显然偏颇方式惹得发火，大都在他创作出最佳作品的数年间对他忽视不理。（颜元叔译）

例 1-129　Some feminists, particularly in America, <u>disappointed by the failure to ensure passage of the *Equal Right Amendment* and by threats to welfare and abortion rights</u>, seized on this issue as a symbol of woman's second-class status and her vulnerability.

🔤 一些女权主义者，尤其是美国女权主义者，由于推动《平等权利修正案》未获通过，要求福利和堕胎权又遭到威胁，失望之余便抓住男性暴力这个问题不放，认为这是女性二等公民地位和脆弱无助的象征。（朱刚和麻晓蓉译）

例 1-130　That gloomy remark, <u>made to me the other day by a prominent U. S. State Department official</u>, dramatizes the frustrations currently nagging senior members of the Ford Administration as they wage a losing fight against efforts by Congress to play a larger role in foreign policy.

🔤 这是几天前一位美国国务院要员对我说的丧气话，生动地描绘出福特政府高级人员的挫折感，当他们面对国会争取外交决策的更大角色而发动无胜算之战的时候。（颜元叔译）

例 1-131　The rhetoric <u>generated by this dispute</u> has attained bitter and sometimes unprintable proportions.

🔤 这次争论引发的言辞已经达到刻薄而有时候是不宜付印发表的程度。（颜元叔译）

例 1-132　Hume is one of the most attractive figures in the history of philosophy, <u>loved and esteemed by his friends</u>, <u>combining benevolence with one of the most acute and skeptical minds of the century</u>（过去名词结构），<u>without a trace of that Angst which Existentialists and other modern philosophers have associated with doubt</u>.（介词结构）

🔤 休谟是哲学史上最有吸引力的人物之一，受到他朋友的敬爱和尊重。他把仁人之心同本世纪最敏锐和最赋怀疑气质的头脑结合起来，而丝毫没有存在主义者和其他现代哲学家与怀疑联系在一起的焦虑。（董乐山译）

例 1-133　Workers <u>continuously exposed to cold conditions</u>, such as deep sea divers, appear to accumulate much higher than normal amounts of brown fat deposits, indicating that brown fat can be regenerated in adults. (前者为过去分词结构，后者为现在分词结构)

㊎ 持续暴露在寒冷条件下的工人，如深海潜水员，似乎积累的棕色脂肪远远高于正常水平，这表明棕色脂肪可以在成人身上再生。

例 1-134 The most inclusive category, the equivalent of 'Vehicles' in our example, is the kingdom, followed by the phylum, class, order, family, genus (过名词结构), with the species being the smallest, least inclusive, formal category. (介词结构)

㊎ 相当于"车辆"级别的是"界"，下面依次为"门""纲""目""科""属""种"；"种"是最小的、最不具包容性的正式分类单位。（冯兴无译）

例 1-135 Philosophy is an under-labourer to science, solely concerned with the logical clarification of the propositions and method of empirical science.

㊎ 哲学是一种从属于科学的工作，它唯一关注的是对命题的逻辑澄清和经验科学的方法。（江怡译）

例 1-136 So as the European economies developed, the EEC's original project, centred on abolition of tariffs in a customs union, was succeeded in the 1980s by the single market programme, then in the 1990s by the single currency.

㊎ 因此，随着欧洲经济的发展，欧洲经济共同体以废除关税为核心的最初的关税同盟计划，在20世纪80年代被单一市场计划所取代，并进而在90年代被单一货币计划所取代。（戴炳然译）

例 1-137 Determined to keep its border controls, Britain opted out of the Amsterdam Treaty's provisions on freedom of movement; and Ireland, enjoying open frontiers with the UK, had to do the same. （前者为过去分词结构，后者为现在分词结构）

㊎ 英国决心保持其边境控制，选择不参加《阿姆斯特丹条约》关于人员流动的规定；与英国开放边境的爱尔兰，也不得不如此。（戴炳然译）

例 1-138 These centrioles occur in pairs, positioned at right angles to each other.

㊎ 这些中心粒成对出现，彼此成直角排列。

例 1-139 The molecular interactions between kinesin and microtubules have been determined by resolving molecular detail in the electron microscope, helped by technology that permits instantaneous freezing of the cell, retaining molecular arrangements exactly as they were in life.

🔵译 借助于使细胞瞬间冷冻及保持与活体中完全相同的分子排列技术，通过电子显微镜解析分子细节，已确定驱动蛋白和微管之间的分子相互作用。

例 1-140　The mitotic spindle is formed from cytoplasmic microtubules, <u>organized by a pair of centrioles which have previously replicated and migrated to either end of the cell</u>.

🔵译 有丝分裂纺锤体由细胞质微管形成，微管由一对此前已复制并迁移到细胞两端的中心粒组织组成。

例 1-141　<u>Based on its treaty obligation to ensure that 'the law is observed'</u>, in judgments in 1963 and 1964 the Court established the principles of the primacy and the direct effect of the Community law, so that it would be consistently applied in all the member states.

🔵译 基于其负有条约规定的保障"法律得到遵守"的义务，法院通过1963年和1964年的裁决，确立了共同体法优先与直接有效的原则，从而使之能始终如一地在所有成员国中得到贯彻。（戴炳然译）

例 1-142　Reconstructions of past configurations of the continents, <u>largely based on palaeomagnetics and detailed stratigraphy</u>, indicate that at the time of their origin all the continents were lying clustered together in a single gigantic landmass, known as Pangaea ('all Earth').

🔵译 主要依据古地磁和详细的地层学研究而对过去各大陆形态所进行的重建显示，在所有大陆起源的时候，它们都聚集在一起，是一个单一的巨大陆块，称为泛古陆（"整个地球"）。（史立群译）

例 1-143　Though without the means of enforcement proper to a state, respect for the law, <u>based on the treaties and on legislation enacted by its institutions</u>, provided cement that has bound the Community together.

🔵译 尽管缺乏对国家主体的严格意义上的强制手段，但建立在条约和共同体机构立法之上的对法律的尊重成为一种黏合剂，将共同体紧密地联结在一起。（戴炳然译）

（三）分词形式的独立主格结构

值得注意的是，上述分词结构要与分词形式的独立主格结构（absolute construction 或 nominative absolute）相区别。分词结构的逻辑主语通常为句子中的修饰词或中心词（通常句子主语也作分词结构的主语），或者是前面的句子部分；而分词形式的独立主格结构则是自带有自己主语的状语修饰短语（称其为短语，是因为其无法独立成句），分词前面的名词不是句子中的主语、宾语或同位语的一部分，因而独立主格结构是一种松散或游离的结构。独立主格结构功能上相当于状语从句，修饰句子中的其他部分或句中的某个动词，表示时间、原因、条件、伴随状况或动作条件等，例如：

例 1-144 Two days having elapsed, we again set forward.

[译] 两天过去了，我们又出发了

例 1-145 The pipe having a small cross-section, the water flow per second will be small.

[译] 如果管的横截面积很小，那么每秒钟的水流量也很小。（范武邱译）

例 1-146 Death from accidental poisoning has increased almost threefold in the past 30 years, women being more likely than men to die in this way.

[译] 在过去的 30 年里，意外中毒引起的死亡几乎增加了 3 倍，这样死亡的妇女可能比男性要多。（洪班信译）

例 1-147 The nuclear envelope consists of two distinct membranes, the outmost being formed by endoplasmic reticulum, which is separated from the inner nuclear membrane by a perinuclear space.

[译] 核膜由两层不同的膜组成，最外层由内质网形成，核周间隙将内质网与核内膜分开。

例 1-148 The independence of a central bank being a new experience for all except the Germans, the question of the ECB's accountability has also been raised.

[译] 由于应对中央银行的独立性对德国以外的所有其他国家都是前所未有的经历，于是出现了欧洲央行所负之责的问题。（戴炳然译）

例 1-149 Interphase chromosomes occupy about half of the internal nuclear space, the rest being filled by a host of other nuclear components, such as nucleoli and Cajal bodies.

[译] 间期染色体占据了细胞核内部空间的一半左右，其余的空间由许多其他核成分如核仁和卡哈尔体填充。

例 1-150 All things considered, the ultrasonic wave is the best choice for cleaning the cracks.

[译] 如果通盘考虑，运用超声波是清洁缝隙的最佳选择。（范武邱译）

例 1-151 Radioactivity discovered, we made great progress in medicine.

🔵 放射性被发现后,我们在医学方面取得很大进展。(洪班信译)

此外,独立主格结构可以是"with 或 without+名词+分词"的复合独立主格结构(参照第五节介词结构部分)。独立主格结构也可以是名词后面带不定式的独立主格结构,例如:

例 1-152 An important lecture to be given tomorrow, the professor has to stay up late into the night.

🔵 因为明天要发表一个重要的演讲,教授不得不熬夜到很晚。

三、同位语结构

英语句子中,往往在一个名词后面紧跟一个同位语结构,对前面的名词进行解释、说明和补充。这个同位语可以是一个名词词组,也可以是名词后面跟一个定语从句或名词从句。

例 1-153 Femininity, as we know it, is romantic nonsense, something that has to be carefully contrived and preserved.

🔵 正如我们所知,女子气质是浪漫的胡编乱造,是经过精心谋划刻意保持下来的东西。(朱刚和麻晓蓉译)

例 1-154 As we are all acutely aware, we live in a scientific world, a world where we are expected to provide empirical evidence for our claims or find those claims rightly rejected.

🔵 我们深刻地意识到,我们生活在一个科学的世界中,在这个世界中我们需要对我们的说法提供实践经验的证明,或者恰当地驳斥那些说法。(江怡译)

例 1-155 This goes against everything we know about what is means to read a book in real life, life, that is to say, which is uncorrupted by educational purpose.

🔵 这与我们所知的在真实生活中读一本书所指的意思完全背道而驰,所谓真实的生活是未被教育目的腐化的生活。(颜元叔译)

例 1-156 Otherwise education becomes too much like another kind of real life, the kind in which nobody reads the book, everyone reads the reviews, and everyone talks as if he knew the book.

🔵 否则教育就变得太像另一种真实的生活,即其中没有人看这本书却人

人看书评而且人人讲起来好像他晓得这本书的那种生活。(颜元叔译)

例 1-157　The mythology of reason then functions as what we might call an ideology in politics, <u>an ideology that is both critical and emancipatory</u>.

译　于是，理性的神话就具有了我们可以称作政治意识形态的功能，这种意识形态既是批判的也是解放的。(江怡译)

例 1-158　The obsessive concern of Heidegger's thinking from beginning to end is the question of being, <u>the question that is raised by metaphysical enquiry</u>.

译　海德格尔的思想自始至终迷恋不已的正是存在问题，这是由形而上学探究带来的问题。(江怡译)

例 1-159　We tend to imagine that there once existed a degree of neighbourliness which has been replaced by ruthless anonymity, <u>a state where people pursue contact with one another primarily for restricted, individualistic ends: for financial gain, social advancement or romantic love</u>.

译　我们往往会猜想，曾经存在过某种守望相助的邻里关系，可惜它后来被冷漠无情的匿名社会关系取代了。在如今这个匿名社会里，人们寻求相互间的交流接触基本上只是为了特定的个人目的，如出于经济上牟利、社会上晋升或者感情上爱恋的需要。(梅俊杰译)

例 1-160　Both Continental and analytic philosophy are, to a great extent, sectarian self-descriptions that are the consequence of the professionalization of the discipline, <u>a process that has led to the weakening of philosophy's critical function and its emancipatory intent, and to its progressive marginalization in the life culture</u>.

译　欧陆哲学和分析哲学在很大程度上都是宗派性的自我描述，这是学科专业化的结果，这个过程导致了哲学批判功能及其解放的目的的削弱，以及在文化生活中逐渐地边缘化。(江怡译)

例 1-161　One way of describing the activities of companies and religions is as forms of commodification - <u>the process whereby haphazardly available, ill-defined goods are transformed into named, recognizable, well-stocked and well-presented entities</u>.

译　公司和宗教的活动可用一种方式加以描述，即他们都采纳了商品化的形态。所谓商品化指的是一个转化过程，就是把一堆凌乱杂陈、缺乏定义的货品转变为有名有牌、辨认容易、码放整齐、陈列得体的商品。(梅俊杰译)

例 1-162 All, however, are apparently reducible to instances of the fundamental contradiction between 'nature' and 'culture', a contradiction which stems from the conflict that humans experience between themselves as animals, and so a part of nature, and themselves as human beings, and so a part of culture.

[译] 不过，所有这些矛盾似乎都可以简化为“自然”与“文化”这一基本矛盾的实例；它源自于这样一种冲突，即人类既将其成员体验为动物，因此也是自然的一部分，又将其体验为人类，因此也就是文化的一部分。（刘象愚译）

例 1-163 In the ancient picture, the wisdom that philosophy teaches us to love is identical with the pursuit of the good life, a life of reflection and contemplation that would, by definition, be a happy life.

[译] 在古时，哲学教导我们热爱的智慧，就是追求美好的生活，一种进行反思冥想的生活；按照释义来看，这将会是一种幸福的生活。（江怡译）

例 1-164 These two ideas fuelled the rejection of skepticism, relativism, and what was called 'psychologism', the view developed in Germany in the early 19th century that all logical and philosophical problems are reducible to psychological mechanisms.

[译] 这两个观念促进了抛弃怀疑论、相对主义和所谓的“心理主义”，后者是在 19 世纪德国盛行的观点，认为逻辑问题和哲学问题都可以还原为心理机制。（江怡译）

例 1-165 Endosomes, lysosomes, and peroxisomes all contain various mixtures of enzymes, proteins that catalyse chemical reactions.

[译] 内体、溶酶体和过氧化物酶体都含有各种酶（催化化学反应的蛋白质）的混合物。

例 1-166 Large external material can be physically engulfed by the membrane, a process known as phagocytosis.

[译] 大的外部物质可以被膜所吞没，这一过程称为吞噬作用。

例 1-167 As they mature, the DNA is replicated several times but the cell does not divide, a condition known as polyploidy which allows cells to increase in size.

[译] 当它们成熟时，DNA 被复制几次，但细胞不分裂，这种情况称为使细胞体积增加的多倍性。

例 1-168 Philosophy as an acute reflection upon history, culture, and society leads to the awakening of critical consciousness, what Husserl would call the reactivation of a sedimented tradition.

☯ 哲学作为对历史、文化和社会的敏锐反思，带来的是批判意识的觉醒，胡塞尔称之为已积淀的传统的复活。（江怡译）

例 1-169 Because it enhances productivity in the economy, there is benefit for most people, whether they take it in the form of consuming more or working less.

☯ 由于它提高了经济生产率，不管是通过增加消费量的形式还是减少工作量的形式，对绝大多数人都有好处。（戴炳然译）

例 1-170 For much of the Continental tradition, philosophy is a means to criticize the present, to promote a reflective awareness of the present as being in crisis, whether this is expressed as a crisis of faith in bourgeois-philistine world (in Kierkegaard), a crisis of the European sciences (in Husserl), of the human sciences (in Foucault), of nihilism (in Nietzsche), of the forgetfulness of Being (in Heidegger), of bourgeois-capitalist society (in Marx), of the hegemony of instrumental rationality and the domination of nature (in Adorno and Max Horkheimer), or whatever.

☯ 对欧陆传统中的大多数哲学家来说，哲学是一种批判现实的手段，是为了推进对处于危机中的现实的反思意识，无论这是被表达为低俗的平庸世界的信仰危机（克尔恺郭尔），还是欧洲自然科学的危机（胡塞尔），或者是人文科学的危机（海德格尔）、虚无主义的危机（尼采）、遗忘存在的危机（海德格尔）、小资产阶级资本主义社会的危机（马克思）、工具理性霸权和对自然支配的危机（阿多诺和霍克海默），或者是其他的什么危机。（江怡译）

四、形容词结构

形容词结构也可用作状语，当位于英语句子结尾时，可用来补充说明前面成分或整句所表达的状态、条件和能力；当位于句首时，可对后面的主语进行附带说明，或对整句进行评价性说明，或可看作省去 being 的分词结构。

例 1-171 By contrast, a popular culture is a large heterogeneous group, often highly individualistic and constantly changing.

☯ 与民间文化相反，大众文化是一种多元文化大群体，常常表现出高度的个人主义，经常发生变化。（谭卫国译）

例 1-172　At this point, leucocytes migrate between the endothelial cells that line the blood vessels (rather like elbowing a way through a crowd), <u>ready to confront invading bacteria</u>, and maybe commit suicide by bursting to release their antibacterial contents.

🔆 此时，白细胞在血管内皮细胞之间迁移（就像挤过人群一样），准备对抗入侵的细菌，并可能通过细胞破裂自杀来释放其抗菌成分。

例 1-173　Two pathways emerged, <u>dependent on whether apoptosis was triggered externally (extrinsic) or internally (intrinsic)</u>.

🔆 依据细胞凋亡是由外部触发还是内部触发，有两种细胞凋亡途径。

例 1-174　The necessarily massive repertoire of antibodies is created by splicing separate pieces of the large immunoglobin genes together to make immunoglobulin proteins with different active sites, <u>each capable of binding to just one specific antigen</u>.

🔆 通过将大的免疫球蛋白基因的不同片段拼接在一起，形成具有不同活性位点的免疫球蛋白，产生这样大规模的抗体库必需的，因为每一个活性位点只能结合一个特定抗原。

例 1-175　<u>Large or small</u>, all the circuits will contain the same kinds of components.

🔆 所有的电路不论大小，都含有相同的元件。（秦获辉译）

例 1-176　<u>Contrary to common belief</u>, forces are not transmitted only by 'direct contact'.

🔆 与一般的观念相反，力并不是仅仅靠"直接接触"传递的。（秦获辉译）

例 1-177　<u>Accurate in operation and high in speed</u>, computers can save man a lot of time and labor.

🔆 由于计算机运算快速准确，所以能节省人类大量的时间和劳力。（秦获辉译）

五、介词结构

句子中的介词结构可以有效地扩展句意，补充说明谓语动作词所采取的手段、方式，或所达成的目的和结果，多数作状语使用。其中最常用的结构有"for +名词""by + 动名词""In order to + 动词"结构（可缩略为动词不定式"to + 动词"结构）和"with + 名词"。

例 1-178　The most boring and unproductive question one can ask of any religion is whether or not it is true — <u>in terms of being handed down from heaven to the sound of trumpets and supernaturally governed by prophets and celestial beings.</u>

译　关于任何宗教，人们提出的最无聊、最徒劳的问题——它是不是真的。这里所谓真，是指宗教自茫茫上苍下凡到尘世俗界，由先知和天神以超自然的方式司管理。（梅俊杰译）

例 1-179　Following Europe's poor showing in the Gulf War, defence was mentioned in the treaty, <u>but in ambiguous terms to accommodate both the French desire for an autonomous European defence capacity and British opposition to any such thing, for fear that it could weaken Nato.</u>

译　鉴于欧洲在海湾战争中不如人意的表现，条约提及了防务，但用词模棱两可，以既顾及法国建立欧洲自主防卫能力的愿望，同时又迎合英国反对建立这种能力的立场（英国担心这会削弱北大西洋公约组织）。（戴炳然译）

例 1-180　Blair has emphasized deregulation and flexibility in his approach to the EU, <u>on the grounds that it will make the European economy more competitive and increase employment.</u>

译　在对欧盟的方式上，布莱尔强调放松管制和灵活性，理由是这可提高欧洲经济的竞争力和促进就业。（戴炳然译）

例 1-181　It argued that the euro-zone's 'one size fits all' monetary policy would not fit Britain and would thus cause inflationary or deflationary pressures, <u>on the grounds that Britain's economic structures differed too much from those of the Continent.</u>

译　它称欧元区"一个尺码适合全体"的货币政策，不适合英国并会带来通货膨胀或通货紧缩压力，理由是英国的经济结构与欧洲大陆国家差别太大。（戴炳然译）

例 1-182　Freud attacked philosophy <u>on the grounds that, unlike science, it attempted to present a picture of the universe which was too coherent, too lacking in gaps.</u>

译　弗洛伊德攻击哲学的原因是他认为哲学不同于科学，哲学试图展现一个过于连贯、没有空白的宇宙图景。（尹莉译）

例 1-183　<u>On the basis of our transcriptome data</u>, we hypothesized that *phr1; phl1* would express an altered response to pathogen infection.

🔄 根据我们的转录组数据，我们假设 *phr1;phl1* 可以响应于病原体感染而改变表达。

例 1-184 On the basis of evidence from fossils, rocks, and general shape correspondence, Alfred Wegener, a German meteorologist, suggested in 1912 that at times in the past the continents of the Earth must have occupied different positions to the ones they are in today, with, for example, the Americas and Eur-Africa nestled together in the Permian Period.

🔄 基于化石、岩石以及总体形态一致的证据，德国气象学家阿尔弗雷德·魏格纳于 1912 年提出，在过去的年代里，地球上的各个大陆一定占据着与它们今天所处的地方不同的位置，例如，在二叠纪时期，美洲与欧洲和非洲紧靠在一起。（史立群译）

例 1-185 Students are made to read more than they can ever enjoy, too little of too many things, in a way calculated to destroy personal involvement with the writer.

🔄 学生被迫去读的东西根本是他们不可能欣赏喜欢的，所读甚多，却收获甚少，而且是以刻意要破坏读者亲身感受作者的方式阅读。

例 1-186 We cannot read an author for the first time in the same way that we read the latest book by an established author.

🔄 我们不能以阅读一个成名作家最新出版作品的那种态度来阅读一个新作家的第一部作品。（朱树飓译）

例 1-187 And it subjects it to the pressure of technical change, in the way I have just been describing, until the whole basis of our culture has imperceptibly been remade.

🔄 科学也使文化经受技术更新的压力，按照我以上表达的方式，直至我们文化的整个基础不知不觉焕然一新。（杨自伍译）

例 1-188 In the absence of any great body of work in this area of research, it is hard to assess the true significance of these studies, but they are extremely intriguing.

🔄 由于在这个研究领域缺乏任何系统全面的工作，因此很难评估这些研究的真正意义，但它们非常有趣。

例 1-189 The brighter the student, the more he is asked to read, until he develops prodigious skill in reading quickly and cleverly, for purpose of taking examinations and talking in discussions.

🔘 译 学生愈聪明,被要求阅读的东西愈多,直到他有了读得又快又精明的惊人技巧,以便应试及在讨论中发言。(颜元叔译)

例 1-190 The foibles of citizens are placed beyond comment or criticism — for fear of turning government into that most reviled and unpalatable kind of authority in libertarian eyes, the nanny state.

🔘 译 自由主义者所担心的是,对小节的干预可能会将政府打造成一个保姆国家,在他们眼里,那是最应当加以讨伐、最令人厌恶的政权类型。(梅俊杰译)

例 1-191 For wild soil experiment 16S sequencing, we processed libraries according to Caporaso et al. (2018).

🔘 译 为进行野外土壤试验 16S 测序,我们根据 Caporaso 等(2018)方法对文库进行了处理。

例 1-192 For wild soil census analysis, sequences from each experiment were pre-processed following standard method pipelines from refs. 2, 19.

🔘 译 为了对野生土壤调查结果进行分析,根据参考文献 2,19 中的标准方法管道对每个试验的序列进行预处理。

例 1-193 For the demonstration that sucrose is required for the induction of PSR in sterile conditions, plants overexpressing the PSR reporter construct *IPS1: GUS* were grown in Johnson medium containing 1mM Pi or 5μM Pi supplemented with different concentrations of sucrose.

🔘 译 为了证明在无菌条件下诱导 PSR 需要蔗糖,过表达 PSR 报告基因构件 *IPS*1: *GUS* 的植物培养在含有 1mmol/L Pi 或 5μmol/L Pi 及添加不同蔗糖浓度的约翰逊培养基(Johnson medium)上。

例 1-194 Arnold responded in the 1882 Rede Lecture in Cambridge, 'Literature and Science', by claiming that both literature and science could be integrated into a wider, more Germanic, understanding of science as Wissenschaft, of knowledge in the broad sense.

🔘 译 1882 年阿诺德在剑桥的里德讲座"文学与科学"中回应道,文学与科学两者都可以被整合为一种更普遍的、更为德国式的理解,即把科学理解为人文科学,理解为更为广义的知识。(江怡译)

例 1-195 In my view, this is the problem that Continental philosophers return to again and again, either by trying to find a new way of responding to the problem, as for example in Habermas and Derrida, or by refusing the historical and philosophical terms in which the problem is posed, for example in Rorty.

[译] 我认为，这就是欧陆哲学家们一再回归的问题，他们或者试图找到回应这个问题的方法，如哈贝马斯和德里达，或者是拒绝造成这个问题的历史和哲学术语，如罗蒂。(江怡译)

例 1-196 By identifying emotions with rapid-response interruption mechanisms, Simon may have been too narrow.

[译] 西蒙将情绪定义为迅速反应的中断机制可能过于狭隘。(石林译)

例 1-197 By laying us open to the emotional influence of others, sympathy gives them an extra way of inducing emotions in us for the purposes of persuasion.

[译] 由于同情可以让我们受到他人情绪的影响，因此他人就可以通过激发情感说服我们。(石林译)

例 1-198 By dividing a diploid cell twice, four haploid gametes are produced.

[译] 二倍体细胞分裂两次产生四个单倍体配子。

例 1-199 In order to ensure that only states which had achieved monetary stability should participate in the euro, five 'convergence criteria' were established regarding rates of inflation and of interest, ceilings for budget deficits and for total public debt, and stability of exchange rates.

[译] 为了确保只有那些达到货币稳定的国家才能加入欧元区，条约制定了5项"趋同标准"，涉及通胀率、利率、预算赤字上限、公共债务总额上限，以及汇率稳定性。(戴炳然译)

例 1-200 Students are always reading to deadlines, in order to return books to the library, in order to answer questions and prove only that they have covered the ground.

[译] 学生从来都是限期读书，以便及时将书还给图书馆，以便回答问题，并且只为证明他们都读过了。(颜元叔译)

例 1-201 The third of what became known as the 'structural funds', in order to underline that their aim was not just to redistribute money but rather to improve economic performance in the weaker parts of the Community's economy, was the 'Guidance Section' of the European Agricultural Guarantee and Guidance Fund

(EAGGF).

🔹译 "结构性基金"这一称呼在于强调其目的不仅是为了资金再分配,更是为了改善共同体经济较弱部分的经济状况。构成结构性基金第三部分的是欧洲农业保证与指导基金(EAGGF)的"指导部分"。(戴炳然译)

英语句子中往往广泛使用"with(或 without)+名词(动名词或代词)"结构,表示拥有属性、伴随状况或条件状态等。其后还可跟介词短语(as, of, in, on, from 等)、形容词短语、定语从句、分词短语(现在分词和过去分词)或不定式短语,或这些结构的复合形式,来进一步修饰 with(或 without)后面的名词(动名词或代词)。其中"with(或 without)+名词+分词"结构也称为分词复合结构,功能上相当于复合的独立主格结构,其中 with(或 without)后面的名词为分词的逻辑主语。"with(或 without)+名词+不定式短语"也是一种复合的独立主格结构。例如:

例 1-202 Never had the educated classes in Europe formed a more cosmopolitan society, with French as the lingua franca and frequent travel — the age of the Grand Tour — especially in the first half of the century when wars were less frequent.

🔹译 欧洲受过教育的阶级从来没有形成过比这更加世界主义化的社会,他们以法语为通用语言,经常出国游历——这是一个伟大的旅行时代——特别是在十八世纪上半叶战争不甚频仍期间。(董乐山译)

例 1-203 A key assumption of modern Western political thinking is that we should be left alone to live as we like without being nagged, without fear of moral judgement and without being subject to the whims of authority.

🔹译 现代西方政治思想中的一个关键前提假定就是,我们应当在不受责骂的状态下如自己所愿地自由生活,既然不必恐惧他人的道德评判,也不应屈从于某一权威一时兴起的意念。(梅俊杰译)

例 1-204 If the universe expanded, so did the known limits of the earth itself, with the voyages of exploration and the discovery not only of the American Indian peoples of the New World but also of other historic non-Christian civilizations in China, India and Islamic world.

🔹译 宇宙开阔了,地球本身的已知界限也开阔了,许多人作了探险的航行,不仅发现了新世界的美洲印地安人,也在中国、印度以及伊斯兰世界发现了其他非基督教的历史文明。(董乐山译)

例 1-205 With the notable exception of the pioneering work of Charles Taylor, Hegel was until fairly recently a rather shadowy figure in the Anglo-American philosophical canon.

[译] 除了查尔斯·泰勒所做的显著的开创性工作之外，黑格尔在英美哲学经典中一直是位相当模糊的人物，这种情况直到最近才有所改观。(江怡译)

例 1-206 With a difference of 500, 000 volts, some of the negatively charged electrons in the core are forced into the polyethylene insulation, where they become trapped.

[译] 在 50 万伏位差的情况下，芯线中一些带负电荷的电子被迫进入聚乙烯绝缘层并在那里滞留。(闫文培译)

例 1-207 With all the help from the machines, farming still requires hard work and long hours.

[译] 尽管有了各种机械，干农活还是很累，耗时也很长。(闫文培译)

例 1-208 So a deal was done, with agreement on a higher ceiling for tax resources allocated to the Community and an annual rebate for Britain at around two-thirds of its net contribution.

[译] 于是达成了交易，大家同意提高共同体从税收中提取预算收入的限额，并答应每年给英国相当于其对共同体预算净贡献三分之二左右的返回款。(戴炳然译)

例 1-209 Most cells throughout our bodies will be replaced over the course of our lifetime, with an average of seven to ten years according to Jonas Frisen, from the Karolinska Institute in Stockholm.

[译] 据斯德哥尔摩卡罗琳斯卡研究所的乔纳斯·弗里森所说，在我们的一生中，我们身体中的大多数细胞平均每 7~10 年将被替换一次。

例 1-210 To choose a more prosaic image, the texts of the Continental tradition make up a kind of documentary archive of philosophical problems, with a distinct relation to their context and our own and marked by a strong consciousness of history.

[译] 若用一种更为平淡的意象表述，欧陆传统的文本构成了一种哲学问题的记录档案，这与它们的语境以及我们自己的语境都有着明显的关联，具有一种强烈的历史意识。(江怡译)

例 1-211 In order to keep sectors that employed a high proportion of women competitive, France demanded that its partners introduce equal pay too. With the general movement towards gender equality, this was to become one of the most popular European laws.

译 为使那些大量雇佣女性的部门保持竞争力,法国要求其伙伴国也实行同工同酬。由于性别平等渐成趋势,同工同酬成为最出名的欧洲法律之一。(戴炳然译)

例 1-212 After the Renaissance, the next step I want to look at in the development of the humanist tradition is the eighteenth-century Enlightenment, with a particular interest in the philosophes — not professional philosophers, but described by their historian Peter Gay as 'a loose, informal, wholly unorganized coalition of cultural critics, religious skeptics, and political reformers from Edinburgh to Naples, Paris to Berlin, Boston to Philadelphia'.

译 在文艺复兴以后的人文主义传统的发展中,我下一步要考察的是十八世纪的启蒙运动,特别着重于哲学家——不是职业的哲学家,而是研究他们历史的彼得·盖伊所说:"一批从爱丁堡到那不勒斯、从巴黎到柏林、从波士顿到费城的文化批评家、宗教怀疑派和政治改革家的松散、非正式、完全无组织的联合。"(董乐山译)

例 1-213 As proportional representation has been used in all the other states, the balance between the mainstream parties has been fairly stable, with neither the centre-right nor the centre-left able to command a majority.

译 因为其他所有国家都实行比例代表制,各主流党派间的均势相当稳定,中间偏右党派与中间偏左党派均不能占多数。(戴炳然译)

例 1-214 While moving closer together on agriculture, the Community and the USA have been diverging over environmental, cultural, and consumer protection issues, with the Europeans favouring standards which lead to restriction of their imports from the USA and which the Americans regard as protectionist.

译 共同体与美国在农业上趋于接近,但在环保、文化与消费者保护问题上一直存在分歧:欧洲实行的标准限制了来自美国的进口,美国则认为那是贸易保护主义。(戴炳然译)

例 1-215 But most important has been the sustained success of the American economy, with its low unemployment and high growth, from which the conclusion may be drawn that flexibility suits the new wave of technological development.

🔁 但非常重要的事例是，美国的低失业率与高增长带来了该国经济上的持续成功；从中或许可以得出结论：灵活性适合于技术发展的新浪潮。（戴炳然译）

例 1-216　In a word, the social heritage does not ensure the future of culture with the same probability with which it provides the conditions of civilization.

🔁 总而言之，社会遗产为文明进步提供环境条件时给了相当成功把握，却不能以同样的把握担保文化的未来。（颜元叔译）

例 1-217　Freud is now a historical figure. It is possible to discuss both his achievements and his limitations objectively, without being accused either of swallowing psychoanalysis whole as an uncritical disciple, or else of rejecting it because of personal resistance or lack of insight.

🔁 弗洛伊德现在已经成为历史人物。我们可以客观地讨论他的成就和局限，既不像一位盲从的信徒那样全盘接受精神分析，也不因为个人抵触或缺乏洞见而完全将其摒弃。（尹莉译）

例 1-218　Loss of surface cells one at a time maintains a constant overall thickness, with no tearing which might allow bacteria to penetrate more deeply.

🔁 表面细胞的一次损失一个，总厚度保持恒定，这样就不会有可使细菌穿透皮肤的大面积撕裂。

例 1-219　Problems are more acute in the Muslim theocracies. Saudi Arabia is an extreme example, with its heavy and compulsory veiling of women, who cannot even walk on the street unless accompanies by a male relative, and need male permission to travel and work.

🔁 在穆斯林神权国家，问题更加尖锐。沙特阿拉伯是一个极端的例子：妇女被强制佩戴厚重的面纱，在没有男性亲属陪同时甚至都无法上街，旅行和工作都需要征得男性的许可。（朱刚和麻晓蓉译）

例 1-220　Without the ability of divining the emotions felt by others, we would lose many opportunities to learn from their experience, with the result that we would have to learn everything the hard way — on our own.

🔁 如果没有猜测他人情绪的能力，就会失去许多他人的经验中学习的机会，使我们不得不以一种更困难的方式学习——自己摸索。（石林译）

例 1-221　The final piece in the jigsaw of DNA structure was produced by Watson with the realization that the pairing of the nucleotide bases, adenine with thymine and guanine with cytosine, not only provided the rungs holding the twisting ladder of DNA together, but also provided a code for accurate replication and a template for protein assembly.

🔄 DNA 结构拼图中的最后一块由沃森完成,他认识到核苷酸碱基配对(腺嘌呤与胸腺嘧啶配对,鸟嘌呤与胞嘧啶配对)不仅提供了将 DNA 螺旋梯架固定在一起的梯级,还提供了精确复制的代码和蛋白质组装的模板。

例 1-222 Despite the rapid rate, replication is extremely accurate, with enzymes that proofread and correct any mismatched nucleotide, usually leaving only one error in every billion nucleotides.

🔄 尽管复制的速度很快,但复制是非常准确的,因为有酶可以校对和纠正任何配对错误的核苷酸,通常每十亿个核苷酸只有一个错误。

例 1-223 Relations with Russia have not been easy, with its combination of unstable politics and an economy lacking a sound legal and administrative framework.

🔄 由于俄罗斯政治的不稳定以及经济缺乏坚实的法律与行政体制,欧盟与它的关系并不一帆风顺。(戴炳然译)

例 1-224 And because cockroaches live only for about 100 days, that resistance can evolve quickly, with genes from the most resistant cockroaches being passed to the next generation.

🔄 由于蟑螂只活 100 天左右,这种抵抗力会迅速进化,最具抵抗力的蟑螂的基因会传给下一代。

例 1-225 All this frenzied metabolic activity, as well as exposure to the continual threat of bacterial invasion, has resulted in the life of an enterocyte being a short time, with each cell lasting no more than two or three days before replacement.

🔄 所有这种激烈的代谢活动,以及暴露在细菌入侵的持续威胁下,导致肠细胞的寿命很短,每一个细胞在替换前不超过 2~3 天。

例 1-226 In a study of 375 adults who have successfully maintained weight loss and who engage in moderate-to-vigorous intensity physical activity, most reported consistency in the time of day that they exercised, with early morning being the most common time.

🔄 在一项对 375 名成年人成功地保持了体重减轻并进行了中等强度到高

强度体力活动的研究中，大多数人报告说他们每天锻炼的时间是一致的，早晨是最常见的时间。

例 1-227　The body with a constant force acting on it moves at constant acceleration.

㊁ 若物体受到某个恒力的作用，则该物体就会做匀加速运动。（闫培文译）

例 1-228　But with obesity also linked to heart disease and other serious ailments, fighting fat has become a matter of life or death.

㊁ 不过，由于肥胖症与心脏病以及其他严重疾病也有关联，与肥胖做斗争已成为生死攸关的问题。（闫培文译）

例 1-229　Solar output goes through 11-year cycles, with high numbers of sunspots seen at their peak.

㊁ 太阳辐射输出完成了 11 年的周期，高峰期出现大量的太阳黑子。

例 1-230　Considering the health consequences of being overweight, it is surprising that fat at the cellular level has received relatively little attention, with lipid droplets thought of as no more than simple storage depots.

㊁ 考虑到超重对健康的影响，令人惊讶的是，细胞水平的脂肪受到的关注相对较少，脂滴被认为只是简单的储存库。

例 1-231　Interestingly, China appears to have made the most progress in p53-based treatments, with a drug called Gendicine have been approved for head and neck cancer in 2003, whereas the US Food and Drug Administration by 2010 had not approved any p53-based treatments.

㊁ 有意思的是，看起来中国在基于 p53 的治疗方面取得了最大的进展，2003 年一种称为金雀花碱的药物被批准用于头颈癌，而美国食品和药物管理局到 2010 年还没有批准任何基于 p53 的治疗。

例 1-232　With a majority of member states now significant net contributors to the budget and public finances under pressure with the introduction of the euro, the Commission was constrained to stay below the ceiling of 1.27 percent of Union GDP for its total tax revenue.

㊁ 随着大多数成员国成为预算的重要净贡献国，同时在实行欧元后公共财政面临压力，委员会不得不将其从欧盟税收中的提取维持在欧盟 GDP 的 1.27%之下。（戴炳然译）

例 1-233 With the enlargement first to include almost all of Western Europe, and in the coming years most Central and East European countries, the aspiration is approaching reality.

[译] 通过扩大——首先包括几乎所有西欧国家，接着在随后的几年中包括大多数中东欧国家——此愿望正接近实现。（戴炳然译）

例 1-234 By the end of the 1990s, moreover, enlargement to the East was approaching, with the prospect of a large farm population likely to produce big surpluses if paid present EU prices.

[译] 另外，到 20 世纪 90 年代末，随着东扩的临近，欧盟面对的前景是：如果继续执行欧盟的现行价格，庞大的农业人口可能产生农产品的巨量过剩。（戴炳然译）

六、动词不定式

动词不定式由“to +动词原形”构成，是一种非谓语动词结构。动词不定式具有动词、名词、形容词和副词的特征，因此，可在句中做主语、宾语、宾补、表语、定语和状语等。这里主要关注动词不定式作状语的情形（科技论文经常使用）。作目的状语时，动词不定式一般置于句首，表达句子谓语动作词的目的、原因或要达到的结果。

例 1-235 To reach sites of injury or infection, leucocytes must leave the circulatory flow.

[译] 为了到达受伤或感染部位，白细胞必须离开血液循环。

例 1-236 To accommodate one and a half metres of double-stranded DNA within a spherical nucleus roughly one thirty-thousandth of this length, it is clear that the DNA has to be packed in a fairly sophisticated manner.

[译] 为了将 1.5m 的双链 DNA 放在一个球形的、长度约是 DNA 长度 1/30,000 的细胞核内，很明显，DNA 必须以相当复杂的方式进行包装。

例 1-237 To investigate the capacity of various leaf cell types to recognize and respond to pathogenic bacteria, cell death was used as a proxy for effector recognition.

[译] 为研究不同叶细胞类型对病原菌的识别和响应能力，以细胞死亡作为效应子识别的指标。

例 1-238 To determine the role of phosphate starvation response in controlling microbiome composition, we analysed five mutants related to the Pi-transport system (*pht*1; 1, *pht*1; 1; *pht*1; 4, *phf*1, *nla* and *pho*2) and two mutants directly involved in the transcriptional regulation of the Pi-starvation response (*phr*1 and *spx*1; *spx*2).

[译] 为确定磷饥饿反应在控制微生物组成中的作用，我们分析了与 Pi 转运系统相关的 5 个突变体(*pht*1; 1, *pht*1; 1; *pht*1; 4, *phf*1, *nla* 和 *pho*2)和直接参与 Pi 饥饿反应转录调控的 2 个突变体(*phr*1 和 *spx*1; *spx*2).

例 1-239 To explore PHR1 function in the regulation of plant immunity further, we generated transcriptomic time-course data for treatment-matched Col-0 seedlings following application of methyl jasmonate (MeJA) or the SA analogue benzothiadiazole.

[译] 为了进一步探讨 PHR1 在植物免疫调控中的功能，利用茉莉酸甲酯(MeJA)或 SA 类似物苯并噻二唑处理后，我们得到与处理一致的 Col-0 实生苗的转录时间进程数据。

例 1-240 To isolate and quantify bacteria from plant roots in the SynCom experiment, plant roots were harvested, and rinsed three times with sterile distilled water to remove agar particles and weakly associated microbes.

[译] 为了在 SynCom 实验中从植物根系中分离和量化细菌，采集植株根系，并用无菌蒸馏水冲洗 3 次，以去除琼脂颗粒和弱相关微生物。

七、造句原则

(一)长句和复杂句造句原则

总体上讲，英语句子以主从关系为主，英语句子(尤其构造复杂的长句)结构类似树状结构，主句结构或主谓结构类似于树的主干，其他从句或结构为次要或从属成分，类似于树的次级树枝与树叶；汉语则以并列关系小句或动词短语为主，没有主干或结构焦点，小句和动词短语按时间或逻辑顺序排列，相互之间关系松散，类以于顺序排列但无主次之分的竹节。英语句子无论多么复杂，一定要有主语(与汉语中较多的无主句形成对照)，且在主句或分句中只能有一个主语(与汉语较多的小句、分句和流水句中多个主语随意变换形成对照)；同样，不论句子中有多少个动词，除并列结构外，必须有且只能有一个谓语动词，其余的动词为非谓语动词形式。汉语则没有非谓语形式，句子中既能没有动词谓语，也能有很多动词谓语(连动谓语)。此外，汉语句子中各个成分一般按时间、空间或逻辑关系前后顺序排列，成分之间无须或较少用语言形式手段相连接，没有明显的语义形态标记，而英语句子中各个成分之间以主谓结构为核心通过语言形式手段连接，前后排列没有一定顺序。

在构造层次较多、形式复杂的句子时，在句子的核心成分(也就是主谓宾结构或主系表结构)的基础上，通过语义或形式手段连接非谓语动词、同位语结构、介词结构或者各种从句；各种结构中还可再跟从句，而从句中也可再嵌套从句及类似功能的结构。

例 1-241 Cells that are no longer required during development begin to shrink, and their surfaces generate spherical protuberances called blebs, a very active process when observed by time-lapse microscopy, with the surface of the cell resembling boiling mud pools in volcanic sites.(第一个并列分句嵌套定语从句，第二并列分句嵌套同位语结构和介词结构)

[译] 在发育过程中不再需要的细胞开始收缩，它们的表面产生称为泡的球形凸起，当用延时显微镜观察时可看到这个非常活跃的过程，细胞的表面类似于火山喷发产生的沸腾泥浆池。

例 1-242 A different and more intriguing cell death is one which is a very necessary process in all multicellular organisms, originally identified in studies of development but subsequently as a ‘suicide pathway’ for all cells that have failed to reproduce themselves in a satisfactory manner, ending any threat posed by the continued replication of ‘rogue’ cells.(定语从句中嵌套过去分词结构、定语从句和现在分词结构)

[译] 一个不同而更有趣的细胞死亡是所有多细胞生物中一个不可或缺的过程，最初是在发育研究中鉴定，但随后发现是所有未能以合适方式自我繁殖细胞的“自杀途径”，它可终结“流氓”细胞持续复制所造成的任何威胁。

例 1-243 The fact that such a question can be formed at all is evidence that metaphysics feeds off certain ambiguities inherent in ordinary language that could and should be eliminated through logical reform.(主语从句，定语从句，定语从句还嵌套定语从句)

[译] 可以形成这样一个问题本身就表明，形而上学正是利用了日常语言固有的某些模糊性，这些模糊性是可以并应当通过逻辑重组而得以消除的。(江怡译)

例 1-244 Philosophy is that moment of critical reflection in a specific context, where human beings are invited to analyse the world in which they find themselves, and to question what passes for common sense in the particular society in which they live by raising questions of the most general form: 'What is justice?' 'What is love?' 'What is the meaning of life?'. (表语从句，表语从句嵌套非限制性定语从句，非限制性定语从句再嵌套限制性定语从句)

🔵 哲学是在专门语境中进行批判性反思的时刻，人类由此得以有机会分析他们找寻到自我的世界，质疑在他们所生活的社会中被看作常识的东西，在这个社会中他们提出最有概括性的问题：例如，"正义是什么？""爱是什么？""生命的意义是什么？"。（江怡译）

例 1-245   All eukaryotic cells share the same basic layout, in that they are surrounded by membrane, and filled with cytoplasm within which there is a variety of membrane-bound organelles that perform specialized tasks. (非限制性定语从句，非限制性定语从句嵌套限制性定语从句，限制性定语从句再嵌套限制性定语从句)

🔵 所有真核细胞都有相同的基本布局，它们被膜包围，充满细胞质，在细胞质内有各种膜结合的、执行特定的任务细胞器。

（二）造句"尾重原则"

英语造句一般遵循"尾重原则"（principle of end weight），也就是短的（通常也是简单的）结构放在前面，长的（通常也是复杂的）结构置于在句尾。英语句子通常从一个较短的主句或结构开始，然后在句尾添加解释或支持它的更长和更复杂的结构。长的句子成分（主语、直接宾语、间接宾语、定语从句、状语从句等）或长的并列结构成分置于句尾，这会使句子更加平衡（既不头重脚轻，也不笨拙），而且更加容易理解，这种原则的修改例句如下：

例 1-246   The rate at which the American people are using up the world's supply of irreplaceable fossil fuels and their refusal to admit that the supply is limited is the real problem.

本例句主语过长，可修改为：

The real problem is the rate at which the American people are using up the world's supply of irreplaceable fossil fuels and their refusal to admit that the supply is limited.

🔵 真正的问题是美国人民消耗世界上不可替代的化石燃料的速度太快，以及他们拒绝承认供应是有限的。

例 1-247 The discovery of a baby mammal in Siberia has provided biochemists, anthropologists, immunologists, zoologists, and paleontologists with ample material.

本例句宾语过长，可修改为：

The discovery of a baby mammal in Siberia has provided ample material for biochemists, anthropologists, immunologists, zoologists, and paleontologists.

🔵 译 在西伯利亚发现的一种哺乳动物幼崽，为生物化学家、人类学家、免疫学家、动物学家和古生物学家提供了丰富的材料。

英语的"尾重现象"很多情况下是由几乎可以无限制地"向右延伸"的行文习惯造成的。例如：

例 1-248 Its trustees appointed as the Museum's first curator a young art historian, Alfred H. Barr, Jr, who brought with him not only a scholarly education but also an eye trained to make clear distinctions of both form and value. (宾语太长而后置)

🔵 译 董事会任命了一位年轻的艺术史家——阿尔弗雷德·巴尔担任博物馆的首任馆长，他不仅带来了其学者式的教育背景，还带来了能明辨艺术形式和价值的训练有素的眼光。(朱扬明译)

例 1-249 Millions long for immortality who don't know what to do with themselves on a rainy Sunday afternoon. (主语的定语从句太长而后置)

🔵 译 许多人希望长生不死，却不晓得如何过一个下雨的周日下午。(高瑞武等译)

例 1-250 Most were unsuccessful, finding their paths to fame choked by their own numbers and obstructed by protocols of privilege. (修饰 paths 的过去分词结构太长而后置)

🔵 译 他们中绝大多数没有成功，怀有同样梦想的人过多使得成名之路困难重重，同时还要受到种种规矩的限制。(朱扬明译)

例 1-251 The city's art market by then had sufficient critical mass, in terms of the number of its dealers and its seriously wealthy collectors, and an associated corps of art critics – informed, ambitious writers (and sometimes artists) reviewing exhibitions, staking out positions, shaping the tastes of their assorted publics. (介词结构太长而后置)

🔵 译 就人数而言，纽约的艺术市场当时已拥有了充足的批评力量，包括艺术经纪人、非常富有的收藏家以及相关的艺术批评团队,那些见多识广、雄心勃勃的作家(有时也是艺术家),撰写展评,阐明立场,并塑造对应的公众审美品位。(朱扬明译)

例 1-252 The appointment was shrewd, for this combination of qualities enabled Barr to undertake, by means of a series of themed exhibitions, the ambitious project of laying down a historical narrative of modernism that placed the Museum's collection at its centre. (状语从句太长而后置)

译 这一任命是明智的,因为这些优点的结合使巴尔能借助一系列主题展览,展开他雄心勃勃的计划,即以该馆的收藏为中心,对现代主义进行一次历史的叙述。(朱扬明译)

例 1-253 In the early 1800's cattle still roamed free over the prairies and plains of the western United States, making scientific breeding impossible and creating the law of the open range, which allowed free access to water and grazing lands but discouraged farming. (并列的两个现在分词短语,较长的分词短语后置)

译 19世纪初期,美国西部的牛群依然是在草地和旷野上漫无边际地放牧,这使得科学育种无法实现,同时,还导致产生了一项牧区开放的法令,法令允许自由选取水源和牧地,但损害了农业耕作。(王蓝译)

有时,可以利用倒装句将很长的主语后置,既符合"尾重原则",同时又对主语加以强调,或者使上下句衔接更紧。例如:

例 1-254 Fundamental to the bewilderment that underpins much public response to modern art is a suspicion of its sincerity, of the view being 'conned' or being found wanting – of this art being made by artists hungry for notoriety and sold through dealers whose main interest is in making money – a suspicion that is only heightened by revelations of the role of conspicuous art dealers and/or collectors such as Charles Saatchi in its promotion and display. (主语后置加以强调)

译 观众对现代艺术大多表现出迷惑不解,从根本上来讲,是怀疑它的真诚性,怀疑自己被"哄骗"或被证明缺乏鉴赏力,即怀疑这种艺术是那些渴望成名的艺术家所为,再由以赚钱为主要目的的艺术经纪人兜售。而诸如查尔斯·萨奇这样著名的艺术经纪人兼/或收藏家在现代艺术宣传和展览方面所发挥的作用被披露,更是加深了这种怀疑。(朱扬明译)

例 1-255 The agriculture of the next decades must satisfy demands for nutritious food, fibre and animal feed in a highly variable climate, and also mitigate the effects of agriculture on the environment. This is a tall order. Key to addressing the challenge is <u>a deeper understanding of genetic variation and the molecular, cellular and developmental pathways</u> by which plants dynamically respond to and interact with their environment and pathogens, while maintaining growth, efficiency of nutrient use and fitness. (为了加强上下句的衔接而倒装)

译 未来几十年的农业必须在高度多变的气候条件下满足对营养食品、纤维和动物饲料的需求，并减轻农业对环境的影响。这是一个苛刻的要求。更深入地了解植物的遗传变异，以及更深入地了解植物在保持生长、养分利用效率和适应性的同时，对环境和病原体作出动态反应和相互作用的分子、细胞和发育途径，是应对这一挑战的关键。

例 1-256 The application of the science of genetics to plant breeding occupies a strategic place in the enhancement of crop productivity. Upon its success depends <u>the effectiveness of many other efforts to provide adequate food supplies for direct consumption by man, feed for his animals and agricultural raw materials for his industries</u>. (为了加强上下句的衔接而倒装)

译 把遗传科学应用于植物育种工作在提高作物产量方面占有战略地位。人们为提供自己直接消费所需的食物、为提供牲畜所需的饲料以及为提供工业所需的农业原料作了很多努力，而这些努力的有效性都有赖于上述育种工作的成就。(王蓝译)

（三）平衡与对称原则

句子要讲究结构美感和朗朗上口，需要句子的各个部分相互平衡和对称（balance and symmetry），在声音、韵律、结构和意思方面做到协调和呼应。其中最主要的是在并列句的两端，或并列和排比结构中各个成分之间达到对称和平衡，尤其是在结构和长度上要大体一致，这样在阅读朗诵时语音铿锵，文本的可读性就强，也就是所谓并列平衡。并列关系的标记词包括 and, or, nor, but 和 yet 等。此外，在语法上处于非并列关系的短语和从句也可以实现对称和平衡，如从句和主句、主语和宾语、直接宾语和介词宾语之间的平衡，这类平衡称为非并列平衡。

并列平衡的示例如下：

例 1-257 Wit consists in knowing <u>the resemblance of things that differ</u> and <u>the difference of things that are alike</u>.

译 智慧就是理解异中有同，同中有异。（高瑞武等译）

例 1-258 True wisdom is to know what is best worth knowing, and to do what is best worth doing.

译 真正的智慧就是知道最值得知道的和做最值得做的。（黄闯译）

例 1-259 Men may be divided almost any way we please, but I have found the most useful distinction to be made between those who devote their lives to conjugating the verb 'to be', and those who spend their lives conjugating the verb 'to have.'

译 人，随便怎么分类都可以，不过我发觉最好的区分是：一种人毕生致力于"有为"，另一种人毕生致力于"拥有"。（高瑞武等译）

例 1-260 In science the credit goes to the man who convinces the world, not to the man to whom the idea first occurs.

译 在科学领域，荣誉属于那些使世界信服的人，而不是属于那些首先有这种想法的人。（黄闯译）

例 1-261 There are two ways to study butterflies: chase them with nets then inspect their dead bodies, or sit quietly in a garden and watch them dance among the flowers.

译 研究蝴蝶的方法有二种：用网捕捉，研究死蝶；静坐花园，看蝴蝶花间起舞。（高瑞武等译）

例 1-262 A true great man will neither trample on a worm, nor sneak to an emperor.

译 真正的伟人既不会践踏小人，也不会在皇帝面前卑躬屈膝。（黄闯译）

例 1-263 Good art is not what it looks like, but what it does to us.

译 好的艺术不在于像什么，而在于它对我们引起什么感受。（高瑞武等译）

例 1-264 The only real voyage of discovery consists not in seeking new landscapes but in having new eyes.

译 真正的发现之旅不在于寻找新的风景，而在于具有独到的眼光。（黄闯译）

例 1-265 The natural flights of the human mind are not from pleasure to pleasure but from hope to hope.

译 人心的自然趋向并非不断追求逸乐，而是不断追求希望。（高瑞武等

译）

例 1-266 To acquire knowledge, one must study; but to acquire wisdom, one must observe.

🔘译 要获得知识，必须学习；要获得智慧，却有赖观察。（高瑞武等译）

例 1-267 The world is moved not only by the mighty shoves of the heroes but also by the aggregate of the tiny pushes of each honest worker.

🔘译 世界前进，不单是靠英雄大力推动，也靠每位辛勤工作的人一起轻轻推进。（高瑞武等译）

例 1-268 The absence of pesticides and the emphasis on natural fertilizer are designed not only to keep the experiment as untainted as possible, but also to protect the health of the human consumers.

🔘译 不使用农药和强调天然肥料的目的不仅是为了使实验尽可能不被污染，也为了保护食用者的健康。（杨海民译）

例 1-269 Long and steep is the path to virtue while smooth is the way that leads to wickedness.

🔘译 通向美德之路漫长陡峭，通向邪恶之路平坦异常。（黄闻译）

例 1-270 The superior vena cava collects the blood from the head and neck, while the inferior vein collects blood from the lower parts of the body below the diaphragm.

🔘译 上腔静脉接纳来自头部和颈部的血液，而下腔静脉接纳来自身体膈以下各部位的血液。（洪班信译）

例 1-271 Prosperity is not without many fears and disasters whereas adversity is not without comforts and hopes.

🔘译 幸运中并非不掺杂各种担心与烦恼，而厄运中也并非不存在欣慰与期望。（黄闻译）

例 1-272 The utilization of glucose by most tissues is insulin dependent whereas the utilization of glucose by brain is insulin independent.

🔘译 大多数组织对葡萄糖的利用均有赖于胰岛素，而脑组织对葡萄糖的利用则不依赖胰岛素。（洪班信译）

更多的并列平衡例子参见第二单元的对称句与平行句部分。

非并列平衡的句例如下：

例 1-273 What is right is often forgotten by what is convenient.

译 正义往往因权宜而所弃。（高瑞武等译）

例 1-274 Reading without reflection is like eating without digesting.

译 读而不思，犹食而不化。（高瑞武等译）

例 1-275 The best way to predict the future is to create it.

译 预测未来最好的办法莫过于自己创造未来。（高瑞武等译）

例 1-276 When lose the right to be different, we lose the privilege of be free.

译 当我们丧失了独立独行的权利，享受自由的特权也会随之丧失。（高瑞武等译）

（四）英语思维造句原则

一般来说，语言是思维的工具和载体，因此，思维方式也反映在语言形式中，具体来说，就是反映在造句方法中。学习英语的造句方式，根本上说，就是学习西方人反映在英语中的思维方式。西方人重分析思维，因此，反映在语句中有多样的词形变化与语法形式（动词的单复数、非谓语形式、时态、语态变化等）及灵活的语序结构（状语结构可在句首和句尾，也可在句中；主从复合句中表示条件、让步、假设和原因的从句可置于主句前，也可置于主句后）。西方人重抽象思维和客体思维，反映在语句中就是多以抽象名词和非生物名词做主语，并且大量使用被动句。西方人思维方向和角度在句子中也有反映，如与汉语习惯不同的正反（肯定与否定）表达、更常使用比较结构等。

英语常用物称表达法或非人称表达法造句，即利用无生命的事物或抽象名词作主语（无灵主语）进行造句。但过多利用抽象名词或名词化结构进行造句，会使句子呈现静态化。例如：

例 1-277 A new idea suddenly came to/occurred to/struck him, but the absurdity of it made him laugh.

译 他突然想到/有一个新主意，但因为主意太过荒唐，他自己笑了起来。

例 1-278 These discoveries may shed light on the origins of the universe.

译 这些发现会有助于理解宇宙的起源。

例 1-279 Technology advancements allow police investigators to crack phone passcodes and access previously deleted information.

译 技术的进步使得警方调查人员能够破解电话密码并获得之前删除的信息。

例 1-280 The circadian rhythms generated by our internal biological clocks vary from individual to individual.

🔄 我们体内生物钟产生的昼夜节律因人而异。

例 1-281 The mixture of waves which constitutes sunlight has to struggle through the obstacles it meets in the atmosphere just as the mixture of waves of the seaside has to struggle past the columns of the pier.

🔄 组成太阳光的各种光波必须穿过它在大气层中所遇到的各种障碍物，正如海边大大小小的波浪必须绕过码头上的铁柱一样。（倪秉华译）

例 1-282 The work may someday lead to new methods of rehabilitation for people suffering from cognitive disabilities resulting from head injury, brain infection or stroke.

🔄 有朝一日，这项研究也许能为那些因头部损伤、脑感染或中风而丧失认识能力的人带来康复的新疗法。（李鲁译）

例 1-283 Exceptions like these may provide hints about the kinds of information the brain finds easiest to remember or process.

🔄 像这样一些例外情况也许能提供线索，使人们弄清大脑最容易记忆或处理哪些类型的信息。（李鲁译）

例 1-284 Human beings are social animals after all, connecting with people close to you will make you feel better.

🔄 人类毕竟是群居动物，与身边的人交往会让你感觉更好。

例 1-285 Renaissance is a term used to mean a period of rebirth by the Italians which saw changes in culture and great achievements.

🔄 文艺复兴是意大利人用来表示复兴（或重生）时期的一个术语，文艺复兴时期文化发生变革，并取得巨大成就。

例 1-286 Ignorance of the law excuses no man from practicing it.

🔄 任何人也不能以不知法律为借口，不受法律制裁。（刘宓庆译）

例 1-287 This recuperation of scrap materials for aesthetic play opened up a whole new field of art practice, and from 1914 a generation of artists explored the interface between painting and printed ephemera.

🔄 这种将废料回收为艺术服务，给艺术实践开创了一个全新的领域，从1914年开始，一代艺术家们不断探索绘画与印刷速耗品之间的边缘区域。（朱扬明译）

例 1-288 The observation that some individuals cannot differentiate among most human-made objects, for example, suggests that some parts of the brain may deal primarily with objects displaying straight edges — most of which are hand-made — while other parts of the brain focus on objects featuring the uneven outlines typical of animals and plants.

[译] 例如，有些人不能区分大多数人造物体此一观察结果表明，也许大脑的某些部位主要负责处理边棱呈直线的物体——其中大部分是手工制品——而大脑的其他部位却着重识别外形不规则的东西（外形不规则是动物和植物的典型特征）。（李鲁译）

例 1-289 The research, conducted by Harvard scientists, indicated that a fish diet may low the process of inflammation by altering the chemistry of white blood cells. Preliminary evidence both in animals and humans suggests that such a diet may help relieve symptoms of arthritis and perhaps other inflammatory diseases.

[译] 哈佛大学的科学家们进行的此项研究表明，鱼类食物会改变白血球的化学组成，从而减缓发炎的过程。动物实验和人体实验的初步证据表明，这种食物可能有助于减轻关节炎的症状，也许还可缓解其他炎症。（陈碚利译）

例 1-290 Automation involves a detailed and continuous knowledge of functioning of the machine system, so that the best corrective actions can be applied immediately when they become necessary.

[译] 自动化要求不断详细了解机器系统的操作，一旦必要时，以便立即采取最佳校正措施。（傅敬民等译）

例 1-291 Their engaging elusiveness of reference and the appeal of their densely worked surfaces invite a reflectiveness of response on our part, whose reward is to enrich our understanding of how visual meanings can be construed from disparate marks, images, and associations — in short, of what might be called the 'poetry' of painting.

[译] 其中难以捉摸的意义和稠密的画面处理产生的吸引力使我们作出思考性的回应，丰富了我们对于如何从完全另类的符号、图像和联想中推断其视觉意义（简言之，什么可称为画中“诗”）的理解。（朱扬明译）

英语多用被动语态进行造句，因此句子不强调施动者，而突出动作和行为（参阅第二单元的主动句与被动句部分）。有些说法更是习惯利用被动语态来表达，例如：

[译] **例 1-292** The activation of receptor tyrosine kinases is characterized by dimerization and phosphorylation.

[译] 受体酪氨酸激酶的激活具有二聚化和磷酸化的特征。

例 1-293 The empirical method of thought, on which all the scientific achievements of the past were founded, is opposed to the most fundamental principles of logic.

[译] 过去所有科学成就都是建立在经验思维方法的基础之上，这种经验思维方法与逻辑思维的最基本原则正好相反。

例 1-294 More consideration should be given to the development of engineered waste forms for used nuclear fuel.

[译]（我们）应更多地考虑开发使用过的核燃料的工程废料形式。

例 1-295 A distinction should be made between the primary and secondary contradictions.

[译]（我们）要区分主要矛盾和次要矛盾。

英语多用比较结构进行造句来加以强调。例如：

例 1-296 Life affords no greater responsibility, no greater privilege, than the raising of the next generation.

[译] 养育下一代是人生最大的责任，也是最大的特权。（高瑞武等译）

例 1-297 Nothing can bring out our weaknesses more than power.

[译] 没有什么比权力更能使人暴露弱点。（高瑞武等译）

例 1-298 No better entertainment than children has ever been invented.

[译] 世上所有发明，没有一件比小孩子更加好玩。（高瑞武等译）

例 1-299 None did so more single-mindedly than the German artist Kurt Schwitters, whose endless yet inexhaustibly inventive production of collages of tickets, cards, adverts, new photos, and the like gave compelling expression to the modern city life in whose interstices, coat pockets, and kitchen drawers such items accumulate.

[译] 其中德国艺术家库尔特·施韦特斯做得最专一，他用车票、卡片、招贴、新闻照片等制作了许许多多拼贴艺术的创新作品，引人入胜地展现了现代城市生活。他所使用的这些材料在现代城市生活的边边角角、大衣口袋、厨房抽屉中都能找到。（朱扬明译）

例 1-300 None did so more directly and confrontationally than German artist Hans Haacke, in a series of documentary 'installations' in which he laid out the results of research he had conducted into aspects of the museums who had invited him to exhibit — material that tended to look embarrassingly like those museums 'dirty linen'.

[译] 而在直接性和对抗性上没有人能比得上德国艺术家汉斯·哈克，他在一系列纪实性"画廊展览"中展现了他对那些邀请他作展览的博物馆的某些方面所作的调查结果——那些看上去令人尴尬的博物馆"家丑"。(朱扬明译)

此外，英语思维在前后与正反表达上与汉语也有很大的不同。例如：

例 1-301　Misery follows war.

[译] 战争导致苦难。(刘宓庆译)

例 1-302　Sympathy is welcome to the unfortunate.

[译] 不幸者容易博得同情。(刘宓庆译)

例 1-303　The significance of these changes cannot be overestimated.

[译] 这些改变的重要性再怎么估计也不过分。

例 1-304　There's nothing like unspoken communication in any collaboration.

[译] 合作中没有什么比默契更重要的了。

例 1-305　You are not mature until you expect the unexpected.

[译] 你对意料不到的事情也能顾虑到，才算成熟。(高瑞武等译)

例 1-306　One never realizes how much and how little he knows until he starts talking.

[译] 人一开口才发觉自己所知何其广泛而又何其不足。(高瑞武等译)

例 1-307　Until you become a parent, you can't begin to discover your capacity for strength, love and fatigue.

[译] 有了儿女，你才会发觉自己有那么大的力量、那么多的爱心，以及那么耐得住疲劳。(高瑞武等译)

英语造句的这些特点应该在阅读和写作中多加体会，才能造出更地道的英语句子。关于造句最后一点要说的是，学术英语造句应该多用名词和动词，尽可能少用形容词和副词。埃尔文·布鲁克斯·怀特(E. B. White)曾说过："Write with nouns and verbs, not with adjectives and adverbs. In general, it is nouns and verbs, not their assistants, that give good writing its toughness and colour."即，写作时要以动词、名词为主，而非形容词和副词。一般来讲，动词、名词才能为作品赋予力量与色彩，而不是它们的助手(形容词与副词)。

第二单元
句型变化

英语句子从长短来讲，可分为长句和短句；从关键信息在句子中所处的位置来讲，可分为松散句和尾重句；从语态来讲，可分为主动句和被动句；从语法结构上来讲，可分为简单句、并列句和复合句，还有特殊的对称句和平行句；从功能上讲，可分为陈述句、疑问句、祈使句和感叹句。

英语写作应该根据需要，在长短和句型上有所变化。可以用长句，也可以用短句；可用简单句，也可用复合句；可用肯定句，也可用否定句或疑问句；可用正常语序，也可改变某些修饰成分位置或倒装语序；可用松散句，也可用尾重句；可用主动句，也可用被动句；在某些情况下还可用对称句或平行句。总之，要根据行文和表达需要，在长短、语序、语态、句式上灵活地穿插变化，以取得特定的修辞效果。本单元主要从长句与短句、松散句与尾重句、主动句与被动句、对称句或平行句进行论述。

一、长句与短句

英语长句和短句没有明确的区分，但一般将20个单词以上的称为长句，20个单词以下的称为短句。

长句和短句的选择会影响文章的可理解性、节奏和修辞效果。从可理解性的角度上讲，一般来说，句子越长，越难理解；句子越短，越容易理解。因此，有些写作书会建议作者将句子的平均长度限定在15~20个单词以内。但从节奏上讲，要长短句结合，避免全是长句或全是短句，这样表达才能产生富有活力的节奏，因此也有写作书建议，避免使所有句子长度都维持在18~19个单词。需要说明的是，简单句并不一定都短，复合句也不一定很长。从修辞效果上讲，长句结构复杂、信息容量大，更擅长详细和从容地描述、解释和推理，有描述周到、推理严密、滴水不漏和面面俱到之感，用于阐述复杂的概念，表达复杂的思想或严密的逻辑。短句结构简单、语法明确，有直接有力、清楚易懂、活泼明快、言简意赅等特点。短句在长句前后使用，可以突出或强调所陈述的事实或所表达的思想。短句在学术英语中更适合论断和概括，特别是在语法简单时有格言警句的修辞效果，让人印象深刻。全是长句时，感觉语气臃肿、笨重、迟缓；全是短句时，虽然语气轻快，但有幼稚之感。因此若全是长句或短句，节奏单调，都会让人生厌。

长句如约翰·斯图亚特·密尔（John Stuart Mill）《论自由》（*On Liberty*）的一段：

例 2-1　Though society is not founded on a contract, and though no good purpose is answered by inventing a contract in order to deduce social obligations from it, every one who receives the protection of society owes a return for the benefit, and the fact of living in society renders it indispensable that each should be bound to observe a certain line of conduct towards the rest. This conduct consists, first, in not injuring the interests of one another; or rather certain interests, which, either by express legal provision or by tacit understanding, ought to be considered as rights; and secondly, in each person's bearing his share (to be fixed on some equitable principle) of the labors and sacrifices incurred for defending the society or its members from injury and molestation.

🔴译　尽管社会并非建立于一纸契约之下，尽管没有任何善的目的可以靠发明社会契约以便推导出社会义务来满足，每个得到社会保护的人都应当作出回报。人人生活在社会中，这个事实本身就决定了每个人与其他人相处时势必要遵守某种行为规范。这种行为包括：首先，不损害他人的利益，或者，更确切地说，某些应当被成文的律法或默契视为权利的利益；其次，每个人应当担负起他的一份责任（由一些公平的原则所规定），为保卫社会或其成员免于伤害和骚扰而付出辛劳和牺牲。（吴简清译）

短句如戴维·赫伯特·劳伦斯（D. H. Lawrence）《给他一个模式》（*Give Her a Pattern*）的一段：

例 2-2　Women are not fools. They have their own logic, even if it's not the masculine sort. Women have the logic of emotion, men have the logic of reason. The tow are complementary and mostly in opposition. But the woman's logic of emotion is no less real and inexorable than the man's logic of reason. It only works differently.

🔴译　女人不是傻瓜。她们有自己的道理，即便不是男子汉的那一套。女人有的是感情的道理，男人有的是理智的道理。二者相辅相成而多半又彼此对立。可是女人感情的道理绝不比男人理智的道理少一分真实和威力。它不过是起作用的方式不同。（杨自伍译）

长短句结构如特里·伊格尔顿（Terry Eagleton）《人生的意义》（*The Meaning of Life: A Very Short Introduction*）的一段：

例 2-3　As for wealth, we live in a civilization which piously denies that it is an end in itself, and treats it exactly this way in practice. One of the most powerful indictments of capitalism is that it compels us to invest most of our creative energies in matters which are in fact purely utilitarian. The means of life become the end. Life consists in laying the material infrastructure for living. It is astonishing that in the twenty‑first century, the material organization of life should bulk as large as it did in the Stone Age. The capital which might be devoted to releasing men and women, at least to some moderate degree, from the exigencies of labour is dedicated instead to the task of amassing more capital.

● 译 至于财富,我们生活在这样一个文明当中,这种文明否认财富是自身的目的,并且在实际上也正是以这一态度对待财富的。对资本主义最有力的控诉之一是,它驱使我们把大部分创造性能量投入到纯粹功利性的事物中。人生的手段成了目的。人生成了为生活奠定物质基础的活动。令人震惊的是,人生的物质组织活动在21世纪和在石器时代竟然同样重要。本该用于在某种程度上将人类从劳动的迫切需求当中解放出来的资本,现在却用来积累更多的资本。(朱新伟译)

二、松散句和尾重句

松散句(loose sentence)是指主要意思出现在句首,而句尾则为补充交代的信息或细节,或者说句子前面呈现主要信息和实质内容,后面为修饰成分对前面信息进行细节补充和阐述解释。通常在主从复合句中,主句在前,从句断后,这样的主从复合句可视作松散句。

尾重句或掉尾句或圆周句(periodic sentence)是指关键信息或重点意思置于句尾,而次要的、背景的信息置于句首,只有读完全句才能了解该句的完整含义。

第三类为结构平行或相对平衡的平衡句,句首句尾并无句子重点与非重点之分。

松散句和尾重句各有其修辞功能。松散句由于主要意思在句首出现,因此读者可快速把握句意,具有开门见山、简明清晰、自然朴实的修辞风格,在新闻和科普作品中较为常见。实际上,由于英语具有将较长的定语从句或类似的功能结构(如同位语或分词结构)置于句尾的习惯,因此,松散句在一般写作中也较为常见。英语句子具有向右无限延伸的能力,也就是后面成分可不断地对前面成分进行补充和阐释,因此,松散句几乎能想写到哪里就写到哪里,是可以在任意位置结束的句子,或者说后面的分句或成分通常可独立成句，因此，松散句组成松散，不属于严谨的正式文体。

尾重句把要强调的部分或主要意思刻意置于句尾，作为整句的高潮，而前面则为铺垫成分(如较长的状语成分)，用于交代背景或条件。尾重句用于说理，给人一种逻辑严谨、推进有力的感觉；用于叙述或描写，句首可制造一种氛围或悬念，吸引读者的注意，或给人一种欲扬先抑、蓄势待发的修辞效果。随着向句尾推进而递进地蓄积能量，在句尾达到高潮而爆发。尾重句多在正式庄重的文体(如法律或演讲)中使用。

但是，一般要求句子具有统一性，也就是表达一个完整意思，而松散句结构松散，可在主要意思之后随意增加语句成分或在任意位置结尾，因此，不容易保持"统一性"。同时，句尾通常作为强调位置，松散句可能以无足轻重的成分结尾，使得句子相对没有力度，绵软无力。段落中偶尔使用松散句，会显得轻松随意，如果连续大量使用，与过多使用尾重句一样，会显得单调、乏味、僵硬、死板。因此，学术英语写作宜多种句法相互调剂。

松散句示例如下：

例 2-4 The doubts persist to this day, based on concern about human rights, democratic stability, a low level of economic development, and high rate of inflation, combined with a size of population, some 70 million and rising fast, which makes such things harder to accommodate.

🔲 **译** 基于对该国(土耳其)人权、民主稳定性、低水平经济发展与高通货膨胀率等问题的担忧，这种怀疑一直持续至今；另外，该国(土耳其)人口达7000万左右，且增长迅速，更使上述问题难以接受。(戴炳然译)

例 2-5 This was taken up by the German Chancellor, Helmut Schmidt, who saw it as a way to spread the burden of a difficult relationship with the USA that resulted from the weakness of the dollar and the strength of the mark, and who was also influenced by Monnet's ideas.

🔲 **译** 这个想法得到德国总理赫尔穆特·施密特的支持，一方面是因为他认为这能分散美元疲软和马克坚挺所导致的德美关系困难的压力，另一方面是因为他深受莫内的影响。(戴炳然译)

例 2-6 The company's success appeared to bear out the principles of efficiency laid down at the turn of the twentieth century by the Italian economist Vilfredo Pareto, who theorized that a society would grow wealthy to the extent that its members forfeited general knowledge in favour of fostering individual ability in narrowly constricted fields.

[译] 这家公司的成功证实，意大利经济学家维尔弗雷多·帕累托在20世纪初制定的效率原则似乎是正确的。帕累托的理论指出：一个社会的富有必须以其成员放弃常识，转而去培养在狭窄的领域里的个人能力为代价。（袁洪庚译）

例 2-7 So they sought alternative channels of advancement, exhibiting together in informal groupings, networking between their multiplying café-based milieux to promote, compare, and contest new ideas and practices, about which they wrote in a proliferating range of ephemeral little magazines, with consequences that we shall explore in Chapter 1, for this hive of activity was where both avant-garde art and the avant-garde community — and thus, 'modern art' — had their origin.

[译] 于是，他们寻求其他发展途径：结成非正式的团体集体举办展览，在不断扩大的以咖啡馆为基地的圈子中进行串联，宣传、比较和质疑彼此新的艺术观念和创作实践。他们为数量激增但往往是昙花一现的小型杂志撰稿，介绍这些新观念和新实践，其结果我们将在本书的第一章中进行探讨。正是在这种喧闹繁忙的活动中诞生了前卫艺术和前卫艺术群体，以至起源了“现代艺术”。（朱扬明译）

例 2-8 This leviathan is headed not for the better-known bits of the river, where tourists buy ice-creams to the smell of diesel engines, but to a place where the waters are coloured a dirty brown and the banks are gnawed by jetties and warehouses — an industrial zone which few of the capital's inhabitants penetrate, though the ordered running of their lives and, not least, their supplies of Tango fizzy orange and cement aggregate depend on its complex operations.

[译] 这艘巨型轮船的目的地并非泰晤士河上比较知名的地段，游客在那些地方顶着柴油机散出的难闻气味买冰淇淋吃。它要去的地方河水已呈污糟糟的褐色，两岸凌乱地分布着码头和货仓。这是一片伦敦居民很少造访的工业区，不过他们有条不紊，所需要的探戈橙汽水和已搅拌成浆的水泥均得依赖其复杂运转。（袁洪庚译）

例 2-9 This gargantuan granary is evidence that we have become, after several thousand years of effort, in the industrialized world at least, the only animals to have wrested ourselves from an anxious search for the source of the next meal and therefore to have opened up new stretches of time — in which we can learn

Swedish, master calculus and worry about the authenticity of our relationships, avoiding the compulsive and all-consuming dietary priorities under which still labour the emperor penguin and Arabian oryx.

🔵 巨大的谷仓表明，至少是在工业化世界里，经过几千年的努力，我们虽然费尽气力，却终于成为唯一一群不必焦虑不安地为下顿饭犯愁的动物。因此我们有闲暇学习瑞典语，掌握微积分，为我们的人际关系是否真诚可信担忧，不必被迫优先考虑耗尽全部精力的觅食问题，而帝企鹅和阿拉伯羚羊仍在为此艰苦奋斗。（袁洪庚译）

例 2-10　Nevertheless, no quayside can ever appear entirely banal, because people will always be minuscule compared to the great oceans and the mention of faraway ports will hence always bear a confused promise of lives unfolding there which may be more vivid than the ones we know here, a romantic charge clinging to names like Yokohama, Alexandria and Tunis — places which in reality cannot be exempt from tedium and compromise, but which are distant enough to support for a time certain confused daydreams of happiness.

🔵 不过码头永远不会显得全然平淡无奇，因为与海洋相比，人类总是微不足道的。而每当人们提到远方的港口城市，总是对那些地方可能展示的生活怀有一种迷茫的希望，认为它会比我们熟悉的所有生活方式更具有活力。与横滨、亚历山大和突尼斯一类的港口紧密联系在一起的是一种浪漫情怀，实际上这些地方亦不免沉闷和平庸，只是它们距离我们甚远，暂时尚能使我们沉湎于毫无道理的沉思遐想之中，并因此心满意足。（袁洪庚译）

尾重句示例如下：

例 2-11　In the pragmatist, streetwise climate of advanced postmodern capitalism, with its skepticism of big pictures and grand narratives, its hard-nosed disenchantment with the metaphysical, 'life' is one among a whole series of discredited totalities.

🔵 置身于发达的后现代资本主义的实用主义和市侩气息中，加上对远大前景和宏大叙事的怀疑、对形而上事物的固执的祛魅，"人生"和许多其他总体性概念一样已经名声扫地。（朱新伟译）

例 2-12　For individual women artists who were faced with a modernism that was defined in terms of 'masculine' qualities, by an avant-garde whose behaviour and protocols denied them the space from which to challenge this, there were few alternatives to invisibility.

[译] 对于女性艺术家而言，因为她们面对的是以“男性气质”特征界定的现代主义，而且作出此界定的前卫派其行为和准则都拒绝女性进入其领域对此进行挑战，这就使得女性艺术家除了默默无闻，几乎没有别的选择。(朱扬明译)

例 2-13 Long before researchers began to accumulate material evidence about the many ways modern humans resemble other animals, and long before Charles Darwin and Gregor Mendel laid the foundations of our understanding of the principles and mechanisms that underlie the connectedness of the living world, Greek scholars had reasoned that modern humanity was part of, and not apart from, the natural world.

[译] 早在研究人员开始收集人类与其他动物相似性的物证之前，远在查尔斯·达尔文和格雷戈尔·孟德尔为我们奠定理解生命世界关联性的基本原理和机制之前，古希腊学者就已推断：现代人是自然界生命系统的一部分，而非脱离于自然界。(冯兴无译)

例 2-14 When we are dreaming, even without the help of the chemical unification conferred by noradrenaline and serotonin, and even without the focus and control of thought and action conferred by the part of the brain called the dorsolateral prefrontal cortex, our experience is nevertheless convincingly integral and convincingly real.

[译] 即便没有去甲肾上腺素和 5-羟色胺帮助进行化学整合，甚至没有前额叶背外侧皮质对思维和动作实施控制和集中，我们在做梦时的体验仍然是完整、真实且有说服力的。(韩芳译)

例 2-15 Given the massive numbers of potential antigenic sequences, which can be as small as two or three consecutive amino acids in a protein, a chemically modified sugar molecule, or even the shape of the protein, there are millions of different T-memory cells.

[译] 鉴于存在大量的潜在抗原序列，抗原序列可以小到只有蛋白质上 2~3 个连续的氨基酸，抗原还可以是一种经化学修饰的糖分子，甚至是具有蛋白质形状分子，因此有数以百万计的不同记忆 T 细胞。

三、主动句与被动句

主语为施事主语的句子是主动句，而主语为受事主语的句子是被动句。

主动句与被动句除语法结构外，还具有不同的修辞功能。主动句有叙述功能，被动句有说明功能。相对而言，主动句直接、简洁，而被动句则没有这种优势。被动句可省略行为主体或施动者，突出动作承受者或动作本身的重要性，具有客观性的特点。学术英语大量使用被动语态，以实现叙述的客观性和规范性。

主动句常用于叙述文体，例如：

例 2-16 ①In 1540 Vesalius visited Bologna where, for the first time, he was able to compare the skeletons of a monkey and a human. ②He realized the textbooks used by his professors were based in a confusing mixture of human, monkey, and dog anatomy, so he resolved to write his own, accurate, human anatomy book. ③The result, the seven-volume De Humani Corporis Fabrica Libri Septem, or 'On the Fabric of the Human Body', was published in 1543. ④Vesalius performed the dissections and sketched the drafts of the illustrations: the Fabrica is one of the great achievements in the history of biology. ⑤Vesalius' successful efforts to make anatomy more rigorous ensured that scientists would have access to reliable information about the structure of the human body.

译 ①1540年，维萨留斯在博洛尼亚访问参观时才得以首次比较猴子与人类的骨骼。②他发现，教授使用的教科书把人、猴子和狗的解剖结构混在一起，因此，他决心自己写一本准确的人体解剖书。③在1543年，他出版了包含7卷内容的《人体构造》一书。④维萨留斯亲自解剖并绘制了草图来演示解剖过程，此书是生物学历史上的杰作之一。⑤其研究为后来科学家进行人体结构的研究提供了可靠的参考资料。（冯兴无译）

上述5句话中，除第③句为被动句外，其余的都是主动句，并且主动句的主语不必非是人，还可以是抽象名词，如第⑤句的主语为 Vesalius' successful efforts.

被动句多出现在科技说明文体中，在英语科技论义的"材料与方法"部分往往大量使用被动句，例如：

例 2-17 As oil is found deep in the ground, its presence cannot be determined by a study of the surface. Consequently, a geological survey of the underground, rock structure must be carried out. If it is thought that the rocks in a certain area contain oil, a 'drilling rig' assembled. The most obvious part of a drilling rig is called 'a derrick'. It is used to lift sections of pipe, which are lowered into the hole made by the drill. As the hole is being drilled, a steel pipe is pushed down to prevent the sides from falling in. If oil is struck, a cover is firmly fixed to the top of the pipe and the oil is allowed to escape through a series of valves.

[译] 由于石油深埋于地下，研究地面不能确定石油之有无，因此，必须对地下岩层结构进行地质勘探。如果认为某一地区的岩石中蕴含石油，就装配一台“钻机”。钻机最明显的部分称为“井架”。井架用来升吊油管，油管深入放置于由钻头打出的洞中。在钻洞过程中，要把一根钢管往下推，以防止洞壁坍塌。如果钻到石油，油管顶部加盖紧固，就可使石油通过系列阀门逸出。

如下情况宜用被动语态：①如果写作者不知或者众所周知或无须知道谁是动作的执行者或施动者时，或者强调过程和受动者而不是施动者时，可用被动语态。②当使用被动语态，被动句的主语更具体、更简短，句子更清晰时，可用被动语态。③当被动句能按照旧信息向新信息排列时，当被动句能更好地实现上下句之间的连贯和过渡时，可用被动语态。④被动句可以将重点阐述的内容置于句尾，句子更显平衡得体，避免头重脚轻时使用被动语态。例如：

例 2-18 Because he was not a trained geologist, Wegener's views were ignored, or dismissed as irrelevant and unprovable speculations.

[译] 由于魏格纳不是一位经过训练的地质学家，他的观点被人们忽略了，或者被认为是无意义的或无法证明的猜测而不予接受。(史立群译)

例 2-19 This type of approach has been developed in recent years to probe for coincident patterns in the evolutionary history of dinosaurs and whether their evolutionary history is echoed in their geographic distribution.

[译] 这种研究方法近年来已得到发展，用于探索恐龙进化历史上出现的一致模式，以及它们的进化历史是否与其地理分布相呼应。(史立群译)

例 2-20 An attempt was being made to find out whether an overall signal did emerge that was suggestive of a tectonic influence on the evolutionary history of all dinosaurs.

[译] 科学家正试图查明是否的确存在一个总的信号，表明地壳构造格局对恐龙整个进化历史的影响。(史立群译)

例 2-21 Considerable attention has been directed toward understanding fine details of the internal structure of dinosaur bone.

[译] 研究者对了解恐龙骨骼的内部详细结构给予了极大的关注。(史立群

译)

例 2-22 Anti-clerical criticism of the Church for its wealth, its corruption and worldliness could now be supported by a naturalistic view of the cosmos, a triumphant scientific method and the critical, sceptical, empiricist habits of thought which these engendered.

🔵译 对教会拥有巨额财富、腐化堕落和追名逐利的批评，如今可得到自然主义的宇宙观，成功的科学方法，和由此产生的持批判态度的、怀疑的、经验主义的思想习惯所支持。（董乐山译）

例 2-23 This tide of unease was reversed and replaced by a new mood of optimism in the first half of the eighteenth century. The grounds for such a change of mood had been predicted well before then, in the early years of the seventeenth century, by Francis Bacon (1561—1626) who rejected tradition in all branches of learning and staked everything on an experimental science which would free man from the burden of original sin and restore to him that control over nature which had been lost with the Fall.

🔵译 这种不安的潮流在18世纪上半叶被一股新的乐观情绪所逆转和代替了。这种情绪的转变早在17世纪早期就被弗朗西斯·培根（1561—1626）预言。培根在所有学科中摒弃传统，把一切都押在试验性的科学上，认为这能把人从原罪的负担下解放出来，恢复由于堕落而丧失的对自然的控制。（董乐山译）

例 2-24 For its hard tissues to be preserved as fossils, the bones and teeth of a dead hominin would need to have been covered quickly by silt from a stream, by sand on a beach, or by soil washed into a cave.

🔵译 人类骨骼和牙齿等硬组织若要变成化石存留下来，死后的尸体需要能被溪流挟带的泥沙、海滩上的沙粒，或冲进山洞的泥土迅速填埋。（冯兴无译）

例 2-25 The final piece in the jigsaw of DNA structure was produced by Watson with the realization that the pairing of the nucleotide bases, adenine with thymine and guanine with cytosine, not only provided the rungs holding the twisting ladder of DNA together, but also provided a code for accurate replication and a template for protein assembly.

🔵译 DNA结构拼图中的最后一块由沃森完成，他认识到核苷酸碱基配对

(腺嘌呤与胸腺嘧啶配对，鸟嘌呤与胞嘧啶配对)不仅提供了将 DNA 螺旋梯架固定在一起的梯级，还提供了精确复制的代码和蛋白质组装的模板。

例 2-26 The movements of these heads are energized by the breakdown of adenosine triphosphate to adenosine diphosphate, which releases the energy required to promote the muscle contraction.

[译] 这些(肌球蛋白丝)头运动是靠三磷酸腺苷分解成二磷酸腺苷提供能量的，三磷酸腺苷分解释放出促进肌肉收缩所需要的能量。(李少如译)

被动句和主动句穿插使用，可使句子的衔接更好，例如：

例 2-27 This analysis has been challenged by the economist Robert Frank. Frank argues that it is actually advantageous to have the capacity for guilt, because people who are known to have a conscience are more likely to be trusted by others.

[译] 经济学家罗伯特·弗兰克对这一观点提出了质疑。他认为会内疚实际上是有益的，因为人们更容易信任那些他们认为有良知的人。(石林译)

例 2-28 The ease and accuracy of recall are also influenced by the mood we are in when we remember something. Dozens of experiment conducted by the psychologist Gordon Bower show that, when we are in happy mood, we tend to recall pleasant events more easily and more accurately than unpleasant ones.

[译] 回忆的难度和准确性还受到回忆时的心境影响。心理学戈登·鲍尔所做的许多实验表明，在我们心情好时，回忆愉快事件比回忆不愉快的事件更容易、更准确。(石林译)

例 2-29 As philosopher of science Karl Popper has emphasized, a good theory is characterized by the fact that it makes a number of predictions that could in principle be disproved or falsified by observation.

[译] 正如科学哲学家卡尔·波普强调的那样，一种好的理论，其特征是能做出许多原则上可以被观测结果所否定或证伪的预言。(谭卫国译)

例 2-30 Thyreophorans are a major group of ornithischians that are characterized by bearing bony plates in their body wall, clubs or spikes adorning their tails, and for having an almost exclusively quadrupedal method of locomotion.

[译] 覆质甲龙亚目是鸟臀目中的一个主要类群，其特点是它们的体壁上具有骨板，尾巴上装饰有尾槌或长钉状构造，运动方式几乎毫无例外地为四足行走。(史立群译)

目前，很多科技论文大量使用 We 作主语的主动语态。虽然有人认为科技论文中使用 we 作主语会有主观性的感觉,但目前此类用法已成趋势。这样做除了具有主动语态的优势外,更能强调动作完成者及成果归属者。当动词为元话语动词(包括言语行为动词 suppose, claim, assume, suggest 等,及心理动词 think, consider, believe, doubt 等),更宜使用 We 作主语的主动语态,因为这些动词所表达的动作对作者而言是独有的。但也有人认为,适当使用第一人称代词,但不要用得太多,以滋生靠不住或自以为是的感觉。

下面论文 *Root microbiota drive direct integration of phosphate stress and immnity*(根微生物群促进磷胁迫与免疫的直接整合)中的例子,显示科技英语期刊论文中使用主动语态及主语"我们(We)"和"我们的(Our)等"已成趋势。

例 2-31 Here we establish that a genetic network controlling the phosphate stress response influences the structure of the root microbiome community, even under non-stress phosphate conditions. We define a molecular mechanism regulating coordination between nutrition and defence in the presence of a synthetic bacterial community. We further demonstrate that the master transcriptional regulators of phosphate stress response in *Arabidopsis thaliana* also directly repress defence, consistent with plant prioritization of nutritional stress over defence. Our work will further efforts to define and deploy useful microbes to enhance plant performance.

🔄 本文中,我们确立了控制磷胁迫反应的一个遗传网络;磷胁迫反应影响根微生物群落结构,即便在无磷胁迫条件下也会影响根微生物群落的结构。我们阐述了合成细菌群落存在的情况下调控营养和防御之间协调的一种分子机制。我们进一步证明,拟南芥体内磷胁迫反应的主转录调控因子也直接抑制防御,这与植物对营养胁迫反应优先于防御相一致。我们的工作将进一步推进确定和部署有用的微生物来提高植物的性能。

四、对称句与平行句

对称句或对称结构则通常由形式(结构和长短)上类似,但意思上相对或相反的两个句子组成。这种句式也称为对偶(antithesis)。平行句或平行结构(parallel structure)往往是由两个或两个以上重复的成分组成;重复的成分可以是平行的若干词、短语,也可以是若干句子。这种句式也称为排比(parallelism)。排比中并列使用的词组、短语或句子不仅结构相同或相似,而且意义相关、语气一致。

对称句与平行句形式整齐、节奏鲜明,在叙述和说理方面可以突出论点、增强语势、提高表达力度。排比中平行的各个成分,其语气一般按由弱到强、由浅入深排列,这种富有节奏感、气势逐渐增强的效果不论是抒情还是说理,都能增强文章的表现力和感染力。

对称句示例如下:

例 2-32　In prosperity, our fiends know us; in adversity, we know our friends.

㊋ 得意时,众友识我;失意时,我识良朋。(高瑞武等译)

例 2-33　The reactionary is against progress; the conservative against its abuse.

㊋ 反动派反对进步,保守派反对滥用进步。(高瑞武等译)

例 2-34　In youth we want to change the world; in old age we want to change youth.

㊋ 青年想改造世界,老年想改造青年。(高瑞武等译)

例 2-35　Discipline without freedom is tyranny; freedom without discipline is chaos.

㊋ 只有纪律而无自由是极权,只有自由而无纪律则是混乱。(高瑞武等译)

例 2-36　Without adversity there is no pressure; without pressure there is no change.

㊋ 没有逆境就没有压力;没有压力就没有变化。

例 2-37　Where there is a will, there is a way.

㊋ 有志者事竟成(或译为:事在人为)。

例 2-38　A man who enjoys responsibility usually gets it. A man who merely likes exercising authority usually loses it.

㊋ 承担责任者恒膺重任,只受弄权者恒失权力。(高瑞武等译)

例 2-39　And so, my fellow Americans, ask not what your country can do for you; ask what you can do for your country.

㊋ 所以,我的美国同胞,不要问你们的国家能为你们做些什么;要问你们能为你们的国家做些什么。

例 2-40　They do not suffer from hunger, but they do suffer from malnutrition.

㊋ 他们是没有遭受饥饿,但他们确实营养不良。

例 2-41　God, it appeared, was a mathematician whose calculations were accessible to human reason, and Nature, instead of being an arbitrary collection of mysterious powers of which man had to live in continual fear, was revealed as a system of intelligible forces.

🔵 看来，上帝不过是个数学家，他的计算是人的推理能力所及的，大自然不再是人类连续不断地怀着恐惧心理生活于其中的神秘力量的随意汇集，而已被显示是一种可知力量的体系。（董乐山译）

平行句示例如下：

例 2-42　Myth was assumed to be part of religion, which was assumed to be the primitive counterpart to science, which in turn was assumed to be wholly modern.

🔵 神话被认为是宗教的一部分，宗教被认为是科学的原始对应物，而科学则被认为是完全现代的。（刘象愚译）

例 2-43　Freedom of thought and freedom of expression were the conditions of progress; human invention and intelligence the keys, scientific empiricism the most powerful agent.

🔵 思想自由和言论自由是进步的条件，人的发明和智力是钥匙，科学经验则是最有力量的触媒剂。（董乐山译）

例 2-44　My plea is for the restoration of the personal element in modern life and in modern education at a time when everything is pushing us into collective states of mind, when intellectuals huddle together in committees that issue reports in anonymous prose, when so many people are willing to strip themselves of their personal qualities in order to become clusters of approved characteristics.

🔵 我祈求的是恢复现代生活与现代教育中个人的地位，当一切都在把我们推向集体式心态，当知识分子簇拥在以不具名文章发表报告的委员会里，当如此众多的人甘愿剥掉个人特质以求变成为具有被认可的特征的一群。（颜元叔译）

例 2-45　But the question persists and indeed grows whether the computer will make it easier or harder for human beings to know who they really are, to identify their real problems, to respond more fully to beauty, to place adequate value on life, and to make their world safer than it now is.

🔵 但是，电脑是否将使人类真正认识自我、确认真正问题、更全面地对

美共鸣、对人生作恰如其分的评价，及是否把世界变得比现在更安全，这个疑虑一直存在，并且实际上在不断变大。(颜元叔译)

例 2-46 There is much in England that this explains. It explains the decay of country life, due to the keeping-up of a sham feudalism which drives the more spirited workers off the land. It explains the immobility of the public schools, which have barely altered since the eighties of the last century. It explains the military incompetence which has again and again startled the world.

[译] 这一点可以解释英国社会的诸多问题。它解释了乡村生活的衰退，是因为一种伪封建制度的存在，这种制度将很多精力充沛的工人从他们的土地上赶出来。它解释了公学的僵化，这些学校自 19 世纪 80 年代以来简直就没有变化过。它解释了英国军事上的无能，一次又一次地让世界感到震惊。(刘沁秋和赵勇译)

例 2-47 Few human creatures would consent to be changed into any of the lower animals for a promise of the fullest allowance of a beast's; no intelligent human being would consent to be a fool, no instructed person would be an ignoramus, no person of feeling and conscience would be selfish and base, even though they should be persuaded that the fool, the dunce, or the rascal is better satisfied with his lot than they with theirs.

[译] 即使有人对他们说，傻瓜、低能者或恶棍对其生活的满意感比他们现在对自己境遇的满意感高得多，那么也很少有人愿意将自己变为一个低等动物，以便享受动物的全部快感。没有任何有理智的人会愿意将自己变为傻瓜，没有任何受过良好教育的人会是没有知识的人，没有任何具有情感和良知的人会是自私和卑鄙的。(严忠志译)

例 2-48 That Man is the product of causes which had no prevision of the end they were achieving; that his origin, his growth, his hopes and fears, his loves and his beliefs, are but the outcome of accidental collocations of atoms; that no fire, no heroism, no intensity of thought and feeling, can preserve an individual life beyond the grave; that all the labours of the ages, all the devotion, all the inspiration, all the noonday brightness of human genius, are destined to extinction in the vast death of the solar system, and that the whole temple of Man's achievement must inevitably be buried beneath the debris of a universe in ruins—all these things, if not quite beyond dispute, are yet so nearly certain, that no philosophy which rejects them can hope to stand.

🔵 译 人是无法预知自身结局的多种原因的产物。人的起源、人的成长、人的希望与恐惧、人的种种爱与信仰，都只是原子偶然排列的结果；任何激情、任何英雄的行为、任何强烈的思想感情，都不可能在一个人死后还继续维持其生命；各个时代所有的劳动成果、所有的虔诚、所有的灵感、人类天才所有日正中天的灿烂光辉，都注定要在太阳系的巨大毁灭中消亡，人类成就的整个殿堂，必将不可避免地埋葬于坍塌的宇宙废墟之下——这一切即使并非完全无可争议，也几乎是可以肯定的。任何哲学想否定它们都是不可能站得住脚的。（杨岂深译）

例 2-50 When they viewed with complacency the extent of their own mental powers, when they exercised the various faculties of memory, of fancy, and of judgment, in the most profound speculations, or the most important labours, and when they reflected on the desire of fame, which transported them into future ages, far beyond the bounds of death and of the grave; they were unwilling to confound themselves with the beasts of the field, or to suppose, that a being, for whose dignity they entertained the most sincere admiration, could be limited to a spot of earth, and to a few years of duration.

🔵 译 及彼顾盼自得，矜其心智之所能及；及彼穷尽智虑，用诸大学抑或庙堂；及彼挂念声名，欲自使流芳百世，超乎肉身之限；彼殊不愿自拟与田野走兽同伦，亦不愿使彼衷心称颂之尊贵生灵，囿于尺寸之土、数载之岁。（刘怡译）

需要指出的是，对于语法结构（grammatical structure）的安排，对称的、平衡的、协调的结构总是看起来美观，也更容易理解。对于两个语法结构，可借助 both…and…, not only…but also…, neither…nor…或 either…or…等并列连词或关联连词（correlative conjunction）进行协调安排。平行结构中的并列模块（可以是词、词组、非谓语动词或从句）语法上要一致。也就是说，如果是单词平行，那么单词的词性要一致；如果是句子平行，句子的语法结构要相同；如果非谓语结构平行，那么不定式对不定式，分词对分词。英文句子一般避免头重脚轻，长的、复杂的语法结构宜置于句尾，或者置于并列结构中的后面位置。

例 2-52 In this essay, I will take the most notorious of textbook baddies and try to display their theory as <u>both</u> reasonable in its time <u>and</u> enlightening in our own.

> 译 在本文中,我要举出课本中名声最臭的坏蛋,力求证明他们的理论在当时是合理的,而且在我们今天也有启发性。(杨自伍译)

例 2-53　Most cities in the world today use outdoor lighting that is <u>not only</u> far too bright, <u>but also</u> directed to places where it is not needed.

> 译 当今世界上的大多数城市都使用户外照明,这种照明不仅过于明亮,而且指向不需要的地方。

例 2-54　As the ends of such a partnership cannot be obtained in many generations, it becomes a partnership <u>not only</u> between those who are living, <u>but</u> between those who are living, those who are dead, and those who are to be born.

> 译 由于这样一种合作关系的结果是无法在多少世代之内取得的,于是就变成了一种合作关系,它不仅存在于活着的人之间,而且存在于活着的人、死去的人、将要诞生的人之间。(杨自伍译)

例 2-55　Narrative history is <u>neither</u> as simple <u>nor</u> as straightforward as it might seem. It requires arrangement, composition, planning just like a painting – Rembrandt's '*Night Watch*', for example.

> 译 历史叙述并不像看起来那么简单那么直白。它如同一幅画,需要布局、组织、谋划,如伦勃朗的《夜巡》。(吴简清译)

例 2-56　Leaders <u>provide</u> answers as well as direction, <u>offer</u> strength as well as dedication, <u>and speak</u> from experience as well as understanding of problems they face and the people they work with.

> 译 领导者不仅给予方向性指导,也对问题和要求给予具体解答,不仅示以献身精神而且给予力量。他们说话既根据经验,也根据对问题的认识和对同事的了解。(王炤译)

例 2-57　For many young people, the dream of a lifetime is to <u>travel</u> the world, <u>explore</u> different cultures and landscapes, <u>taste</u> new foods and flavors, <u>and listen</u> to the distinctive sounds of international music and languages.

> 译 对于许多年轻人来说,一生的梦想是周游世界,探索不同的文化和景观,品尝新的食物和风味,聆听国际音乐和语言的独特声音。

例 2-58　Leadership is all about <u>getting</u> people consistently to give their best, <u>helping</u> them to grow to their fullest potential, <u>and motivating</u> them to work toward a common good.

🅣 领导艺术全在于使下级工作人员不断地发挥所长，帮助他们最大限度地发掘潜力，推动他们为共同事业而奋斗。（王焰译）

例 2-59 In the affairs of life or of business, it is <u>not</u> intellect that tells so much as character, <u>not</u> brains so much as heart, <u>not</u> genius so much as self-control, patience, and discipline, regulated by judgment.

🅣 在生活和事业的种种事务之中，人品比智力的作用要大，头脑的作用远不如心地，天资也不如由判断力所制约的自制、耐心与修养。（周华等译）

例 2-60 The whole mammalian type of jaw mechanism is dependent upon <u>very complex jaw muscles, a complex nervous control system, and a specially constructed set of skull bones</u> to withstand the stresses associated with this chewing method.

🅣 所有类型哺乳动物的颌骨机制都需要复杂的颌部肌肉、复杂的神经控制系统，以及一套具有特殊结构的头骨，以便承受这种咀嚼方式所带来的压力。（史立群译）

例 2-61 As regards external events, ego performs that task <u>by becoming aware of stimuli, by storing up experiences about them (in the memory), by avoiding excessively strong stimuli (through flight), by dealing with moderate stimuli (through adaptation) and finally by bringing about expedient changes in the external world to its own advantage (through activity)</u>. As regards internal events, in relation to the id, it performs that task <u>by gaining control over the demands of the instincts, by deciding whether they are to be allowed satisfaction, by postponing that satisfaction to times and circumstances favorable to the external world or by suppressing their excitations entirely</u>.

🅣 对于外界事件，自我这样来发挥功能：通过意识到刺激的存在，存储有关它们的经历（于记忆中），（通过逃离）避免过度强烈的刺激，（通过适应）处理温和的刺激，最后（通过活动）对外界作出利己的权宜变化。对于关系到本我的内心事件，自我如此发挥功能：它对本能的要求施加控制、决定是否允许它们获得满足、将这种满足的获得拖延至与外界契合的时间和场合，或者完全地抑制它们引起的兴奋。（尹莉译）

两个或一对并列成分，可用连词 and 连接，也可不用 and 但用逗号分隔；但如果为了强调第二个成分时，可用逗号在连词（and/but/or）前面分隔。当一对并列成分较长，读者不易搞清其范围时，可用逗号在连接两个并列成分的连词前面分隔。在两个以上的并列成分之间可用逗号分隔，最后一个并列成分之前使用 and/or；and/or 前面使用或不使用逗号分隔的例子均有，但在 and/or 前面使用逗号，也就是所谓的"系列逗号或连续逗号（serial comma）"；and 前面使用逗号在某些情况（and 前后的两个并列成分有可能是一种事物）下可保证不会造成误解，如 They have mobile phones in the following colors: silver, pink, blue, red, black, yellow and green. 就很容易让人理解为"他们的手机有银色（silver）、粉红色（pink）、蓝色（blue）、红色（red）、黑色（black）、黄绿色（yellow and green）6 种"，而如果改用系列逗号如 They have mobile phones in the following colors: silver, pink, blue, red, black, yellow, and green. 则可确定无疑地理解为"他们的手机有银色、粉红色、蓝色、红色、黑色、黄色（yellow）和绿色（green）7 种"。两个以上的并列成分，如果为了让读者感受到并列成分累积的力度，在最后一个并列成分之前可不使用 and/or。如果并列结构中的成分过长或读者容易混淆并列成分的层次和范围，除使用逗号将并列的成分分开外，还可重复并列成分之前的单词（如介词或连词），以便于读者识别并列的成分范围，避免错觉、歧义或模糊含义。当一系列并列成分内部还有逗号分隔时，可在并列成分之间用分号分开。

例 2-62　The Renaissance leapt ahead into its own necessary future, into the development and near perfection of machines.

🔵 文艺复兴时期大步迈进了它必然到来的未来，迈进了机器发展和近乎完善的阶段。（杨自伍译）

例 2-63　Systems which attempt to question it, deal in sounds instead of sense, in caprice instead of reason, in darkness instead of light.

🔵 尝试对此提出质疑的各种体系，论述时是以声音代替道理，以奇想代替理性，以黑暗代替光明。（杨自伍译）

例 2-64　According to the textbooks, preformationists believed that a perfect miniature homunculus inhabited the human egg (or sperm), and that embryological development involved nothing more than its increase in size.

🔵 据课本所称，预成论者相信，一个完整的微型胎体存在于人卵（或者说精子），胚胎生长无非只是越变越大而已。（杨自伍译）

例 2-65　In my view, scientism rests on the fallacious claim that the theoretical or natural scientific way of viewing things provides the primary and most significant access to ourselves and our world, and that the methodology of the natural sciences provides the best form of explanation for all phenomena.

🔵译 在我看来，科学主义是基于这样一种错误的主张，即认为看待万物的理论方式或自然科学方法提供了使我们了解自我和世界的主要的和最为重要的方式，而自然科学的方法论则提供了解释一切现象的最好方式。（江怡译）

例 2-66 The principle of utility recognizes his subjection, and assumes it for the foundation of that system, the object of which is to rear the fabric of felicity by the hands of reason and of law.

🔵译 功利原理承认这种屈服，而且假定它是那个体系的基础，而体系的宗旨则是假借理性之手和法律之手来扶植幸福的机理。（杨自伍译）

例 2-67 Absolute dating methods are mostly applied to the rocks in which the hominin fossil was found, or to non-hominin fossils recovered from the same horizon.

🔵译 绝对测年方法主要应用于发现人类化石的岩层的年代测定，或用于从相同层位发现的非灵长类化石的年代测定。（冯兴无译）

例 2-68 Absolute dating methods rely on knowing the time it takes for natural processes, such as atomic decay, to run their course, or they relate the fossil horizon to precisely calibrated global events such as reversals in the direction of the earth's magnetic field.

🔵译 绝对测年方法依赖对自然进程如原子衰变所需时间的了解，或者能将化石层与精确标定的全球性事件如地球磁场方向的反转相联系。（冯兴无译）

例 2-69 To be truly happy is a question of how we begin and not of how we end, of what we want and not of what we have.

🔵译 所谓真正的幸福，指的是如何开端，而不是如何结束；指得是我们渴望着什么，而不是我们占有着什么。（刘柄善译）

例 2-70 Most commonly we come to books with blurred and divided minds, asking of fiction that it shall be true, of poetry that it shall be false, of biography that is shall be flattering, of history that it shall enforce our own prejudices.

🔵译 通常我们总是三心二意带着模糊的观念去看书：要求小说情节真实，要求诗歌内容虚构，要求传记阿谀奉承，要求历史能加深我们的偏见。（江怡译）

例 2-71 Our life is an apprenticeship to the truth, that around every circle another can be drawn; that there is no end in nature, but every end is a beginning;

that there is always another dawn risen on mid-noon, and under every deep a lower deep opens.

🔵译 我们一生都在学习这样的真理：围绕每一个圆都可以再画一个圆；自然界中没有终点，而每个终点都是一个开端；正午时分总有另一缕曙光升起，每个深渊下面还有一个深渊。（彭发胜译）

例 2-72 Then there is a still higher type of courage – the courage to brave pain, to live with it, to never let others know of it and to still find joy in life; to wake up in the morning with an enthusiasm for the day ahead.

🔵译 然而还有品格更高一层的勇气——这种勇气就是勇敢面对痛苦，忍受痛苦，决不让他人知道痛苦，而且依然能够在生活之中找到欢乐；清晨醒来时还能够怀着满腔热情去迎接新的一天的到来。（周华等译）

例 2-73 The province of the epic is the poetical narrative of real or supposed events, and the representation of real, or at least natural, characters; and history, in its noblest examples, is an account of occurrences in which great events are commemorated, and distinguished men appear as agents and actors.

🔵译 史诗的领域包括对真实或虚构事件的诗化描述，以及对真实、或至少是自然的人物性格的描写；而史书，从最为卓越的几部典范之作中可以看出，它是对历史事件的记叙，其中记载着重大事件，还有出类拔萃的人物不时以代理人或演员的身份登台亮相。（石敏译）

例 2-74 There is room for an amateur to say something about Buddha faces, because the experts tend rather to avoid so indefinite a topic, while there are two likely misunderstandings for a man in the street: that the Buddhas have no expression at all, an idea set on foot by Lafcadio Hearn, who had a genuine feeling for the East but was almost blind; or else that they all sneer, a thing G. K. Chesterton, for instance, often says, which is less easy to answer.

🔵译 关于佛的尊容，门外汉有机会说上几句，因为专家们往往避而不谈这样一个定义不明的话题，然而一个普通人可能有两种误解：认为佛根本没有表情，这个想法始于拉夫卡迪奥·赫恩，他对东方怀有真诚的感情，但是却几乎一无所知；或者认为佛在嗤笑，例如吉·凯·切斯特顿经常这么说，这是一个更不容易回答的问题。（穆国豪译）

例 2-75 Our life is a brief span measuring some sixty or seventy years in all, but nearly one half of this has to be spent in sleep; some years have to be spent over our meals; some over dressing and undressing; some in making journeys on land and voyages by sea; some in merry-making, either on our own account or for the sake of others; some in celebrating religious and social festivities; some in watching over the sick beds of our nearest and dearest relatives.

🔵译 人生短暂，总共不过六七十年，可是将近一半时间必须用于睡眠；吃饭时间总加起来也得几年工夫；穿衣脱衣又是几年；水路陆路旅行又是几年；再加上几年娱乐时间——不论是为自己还是为别人；几年宗教节日和社会节日的庆祝活动；我们的近亲至亲病了，侍奉汤药也得几年工夫。（王焰译）

例 2-76 The previous history of metaphysics has attempted to answer the being-question in various ways: for Plato, it is answered through the notion of 'form', namely that knowledge of a thing is knowledge of the form of a thing; for Aristotle, it is expressed with the notion of 'substance'; for Thomas Aquinas, it is answered with reference to the 'self-caused cause', that is God; for Hegel, it is 'Spirit'; for Nietzsche, it is 'will to power'; and so on.

🔵译 形而上学先前的历史一直在试图以各种方式回答存在问题：在柏拉图看来，它可以通过"形式"概念加以回答，即关于事物的知识就是关于事物形式的知识；在亚里士多德看来，它可以表达为"本体"概念；在托马斯·阿奎那看来，它可以用"自有之因"，即上帝，来回答；在黑格尔看来，它就是"精神"；在尼采看来，它就是"权力意志"；如此等等。（江怡译）

例 2-77 These processes ('dream-work') included condensation, the fusing together of different ideas and images into a single image; displacement, in which a potentially disturbing image or idea is replaced by something connected but less disturbing; representation, the process by which thoughts are converted into visual images; and symbolization, in which some neutral object stands for, or alludes to, some aspect of sexual life or those persons connected with it which the dreamer would prefer not to recognize.

🔵译 这个过程（指上文的"梦工作"）包括凝缩，即不同想法和形象融合在一起；转移，即一个潜在令人不安的形象或想法被相关的、但不是那么令人烦扰的事物所替代；表现，即思想被转化为视觉形象；象征，即某种中性的事物代表或者暗指性生活的某个方面，或者与之相关的、梦者不愿意辨认的一些人物。（尹莉译）

例 2-78 This questioning has been conducted via a range of gestures that has run from the iconoclastic, such as Picasso's use of newspaper and wallpaper, old tin cans, and other junk to make his collages and sculptures; through the provocative, as in Pollock's abandonment of paintbrushes, oils, and painterly dexterity for the crudeness of household enamel poured straight from the tin; or Warhol's deadpan adoption, in his soup can prints and brillo box sculptures, of the impersonal techniques of advertisement billboards and packaging; to the blatantly challenging, such as Duchamp's nomination of a urinal (and, more recently and exotically, Hirst's nomination of a dead shark) as a work of art.

[译] 这种质疑通过各种方式进行表达，从反传统，如毕加索用报纸、壁纸、旧锡罐及其他杂物制作拼贴画和雕塑——到挑衅，如波洛克放弃画笔、颜料和创作技巧，改为随意地从锡罐中泼洒家用亮光涂料，或是安迪·沃霍尔在汤罐头版画和布日罗啤酒盒做的雕塑中采用广告和包装业所使用的非个性化的技法——再到公然地挑战，如杜尚将一个小便器(后来，赫斯特以更奇异的方式将一条死鲨鱼)命为艺术品。(朱扬明译)

第三单元

简洁清晰

文章贵简洁。王充在《论衡·自纪》中指出："文贵约而指通，言尚省而趋明。"刘勰在《文心雕龙·议对》中也说："文以辩洁为能，不以繁缛为巧。"刘知几在《史通·叙事》中提到："叙事之工者，以简要为主。简之时义大矣哉！"安东·契诃夫(Anton Chekhov)说："Conciseness is the sister of talent."（简洁是天才的姐妹）。亚历山大·蒲柏(Alexander Pope)有言："Words are like leaves; and where they most abound, Much fruit of sense beneath is rarely found."（言词就像树叶，最茂密的树叶之下很难找到丰硕的意义之果）。

清晰更重要。威廉·津瑟(William Zinsser)认为："写作的四个基本前提应该是清晰、简洁、简单和人性。"(Four basic premises of writing should be clarity, brevity, simplicity and humanity.)。清晰是排在第一位的。为什么如此？因为比利·科克斯(Billy Cox)说过："清晰就是力量"(Clarity is power)，而托马斯·伦纳德(Thomas Leonard)也有言："清晰才能聚焦"(Clarity affords focus)。

简洁和清晰可在段落和篇章上用力，也可以在措词和句法上用力。但其实写作问题就是思维问题，只有思路清晰，才能做到写作简洁和清晰。大卫·麦卡洛(David McCullough)说："Writing is thinking. To write well is to think clearly."（写作就是思考。写得好就是要思维清晰），而比尔·惠勒(Bill Wheeler)也说："Good writing is clear thinking made visible."（好的写作就是将清晰的思维呈现出来）。

一般文章应当做到简洁和清晰，学术文章更应该如此。因为学术文献浩如烟海，需要读的文献实在太多，所以应为读者着想，让学术文章应尽可能简洁、清晰，不仅节省读者时间与精力，也有利于自己学术成果的交流和推广。本单元主要从措词和语法角度说明如何简洁和清晰地写作，重点是选择合适的词语和句式。

一、简洁

（一）讲究措词

尽管乔治·奥威尔(George Orwell)说过"Never use a long word where a short one will do."（能用短词的时候就别用长词），但学术写作一般讲究措词要正式。而正式词通常都为长单词，例如，日常用词 about 与对应的正式词是 approximately，begin 对应的正式词是 commence 或 initiate，many 或 much 对应的正式词是 substantial proportion, buy 对应的正式词是 purchase, before 对应的正式词是 prior to.

那么，如何在措词方面做到简洁呢？乔治·奥威尔（George Orwell）说过："If it is possible to cut a word out, always cut it out."（如果能够删除某个词，就删除它）。

（1）不要使用成对的单词。如 each and every, first and foremost, basic and fundamental, full and complete 等。

（2）去掉意义上的冗词。如 <u>unexpectedly</u> surprise, <u>terrible</u> tragedy, <u>future</u> plans, <u>final</u> outcome, <u>true</u> facts 等，划线的为前面意义上多余的形容词。

（3）去掉多余的范畴词。如 large in <u>size</u>, round in <u>shape</u>, pink in <u>color</u>, shiny in <u>appearance</u>, in an accurate <u>manner</u>, <u>area</u> of mathematics, period of <u>time</u>, educational <u>system</u>, public recreational <u>activities</u> 等。

（4）用词代替词组。如 about 代替 in the matter of, to 代替 in order to, for 代替 for the purpose of, by 代替 by means of, if, when 代替 in the event that, now 代替 at the present time, at this point of time, because 代替 for the reason that, due to the fact that, owing to the fact that, because of the fact that, by virtue of the fact that, since 代替 in view of the fact that, like 代替 in the nature of, always 代替 at all time, daily 代替 on a daily basis, finally 代替 in the final analysis 等。

（5）用肯定词代替否定词。如 different 代替 not the same, rarely 代替 not often, few 代替 not many, continue 代替 not stop, omit 代替 not include, overlook 代替 not notice, prevent 代替 not allow 等。

（6）在一般英语写作中，滥用模糊限制语（hedge）和强势语（intensifier）没有必要。《清晰与优雅的风格课程》（*Style lessons in clarity and grace*）中列举的模糊限制语包括副词 possibly, perhaps, apparently, arguably, usually, often, sometimes, almost, somewhat, certain, particular, to a certain extent 等，形容词 some, many, most 等，动词 seem, suggest, indicate, may, might, can, could 等。强势语包括副词 very, quite, rather, certainly, really, actually, undoubtedly, practically, basically, generally, obviously, clearly, inevitably 等，形容词 basic, fundamental, crucial, essential 等，动词 show, prove, establish 等。另外，过多使用元话语（metadiscourse）如 I believe, note that, consider now, as you see, I will explain, look at the next example, in regard to, so far as…is concerned 等会使句子的意思不够显豁。

而在科技英语写作中，会经常使用到上述模糊限制语和强势语，只是需要注意意义和程度的区别。例如，prove，establish，confirm，validate，support 表示有证据明确地证明、确定、验证和支持，show，reveal，display，suggest，demonstrate，indicate 等表示一般性地表明或显示某种现象或情况存在或发生，implicate，imply 也是表明的意思，但确定性程度最低。又如，possible 和 probable 都是“可能的”的意思，但存在细微区别：possible 表示客观上“有潜力的、有能力的”，但在概率上是不确定的、可变化的，而 probable 则表示“在概率上是有可能发生的或真的”。也就是说，当你相信某事不只是有能力（possible）发生或真实的，而且相信有可能发生或真实时，就要用 probable. 初学者对 significant 和 obvious，apparent，noticeable，notable，remarkable 的使用也极易混淆。当使用 significant 时，表示在统计学上是“显著的”，因此不能随便乱用，而 obvious，apparent，noticeable，notable，remarkable 只是一般性或非统计学意义上“显然的、明显的、显而易见的、显著的”意思。在推测可能性程度上，must，will，would，should，could，may，might 由 100% 的确定性（must）向下依次降低；在表示推测最常用的 may 和 might 之间，may 表示根据证据或现象上判断有可能发生的或者是事实的，might 表示猜测的、不一定有事实依据的、发生的可能性低于 may 的情况。在事情发生频度上，always，usually，frequently，often，sometimes，occasionally，rarely，seldom，hardly ever，never 从 100% 依次降低。上述词语在意义和程度上的细微差别需要格外注意。此外，学术英语的风格一般应平易典实，避免奇险浮华，因此，也不宜过多使用不必要的形容词和副词。

（二）经营句法

（1）英语中利用定语从句对名词“随举随释”，最能体现英语的特点，本身就是简洁的一种表现。

例 3-1 The observatory, which was launched last year to find other Earths, made the discoveries in its first few weeks of science operations.

[译] 该观测台去年发射的目的是寻找其他地球，在最初几周的科学探测行动中就做出了这些发现。

例 3-2 We propose that peptidases, the most common and abundant proteins found in the laticifers of many plants, are key molecules involved in plant defense mediated by laticifers.

[译] 我们认为肽酶作为许多植物乳管中最常见和最丰富的蛋白质，是乳汁

细胞介导植物防御的关键分子。

例 3-3 Stress causes the body to release cortisol, which can impair memory and has been found to shrink the memory centers in the brain.

🔹 译 压力会使身体释放皮质醇，皮质醇会削弱记忆，并且会使大脑的记忆中枢萎缩。

例 3-4 The costly print advertisements that kept magazines and newspapers alive were migrating to the web, where they earned only pennies on the dollar.

🔹 译 曾一度养活了报纸杂志的昂贵广告费从那时开始向互联网转移，网络广告商只需要消耗较低的成本，就可以赚取较高的利润。（何凯文译）

例 3-5 People who averaged fewer than seven hours of sleep per night in the weeks before being exposed to the cold virus were nearly three times as likely to get sick as those who averaged eight hours or more, a new study found.

🔹 译 一项新的研究发现，人在接触感冒病毒前的一周内，平均每晚睡眠时间低于 7 小时的患病概率是那些睡眠不少于 8 小时的近 3 倍。（达子译）

例 3-6 A human being is an individual who has grown from a fertilized egg which contained genes from both father and mother.

🔹 译 人是从受精卵演化成的个体，这个受精卵既包含着其父亲的基因，也包含着其母亲的基因。（何凯文译）

本例句中，定语从句 who has grown from a fertilized egg 修饰 an individual，而 which contained genes from both father and mother 又修饰 a fertilized egg。

例 3-7 Nitrogen fixation is a process in which certain bacteria use atmospheric nitrogen gas, which green plants cannot directly utilize, to produce ammonia, a nitrogen compound plants can use.

🔹 译 固氮是某些细菌利用大气中绿色植物不能直接利用的氮气来制造植物可以利用的氮化合物氨气的过程。（吴中东和宫玉波译）

本例句有三个层次的修饰关系：第一个层次是 in which certain bacteria use atmospheric nitrogen gas 为 a process 的限制性定语从句；第二个层次是 which green plants cannot directly utilize, to produce ammonia 为修饰 atmospheric nitrogen gas 的非限制性定语从句；第三个层次是 a nitrogen compound plants can use 为 ammonia 的同位语结构。很好地体现了定语从句及相同功能结构在阐明新概念中的作用。

（2）有些定语从句还可进一步简化，如主从复合句中的主系表结构的定语从句去掉 which/who/that be, 保留后面的表语，也就是修改为同位语结构。

例 3-8 In 2008 there were 463, 000 children in foster care, which is a system where the government places orphans and children with parents who are abusive or unable to take care of them in the care of guardians.

从原例句中删除 which is, 将非限制性定语从句改为同位语结构：

In 2008 there were 463, 000 children in foster care, a system where the government places orphans and children with parents who are abusive or unable to take care of them in the care of guardians.

[译] 在 2008 年，46.3 万名儿童得到成长关照系统的保护，政府通过这个系统为孤儿、父母有虐待行为或无法提供实际监护的小孩提供监护人。(何凯文译)

例 3-9 One had, therefore, to encapsulate only a limited number of generations, which were not the potential products of several million years on a twentieth-century geological time chart.

从原例句中删除 which were, 将非限制性定语从句转变为同位语结构：

One had, therefore, to encapsulate only a limited number of generations, not the potential products of several million years on a twentieth-century geological time chart.

[译] 因此，当人们只得概括为数有限的生殖代，而不是根据一张 20 世纪的地质时期表来概括几百万年的潜在产物。(杨自伍译)

例 3-10 Safe Families, which is a non-profit outfit that places children in temporary homes with volunteer families until jobless parents can get back on their feet, saw the number of children it serviced triple in 2012, and it expects that number to double again in 2013.

从原例句中删除 which is, 将非限制性定语从句改为同位语结构：Safe Families, a non-profit outfit that places children in temporary homes with volunteer families until jobless parents can get back on their feet, saw the number of children it serviced triple in 2012, and it expects that number to double again in 2013.

[译] 还有一家名为"安全家"的非营利性机构将小孩安置在临时志愿者家中，直到失业的父母能重拾生计。2012 年该机构帮助的小孩数量增长了三倍，据说到 2013 年还会再翻倍。(何凯文译)

例 3-11 CMS, run by Dr. Incandela, and ATLAS, run by Dr. Gianotti, are fitted to the Large Hadron Collider (LHC), which is the principal piece of equipment at Europe's main particle-physics laboratory, near Geneva, which CERN runs.

从原例句中，删除 which is,将非限制性定语从句改为同位语结构：

CMS, run by Dr. Incandela, and ATLAS, run by Dr. Gianotti, are fitted to the Large Hadron Collider (LHC), <u>the principal piece of equipment at Europe's main particle-physics laboratory</u>, near Geneva, which CERN runs.

🔘 译 Incandela 博士是紧凑型 μ 子螺旋形磁谱仪的负责人，而 Gianotti 博士主要负责超导环场探测器，这两个实验装置与位于日内瓦附近欧洲粒子物理实验室的主要设备——大型强子对撞机——协同工作，由欧洲粒子物理研究总署运营。（何凯文译）

例 3-12 The discovery puts the finishing flourish on the Standard Model, which is the best explanation to date for how the universe works-except in the domain of gravity, which is governed by the general theory of relativity.

从原例句中删除 which is,将非限制性定语从句改为同位语结构：

The discovery puts the finishing flourish on the Standard Model, <u>the best explanation to date for how the universe works – except in the domain of gravity, which is governed by the general theory of relativity.</u>

🔘 译 本次发现为标准模型理论画上了一个完美的句号，该模型对除了广义相对论涵盖的重力范围外宇宙的运行机制做出了最好的解释。（何凯文译）

前面的例子都是复合句中的定语从句修改为复指性修饰语/词（resumptive modifier）的情况，也就是说，同位语结构是对前面紧跟名词的复指或复述。下面的例句是一个定语从句修改为总结性修饰语/词（summative modifier），也就是说，同位语结构是对前面整个句子部分内容的总结和概括。

例 3-13 Social stress may release hormones that affect bone loss, which is a finding that might be linked to the higher incidence of bone fractures after the menopause.

从原例句中删除 which is,将非限制性定语从句改为同位语结构：

Social stress may release hormones that affect bone loss, <u>a finding that might be linked to the higher incidence of bone fractures after the menopause.</u>

🔘 译 社会压力可能释放影响骨质流失的激素，这一发现可能与更年期后更高的骨折发生率有关。

例 3-14 The rise in non-communicable diseases reflects declines in maternal and child mortality over nearly three decades, which is largely the result of economic growth and increasing levels of education.

从原例句中删除 which is, 将非限制性定语从句改为同位语结构：

The rise in non-communicable diseases reflects declines in maternal and child mortality over nearly three decades, largely the result of economic growth and increasing levels of education.

🔄 非传染性疾病的增加反映了近30年来孕产妇和儿童死亡率的下降，这主要是经济增长和教育水平提高的结果。

（3）如果中心词或被修饰词也在定语从句（主动句或被动句）中做主语，那么定语从句也可修改为现在分词结构（原定语从句为主动句）或过去分词结构（原定语从句为被动句）。或者直接将复合句中的定语从句切断，修改为独立句子。

例 3-15 The preformationists must have been blind, antiempirical dogmatists who support an *a priori* doctrine of immutability against clear evidence of the senses – for one only has to open a chicken's egg in order to watch an embryo develop from simplicity to complexity.

从原例句中删除 who, 将限制性定语从句转变为现在分词短语：

The preformationists must have been blind, antiempirical dogmatists supporting an *a priori* doctrine of immutability against clear evidence of the senses – for one only has to open a chicken's egg in order to watch an embryo develop from simplicity to complexity.

🔄 预成论者肯定是盲目的、反经验主义的教条主义者，他们支持一种恒定不变的先验学说而反对感官提供明证——因为人们只要打开鸡蛋便可观察一个胚胎从简单到复杂的生长过程。（杨自伍译）

例 3-16 White House officials who are looking for any sign of a break in the opposition ranks took heart that a group of Republican senators supported increased spending on July 23rd, albeit only for transport, and only in a procedural vote.

从原例句中删除 who are, 将从句改成现在分词短语：

White House officials looking for any sign of a break in the opposition ranks took heart that a group of Republican senators supported increased spending on July

23nd, albeit only for transport, and only in a procedural vote.

🀄 现在已经有一些共和党参议员于7月23日同意增加支出，虽然只针对交通，并且只是程序性投票，但这已使得一直致力于在共和党议员中找寻突破口的白宫官员们振作了起来。（何凯文译）

例 3-17 A new report, 'Sponsor Effect: UK', which is <u>produced by the Centre of Talent Innovation (CTI), a New York think-tank, offers a detailed picture of the female talent pipeline in Britain, based on a survey of about 2,500 graduate employees, mostly of large companies.</u>

从原例句中删除 which is，将非限制性定语从句改为过去分词短语：

A new report, 'Sponsor Effect: UK', produced by the Centre of Talent Innovation (CTI), a New York think-tank, offers a detailed picture of the female talent pipeline in Britain, based on a survey of about 2500 graduate employees, mostly of large companies.

🀄 一家名为人才创新中心的纽约智囊团最近发表了一分标题为"英国赞助者效应"的报告。该报告基于约2500名主要就职于大公司的本科毕业生，详细介绍了英国女性人才的发展道路。（何凯文译）

例 3-18 If people stop taking their ART medicines, some of this dormant viral DNA wakes up, and blood virus levels surge back up again. So any hope of a permanent cure requires getting rid of this reservoir of virus-infected cells, which are found all over the body, including in the bone marrow, brain, and lymph nodes.

从原例句中删除 which are，将非限制性定语从句改为过去分词短语：

If people stop taking their ART medicines, some of this dormant viral DNA wakes up, and blood virus levels surge back up again. So any hope of a permanent cure requires getting rid of this reservoir of virus-infected cells, <u>found all over the body, including in the bone marrow, brain, and lymph</u> nodes.

🀄 如果人们停止服用他们的艺术药物，一些潜伏的病毒DNA就会苏醒，血液中的病毒水平会再次上升。因此，任何对永久性治疗的希望都需要清除这种病毒感染的细胞，这种病毒感染的细胞遍布全身，包括骨髓、大脑和淋巴结。

例 3-19 And, come to think of it, what could be more fantastic than the claim that an egg contains thousands of instructions, which are written on molecules that tell the cell to turn on and off the production of certain substances that regulate the speed of chemical processes?

从原例句中删除 which are, 将非限制性定语从句转变为过去分词短语：

And, come to think of it, what could be more fantastic than the claim that an egg contains thousands of instructions, written on molecules that tell the cell to turn on and off the production of certain substances that regulate the speed of chemical processes?

❥ 再则，有人声称一个卵子包含数以千计的指令，写在分子上晓示细胞开始和停止生产一定特质的时间，而这些物质能调节化学变化过程的速度，不妨来试想一下，还有什么比这个断言更加荒诞不经的呢？（杨自伍译）

下面例句中的分词结构均可视作定语从句的简略形式：

例 3-20　Experts also found that the evolution of the dream animals corresponds to the growth of the baby, ranging from aquatic creatures like tadpoles during the first trimester, to cuddly puppies and bunnies in the second, and to monkeys and gorillas in the final phase.

❥ 专家们也发现：梦见动物与胎儿的生长发育有关，在前三个月时，会梦见诸如蝌蚪一类的水生动物，而后发展到第二阶段是可拥抱的幼犬和小兔，最终是猴子和大猩猩。（史含皤译）

例 3-21　The positive ions and negative electrons are transported to alternate sides of a chloroplast membrane, creating an electrochemical potential similar to that inside a battery.

❥ 正离子和负电子分别被输送到叶绿体膜的两侧，就产生了和电池内类似的电化学势。（李德煜和张会欣译）

例 3-22　Then a drought, which eventually lasted 300 years, crippled the farming communities on which the cities depended, forcing urban dwellers to abandon their empty granaries and silent temples.

❥ 然后是最终持续了300年之久的一次大旱使城市赖以生存的农业社区陷于瘫痪，迫使城市居民离弃他们已被吃空的谷仓和已无人祈祷的神殿。（韩青译）

（4）物称（包括抽象名词）作主语，具有简洁化的效果。由于英汉语的差别，英语常用物称作主语，中国人则不善于使用物称，而多用人称作主语来造句。当使用抽象名词作主语时，如果不滥用、不装腔作势，很多情况下句子会更简洁，概括性强，有客观性和静态化的效果。学术英语中，动词名词化使用较多。名词化是指用名词或名词结构来表达属于动词或动词结构所表达的信息，如用抽象名词来表达动作、行为、变化、状态等。抽象名词作主语可以使表达正式、简洁，造句灵活、自然，便于表达复杂的内容，还有庄重、典雅的文体效果。名词化能够压缩并容纳更多的信息，并凸显抽象的观念，而不是人和动作，因此，对于关注抽象的想法和原因的学术写作，名词化是十分简洁而有用的书面表达。但是，名词化隐去了行动主体的具体场景、主观能动性和动作，不可避免地产生晦涩难懂的文体效果。

例 3-23 Progress and efficiency, for example, make no appeal to the Chinese, except to those who have come under Western influence.

🔵 译 例如，除了那些受到西方影响的中国人外，进步和效率对中国人没有吸引力。

例 3-24 Friction caused by overly tight pants may lead to bladder infections.

🔵 译 过于紧身的牛仔裤所产生的摩擦可能会导致膀胱感染。

例 3-25 Finally, a strange kind of disfigurement can occur when too-tight jeans force fatty tissue into areas above the knee.

🔵 译 最后，过于紧身的牛仔裤会将脂肪组织推到膝盖以上部位，从而产生一种奇怪的畸形。

例 3-26 For example, financial independence makes it easier for women to find a way out of an unhappy marriage.

🔵 译 例如，经济独立让女性更容易找到摆脱不幸婚姻的方法。

例 3-27 Rather than attacking cancer cells, like many drugs, the new treatment harnesses the power of the immune system to fight tumours.

🔵 译 这种新疗法并不是像其他许多药物一样抗击癌细胞，而是调动免疫系统的力量来对抗肿瘤。

例 3-28 The emissions may also heighten the risk of Alzheimer's disease and speed the effects of Parkinson's disease.

🔵 译 汽车尾气也可能增加患老年痴呆症的风险，并加快帕金森氏症的恶化。

例 3-29 The lack of proprieties (of etiquette) would make the most intimate friends turn to be the most decided enemies and the friendly or allied countries declare war against each other.

🔵 译 缺了礼节，最亲密的朋友会变成死敌，友好或结盟的国家会兵戎相见。

（方全译）

例 3-30 Success in any scientific career requires an unusual equipment of capacity, industry, and energy.

译 任何科学事业上的成就，都需要具有不寻常的才能、勤勉和精力。（汪文珍和方全译）

例 3-31 The explanation for the phenomenon of the rising teenage suicide rate involves many complicated factors.

译 对上升的少年自杀率的解释涉及许多复杂的原因。（王炤译）

例 3-32 The application of large enough magnetic fields results in the disruption of superconducting states in materials even at drastically low temperature, thereby changing them directly into insulators — or so was traditionally thought.

译 应用足够大的磁场，即使在极低的温度下，也会导致材料中超导态的破坏，从而直接将其转变为绝缘体——传统上是这样认为的。

例 3-33 The century and a half which preceded the Enlightenment had seen the opening up of the tight, closed world of medieval and Renaissance Europe.

译 在启蒙运动前的一个半世纪里，中世纪和文艺复兴时期的欧洲这个紧紧封闭的世界慢慢开放了。（董乐山译）

例 3-34 Fossilization of a bone begins when chemicals from the surrounding sediments replace the organic material in the hard tissues.

译 骨骼的石化最先是周围沉积物中的化学物质替代硬组织里的有机物质。（冯兴无译）

例 3-35 The formalization of language in logical analysis transforms into a technical instrument.

译 逻辑分析语言的形式化把语言变成了一种技术工具。（江怡译）

例 3-36 The temptation of the educator is to explain and describe, to organize a body of knowledge for the student, leaving the student with nothing to do.

译 教育者总是想替学生解释、描述、组织一套知识，让学生落得无事可做。（颜元叔译）

例 3-37 The rhetoric generated by this dispute has attained bitter and sometimes unprintable proportions.

译 这次争论引发的言辞已经达到刻薄而有时候是不宜付印发表的程度。（颜元叔译）

例 3-38　In addition, advances in cockpit technology and aircraft reliability can lull pilots into complacency, and even erode basic flying skills because computers do so much of the flying on commercial airliners.

译　此外，驾驶舱技术进步和飞机可靠性提高也会使飞行员麻痹大意，甚至会削弱基本的飞行技能，因为商业飞机上计算机系统控制着大部分的飞行程序。（达子译）

例 3-39　Globalization and technology allow foreigners and machines to compete for jobs once done by Americans.

译　全球化和技术进步给外国人和机器提供机会，竞争本应由美国人完成的工作。（何凯文译）

例 3-40　But his willingness to criticize the chaotic regulatory structure imposed on banks after the financial crisis has exposed him to political retribution.

译　他也总是成为政客们报复的对象，因为他对于金融危机后银行面临的混乱监管总是表现得过于心直口快。（何凯文译）

例 3-41　These inventions and discoveries — fire, speech, weapons, domestic animals, agriculture, and writing — made the existence of civilized communities possible.

译　这些发明和发现——火、语言、武器、家畜、农业和文字——使文明社会能够出现。（谭卫国译）

例 3-42　This growing poverty in the midst of growing poverty constitutes a permanent menace not only to peace but also to democratic institutions and personal liberty, for over-population is not compatible with freedom.

译　不断扩大的贫穷不仅对和平构成永久的威胁，而且是对民主制度和个人自由的威胁，因为人口过剩与自由是不相容的。（谭卫国译）

例 3-43　Insecurity and the weakening of union organization have reduced the capacity of employees to resist the employers' demands for harder and better work, demands driven by increased competition and closer state regulation.

译　生活的不确定性，加上工会组织的弱化，削弱了被雇佣者抗拒雇主的劳动力要求的底气，由于日益激烈的竞争以及国家更为严密的管控，雇主要求他们更好地完成更加艰巨的工作。（张罗和陆赟译）

例 3-44　The gap has widened between those trapped in low-wage occupations who face insecure futures and those able to exploit the new opportunities to accumulate wealth.

㊋ 一部分人身陷低工资的职业，面临不确定的未来，一部分人则能够抓住新的机会积累财富，这两类人之间差距越来越大。（张罗和陆赟译）

例 3-45　The quarter century of relatively stable economic growth after 1945 may have shaped a generation's expectations about capitalist normality but it was not historically typical of capitalism.

㊋ 自1945年后的25年，经济发展相对平稳，这或许是一代人心目中规范的资本主义，但这段时期并不是典型的资本主义。（张罗和陆赟译）

例 3-46　The scanty and suspicious materials of ecclesiastical history seldom enable us to dispel the dark cloud that hangs over the first age of the church.

㊋ 教会史之资料贫乏可疑，吾辈难于洞悉其初创时代种种疑窦。（刘怡译）

例 3-47　Our curiosity is naturally prompted to inquire by what means the Christian faith obtained so remarkable a victory over the established religions of the earth.

如是，吾辈之好奇心自当导向此一问题之探究：何以基督教之信仰得以完胜世间既存之一般宗教？（刘怡译）

例 3-48　The sullen obstinacy with which they maintained their peculiar rites and unsocial manners, seemed to mark them out a distinct species of men, who body professed, or who faintly disguised, their implacable hatred to the rest of human-kind.

㊋ 犹太人谨奉渠专属之礼法，遗世独立，其拘谨固执之态，似已自显为一特殊族群，于非其族类者，则直言常存憎恶之心，几无宿物。（刘怡译）

例 3-49　The acquisition of knowledge, the exercise of our reason or fancy, and the cheerful flow of unguarded conversation, may employ the leisure of a liberal mind.

㊋ 世间旷达之士皆得享闲暇之乐，或优游于求知问道之途，或锤炼其理性感性诸思维，亦可言谈无拘，实乃快人心意。（刘怡译）

例 3-50　Such amusements, however, were rejected with abhorrence, or admitted with the utmost caution, by the severity of the fathers, who despised all knowledge that was not useful to salvation, and who considered all levity of discourse as criminal abuse of the gift of speech.

译 而严肃底教父，于此消遣或深恶痛绝，或敬而远之。凡知识不得稍助于"获救"者，彼皆抱鄙视；至于言谈轻浮，更属滥用语言之才，等同罪孽。（刘怡译）

二、清晰

英语句子有多种组织类型，但从读者的阅读习惯来讲，有些句型更为清晰，也更容易为读者所理解，而有些句子则否。总体上而言，简单句比复合句易于理解；并列句比从句层层包埋或嵌套的复杂句易于理解；修饰语置于中心词右侧要比置于左侧易于理解。作者可以高声读出自己写的句子，如果感觉拗口，通常也是难以理解的。或者对自己写的句子进行树状分析，层层包埋的多层树状结构一般难以理解，而用 and, or 或逗号连接起来的一串不太复杂的结构或语句（也就是扁平树枝结构）则更容易理解。从清晰的角度看，利用简单句、并列句和不超过三层的嵌套或包埋结构的复合句写作是比较好的。

鉴于读者用眼睛扫描句子时，最先扫过句子的开头，因此，一个句子的开头是十分重要的。为了使句子表达更为清楚，通常把重点放在句子前 7~8 个词语。如果读者能从句子开头的 7~8 个词语把握整个句子的意思或论述重点，则理解起来就更容易。除了开头，主语和谓语之间及谓语和宾语之间连接紧密，没有被其他成分隔开，能使读者快速阅读句子后面的部分，从而更好地理解和记忆整个句子。

（一）引导性成分不要太长，或直接以主语开头

英语句子中主语是"首脑"，如果直接用主语开头，则更为清晰和直接，易为读者所把握；如果主语前面有引导性短语或分句开头，特别是主语前的引导性成分或分句很长时，虽然是为理解后面部分进行铺垫和准备，但相对而言则不够清晰。因此，从清晰性角度考虑，引导部分最好不要超过 10 个左右的词语。例如：

例 3-51 To find out how persistent the bacterial signature might be, the researchers did a further test where they swabbed the skin of two people, froze one set of samples to minus 4 deg F (−20 deg C) and left the other at room temperature.

译 为了找出细菌指征的持久性，研究人员做了进一步的测试，他们擦拭两人的皮肤进行细菌采样，一组样品在-4℉（−20℃）冷冻保存，另一组则在

室温下保存。

例 3-52 Based on readings from more than 30,000 measuring stations, the data was issued without fanfare by the Met Office and the University of East Anglia Climatic Research Unit.

译 英国气象局和东安格利亚大学气候研究中心悄无声息地发布了这些基于3万多个监测站的数据,确认世界温度上升趋势止于1997年。

例 3-53 Today, thanks to modern transportation and well-organized societies, thousands of people willingly and eagerly leave the surroundings where they were born, and the more often they do so, the less sentiment they are likely to have for those surroundings.

译 今天,由于有了现代交通工具和组织良好的社会,成千上万的人愿意并且渴望离开他们出生的环境。而且,他们离家外出越频繁,对那个环境的情感就可能越少。(谭卫国译)

例 3-54 Because of women's association with mothering and the home, women are associated with the domestic affairs and men are associated with the public affairs.

译 因为妇女与母性和家庭联系在一起,所以妇女同家事密不可分,男人与公务联系在一起。(谭卫国译)

例 3-55 With its matchless armed forces, a web of alliances and omnipresent soft power, the United States is still the world's indispensable nation — as it has show in the rescue efforts in the Philippines.

译 首屈一指的军备、众多的盟友以及无所不在的软实力,使得美国仍是世界上最不可或缺的国家——菲律宾救援行动就是最好的体现。(何凯文译)

对于引导部分较长的句子,可将过长的引导短语和分句修改改成独立的句子。例如:

例 3-56 During the course of work on the brain, which led to the suspicion that it might be brain activation in sleep that causes dreaming, we realized that the most scientifically useful way to define and measure dreaming was to focus on the formal features rather than the content — by this is meant the perceptual (how we perceive), cognitive (how we think), and emotional (how we feel) qualities of dreaming, whatever the details of the individual stories and scenarios might be.

可将引导成分修改成独立句子:

Work on the brain led to the suspicion that it might be brain activation in sleep that causes dreaming. During the course of it, we realized that the most scientifically useful way to define and measure dreaming was to focus on the formal features rather than the content — by this is meant the perceptual (how we perceive), cognitive (how we think), and emotional (how we feel) qualities of dreaming, whatever the details of the individual stories and scenarios might be.

🔵 对大脑的研究使人们认识到,梦可能源于睡眠时大脑的激活,定义和衡量梦最科学有效的方法不是去关注梦的具体内容,而应着重于其形式特点,即抛开千奇百怪的情节差异,去探寻梦的感知、认知和情感特性。(韩芳译)

例 3-57 For France and Germany, which had been at war with each other three times in the preceding eight decades, finding a way to live together in a durable peace was a fundamental political priority that the new Community was designed to serve.

可将引导成分修改成独立句子:

France and Germany had been at war with each other three times in the preceding eight decades. For the two countries, finding a way to live together in a durable peace was a fundamental political priority that the new Community was designed to serve.

🔵 对于过去 80 年中曾 3 次兵戎相见的法国和德国而言,寻找持久和平共处的途径是首要的政治目标,而新的共同体正是为此而构建的。(戴炳然译)

例 3-58 Following consultation with Monnet, who had remained active until then as President of the Action Committee for the United States of Europe in which he had brought together the leaders of the democratic political parties and trade unions of the member states, Giscard successfully proposed both the European Council and the direct elections.

可将引导成分修改成独立句子:

Monnet had remained active until then as President of the Action Committee for the United States of Europe in which he had brought together the leaders of the democratic political parties and trade unions of the member states. Following consultation with Monnet, Giscard successfully proposed both the European Council and the direct elections.

🔵 此时,莫内依然十分活跃,组织各成员国民主政党领袖和工会领导人

成立"欧洲合众国行动委员会",并担任主席。经与莫内磋商,德斯坦建立欧洲理事会与实行议会直选的建议均被采纳。(戴炳然译)

例 3-59　By electrically stimulating the vagus nerve — a large nerve running from the head and neck to the abdomen — with a small electrode at the same time as playing a high-pitched sound, they banished tinnitus from the rats.

可将引导成分修改成独立句子:

Vagus nerve is a large nerve running from the head and neck to the abdomen. By electrically stimulating the vagus nerve with a small electrode at the same time as playing a high-pitched sound, they banished tinnitus from the rats.

🔄 在发出高音的同时,通过用一个小电极电刺激迷走神经——一条从头部和颈部到腹部的大神经,他们给老鼠消除了耳鸣。

例 3-60　Tipped off by a previous paper, which reported that viruses can survive inside blood sucked up by leeches for as long as half a year, Dr. Schnell and her colleagues wondered if DNA from a leech's most recent victim might be recoverable as well.

可将引导成分修改成独立句子:

A previous paper reported that viruses can survive inside blood sucked up by leeches for as long as half a year. Tipped off by it, Dr. Schnell and her colleagues wondered if DNA from a leech's most recent victim might be recoverable as well.

🔄 之前的一项研究表明,病毒在水蛭所吸食的血液中可存活长达半年之久,因此 Schnell 博士和她的同事推断:水蛭最后吸食对象的 DNA 或许也可以被复原。(何凯文译)

例 3-61　Using a technique called the polymerase chain reaction (PCR), which employs enzymes to produce millions of copies of a DNA sequence, the researchers were able to prove that DNA from the goats survived in the leeches for at least four months.

可将引导成分修改成独立句子:

The polymerase chain reaction (PCR) employs enzymes to produce millions of copies of a DNA sequence. Using the technique, the researchers were able to prove that DNA from the goats survived in the leeches for at least four months.

🔄 通过利用 DNA 聚合酶来大量复制已知的 DNA 片段的聚合酶链式反应技术,研究人员能够证明来自山羊 DNA 在水蛭体内可以存活至少四个月。

(何凯文译)

例 3-62 Characterized by their zero electrical resistance or alternatively their ability to completely expel external magnetic fields, superconductors have fascinating prospects for both fundamental physics and applications for e. g., superconducting coils for magnets.

可将引导成分修改成独立句子：

Superconductors are characterized by their zero electrical resistance or alternatively their ability to completely expel external magnetic fields. They have fascinating prospects for both fundamental physics and applications for e. g., superconducting coils for magnets.

译 超导体以其零电阻或完全排除外部磁场的能力为特点，在基础物理和应用方面都有着诱人的前景，如用于磁铁的超导线圈。

此外，在不影响理解句子意思的情况下，可将引导短语或分句后置，使主语置于句首。例如：

例 3-63 Attention has focused on the sudden drops in the currencies of various emerging markets, thanks both to slowing growth and poor economic management in the countries concerned, and to the Fed's decision to begin reducing ('tapering') its bond purchases.

译 一些新兴市场货币的急剧贬值引起了众人的关注，这一方面是由于所涉及国家的经济增长放缓与经济管理不善，另一方面是由于美联储决心开始逐步减少债券买入。（何凯文译）

例 3-64 Human life, according to scientists, developed on this planet because of the unique combination of many factors — the earth's distance from the sun, the composition of our atmosphere, the structure of the earth's surface, the presence of certain organisms on the face of the planet.

译 人的生命之所以在地球上繁衍生息，这是因为许多因素的奇特结合，这些因素包括地球离太阳的距离，大气层的成分，地球表层的结构，地球表面存在的某些生物等。（谭卫国译）

例 3-65 We are simply foolish if we call Anaximander (sixth century BC) an evolutionist because, in advocating a primary role for water among the four elements, he held that life first inhabited the sea; yet most textbooks so credit him.

译 阿那克西曼德（公元前六世纪）在提出四大元素中水起着首要作用时，

认为生命最初栖息于大海,如果我们因此而把他称为进化论者,那就实在是愚蠢;然而大部分课本都认为进化论出自他。(杨自伍译)

(二)避免主谓或谓宾之间插入成分

当读者扫过主语后,如果主语和谓语动词之间有插入成分,则会影响对后面谓语动词的识别;同样的道理,如果谓语动词与宾语之间(或系动词与表语)有插入成分,也会影响对后面宾语的识别。从清晰角度考虑,在主谓之间及谓宾(或系动词与表语)之间,避免插入短语或分句,可使读者快速直达谓语动词与宾语,迅速把握句子的主要意思。事实上,主谓之间及谓宾(或系动词与表语)之间存在插入成分并不少见,尽管从清晰的角度讲并不可取。例如:

例 3-66 And the guilt felt for having killed the father whom one loved as much as hated, and for having forced oneself upon a resisting mother, would be overwhelming.

❶译 而杀死自己又恨又爱的父亲,对抗拒的母亲行使暴力,这样的罪恶感将会是难以承受的。(刘象愚译)

例 3-67 The habit of doing that which you do not care about when you would much rather less doing something else, is invaluable.

❶译 在你宁愿做其他事情的时候,却仍能够从事你不感兴趣的工作,这种习惯是十分可贵的。(汪文珍、方全译)

例 3-68 The British, who had not suffered the shock of defeat and did not share the conviction that there must be radical reform of the European system of nation-states, stood aside from the Community in the 1950s.

❶译 未遭受战败打击的英国人不赞同欧洲民族国家体制必须彻底改革,因而在 20 世纪 50 年代与共同体保持着距离。(戴炳然译)

例 3-69 On becoming President of the Commission in 1977, Roy Jenkins, formerly a leading member of the Labour government, who without being explicitly federalist favoured steps in a federal direction, had looked for a way to 'move Europe forward' and concluded that the time was ripe to revive the idea of monetary union.

❶译 1977 年,前工党政府重要成员罗伊·詹金斯成为共同体委员会主席。他并非明确的联邦主义者,却支持共同体向联邦方向迈进;在探索"推动欧洲前进"的途径后他得出结论,认为将建立货币联盟重新提上日程的时机已经成

熟。(戴炳然译)

例 3-70 Currently, the paramount problem in the field of biomaterials, <u>the science of replacing diseased tissue with human-made implants</u>, is control over the interface, or surface, between implanted biomaterials and living tissues.

🔹 当前在生物材料领域中,也就是在用人造植入物替换患病组织的学科中,首要问题是如何控制被植入的生物材料与活组织之间的界面或表面。(吴中东和宫玉波译)

例 3-71 The weekly sermons of Christendom, <u>that vast pulpit literature which acts so extensively upon the popular mind — to warn, to uphold, to renew, to comfort, to alarm</u> — does not attain the sanctuary of libraries in the ten-thousandth part of its extent.

🔹 基督教世界每星期布道,这种篇什沿繁且对民众精神影响极广的讲坛文学,这种对世人起告诫、鼓励、振奋、安抚或警示作用的布道文学,最终能进入经楼书馆的尚未及其万分之一。(彭发胜译)

例 3-72 The dress has polyvinyl alcohol, <u>a biodegradable substance that is used in laundry bags and washing detergents</u>, knitted into the fabric.

🔹 这件衣服的布料编织有聚乙烯醇,而聚乙烯醇一种用于洗衣袋和洗涤剂的可生物降解物质。

例 3-73 For France the prospect of a completely independent Germany, <u>with its formidable industrial potential</u>, was alarming. The attempt to keep Germany down, <u>as the French had tried to do after the 1914-18 war</u>, had failed disastrously. The idea of binding Germany within strong institutions, <u>which would equally bind France and other European countries and thus be acceptable to Germans over the longer term</u>, seemed more promising.

🔹 对法国而言,以德国巨大的工业潜力,其完全独立的前景是令人担忧的。1914—1918年那场战争之后,法国就曾力图遏制德国,却一败涂地。用强有力的机构来约束德国,同时也约束法国及其他欧洲国家,从而在更长时期可以使德国接受,这一想法似乎更有希望。(戴炳然译)

例 3-74 While the commission, as it stands today, is not the federal executive that Monnet envisaged, it is, <u>with its right of 'legislative initiative' and its functions in executing Community policies and as 'watchdog of the Treaty'</u>, a great deal more than the secretariat of an international organization.

> 尽管今天的委员会还不是莫内所构想的联邦执行机构，但因为拥有"立法动议"权以及执行共同体政策和作为"条约监察者"的功能，它已远远超越了一个国际组织的秘书处。（戴炳然译）

例 3-75　The memory rewards and widespread though ephemeral fame <u>which those agencies have made</u> possible place temptations in the way of able men <u>which are difficult to resist.</u>

> 那些机构可能提供的酬金和闻名遐迩却昙花一现的声誉，在有能力者的道路上所设置的诱惑难以抑制。（杨岂深译）

该句难理解的原因，一是主语的定语从句 which those agencies have made possible 造成主语与谓语动词之间的分隔，二是定语从句 which are difficult to resist 与修饰词或中心词 temptations 之间存在分隔。

这类插入成分可以修改为单个句子或不是插入主谓之间的复合句的从句。例如：

例 3-76　Kleine–Levin Syndrome, <u>a type of periodic hypersomnia from which sufferers make a full recovery between periods of sleep</u>, is more common in males and usually vanishes in adulthood.

可以修改为：

Kleine-Levin Syndrome is a type of periodic hypersomnia from which sufferers make a full recovery between periods of sleep, and is more common in males and usually vanishes in adulthood. Kleine-Levin.

> 综合征是一种间发性睡眠过度症，患者在睡眠期之间完全恢复正常，该病在男性中更常见，但通常在成年后消失。

例 3-77　Many, <u>without being able to attain any general character of excellence</u>, have some single art of entertainment which serves them as a passport through the world.

可以修改为：

Many have some single art of entertainment which serves them as a passport through the world, <u>although they are not able to attain any general character of excellence.</u>

> 还有许多人，他们无法掌握一般类型的精湛技艺，却也自有一套办法讨人喜欢，凭借这套办法，他们犹如有了通行证，同样可以畅行无阻。（聂振雄译）

(三)由旧信息向新信息顺序流动

从清晰的角度讲,句子应该是从旧信息到新信息的顺序流动,也就是说,将旧的信息、读者熟悉的信息、前文已论述过的信息置于句子开头,而新的信息、读者未知的信息、将要在下文论述的信息置于句尾。特别是要引入一个新的专业术语时,宜将其置于句尾,并且用同位词结构与非限制定语从句对句尾的新概念进行定义和解释。例如:

例 3-78 According to the model, that signal is generated as <u>a negative Rossby wave</u>, a wave of depressed, or negative, sea level, that moves westward parallel to the equator at 25 to 85 kilometers per day.

🔵 根据这个模型,该信号是以负罗斯比波产生的。负罗斯比波是压低的或负的海平面波,以每天25~85千米的速度平行于赤道向西运动。(吴中东和宫卞波译)

例 3-79 Two relatively recent independent developments stand behind the current major research effort on <u>nitrogen fixation</u>, the process by which bacteria symbiotically render leguminous plants independent of nitrogen fertilizer.

🔵 共生细菌通过固氮过程使豆科植物不依赖氮肥生长。两个相对较近的独立进展对目前主要固氮研究工作提供了支持。

例 3-80 An inventor has created <u>his perfect woman</u>, a robot who can do the cleaning, remember his favourite drink and read him the newspaper headlines.

🔵 一位发明家创造了一位完美的女人:这是一个机器人,能做清洁工作,能记住他最喜欢的饮料,还能给他读报纸的简要新闻。

例 3-81 The water also contains <u>sulphate</u>, a common energy source for microbes that can't carry out photosynthesis because hey live in environments without oxygen and sunlight.

🔵 这种水还含有硫酸盐,而硫酸盐是因生活环境没有氧气和阳光而不能进行光合作用的微生物的一种常见能源。

例 3-82 Obesity also throws off the action of <u>leptin</u>, a hormone secreted by fat tissue that tells the hypothalamus how much energy the body has stored.

🔵 肥胖也会使瘦素失去作用。瘦素是脂肪组织分泌的一种激素,能告诉下丘脑身体内储存了多少能量。

例 3-83 However, the number of poor people is growing in 'fragile' states, which the authors define as countries which cannot meet their populations' expectations or manage these through the political process.

🔄 但是，穷人的数量在"脆弱"国家一直在增长。这两位作者认为这些国家不能满足他们国人的期望，也不能通过政治过程解决这些问题。（何凯文译）

例 3-84　This may help explain <u>an otherwise weird observation from agriculture</u>, which is that adding antibiotics to cattle feed helps fatten beasts up — though cattle treated in this way put on muscle mass as well as fat.

🔄 这大概可以帮助解释另外一个农业上非常奇怪的现象，即给牲畜的饲料增加抗生素有助于牲畜长膘——尽管这种情况下牲畜不但长脂肪，也长肌肉。（何凯文译）

尽管许多写作书都告诫，句子要从旧信息过渡到新信息，从读者熟悉的信息过渡到读者不熟悉的信息，但也不要胶柱鼓瑟，并非所有的句子都如此安排。如果句子是新概念或新信息位于句首，那么，就需要紧随其后利用定语从句或同位语结构对其加以定义或解释。当然，如前所示，这又会造成主语与谓语的分隔，使句子不够清晰。例如：

例 3-85　<u>Ransomware attacks, which see individuals and organisations locked out of their data unless they pay up,</u> are on the rise.

勒索软件的攻击越来越猖獗，这些攻击会导致个人和组织的数据被封锁，除非他们付费。

例 3-86　Quantum computers, <u>which use light particles (photons) instead of electrons to transmit and process data,</u> hold the promise of a new era of research in which the time needed to realize lifesaving drugs and new technologies will be significantly shortened.

🔄 量子计算机使用光粒子（光子）而不是电子来传输和处理数据。量子计算机有望使我们进入一个研发救命药物和新技术所需的时间大大缩短的新研究时代。

类似句子可以改写。例如：

例 3-87　The Event Horizon Telescope (EHT), which uses a network of telescopes around the globe to turn the Earth into an enormous radio telescope, has taken the first direct image of a black hole.

🔄 事件视界望远镜（EHT）利用遍布全球的望远镜网络，将地球转变成一个巨大的射电望远镜，拍摄了黑洞的第一张直接照片。

该句的主语 The Event Horizon Telescope (EHT)和动词谓语 has taken 之间有一个较长的定语从句 which uses a network of telescopes around the globe to turn the Earth into an enormous radio telescope 相隔。这一句我们可以利用被动句改写，使得主语和动词谓语靠近些：The first direct image of a black hole has been taken by the Event Horizon Telescope (EHT), which uses a network of telescopes around the globe to turn the Earth into an enormous radio telescope. 但这样更改会改变原句的强调对象，原句强调对象是句尾的"the first direct image of a black hole"。

(四)避免抽象名词或较长的名词结构作主语

一般情况下，避免用抽象名词作主语、避免用较长的主语，尤其是避免用很长的名词结构作主语，尽可能用短而具体的个体、事物或机构或话题作主语，会让句子清晰明白。虽然很多语法成分都能用作主语，但使用有血有肉的故事或事件的"主人公"作主语，同时，将表示主要动作的动词作为句子的动词谓语，而不是包埋在抽象名词中，读者更容易把握句意。此外，为了使主语简短、具体、熟悉，可选择动词的主动或被动语态来实现。

一般而言，抽象名词作主语的劣势是，容易使英语句子晦涩、冗长、呈现静态化、缺乏生气、不直接，并可能使读者感觉模糊、晦涩、难懂。当你使用某个抽象名词作主语时，就尽可能不要再用抽象名词作宾语或表语等成分。一个句子中的成分差不多都是抽象名词时，更会增加句子的模糊性，使读者不易理解。因此，很多写作参考书建议多用动词，而不是名词，可使表达具体、直接、动感、活泼、有力、明晰、平易和简洁。

具体修改建议是当主语为抽象名词，谓语为弱势动词或空动词(如 be, do, make, get, have, give, see, observe, note, occur, provide, conduct, produce, cause, lead to, result in 等)时，可识别出句子中真正的施动者或主人公，重写句子，将真正的施动者或主人公作为主语，真正的动作动词作谓语动词。

例 3 88 Governmental intervention in fast-changing technologies has led to the distortion of market evolution and interference in new product development.

❷ 政府对快速变化技术的干预导致市场发展的扭曲和对新产品开发的干扰。

这句从《清晰与优雅的风格课程》(*Style lessons in clarity and grace*)摘出，我们可以看到，例句的主语和宾语都是名词化结构，包含多达 5 个动词转化成的抽象名词：抽象名词 intervention 对应 intervene, distortion 对应 distort, evolution 对应 evolve, interference 对应 interfere, development 对应 develop. 整句话形式上主语为 governmental intervention, 动词谓语为弱化动词 led to (lead to 的过去式), 但背后的动作主体是 government, 真正作用于并列宾语的两个动词是 distort 和 interfere. 因此, 为了清晰起见, 可将这句话改为: When a government intervenes in fast-changing technologies, it distorts how markets evolve and interferes with their ability to develop new products. (当政府干预快速变化的技术时, 它就扭曲了市场的发展方式, 并干扰了市场开发新产品的能力)。

但是可以在以下几种情况下使用抽象名词作主语: 一是当抽象名词短小, 且为人们所熟知熟用, 如前所举的句例, 这种情况反而是抽象名词作主语更为简洁; 第二是很多抽象名词为某些学术英语中通行的行话, 如哲学和法律等专业英语; 第三是用抽象名词取代 the fact that 从句内容时, 会使句子表达更简洁; 第四是抽象名词指代或概括前一个句子或上文内容时, 这种情况下用抽象名词作主语也很简洁和清晰, 第四种情况例如:

例 3-89 It is important, at the outset, for the reader to realize that the fossil record is incomplete and, perhaps more worryingly, decidedly patchy. The <u>incompleteness</u> is a product of the process of fossilization.

🔷 对于读者来说, 很重要的是从一开始就认识到化石记录是不完整的, 以及或许更令人烦恼的是, 它们注定是零零碎碎的。这种不完整性是由石化过程决定的。(史立群译)

例 3-90 All too often fossil discoveries have been ruined, scientifically speaking, in the frantic rush to dig the specimen up, so that it can be displayed by its proud finder. Such <u>impatience</u> can result in great damage to the fossil itself.

🔷 从科学角度来说, 因为骄傲的发现者急于将标本挖出来进行炫耀, 化石发现常因过于仓促的挖掘而遭到破坏。这种缺乏耐心的行为可能给化石本身造成巨大的破坏。(史立群译)

需要指出的是, 学术英语中, 尽管较长的由名词或动名词结构作主语在风格上不够清晰, 但很多情况也在普遍使用。尤其是一些特定的表达为大家所习用, 因此使用长的名词结构作主语并不鲜见, 也不必回避。有时是出于就近呼应上文, 有时是为了强调其他成分。例如:

例 3-91 <u>The identification of a cell wall enzyme acting in the extracellular space mediating plant stem cell divisions</u> suggests we need to take into account a much broader range of proteins in our future search to disentangle the process of root branching.

🔵 对一种作用于细胞外空间，介导植物干细胞分裂的细胞壁酶的鉴定，表明我们在未来理解根分支过程的研究中需要考虑更广泛的蛋白质。

例 3-92　Increasingly, <u>sophisticated knowledge of medicine and anatomy and the association of beauty with health</u> also saw physicians weigh into the debate.

🔵 美貌与健康复杂的医学和解剖学及相关关系知识，也让医生们越来越多地参与了辩论。

例 3-93　Therefore, <u>the current view of latex and laticifer functions</u> is, at least in part, built on conjecture, and needs experimental consolidation.

🔵 因此，目前对胶乳和乳汁细胞功能的看法至少部分是建立在推测之上的，需要实验验证。

例 3-94　Despite progress in understanding the regulatory mechanisms of the MEP pathway, <u>current knowledge of the interplay between the synthesis and emission of isoprene and other cellular processes</u> remains limited.

🔵 尽管在理解 MEP 途径的调节机制方面取得了进展，但目前有关异戊二烯合成和排放与其他细胞过程之间相互作用的知识仍然有限。

例 3-95　Although the importance of latex fluids in plant defense is recognized, <u>the principles orchestrating the integrated activity of different latex compounds against plant enemies</u> still need better description.

🔵 尽管人们认识到胶乳液在植物防御中的重要性，但不同乳胶化合物对植物天敌的整合活性的协调原则仍然需要更好地描述。

例 3-96　<u>The understanding of shared or individual involvement of latex constituents in the defense against specific plant enemies</u> is still in its infancy.

🔵 对乳胶成分共同或个别参与防御特定植物天敌的理解仍处于初级阶段。

例 3-97　<u>The ability to be inquisitive, to probe the natural world and all its products, and to keep asking that beguilingly simple question — why? —</u> is one the essences of being human.

🔵 盘根问底、探究自然界及其所有产物，以及不断提出那个令人着迷的问题——为什么？——是人类的本质特征之一。（史立群译）

例 3-98　<u>The age old dilemma about what brides should do with their wedding dress once their honeymoon is over</u> appears to have been solved by scientists.

🔵 关于蜜月结束后新娘该如何处理婚纱这一古老的难题似乎已经被科学

家们解决了。

例 3-99 <u>A remarkable piece of evidence in support of the notion that there is a relationship between the latent appeal of dinosaurs and the human psyche</u> can be found in mythology and folklore.

㊁ 恐龙的潜在吸引力与人类心灵之间存在某种关系，很多神话和民间传说为这一观点提供了证据。（史立群译）

例 3-100 <u>The probability that any particular person should ever be qualified for the employment to which he is educated</u>, is very different in different occupations.

㊁ 任何人在接受相关教育后能否胜任该工作，根据行业而差异万千。（谢宇译）

例 3-101 <u>The chances that an early hominin' skeleton would have been preserved in the fossil record</u> are very small.

㊁ 早期人类骨骼保存下来成为化石记录的概率非常小。（冯兴无译）

例 3-102 <u>The chances of any such material surviving unaltered for over 65 million years while it is buried in the ground (and subject there to all the contamination risks presented by microorganisms and other biological and chemical sources, and ground water)</u> are effectively zero.

㊁ 任何这样的物质被埋在地下（而且在那里遭遇由微生物、其他生物和化学污染源，以及地下水造成的各种污染风险），经过6500多万年而未被改变的可能性很小。（史立群译）

例 3-103 <u>The resurgence in palaeobiology in the 1960s, and the new insights into dinosaurs prompted by John Ostrom's important work</u>, provided a spur to reinvestigate some of the earliest discoveries.

㊁ 20世纪60年代古生物学的复苏，以及由约翰·奥斯特罗姆的重要工作所带来的对恐龙的新见解，促使人们开始重新研究早期发现。（史立群译）

例 3-104 <u>Feeling that the meaning of your life is a function of a greater whole</u> is not at all incompatible with having a robust sense of selfhood.

㊁ 感觉你的人生意义属于一个更大的整体，这和强烈的自我意识并不矛盾。（朱新伟译）

例 3-105 <u>Using Viagra or any other erectile dysfunction drug to boost female fertility without being constantly monitored by doctors</u> is not advised.

[译] 在没有医生持续监控的情况下服用伟哥或任何其他勃起功能障碍药物来提高女性生育能力，这种做法是不妥当的。(达子译)

例 3-106 Being in constant touch through mobile phones and laptops and tablet computers, for instance, means it is harder to ‘switch off’ and easier to work from home.

[译] 例如，经常使用手机、笔记本电脑和平板电脑意味着更难“关机”，也更容易在家工作。

例 3-107 The reasons why some artists began to have ‘avant-garde’ aspirations in the mid-19th century are complex.

[译] 为何在 19 世纪中期有些艺术家会产生“前卫”意识呢？原因错综复杂。(朱扬明译)

例 3-108 The massive expansion of the Museum of Modern Art in New York over the half-century from its beginnings as the showcase of a couple of private art collections, into the most important collection of modern art in the world and the unrivalled arbiter of cultural taste, is indicative of this co-option.

[译] 经过半个多世纪的大规模扩张，纽约现代艺术博物馆拥有了当今世界最重要的现代艺术收藏和无可匹敌的文化鉴赏权威，恰恰表明了这种拉拢所起的作用。(朱扬明译)

有些情况下，为避免使用过长复合名词结构作主语，可酌情修改成别的语法结构。如：

例 3-109 The presence of constitutive peptidases in latex sap in addition to inducible and de novo synthesized pathogenesis-related proteins (PR-proteins), raises the question about the role that each sap component plays to protect plants and how synergism occurs among sap proteins in the course of herbivory or infection.

[译] 胶乳液中除了含有可诱导的和从头合成的致病相关蛋白(pathogenesis-related protein, PR 蛋白)外，还存在组成性肽酶，这就提出了一个问题，即每种胶乳液组分在保护植物方面发挥何种作用，以及在采食或感染过程中胶乳液蛋白之间如何产生协同作用。

由于抽象名词做主语，而且主语较长，因此并不清晰易懂，如果将主语修改为介词状语结构，用被动语态将主谓结构改为 the questions are then raised, 则更容易识别和理解。

参考方案之一：

Owing to the presence of constitutive peptidases in latex sap in addition to inducible and de novo synthesized pathogenesis-related proteins (PR-proteins), the questions are then raised about the role that each sap component plays to protect plants and how synergism occurs among sap proteins in the course of herbivory or infection.

参考方案之二：

The questions are then raised about the role that each sap component plays to protect plants and how synergism occurs among sap proteins in the course of herbivory or infection, owing to the presence of constitutive peptidases in latex sap in addition to inducible and de novo synthesized pathogenesis-related proteins (PR-proteins).

例 3-110 As the century developed, the increasing magnitude and complexity of problems to be solved and the growing interconnection of different disciplines made it impossible, in many cases, for the individual scientist to deal with the huge mass of new data, techniques and equipment that were required for carrying out research accurately and efficiently.

🔵 本世纪以来，随着时间推移，需要解决的问题日益增多而且复杂，不同学科之间的联系日益增强，因此，在许多情况下，单个科学家不可能处理解决那些为精确有效地开展研究工作所需要的大量新资料、新技术和新设备。（王蓝译）

该句也同样可以将较长的名词结构的主语修改为介词状语结构，则更容易理解。

参考方案之一：

As the century developed, due to the increasing magnitude and complexity of problems to be solved and the growing interconnection of different disciplines, it is impossible, in many cases, for the individual scientist to deal with the huge mass of new data, techniques and equipment that were required for carrying out research accurately and efficiently.

参考方案之二：

As the century developed, due to the increasing magnitude and complexity of problems to be solved and the growing interconnection of different disciplines, the individual scientist impossiblely, in many cases, deals with the huge mass of new data, techniques and equipment that were required for carrying out research accurately and efficiently.

有些情况下，可以通过选择主动或被动语态促使主语简短、具体、熟悉，增加句子的清晰性。也就是说，如果选择被动语态能使句子主语更简短、具体时，就选择被动语态；主动语态亦然。例如：

例 3-111　In response to concerns that the Union needs to do more to attract the support of its citizens, a Charter of Fundamental Rights was also drafted, in parallel with the IGC 2000, by a Convention of MEPs, members of the states' parliaments, and government representatives.

译 人们希望欧盟能采取更多措施以获得民众的支持。为此，在 2000 年政府间会议召开的同时，欧洲议会议员、成员国议会议员和政府代表如开一个大会，起草了一份《基本权利宪章》。

例句中，被动句的主语 a Charter of Fundamental Rights 显然要比其主动句的主语（被动句的施动者）a Convention of MEPs, members of the states' parliaments, and government representatives 要简短而具体。下面两句也类似。

例 3-112　After a revolution of thirteen or fourteen centuries, that religion is still professed by the nations of Europe, the most distinguished portion of human kind in arts and learning as well as in arms.

译 历经十三四世纪之变迁，此宗教仍为欧罗巴诸民族——人类中于艺术、学术及武力最杰出者所信奉。（刘怡译）

例 3-113　The conquest of the land of Canaan was accompanied with so many wonderful and with so many bloody circumstances, that the victorious Jews were left in a state of irreconcilable hostility with all their neighbours.

译 犹太人之片迦南也，奇妙之景与血腥之况常萦，及其胜出，彼固已与其邻族处一难于和解之敌对状态。（刘怡译）

（五）句首铺设主体架构

不论是一个复杂的单句还是复合句，识别句子的框架（单句的主谓宾或复句中主句的主谓宾）是理解其含义的前提步骤。鉴于一个句子的前面 8~9 个单词对读者理解至关重要，因此，如果句子的主体架构（frame）在句子的前面完全呈现，也就是说读者熟悉的、表达重要话题信息的主句的主谓宾尽早出现在句子前部，而将读者不熟悉的技术术语或专业术语及其解释，或者对句子成分信息细节的披露和补充，放在句子后面，将使读者更容易理解和把握。

例 3-114 <u>Japan has one of the most advanced robotics industries in the world</u>, with the government actively supporting the field for future growth.

🔘 日本有世界上最先进的机器人工业之一，政府积极支持该领域的未来发展。

例 3-115 <u>The brain is a complex organ</u> with parallel conscious and unconscious systems that don't always affect the other one-to-one.

🔘 大脑是一个复杂的器官，有平行意识系统和无意识系统，它们并不总是一对一地影响别的系统。

例 3-116 <u>The prototype works</u> thanks to a camera the size of a grain of rice which is put into the glasses frame and connected via a wire to small computer which can be attached to the user's body.

🔘 该原型机的工作原理在于：眼镜框上装有一个米粒大小的摄像机，由电线连接至配戴者随身携带的小型计算机上。

例 3-117 <u>We should not judge the past</u> through anachronistic spectacles of our own convictions — designating as heroes the scientists whom we judge to be right by criteria that had nothing to do with their own concerns.

🔘 我们不该用自身信念形成的不合时代的眼光去评判过去——指明某些科学家是英雄，而我们判断他们正确时所依据的标准则与他们本身关注的问题毫不相干。（杨自伍译）

例 3-118 （The idea of printing organs such as kidneys for transplant has been around for several years.) <u>It works</u> by growing separate cultures of individual cell types, and then spraying them out, layer by layer, in combination with a binding agent called a hydrogel, to build up the correct shape.

🔘 （几年以前，就有人开始琢磨着打印包括肾脏在内的用于移植的各类器官。）通过培养个体互异的各类细胞，将其一层一层喷出来，接着借助于一种水凝胶黏合起来，以实现需要的外形。（何凯文译）

例 3-119 <u>The results were impressive</u>, including the first strong evidence for the presence of *Nesolagus timminsi*, a striped rabbit that ecologists had suspected lived in the area, but which had managed to evade more than 2000 nights of camera surveillance.

🔘 结果令人激动，通过事实第一次强有力地证明了斑纹兔的存在，生态

学家曾经怀疑附近区域生活着这种带条纹的兔子，但是它们却在超过 2000 个夜晚成功地躲避了摄像头的监视。（何凯文译）

例 3-120 Climate change is likely to place even more stress on resources, resulting in as many as a billion people moving from inhospitable regions.

译 气候变化可能会使资源更加紧张，导致多达 10 亿人从不适宜居住的地区迁移。

例 3-121 Pollution from vehicles may damage airways, leading to inflammation and the development of asthma in children who are genetically predisposed to the condition.

译 车辆污染可能会损害呼吸道，导致遗传上易患哮喘的儿童发炎和患上哮喘。

例 3-122 It always receives us with the same kindness, amusing and instructing us in youth, and comforting and consoling us in age.

译 它总是以善意接纳我们，在我们年轻时，好书陶冶性情，增长知识，我们年老时，它又会给我们以宽慰。（姚娟译）

例 3-123 Socrates devoted his life to interrogating the citizens of Athens about morality, attempting to show them that, in spite of their firm convictions, they did not really know what virtue was.

译 苏格拉底毕生致力于向雅典公民提出关于道德观念的问题，使他们明白这样的观点：尽管他们具有坚定的信念，实际上并不知道什么是美德。（严忠志译）

例 3-124 He leaves England in 1831, planning to become a country parson upon his return. He lands in 1836, having seen evolution in the raw, understanding (albeit dimly) its implications and committed to a scientific life as revolutionary thinker.

译 他（达尔文）于 1831 年离开英国，打算回国之后当个乡村教师。而他于 1836 年上岸时，已经认识了自然状态下的进化过程，理解了（虽然是模模糊糊地）进化的含义，作为革故鼎新的思想家献身于科学生涯。（杨自伍译）

例 3-125 Each contract of each particular state is but a clause in the great primeval contract of eternal society, linking the lower with the higher natures, connecting the visible and invisible world, according to a fixed compact sanctioned by the inviolable oath which holds all physical and all moral natures, each in their appointed place.

🔸 每个特定国家的每个契约只是永存社会的伟大原始契约的一项条款，使得低等与高等的本性环环相扣，把看得见与隐没的世界联系起来，依据的是不容违背的誓言所批准的一个固定协议，它约束着一切特质和一切精神的生灵万物，各得其所。（杨自伍译）

例 3-126 There are probably words addressed to our condition exactly, which, if we could really hear and understand, would be more salutary than the morning or the spring to our lives, and possibly put a new aspect on the face of things for us.

🔸 可能，有好些话正是针对我们的境遇而说的，如果我们真正倾听了，懂得了这些话，它们就有利于我们的生活，将胜似黎明或阳春，很可能给我们一副新的面目。（徐迟译）

例 3-127 On the other hand, <u>Newton's theory of gravity was based on an even simpler model</u>, in which bodies attracted each other with a force that was proportional to a quantity called their mass and inversely proportional to the square of the distance between them.

🔸 另一方面，牛顿的引力理论基于更为简单的模式，即物体之间的吸引力与质量成正比，与它们之间距离的平方成反比。（谭卫国译）

例 3-128 <u>The classic example again is the Newtonian theory of gravity</u>, which tells us that the gravitational force between two bodies depends only on one number associated with each body, its mass, but is otherwise independent of what the bodies are made of.

🔸 典型的例子还是牛顿的引力理论，它告诉我们两个物体之间的引力只取决于每个物体相关的一个数——它的质量，而与物体由什么组成无关。（谭卫国译）

例 3-129 <u>Noting is less to be desired</u> that the fate of a young man who, as the Scotch proverb says, in 'trying to make a spoon spoils a horn' and becomes a mere hanger on in literature or in science, when he might have been a useful and valuable member of society in other occupations.

🔸 天下最不足取的事情，莫过于一个年轻人如同苏格兰谚语所说的那样，"勺子没做成，倒毁了羊角"成为在文学或科学领域里滥竽充数的食客；要是去从事其他工作的话，他或许会成为社会上有用和有价值的一员。（汪文珍和

方全译)

例 3-130　Evidence is now mounting that the ability to recognize facial expressions of emotion is subserved by specialized neural circuitry.

🔵 现在，越来越多的证据表明，对面部情绪表达的识别能力是由特定的神经通路实现的。(石林译)

例 3-131　One of these is the rapidity of progress which has made it difficult to do work which will not soon be superseded. (下划线标出主句结构)

🔵 其中之一便是进步之迅速已经使人们不容易从事不会即将被替代的工作。(杨岂深译)

例 3-132　Parkinson's occurs when specialised nerve cells in the brain are destroyed.

🔵 当大脑中的特异神经细胞被破坏时，帕金森化症就会发生。

例 3-133　The true love story commences at the altar, when there lies before the married pair a most beautiful contest of wisdom and generosity, and a life-long struggle towards an unattainable ideal.

🔵 真正爱情的故事是要从神坛之前说起的，因为在这时候结成夫妇的两人之间开始了一场美妙动人的智慧和雅量的竞赛，一场为了某种无法实现的理想而终身进行的斗争。(刘炳善译)

例 3-134　Our story starts in 2008, when a group of researchers published an article (*Here it is without a paywall*) that found political conservatives have stronger physiological reactions to threatening images than liberals do.

🔵 我们的故事始于 2008 年，当时一组研究人员发表了一篇文章《这里没有付费墙》，发现政治保守派对威胁形象的生理反应比自由派强烈。

例 3-135　A good companion is better than a fortune, for a fortune cannot purchase those elements of character which make companionship a blessing.

🔵 益友胜于财富。因为益友优秀的品格使友谊成为一种福气和恩惠，这岂是财富所能换取。(周华等译)

例 3-136　Crises are one of its normal features, for there are so many dynamic and cumulative mechanisms operating within it that capitalism cannot be stable for long.

🔵 危机是资本主义的常态特征之一，因为在资本义主体系内有如些多不断变革的、累积性的运作机制，因此，资本主义经济无法长期保持稳定。(张

罗和陆赟译)

例 3-137 Palaeontology is the science that has been built around the study of fossils, the remains of organisms that died prior to the time when human culture began to have an identifiable impact on the world, that is more than 10, 000 years ago.

[译] 古生物学是建立在化石研究基础上的科学，化石是早于人类文明开始对世界产生可确定的影响——即 1 万年以前的年代已死亡的生物体的遗存。(史立群译)

例 3-138 The long nerve fibers are axons, each of which grows outward from a nerve cell body, sometimes extending as long as a meter.

[译] 长的神经纤维是轴突，每根轴突由神经细胞体长出，有时延伸长达 1 米。(李少如译)

例 3-139 We humans employ this type of jaw mechanism, especially when eating tough foods, but it is far more exaggerated in some classically herbivorous mammals such as cows, sheep, and goats, where the swing of the jaw is very obvious.

[译] 我们人类即采用这种类型的颌骨机制，特别是在吃坚硬食物的时候，但在一些标准的食草哺乳动物中，如牛、绵羊和山羊，动物则要夸张得多，颌骨的摆动非常明显。(史立群译)

第四单元
注重强调

人们在说话和写文章时，总是需要突出强调一些信息，吸引读者注意，或达到某种修辞效果。据说中国古代县官判案时，想要轻判，就说罪犯"虽然罪责难逃，毕竟情有可原"；想要重判，就说罪犯"虽然情有可原，毕竟罪责难逃"。这表明将话语重心置于主句句尾的强调手法，产生的修辞效果实在是非同小可。

在学术英语写作中，强调可以通过将强调的成分置于常规语序的句尾（如果是主从复合句，则置于主句的句尾），改变正常语序置于句首，利用标点符号，多次重复，拆句强调，或专门的强调句型等方式加以实现。

一、句尾是首选强调位置

一般的句子，句尾是强调位置，因此可以将要强调的信息成分（名词或从句）置于句尾以示强调。句子和段落的信息流动，遵循从已知（given information）过渡到未知信息新信息（new information）. 通常句子开头为已知信息，而句子结尾则为新信息或新话题，句尾的新信息或新话题同时也是需要强调的内容。位于句尾强调的新信息往往也是后面句子或段落要展开论述的话题。句尾不要安排表达意义不大或读者不看重的信息词语。句子结尾以介词最弱，最强为名词或带 of 结构的名词词组，形容词强度居中。

例 4-1　In our own time, one of the most popular, influential branches of the culture industry is unquestionably sport. (sport 为要强调的信息)

🔅 在我们的时代，最流行、最有影响力的文化产业之一无疑就是体育。（朱新伟译）

例 4-2　At the apex of the Community's legal system is the Court of Justice, which the treaty requires to ensure that 'the law', comprising the treaty itself and legislation duly enacted by the institutions, 'is observed'. (要突出的信息为 the Court of Justice)

🔅 共同体法制的最高层是法院，条约要求它保障由条约本身以及各机构依据条约而制定的立法所构成的"法律""得到遵守"。（戴炳然译）

例 4-3　Of enormous interest in this regard are two long essays by John Stuart Mill on Jeremy Bentham and Coleridge that appeared in the *London and Westminster Review* in 1832 and 1840 respectively.

🔅 在这方面最有吸引力的是约翰·斯图亚特·密尔分别于1832年和1840

年发表在《伦敦和威斯敏斯特评论》上关于杰里米·边沁和柯勒律治的两篇长文。(江怡译)

例 4-4　Of even greater interest is the fact that the most abundant of the dinosaurs preserved in these sandstones in *Protoceratops*, which are approximately wolf-sized, and have a prominent hooked beak and four begs terminated by sharp-clawed toes.

🔵 更有趣的是,在这些砂岩中保存最丰富的恐龙化石是原角龙,它大致像狼一样大小,长有突出的钩状喙,四条腿的末端长有带尖利爪子的脚趾。(史立群译)

例 4-5　One idea that the biological revolution in dream science forces us to take seriously is that, although it constitutes an undeniably interesting and informative state of altered consciousness, dreaming has not particular function in and of itself.

🔵 梦科学的生物学革命迫使我们去重视这样一个问题,尽管梦构成了一个绝对有趣而又内涵丰富的、以意识改变为特点的状态,但梦本质上并无特殊的功能。(韩芳译)

主从复合句中,主句和从句的位置可以调换,也就是说都可位于句首或句尾,但要注意句尾是强调位置。相对而言,读者更重视位于主句句尾所呈现的信息,也就是主句句尾的正面信息有更大的肯定效果,反之,主句句尾的负面信息有更大的否定效果。例如:

例 4-6　Although outflanked by the ambitious, brilliant, and crucially full-time, scientist Owen, Mantell spent much of the last decade of his life continuing research on 'his' *Iguanodon*.

🔵 尽管被野心勃勃、才华横溢,并且关键是全职的科学家欧文的光环所掩盖,曼特尔在生命的最后十年里,大部分时间仍在继续研究"他的"禽龙。(史立群译)

例 4-7　Although it isn't certain which pollutant is responsible, previous research has suggested that exposure to NO_2 is key — and traffic emissions can contribute up to 80 per cent of ambient NO_2 in cities.

🔵 虽然还不确定是哪种污染物造成的,但之前的研究表明,接触二氧化氮是关键,而且交通排放(二氧化氮)可占到城市环境中二氧化氮的80%。

在 not only…but also…等并列句中,强调位置也是位于句尾的并列成分。

例如：

例 4-8　Those who are engaged in scientific work need not only leisure for reflection and material for their experiment, but also <u>a community that respects the pursuit of truth and allows freedom for the expression of intellectual doubt as to its most sacred or established institutions</u>.

🅣 从事科学工作的人不仅需要反思的闲暇和试验的材料，而且需要一个尊重追求真理、使人有权对最为神圣的或既成制度自由表达质疑的社会。（严忠志译）

例 4-9　Our tendency to parse complex nature into pairings of 'us versus them' should not only be judged as false in our universe of shadings and continua, but also (and often) <u>harmful</u>, given another human propensity for judgment — so that 'us versus them' easily becomes 'good versus bad'.

🅣 我们倾向于将复杂的自然分为成对的"他方和我方"，这不仅在我们这个渐变与连续的世界里是错误的，而且（通常）是有害的，鉴于人类还有另一种判断倾向——将"我方与他方"之分很容易变成"好与坏"之分。（马锦儒等译）

如果为了进行强调出现在句首的词语，或者避免新信息位于句首，有几种方法将需要强调的词语后移。一是利用 what 引导的主句从句改写句子，将需要强调的词语置于句尾；二是利用 it 作形式主语，将需要强调的主语从句置于句尾；三是利用 there be 句型，将需要强调的词语置于 there be 后面，然后再用从句代替原来的主句；四是修改成倒装句，如将主谓结构或主系表结构前后颠倒，将需要强调的主语置于句尾。五是可以利用被动语态或主动语态对句子进行改写，将需要强调的词语置于句尾。不论以哪种方式进行强调，很多情况下注意使句子中较长的结构置于句尾，避免头重脚轻，从而显得平衡得体。例如：

例 4-10　<u>The fact that after they (horses) first appeared, they then became even smaller and then dramatically increased in size, and that exactly corresponds to the global warming event, followed by cooling,</u> is surprising.

可修改为：

What's surprising is <u>that after they first appeared, they then became even smaller and then dramatically increased in size, and that exactly corresponds to the global warming event, followed by cooling</u>.

译 令人惊讶的是，在马诞生后过了一段时间，它们的个子变得更小，之后个头又显著变大，而这些变化与全球变暖和变冷正好是对应的。

例 4-11 The fact that the working and replacement teeth are held together in an ever-growing magazine as if they were all contributing to one giant, grindstone-like tooth is unusual, even by reptile standards.

可修改为：

What is unusual, even by reptile standards, is that the working and replacement teeth are held together in an ever-growing magazine as if they were all contributing to one giant, grindstone-like tooth.

译 但是，即便是以爬行动物的标准来看也非同寻常的是，工作齿和替换齿在一个不断生长的匣中被固定在一起，就好像它们都是一个像磨石一样的巨大牙齿的一部分。（史立群译）

例 4-12 The fact that even when the body is full grown, its bones continue to be remodeled in response to ever-changing patterns of stress and strain may be less obvious.

可修改为：

What may be less obvious is that even when the body is full grown, its bones continue to be remodeled in response to ever-changing patterns of stress and strain.

译 即使当身体完全长成后，骨骼也会对不断变化的压力和张力作出反应，继续重新塑造，但这可能不那么显而易见。（史立群译）

例 4-13 The idea of pulling together shops, warehouses, delivery fleets and technology into 'market ecosystems' that no one else can match, quickens hearts in Bentonville, Walmart's headquarters.

可修改为：

What quickens hearts in Bentonville, Walmart's headquarters, is the idea of pulling together shops, warehouses, delivery fleets and technology into 'market ecosystems' that no one else can match.

译 真正令沃尔玛总部本顿维尔心脏跳动加速的是将商店、仓库、送货团队和科技联合成无人能及的"市场生态系统"的理念。（何凯文译）

例 4-14 That microprocessors will probably exist in everything from light switches to pieces of paper will be startling.

可修改为：

What will be startling is that microprocessors will probably exist in everything from light switches to pieces of paper.

[译] 令人吃惊的是微处理器有可能存在于从电灯开头到一张纸片的所有物体中。（李铁刚和孙艳华译）

例 4-15 A government which would provide a comfortable life for them was the people wanted; and with this as the foremost object, ideas of freedom and self-reliance and responsibility were obscured to the point of disappearing.

可修改为：

What the people wanted was a government which would provide a comfortable life for them; and with this as the foremost object, ideas of freedom and self-reliance and responsibility were obscured to the point of disappearing.

[译] 人民向往的是会为他们提供舒适生活的一种政体；把这种想法作为首要目标的话，自由、自力和责任等概念就被掩盖起来，直到消失的地步。（杨自伍译）

例 4-16 Galileo's spirit of going direct to Nature, and verifying our opinions and theories by experiment, has led to all the great discoveries of modern science.

可修改为：

It is Galileo's spirit of going direct to Nature, and verifying our opinions and theories by experiment, that has led to all the great discoveries of modern science.

[译] 正是伽利略的这种直接到大自然中通过实验证明我们的判断和理论的精神，带来了所有现代科学的伟大发现。（唐力行译）

例 4-17 A person of that temper, however bent on any pursuit, is impossible to be deprived of all sense of shame, or all regard to sentiments of mankind.

可修改为：

It is impossible for a person of that temper, however bent on any pursuit, to be deprived of all sense of shame, or all regard to sentiments of mankind.

[译] 无论执着地追求什么，那种性情的人是不可能丧失廉耻心的，也不会全然不顾人类的思想感情。（杨自伍译）

例 4-18 Three planets outside the system, known as exoplanets, could potentially be colonized by future generations, according to experts' belief.

可修改为：

There are now three planets outside the system, known as exoplanets, which experts believe could potentially be colonized by future generations.

[译] 目前太阳系外有3颗“系外行星”被专家认为人类未来可能移居。

例 4-19 A sagacity which is far from being contradictory to the right reason, and is superior to any occasional exercise of that faculty which supersedes it, and does not wait for the slow progress of deduction, but goes at once, by what appears a kind of intuition, to the conclusion, exists in the commerce of life, as in Art.

可修改为:

There is in the commerce of life, as in Art, a sagacity which is far from being contradictory to the right reason, and is superior to any occasional exercise of that faculty which supersedes it, and does not wait for the slow progress of deduction, but goes at once, by what appears a kind of intuition, to the conclusion.

[译] 在生命的交流中，也像艺术中一样，存在着一种灵慧，它与正常的理性绝无相悖之处，尽管偶尔可以运用某种官能来代替，但都不及它优势。它不必费时去进行缓慢的演绎，而是通过表现为直觉的某种东西直接得出结论。(石敏译)

例 4-20 A raft of esoteric job titles such as Packaging Technologist, Branding Executive, Learning Centre Manager, Strategic Projects Evaluator came along with such specialization.

可修改为:

Along with such specialization came a raft of esoteric job titles: Packaging Technologist, Branding Executive, Learning Centre Manager, Strategic Projects Evaluator.

[译] 于是，随着分工专业化，许多神秘的工作岗位应运而生，如包装技术员、商标主管、学习中心经理、战略目标评估师等。(袁洪庚译)

例 4-21 The field of endeavour known as logistics, a name rooted in the Ancient Greek military figure of the logistikos or quartermaster, who was once responsible for supplying an army with food and weaponry, is critical to both our imaginative impoverishment and our practical enrichment.

可修改为:

Critical to both our imaginative impoverishment and our practical enrichment is the field of endeavour known as logistics, a name rooted in the Ancient Greek military figure of the logistikos or quartermaster, who was once responsible for supplying an army with food and weaponry.

🔄 与观念的贫穷和实际生活的富足密切攸关的工作领域是物流管理学，此名称源于古希腊军队里的 logistics，此人负责为部队提供食物和武器。（袁洪庚译）

例 4-22　Good health is the No. 1 most important thing in your life.

可修改为：The No. 1 most important thing in your life is good health.

生活中最重要的事情是身体健康。

例 4-23　Detection systems that operate like search engines, scouring the Web for passages that match portions of student essays are most promising.

可修改为倒装句：

Most promising are detection systems that operate like search engines, scouring the Web for passages that match portions of student essays.

🔄 最为人们看好的是像搜索引擎那样运行的检测系统，该系统在网上搜索，寻找与学生论文相匹配的段落。

例 4-24　That we are profoundly ignorant about nature is the only solid piece of scientific truth about which I feel totally confident.

可修改为：

The only solid piece of scientific truth about which I feel totally confident is that we are profoundly ignorant about nature.

🔄 我感到完全有把握的、唯一确凿的科学真相是我们对自然极其无知。（马锦儒等译）

例 4-25　The nucleoproteins of the nucleus that contain deoxyribonucleic acid (DNA), which constitutes the genes, are of particular importance.

可修改为倒装句：

Of particular importance are the nucleoproteins of the nucleus that contain deoxyribonucleic acid (DNA), which constitutes the genes.

🔄 特别重要的是细胞核内的核蛋白，核蛋白包含脱氧核糖核酸（DNA），DNA 构成基因。（李少如译）

例 4-26　The ability to supply sufficient oxygen to muscles to allow high levels of aerobic activity must be intimately associated with the efficiency of the heart and circulatory system.

可修改为倒装句：

Intimately associated with the efficiency of the heart and circulatory system must be <u>the ability to supply sufficient oxygen to muscles to allow high levels of aerobic activity</u>.

译 与心脏和血液循环系统效率密切相关的应该是给肌肉供应足够的氧的能力，以使动物能够进行高水平的有氧活动。（史立群）

例 4-27 <u>A growing appreciation of the importance of biological diversity, the number of species in a particular ecosystem, to the health of the Earth and human well-being</u> has been coincident with concerns about the accelerating loss of species and habitats.

可修改为倒装句：

Coincident with concerns about the accelerating loss of species and habitats has been <u>a growing appreciation of the importance of biological diversity, the number of species in a particular ecosystem, to the health of the Earth and human well-being</u>.

译 在对物种及其栖息地的加速毁灭予以关注的同时，人们也越来越多地意识到生物多样性——在特定生态环境中特种的数目——对于地球和健康和人类福祉的重要性。（马锦儒等译）

例 4-28 <u>The strong tide of human woe</u> flows beneath the sparkling surface of these dilemmas.

可修改为倒装句：

Beneath the sparkling surface of these dilemmas flows <u>the strong tide of human woe</u>.

译 在这两难困境的波光粼粼的表面之下，奔流着人类悲哀的汹涌波涛。（马锦儒等译）

例 4-29 <u>The claim that the life of each individual is significant in the divine scheme of things</u> is closely allied with this belief.

可修改为倒装句：

Closely allied with this belief is <u>the claim that the life of each individual is significant in the divine scheme of things</u>.

译 与这一信念紧密相关的是这样一个观点，即每个个体的生活在神对事

物的安排中是有意义的。(严忠志译)

例 4-30　Great numbers of ribosomes that synthesize proteins, most of which pass directly from the endoplasmic reticulum and then are transported to other parts of the cell, are attached to many areas of the endoplasmic reticulum.

可修改为倒装句:

Attached to many areas of the endoplasmic reticulum are great numbers of ribosomes that synthesize proteins, most of which pass directly from the endoplasmic reticulum and then are transported to other parts of the cell.

🔅 内质网的很多部位附着有大量能合成蛋白质的核糖体,而大多数合成的蛋白质直接通过内质网,然后被运输到细胞的其他部分。(李少如译)

例 4-31　The fact that, at present, cloning is very inefficient procedure, is overlooked in the arguments about the morality of artificially reproducing life.

可修改为倒装句:

Overlooked in the arguments about the morality of artificially reproducing life is the fact that, at present, cloning is very inefficient procedure.

🔅 围绕人工繁殖生命的伦理问题争论中忽略了一个实际情况,那就是就目前来说克隆是个效率很低的过程。(马锦儒等译)

例 4-32　Large globular protein molecules are interspersed in this lipid film.

可修改为倒装句:

Interspersed in this lipid film are large globular protein molecules.

🔅 散布于此脂质膜中有大的球形蛋白质分子。

例 4-33　Eurofins Scientific, a Luxembourg-based provider of forensic services that conducts hundreds of millions of tests every year for police forces and security agencies worldwide, was hit with a ransomware attack in early June.

可修改为:

In early June, a ransomware attack hit Eurofins Scientific, a Luxembourg-based provider of forensic services that conducts hundreds of millions of tests every year for police forces and security agencies worldwide.

🔅 总部位于卢森堡的法医服务提供商 Eurofins Scientific 每年为全世界的警察部队和安全机构进行数亿次测试,6月初遭到勒索软件攻击。

例 4-34　A cure for tinnitus, the persistent ringing in the ears that blights the lives of hundreds of thousands of Britons, may have been developed by scientists.

可修改为：
Scientists may have developed a cure for tinnitus, the persistent ringing in the ears that blights the lives of hundreds of thousands of Britons.

🔹 科学家可能已经可以治疗耳鸣了，耳朵中持续的耳鸣使成千上万的英国人痛苦不堪。（达子译）

二、句首是重要强调位置

读者在阅读句子时，首先接触句首，因此，除了句尾，句首通常是仅次于句尾的重要强调位置。对于正常语序无法实现强调时，也可以改变句子语序，也就是改变正常的状语位置、主谓宾语序或主句从句语序，将要强调的成分置于句首，以便突现出来。

（一）状语成分置于句首

状语成分在正常语序中一般位于句中（如修饰的谓语动词前后）或句尾，如果置于句首，有时起承接上文的作用，有时为将重要成分后置（句子倒装）让路，有时也有强调作用。

例 4-35 Laboriously I checked their ages, starting with companies at the beginning of the alphabet.

🔹 从首字母排在字母表最前面的公司开始，我费劲地查出了他们的年龄。

例 4-36 On rather weak biochronological evidence the Omo I cranium had been dated to c. 120 KYA, but a recent attempt to date the Omo I crainium using isotope dating had suggested a substantially older date, closer to 200 KYA.

🔹 根据原来不充分的生物年代学证据预测，奥莫 I 号头骨的年代为距今约 12 万年，但最近用同位素年代测定法对奥莫 I 号头骨的测年结果表明，它的年代还要更早，距今约 20 万年。（冯兴无译）

例 4-37 With very few exceptions Western philosophers living in and immediately after thd *Dark Ages* (5th to 12th centuries) supported a biblical explanation for human origins.

🔹 处于"黑暗时代"及随后时代（公元 5~12 世纪）的西方哲学家几乎毫无例外地支持《圣经》对人类起源的解释。（冯兴无译）

例 4-38 For several reasons it focused on mtDNA and not on nuclear DNA.

🔹 出于几方面的原因，该研究集中在线粒体 DNA 而不是核 DNA 上。（冯兴无译）

例 4-39 In some group of dinosaurs, notably the theropods and the giant sauropodomorphs, there are some tantalizing anatomical hints concerning lung structure and function.

[译] 在一些恐龙类群中，尤其是兽脚亚目和巨大的蜥脚形亚目恐龙，存在某些与肺部结构和功能有关的解剖迹象。(史立群译)

例 4-40 The recent development of dynamic brain imaging technology, especially magnetic resonance imaging (MRI), makes this project particularly promising. For the first time in human history, we can see the regional activity of the brain as people wake, sleep, and dream.

[译] 最近发展起来的动态脑成像技术尤其是核磁共振成像让这一计划如虎添翼，在人类历史上第一次让我们看到人类清醒、睡眠和做梦时的大脑局部活动。(韩芳译)

例 4-41 Until the Amsterdam Treaty, there was no treaty provision requiring respect for fundamental rights within the member states themselves.

[译] 在《阿姆斯特丹条约》缔结之前，还没有任何条约规定要求在成员国本国之内尊重基本权利。(戴炳然译)

(二)从句中要强调的成分置于句首

将从句中的要强调的成分置于句首，而将主句成分作为插入成分置于句中。例如：

例 4-42 A scientist's political opinions, it is assumed, his opinions on sociological questions, on morals, on philosophy, perhaps even on the arts, will be more valuable than those of a layman. The world, in other words, would be a better place if the scientists were in control of it.

[译] 据称一位科学家的政治观点，对社会问题、道德、哲学、甚至对艺术的看法，都要比一位科盲来得高明。换句话说，世界如果由科学家来控制的话就会变得更好。(吴简清译)

例 4-43 Science, we are growing aware, is a method and a force of its own, which has its own meaning and style and its own sense of excitement.

[译] 我们日益意识到了，科学乃是一种方法而且自有其力量，有其自身的意蕴和风格以及自身的刺激感。(杨自伍译)

例 4-44 Such stereotypes are, I fear, only confirmed by debates in the press and by the remark of some professional philosophers who really should know better.

🔸 译 我担心，这种成见会因为新闻界的争论和某些糊涂的专业哲学家的评论而进一步加深。（江怡译）

例 4-45 Femininity, she argues, is too often an artificial, class-based construct, no more than an anxious demonstration of gentility, or would-be gentility.

🔸 译 他指出，女子气通常只是一种人为的构建，建立在阶级基础之上，不过就是对教养——或者说所向往的教养——一种急切的展示。（朱刚和麻晓蓉译）

例 4-46 It is hardly surprising, given the poverty of their education and the narrowness of their lives, he argues, that women have not yet produced 'great and luminous ideas'.

🔸 译 他认为，鉴于女性所受教育之匮乏，生活圈子之狭窄，女性尚未提出什么"真知灼见"并不令人惊讶。（朱刚和麻晓蓉译）

（三）实质信息置于句首

新闻报道的标题、消息中的导言往往将最重要的实质信息置于句首以示强调，而将消息来源、研究者或发布者的信息置于句尾。

例 4-47 Cocaine found in shrimp, shocking study reveals.

🔸 译 令人震惊的研究揭示虾体内发现可卡因。

例 4-48 Chronic diseases, such as stroke, ischemic heart disease, and lung cancer, now represent the leading causes of premature death in China, according to a new scientific study.

🔸 译 一项新的科学研究表明，中风、缺血性心脏病和肺癌等慢性疾病现在是中国人早死的主要原因。

例 4-49 Global warming could make humans shorter, warned by scientists who claim to have found evidence that it caused the world's first horses to shrink nearly 50 million years ago.

🔸 译 科学家警告说，全球变暖可能会使人类变矮。科学家宣称已经找到证据，近 5000 万年前全球变暖就曾让世界上最早的马个头变小。

例 4-50 The amount of debris orbiting the Earth has reached 'a tipping point' for collisions, which would in turn generate more of the debris that threatens astronauts and satellites, according to a U. S. study released.

🔸 译 据美国发布的一份报告，地球轨道上太空垃圾的数量已经达到"临界点"，有撞击风险，而后可能产生更多碎片，威胁宇航员和人造卫星的安全。

例 4-51　Adolescents exposed to elevated levels of pesticides are at an increased risk of depression, according to a new study led by Jose R. Suarez-Lopez, MD, PhD, assistant professor in the Department of Family Medicine and Public Health at University of California San Diego School of Medicine.

译　加利福尼亚大学圣迭戈医学院家庭医学和公共卫生系助理教授 Jose R. Suarez Lopez 博士领导的一项新研究表明，暴露于高水平杀虫剂的青少年患抑郁症的风险更大。

例 4-52　Higher 'trunk fat' in women was associated with an increased incidence of atherosclerosis or hardening of the arteries, while more leg fat predicted lower risk of this type of coronary artery disease, a new study published Monday in the *European Heart Journal* finds.

译　周一发表在《欧洲心脏杂志》上的一项新研究发现，女性的"躯干脂肪"越多，动脉粥样硬化或动脉硬化的发生率就越高，而腿部脂肪越多，这类冠状动脉疾病的风险就越低。

三、标点符号突出强调

利用冒号和破折号，可以将要强调的成分置于这类标点符号后面，通常情况下，这些位置也正好是句尾的强调位置。例如：

例 4-53　As Michel Jouvet shows in his novel *Château du Rêve*, most of our vaunted twentieth-century discoveries about sleep could have been made earlier by the most useful scientific instrument of all: <u>direct observation</u>.

译　正如米歇尔·朱维特在小说《梦的城堡》中描述的，我们所吹嘘的那些 20 世纪的睡眠科学发现，其中的大部分本可以通过最有用的科学手段更早发现，那就是直接观察。（韩芳译）

例 4-54　I begin by taking a slightly different tack and sketching a larger problem that faces contemporary philosophy: <u>the relation between wisdom and knowledge</u>.

译　我首先会采取不同的策略，勾画出当代哲学面临的一个更大的问题，即智慧与知识之间的关系。（江怡译）

例 4-55　*Iguanodon* appears to present us with a conundrum: it does not fit any of the expected models.

译 禽龙似乎给我们出了一道难题：它与任何预期的模式都不相符。（史立群译）

例 4-56 The discovery of two quite similar types of dinosaur that evidently lived in the same place, at the same time, prompted him to ask the simple and yet obvious question: <u>are they males and females of the same species?</u>

译 两种显然生活在同一地点、同一时间的非常类似的恐龙类型的发现，促使他提出了一个简单而明显的问题：它们是同一个种的雄性和雌性吗？（史立群译）

例 4-57 The motors for its emergence, however, were not mystification and profiteering, but two other factors that were central to the growth of Western capitalism itself: <u>individualism and the rage for the new.</u>

译 尽管如此，现代艺术出现的动力并非神秘化和牟利，而是另外两个主宰着西方资本主义自身发展的核心因素——个人主义和对新生事物的激情。（朱扬明译）

例 4-58 Human nature is not intrinsically corrupt — <u>it is intrinsically good.</u>

译 人的本性并非本来堕落，而是天生善良。（严忠志译）

四、通过重复加以强调

强调的一个最简单的方法是，将你要强调的关键词或主要观点多次重复，以便给读者留下深刻印象。一般而言，英语句子尽量避免重复实词，这一点与汉语不同，如果英语有意重复实词，那通常就是为了强调。但这种重复不一定是完全相同的词语，可以是同根词、同义词、近义词或范畴词，也可以是代词，或者意义相同但结构不同的句子来强调重要信息。

例 4-59 <u>Thought</u> is subversive and revolutionary, destructive and terrible, <u>thought</u> is merciless to privilege, established institutions, and comfortable habit. <u>Thought</u> looks into the pit of hell and is not afraid. <u>Thought</u> is great and swift and free, the light of the world, and the chief glory of man.

思想具有颠覆性、革命性、破坏性，会引起可怕的后果。思想对权势，对既定的制度和令人安逸的旧习惯毫不留情。思想审视地狱的深渊却毫不畏惧。思想伟大、敏捷、不受束缚，它给世界带来光明，它是人类无上的荣光。（杨自伍译）

例 4-60 To be sure, beauty is a form of <u>power</u>. And deservedly so. What is lamentable is that it is the only form of power that most women are encouraged to seek. This power is always conceived in relation to men; it is not the power to do but the power to attract. It is a power that negates itself. For this power is not one that can be chosen freely – at least, not by women — or renounced without social censure.

🔸 可以肯定，美是力量的一种形式。理应如此。可悲的是，它是鼓励多数女性去追求的力量的唯一形式。这种力量总被设想成与男性有关；它不是作为的力量，而是吸引的力量。它是一种否定自身的力量。因为这种力量是无法自由选择——至少女性不能——或者说要摈弃这种力量时不可能不受到社会的谴责。（杨海红译）

例 4-61　Death cancels everything but truth, and strips a man of everything but genius and virtue. It is a sort of natural canonization. It makes the meanest of us sacred; it installs the poet in his immortality, and lifts him to the skies.

🔸 死亡勾销了一切，唯有真理长存，剥夺了人的一切，唯有天才和品德长存。死亡是一种自然而然的超凡入圣。死亡使我们身上最卑鄙的也变成神圣的；死亡使这位诗人流芳千古，使他升天了。（杨自伍译）

五、通过拆句加以强调

将要强调的成分从一个长句中分离出来，单独成句，从而起到强调作用。例如：

例 4-62　True learning is not a matter of the formal organization of knowledge of books. It is a series of personal experience.

原本可以写成：

True learning is not a matter of the formal organization of knowledge of books but is a series of personal experience.

🔸 真正的学习不是对书本知识进行外在形式组织的问题。它是一系列个人体验问题。

例 4-63　Virtue is not a gift, a sign of the gods' favor. It is the result of training, of the application of intelligence to living.

🔸 美德不是上天赐予的礼物，不是神灵恩宠的表现。它是训练的结果，是将理性应用于生活的结果。（严忠志译）

例 4-64　Science is not a heartless pursuit of objective information. It is a creative human activity, its geniuses acting more as artists than as information processors.

● 译 科学并不冷酷无情地追求客观资料。科学是一种创造性的人类活动，科学上的天才表现更像艺术家而非信息处理机。(杨自伍译)

例 4-65 In response to the disorientation, which is caused by the recent memory deficit, the patient with organic delirium makes up stories that are not lies but false beliefs, sincerely — and often fatuously — advanced to cover the huge holes in memory. We call this trait 'confabulation'.

● 译 为了应对短时记忆丢失带来的定向障碍，器质性谵妄病人会编造故事，这些故事不是谎言而是错误的信念，它们被真诚地——通常是愚蠢地——提出，以掩盖记忆的巨大黑洞，我们把这一特质称为"虚构"。(韩芳)

六、专门的强调句型

(一) It is + 要强调的成分 + that/who/when/where 等引导的定语从句

这种强调句型的强调成分可以是主语、宾语、时间及地点等。但要注意强调句的时态，一般现在时用 it is…that…，一般过去时用 it was…that…，现在完成时用 it has been…that….

例 4-66 It has been one of the most destructive modern prejudices that art and science are different and somehow incompatible interests.

● 译 贻害太甚的偏见之一便是认为，艺术与科学是有所不同而又不无相左的趣好。(杨自伍译)

例 4-67 It is this touchstone of praxis that leads philosophy towards a critique of present conditions, as conditions not amenable to freedom, and towards the emancipatory demand that things be otherwise, the demand for a transformative practice of philosophy, art, thinking, or politics.

● 译 正是这种实践的点金石，引导哲学走向对现实境况的批判，它们看作对自由于事无补；引导哲学走向解放的要求，即事情可以是另一种样子，就是哲学、艺术、思想或政治的转变的要求。(江怡译)

例 4-68 It is the specific neurophysiological details of that activation process, not psychological defence mechanisms, that determine the distinctive nature of dream consciousness.

● 译 决定梦意识特性的是激活过程的特异神经生理细节而非心理防御机制。

（韩芳译）

例 4-69 It is this difference in brain chemistry that probably determines the differences between waking and dreaming consciousness.

[译] 可能正是这一大脑化学系统的差异决定了清醒意识和梦意识之间的区别。（韩芳译）

例 4-70 It was the hard financial interest of French agriculture that secured a solid outcome, in a financial regulation that was to be highly disadvantageous for the British, whose small but efficient farm sector differed from those of the six member states.

[译] 倒是法国农业强硬的经济利益，在一项财政规则中获得了切实的效果，由于英国小而高效的农业与 6 个成员国的情况不同，该规则对英国大为不利。（戴炳然译）

例 4-71 It was this epistemological reading of Kant in the work of Peter Strawson and others that dominated the Anglo-American reception of Kant until fairly recently.

[译] 正是彼得·斯特劳森和其他人的著作中对康德的这种认识论的解读，直到最近仍然主导着英美哲学对康德的接受。（江怡译）

例 4-72 It is science, modern natural science, that provides us with the best and most reliable knowledge of how things are the way they are.

[译] 正是科学，也就是近代自然科学，为我们提供了关于事物如何成为它现在这个样子的最好的、最为可靠的知识。（江怡译）

例 4-73 It is the circulatory system that carries nutrients to the tissues and then carries excretory products away from the tissues.

[译] 正是循环系统将营养带进组织，然后又将排泄物带离组织。（李少如译）

例 4-74 Most of the ribosomes are attached to the endopasmic reticulum, and it is their granular appearance that gives the name ‘granular’ (or ‘rough’) endoplasmic reticulum to the portion of the endoplasmic reticulum where they attach.

[译] 大多数核糖体附着在内质网上，而正是由于它们颗粒状的外表，所以它们所附着的内质网部分称为“颗粒性”（或“粗面”）内质网。（李少如译）

例 4-75 It was Freud’s detachment and refusal to become personally involved with his patients that both promoted the phenomena of transference and made those phenomena apparent.

🔘 译 正是弗洛伊德的这种超脱和拒绝与病人进行私交，促成了移情现象的出现并使这些现象明晰起来。（尹莉译）

例 4-76 It was not until the second half of the 19th century that anything like a true women's 'movement' began to emerge in England.

🔘 译 直到19世纪后半叶，英格兰才开始出现真正意义的妇女"运动"。（朱刚和麻晓蓉译）

例 4-77 So, it is through the creative power of art in the form of a mythology of reason that we can intimate the dimensions of a politically transformed life.

🔘 译 所以，正是通过理性神话形式的艺术创造力，我们才能够展示政治上得到改变的生活的各个方面。（江怡译）

例 4-78 It is from these natural sentiments, not from reason, or revelation, that our approval or condemnation of our own and other people's motives and actions, our appraisal of their being productive of a balance of pleasure or pain, are derived.

🔘 译 我们认可或者谴责自己或者别人的动机或行为，我们权衡这些动机和行为究竟是愉快还是痛苦的产物，这一切均来自我们的自然感情，而不是理性，或者天启。（董乐山译）

例 4-79 It is by its gravity that it is drawn aside continually from its rectilinear course and made to deviate towards the earth, more or less, according to the force of its gravity, and the velocity of its motion.

🔘 译 正是由于重力不断吸引，它才偏离直线轨迹，根据重力和其运动速度而不同程度地偏向地球。（马锦儒等译）

例 4-80 It is in advanced Western societies that the gap between knowledge and wisdom seems to widen into an abyss.

🔘 译 正是在先进的西方社会，知识与智慧的鸿沟似乎扩大成了深渊。（江怡译）

例 4-81 It is in this spirit that the interpretation of dreams — particular dreams of specific individuals — can still find a place in personal psychology and psychotherapy.

🔘 译 正是把握了"各人有各自的梦"这一精髓，梦的解析才能依旧在个体心理学和心理治疗方面占据一席之地。（韩芳译）

例 4-82 It is in Nietzsche's hands that nihilism receives its full philosophical statement and definitive expression.

[译] 正是在尼采的手中，虚无主义得到了完整的哲学陈述和明确表达。(江怡译)

例 4-83 It is surely because of Freud was by nature an impersonal investigator that he interpreted his patients' emotional pulses towards him as being entirely repetitions from the past, and discounted the possibility that they might be experiencing genuine feelings in the here-and-now.

[译] 当然，正是因为弗洛伊德本质上是一个客观而超然的探索者，所以他将病人对他的情感冲动理解为一种病人过去情感的完全再现，而低估了病人或许在此时此地对他抱以真实情感的可能性。(尹莉译)

例 4-84 It is because of this variable transmission of signals that the synapse is perhaps the most important single determinant of central nervous system function.

[译] 正是由于这种可变的信号传递，使突触可能成为中枢神经系统功能的最重要的单个决定因素。(李少如译)

例 4-85 It is perhaps because many of us know what it is to spend an afternoon baking biscuits that there is something striking about encountering a company which relies on the labour of five thousand full-time employees to excute the task.

[译] 我们当中有许多人都知道花费一个下午去烘焙饼干是怎么一回事，因此看到居然有一家公司用 5000 名全职雇员去做这件事，不免会大吃一惊。(袁洪庚译)

例 4-86 It is because we are meaning-focused animals rather than simply materialistic ones that we can reasonably contemplate surrendering security for a career helping to bring drinking water to rural Malawi or might quit a job in consumer goods for one in cardiac nursing, aware that when it comes to improving the human condition a well-controlled defibrillator has the edge over even the finest biscuit.

[译] 正是因为我们是关注意义的动物，不仅仅致力于物质追求。因此我们可心顺理成章地考虑放弃安全的生活，而从事将饮用水送到马拉维乡村去的工作，或者是辞去生产消费品的工作，去护理心脏病人，我们明白，谈到改善人类的生活状态，一部操作得当，供心脏病人使用的除颤器可比一包最精

美的饼干强多了。(袁洪庚译)

例 4-87　It was Freud who reinstated the dream as a phenomenon deserving study.

🔵译 正是弗洛伊德使梦重新成为一个值得研究的对象。(尹莉译)

例 4-88　It is when the force of this paradox begins to be felt existentially that the neglected question of the meaning of life come back with a real and frightening vengeance: 'I seem to have everything I need and want, but what is the point of my life?'

🔵译 正是由于在存在上开始感觉到了这种悖论的力量，被忽视了的生命意义问题才更强烈地被重新提了出来："我似乎拥有了我所想要的一切，但我生活的意义究竟是什么呢？"(江怡译)

(二) not…, but / rather…句型

利用…but / rather…或 not…but / rather…将要强调的成分置于句尾的意思转折之后，如 but / rather 之后的句子成分。

例 4-89　Changes in theory are not simply the derivative results of new discoveries but the work of creative imagination influenced by contemporary social and political forces.

🔵译 理论上的变化不单单是新发现的派生结果，而是受到当世社会及政治力量影响的创造性想象力的活动。(杨自伍译)

例 4-90　In other words, I mean that for this theory what is perceived is not a partial vision of a complex of things generally independent of that act of cognition; but that it merely is the expression of the individual peculiarities of the cognitive act.

🔵译 换言之，我指的是，对于这种理论来说，感知得到的并非对一般不依傍认识活动的事物综合体的局部看法，而仅仅是认识活动上个人特性的表达。(杨自伍译)

例 4-91　A personal essay frequently is not autobiographical at all, but what it does keep in common with autobiography is that, through its tone and tumbling progression, it conveys the quality of the author's mind.

🔵译 一篇个人散文通常根本不是自传性的，而它与自传确实相同的是通过语气及波动的进展，传达出作者思维的品质(张宏译)

例 4-92　Ability by itself, even literary ability of a high order, is not sufficient; it is necessary to have a vogue, to create or satisfy a special demand, to hit the taste of the age.

[译] 才气本身，甚至绝高的才气本身，往往都不济事；那得去兴起一股时尚潮流，开创或迎合一种特殊需求和碰对某个时代的品位。（高健译）

例 4-93 A successful writer of plays may make a fortune, a novelist or a journalist of the first rank may earn a handsome income; but to achieve conspicuous mundane success in literature, a certain degree of good fortune is almost more important than genius, or even than talent.

[译] 一名成功的剧作家当然可能发上笔财，一名一流小说家或记者也不难挣得可观收入，但是要想凭文学而取得轰动效应，名利双收，那就远远不仅是个天才，甚至不仅是人才的问题，而是得靠撞大运了。（高健译）

例 4-94 The wonderful thing to me is, not that there is so much desire in the world to express our litter portion of the joy, the grief, the mystery of it all, but there is so little.

[译] 对我来说，那令人惊异的东西并非世上想要表达我们这类悲喜隐衷的一腔区区之忱竟然是如此巨大，而是恰恰相反，这种念头可说相当贫乏。（高健译）

例 4-95 The difference is the claim, not to objectivity, but to a universality which rises above personal interest or preference. To say ‘This is beautiful’ does not state that there is universal agreement; but is imputes it, claims that this is something which all men of reason would assent to if once they had fully grasped it.

[译] 不同之处不在于客观性，而在于超乎个人兴趣或爱好的普遍性。说“这是美丽的”并不是说存在有着普遍的一致；但是它暗示了这种意思，它声称，确实存在着某种东西，只要让理性的人充分了解，他们全都会同意的。（董乐山译）

例 4-96 We are asking not to know our students by what they say in writing or in speech, but to know whether or not they possess correct information as revealed in mechanical tests that can be graded like eggs, by nonhuman means.

[译] 我们没有要求从学生们写作和发言的内容上了解他们，而是要求了解他们是否拥有可借机械化考试显示出来的正确信息，就像可以用非人性的方法给鸡蛋评级一样。（颜元叔译）

例 4-97 The biggest single need in computer technology is not for improved circuitry, or enlarged capacity, or prolonged memory, or miniaturized containers, but for better questions and better use of the answer.

[译] 电脑科技最重大的一项需求不是要改良的电路图、或扩大的能力、或加长的记忆、或缩小的机体，而是需要更好的问题与更佳利用的答案。(颜元叔译)

例 4-98 This environing world is not the value-neutral objective world of science, but the world that is always already coloured by our cognitive, ethical, and aesthetic values.

[译] 这个周遭世界并不是价值中立的客观的科学世界，而是已经由我们的认识、伦理和审美价值赋予色彩的世界。(江怡译)

例 4-99 A book is essentially not a talked thing, but a written thing, and written, not with a view of mere communication, but of permanence.

[译] 书籍就其本质来讲，不是讲话，而是著述；而著述的目的，不仅止于达意，而且在于流传。(彭发胜译)

例 4-100 It is true that you may fool all the people some of the time; you can even fool some of the people all the time; but you can' t fool all of the people all the time.

[译] 你可以一时欺骗所有人，也可以永远欺骗某些人，但不可能永远欺骗所有人，这是千真万确的。(周华等译)

例 4-101 Thus, to design educational systems for tomorrow (or even for today) we need not images of a future frozen in amber, as it were, but something far more complicated: sets of images of successive and alternative futures, each one tentative and different from the next.

[译] 从而，为了明天(或者即便是为了今天)设计教育体系的话，我们并不需要一个姑且说是冷冻在琥珀中的未来形象，而是更为复杂得多的某种形象：一组组连续性和交替性的未来社会形象，每一个都是试验性的而且不同于下一个。(杨自伍译)

例 4-102 The critique of scientism within phenomenology does not seek to refute or negate the results of scientific research in the name of some mystical apprehension of the unity of man and nature, or whatever. Rather, it simply insists that science does not provide the primary or most significant access to a sense of ourselves and the world.

译 在现象学的范围内批判科学主义，并不是要抛弃或否定以对于人与自然之统一的某种神秘的领悟或其他什么名义得到的科学研究结果。相反，它只是认为，科学并没有为我们提供获得关于自我及世界的认识的主要或最为重要的方式。（江怡译）

例 4-103 What phenomenology provides is a clarifying redescription of persons, things, and the world we inhabit. As such, phenomenology does not produce any great discoveries, but rather gives us a series of reminders of matters with which we were acquainted, but which become covered up when we assume the theoretical attitude of the natural science.

译 现象学所提供的是对个人、万物和我们生于斯长于斯的世界进行澄清的重新描述。这样，现象学就不会带来任何伟大的发现，而是给我们提供了一系列的提醒，即提醒我们所熟知的但当我们主张自然科学的理论态度时就遮蔽起来的事物。（江怡译）

例 4-104 According to this theory, it is not the quality of the sensory nerve impulses that determines the diverse conscious sensations they produce, but rather the different areas of brain into which they discharge, and there is some evidence for this view.

译 根据这个理论，不是感觉神经脉冲的性质而是感觉神经脉冲进入大脑的不同区域决定不同的被意识到的感觉，并且有一些证据支持这种观点。（吴中东和宫玉波译）

例 4-105 The pursuit of private interests with as little interference as possible from government was seen as the road to human happiness and progress rather than the public obligations and involvement in the collective community that were emphasized by the Greeks.

译 在尽可能少的政府干预之下，追求个人利益被视为人类幸福和进步之路，而不是希腊人所强调的公共责任和对集体社区的参与。（马锦儒等译）

例 4-106 Freedom was to be realized by limiting the scope of governmental activity and political obligation and not through immersion in the collective life of the polis.

译 自由应当通过限制政府行为及政治责任的范围来实现，而不是沉浸在古希腊城邦的集体生活中来实现。（马锦儒等译）

(三)比较级结构与否定式比较级结构

常用的结构有：(no)...more...than...，(no)...so...as...等。例如：

例 4-107 All time is precious, but the time of our childhood and of our youth is more precious than any other portion of our existence.

[译] 所有的时间都是宝贵的，而童年和青年时期的时间比一生其他阶段更为宝贵。(王炤译)

例 4-108 When it comes to language, nothing is more satisfying than to write a good sentence.

说到语言，最令人满意的莫过于写出精彩的句子。(吴简清译)

例 4-109 Among all the famous sayings of antiquity, there is none that does greater honour to the author, or affords greater pleasure to the reader (at least if he be a person of a generous and benevolent heart) than that of the philosopher, who, being asked what "countryman he was", replied that he was a citizen of the world.

[译] 一切古代名言之中，最能彰显作者之睿智的，或者说最能给读者(只要是一位心地宽厚而慈善的人)带来极大乐趣的，莫过于那位哲人的话：在被问及"他是哪国人"时，他答道，"世界公民"。(彭发胜译)

例 4-110 There is, we can surely agree, no form of oppression that is quite so great, no construction on thought and effort quite so comprehensive, as that which comes from having no money at all.

[译] 我们完全可以同意，相比根本没有钱所产生的结果，没有一种压迫的形式有这么严重，没有一种对思想和努力所作出的解释有这么面面俱到。

例 4-111 There is hardly anything that shows the short-sightedness or capriciousness of the imagination more than travelling does.

[译] 人的见识短浅与见异思迁在旅行一事上往往表现得最为明显。(彭发胜译)

例 4-112 The more of the details of our daily life we can hand over to the effortless custody of automatism, the more our higher powers of mind will be set free for their own proper work.

[译] 我们把更多的日常生活细节交给无意识去不费力地照管，更多的高级心智能力便可解放出来去做适合它们的工作。(钱满素译)

例 4-113 There is no more miserable human being than one in whom nothing is habitual but indecision, and for whom the lighting of every cigar, the drinking of every cup, the time of rising and going to bed every day, and the beginning of every bit of work, are subjects of express volitional deliberation.

[译] 再没有比这更悲惨的人了：他的一切行为都不曾养成习惯，干任何事情都犹豫不决。对他来说，点每一支雪茄，喝每一杯水，每天何时起床睡觉，每次开始干一点活儿，都需要经过专门的推敲思量。（钱满素译）

例 4-114 This does not require anything more profound than the assumption that organisms that are more closely related, in a genealogical sense, tend to physically resemble each other more closely than they do more distantly related creatures.

[译] 这只需要一个并不深奥的假设，即从系谱的角度来说，亲缘关系较近的生物往往比关系较远的在身体上有更大的相似性。（史立群译）

第五单元

衔接与连贯

句子与句子组成段落，段落与段落组成篇章。不论是段落内部还是篇章内部，都求衔接与连贯。衔接与连贯可以通过意思和形式来实现。前者是指一篇文章或一个典型的段落应该有统一的主题或中心思想，篇章中的段落或段落中句子都应服务于这个主题或中心思想，无关的东西尽量避免。后者是指通过一定的形式和结构实现，如利用连词或过渡性词语、重复中心词（包括相同词语、同源词、近义词和反义词的使用）、使用代词、使用并列结构等。

在构思一篇论文或者一本书的时候，需要考虑如何围绕主题阐述和论证，考虑各个章节如何能够相互配合形成一个整体，得出某种结论，并产生一种超越各部分内容简单集合的意义。从组成篇章的段落类型讲，有引言段、典型段、过渡段和总结段之分。引言段可以通过由总到分、由一般到特殊对所述领域的论述来实现，可以利用某一事件或故事引到主题上来，也可以利用引用名人名言、格言谚语来导入主题。典型段是描写一个事物或论证一个主题的完整段落。过渡段是进行论题或观点转换的段落，在文章中发挥承上启下的作用。结论段是对某一章节或全书的总括性段落，功能是概括和总结中心思想或核心论点。

从组成典型段中的句子来讲，也可分主题句、发展句、转折句和结论句。其中主题句指的是指出段落主题思想的句子，一般出现在句首，也可出现在句中或句尾。发展句是指发展、证明、支持段落主题的句子，包括主要辅助句和次要辅助句。前者指对段落主题进行深入阐述的句子，但又与其他发展句相对独立；后者指对主要辅助句进一步说明的句子。转折句是转变句意或描述角度的句子。结论句是指对段落归纳、总结出的结论性句子。

一、段落展开

段落展开可以采用叙述、描写、例证、定义、分类、例证、对比、比较、推理、分析等方法。段落写作可按时间顺序、过程步骤顺序、空间顺序或逻辑顺序展开。例如，描述事物或关系时，可按由表及里、由远到近、由上到下，或由总体到特殊、由重要到次要等安排。以下就学术英语中两种最常见的典型段进行阐述。

英语中最典型的段落通常有一个主题句。主题句一般位于段首，少数情况下也可位于段尾或其他位置。在主题句位于段首的情况下，首句开门见山地说明本段的中心思想，接下来就是通过各种手段对主题进行阐释和论证。

例如：

例 5-1 Wage labour is both free and unfree. Unlike slaves, who are forced to work by their owners, wage labourers can decide whether they work and for whom. Unlike the serfs in feudal society, who were tied to their lord's land, they can move freely and seek work wherever they choose. These freedoms are, on the other hand, somewhat illusory, since in a capitalist society it is difficult to survive without paid work and little choice of work or employer may be available. Wage labourers are also subject to tight control by the employer and, as we saw in the cotton mills, capitalist production meant a new kind of disciplined and continuous work. Workers had become, as Marx put it, 'wage slaves'.

🔆译 雇佣劳动力既是自由的，又是非自由的。不同于在奴隶主逼迫之下进行劳动的奴隶，雇佣劳动者能自行决定是否工作，为谁工作。不同于封建社会中被封建地主土地束缚的农奴，雇佣劳动者能自由流动，去任何地方寻找工作。但在另一方面，这些自由是虚幻的，因为在资本主义社会要想生存只有通过付出劳动来换取报酬，劳动者对于工作或雇主几乎没法选择。此外，雇佣劳动者受到雇主的严密控制，正如我们在纱厂的例子中看到的那样，资本主义生产意味着一种新型的、经过规训的持续工作。工人们变成了马克思所说的"工资奴隶"。（张罗与陆赟译）

段落第一句"Wage labour is both free and unfree"（雇佣劳动力既是自由的，又是非自由的）即为主题句。接下来通过与 slaves（奴隶）与 serfs（农奴）比较，得出主题的前一半：Wage labour is free（雇佣劳动力自由的）。中间有一句"These freedoms are, on the other hand, somewhat illusory, since in a capitalist society it is difficult to survive without paid work and little choice of work or employer may be available."（但在另一方面，这些自由是虚幻的，因为在资本主义社会要想生存只有通过付出劳动来换取报酬，劳动者对于工作或雇主几乎没法选择。）"加以过渡，将论题过渡到主题的后一半"Wage labour is unfree"（雇佣劳动力是非自由的）。后面通过举纱厂的例子（as we saw in the cotton mills）和马克思所称的"工资奴隶"（as Marx put it, 'wage slaves'）来论证这一点。

此外，还有一种典型的段落模式是：段落前面为一般性的前提或承诺或问题（不同于主题句），将读者置于一个现有的论点或问题之中，然后进行描述和阐释，利用论据进行论证或解读，最后提出设定问题的解决方案，或者获得比前提级别更高的一般性的结论，或者提出层次更高的新概念、新观点或新思想。埃里克·阿约(Eric Hayot)形象地称这种结构为"U形曲线"，并称这不仅是一个段落的结构，而且可以是"任何一个比段落更大的议论文或记叙文单元应该遵循的分形模型或者说扩展模型，这些单元包括：次小节、小节、文章或者一整本书。"例如：

例 5-2 We should not be afraid of cultivating the critical sense. We often hear the warning that criticism destroys enjoyment. Some who like bad poetry would prefer to be left unenlightened. So too would lovers of good poetry. I have often heard it said that to analyse a sonnet by Shakespeare or an ode of Keats destroys it. But I have never met anyone whose real enjoyment of a good poem has been spoil by criticism. Those who object to the criticism of art may be lazyminded, or they may be afraid of losing something which they do not wholly possess. For the love of any work of art is not really secure if it will not stand up to questioning. If a person tell you that he considers worthless a book or a poem which you like, do not refuse to hear him. Let him tell you why he thinks nothing of it; then ask him what he does admire, and why. For if a critic attacks merely for the sake of destruction, you can be sure that there is something wrong with his standards; if on the other hand he can show you that what you like is bad and that to like it may be hindering you from appreciating something better, then he is worth listening to. In the end, the only thing that can destroy a taste for the bad is the appreciation of the good. Constructive criticism is more valuable than destructive.

译 我们不应当惧怕培养批评意识。我们经常听到这样一种警告，批评会破坏欣赏。一些读坏诗的人宁可这么糊涂下去，也不愿意接受点启发教益。就连一些能读好诗的人也常是如此。常听人讲，去分析一首莎士比亚的十四行诗或是济慈的什么颂歌就会毁掉了它。但是我却从未见到过这种情形，一个人对某篇好诗的喜爱曾被批评闹坏。很有可能，这些不赞成对艺术进行批评的人是因为思想懒惰，也或许是担心怕失去些什么(而这些他们其实并不太具有)。因此，对一件艺术品的喜爱来说，凡是经不住追询的喜爱都算不得真正的喜爱。所以如果有谁认为你所喜爱的某部书或某篇诗价值不高，一定不要不听听人家的说法。你可以请他谈谈为什么他对那件作品不太高看；其次，他所特别佩服的又是哪些，以及所以然的道理。如果一名批评家攻击某部作品只是为了去毁掉它，那么可以肯定他的批评标准有问题；但是如果他能证明你喜爱的东西的确不佳，因而喜爱上它就会影响你去欣赏更优秀的作品，那么他的话值得一听。因为，说到底，只有懂得了欣赏那好的，才能不再想要那次的。建设性的批评总比破坏性的批评更有价值。(高健译)

在该段中，先在段首给出一个一般性的论述前提"We should not be afraid of cultivating the critical sense. We often hear the warning that criticism destroys enjoyment."（我们不应当惧怕培养批评意识。我们经常听到这样一种警告，批评会破坏欣赏。），然后经过描述、阐释和论证，最后得出"In the end, the only thing that can destroy a taste for the bad is the appreciation of the good. Constructive criticism is more valuable than destructive."（说到底，只有懂得了欣赏那好的，才能不再想要那次的。建设性的批评总比破坏性的批评更有价值。）这样一个不同于前提，且比前提更高级别的结论。

二、句子衔接

句子是否连贯主要取决于句子是否为整个段落的中心思想服务，句子之间的主题和施动者是否相关，句子的排列是否从旧信息（读者熟悉的信息）向新信息（读者想不到的、不熟悉的信息，或某种新的、复杂的信息）自然过渡。使段落或篇章中心思想统摄全局，避免插入无关的或冗余的语句。一般情况下，围绕中心思想，句子通过相关的情节、概念和观点串联，思想流动的自然顺序和逻辑顺序不被打断，就能实现衔接和连贯。但不少情形下，一定的形式手段或标记能较好地实现衔接和连贯。例如，写作之前确认段落所要论述的主题或系列动作的完成者，将其作为句子的主语进行论述，较易实现句子的连贯。但不一定所有的句子都采用同样的名词做主语，可以采用同义词或范畴词或代词等略加变化，以避免句子单调乏味。此外，上下句的开头和结尾也最为当紧。一般英语句子的最后为强调位置，句子最后的新信息往往也是下一句或下文展开论述的概念或主题。如果引导句结尾的名词正好是下一个展开句的主语，意思承接就更为自然和连贯。此外，英语中大量使用过渡词来实现衔接和连贯，是最常用的形式。

（一）使用连环结构

即通过上一句句尾的词充当下一句主语的连环结构。为了实现这种连环结构衔接，可利用被动语句或倒装句，使前一句句尾的词语（或其代词）充当下一句主语。

例 5-3 Among the first of the new visual media to be explored in these ways was photography. It has been in conversation with painting, indeed, ever since its invention in the 1830s, and the rollcall of artists who have joined this conversation in the last century is too long even to attempt to list them.

🔵译 摄影是最初以此类方式去探索的新视觉媒介之一。事实上，自从19世纪30年代摄影被发明后，它就一直在和绘画进行对话，而上个世纪中参与这一对话的画家举不胜举。（朱扬明译）

例 5-4 Perhaps the most radical of explorations of non-art media, however, and the most influential in the example it set, in both 'co-optive' and 'transgressive' terms, was Picasso's invention of 'collage'. This is the term given to his inclusion of fragments of newspaper, wallpaper, packaging, and other cast-off materials in two- and three-dimensional artworks.

🔵译 从"吸纳"和"超越"的角度看，毕加索发明的"拼贴艺术"或许是对艺术媒介最极端和最有影响力的探索。该名词是由他使用报纸、墙纸、手袋以及其他丢弃材料的碎片，创伤二维或三维的艺术作品而来。（朱扬明译）

例 5-5 An element's atomic number is the number of protons in its nucleus. These, despite being mutually repulsive because they are positively charged, are held together by a phenomenon called the strong nuclear force. Some of this force is also supplied by neutrons, which outnumber protons in most nuclei and have no electric charge.

🔵译 周期表中的序数等于该原子核内的质子数。虽然质子因为所带的正电荷而相互排斥，可是强核力还是将它们聚在了一起。中子也能提供部分强核力，一般情况下它们在数量上超过了同一原子核内的质子而且它们不带电荷。（何凯文译）

例 5-6 One of the most interesting technological trends of the past few years has been the rise of additive manufacturing. This technique, which uses three-dimensional printing to make objects ranging from violins to pilotless aircraft, allows the construction of individual objects at the whim of the designer.

🔵译 最近几年涌现了不少技术发展趋势，其中最有趣的当属加成制造业的兴起。该技术能利用三维打印来制作从小提琴到无人驾驶飞机的各种物件，从而让设计师的无限想象变为现实。（何凯文译）

例 5-7 The rise of modern science may perhaps be considered to date as far back as the time of Roger Bacon, the wonderful monk and philosopher of Oxford, who lived between the years 1214 and 1292. He was probably the first in the middle ages to assert that we must learn science by observing and experimenting on the things around us, and he himself made many remarkable discoveries.

🔄 现代科学的兴起也许要追溯一罗杰·培根的时代。罗杰·培根是牛津杰出的僧侣哲学家,他出生于1214年,死于1292年。他可能是中世纪第一个提出我们必须通过对周围事物进行观察和实验来学习科学的人。(唐力行译)

例 5-8 Located in the nucleus of each cell are approximately 100,000 different types of genes. These are deoxyribonucleic acid (DNA) molecules that are collected in 23 pairs of chromosomes.

🔄 位于每个细胞的细胞核内大约有100,000个不同类型的基因。这些基因是脱氧核糖核酸分子(DNA),它们聚集在23对染色体内。(李少如译)

例 5-9 Inside the membrane of all nerve fibers is an electrical potential of about-90 millivolts, called the membrane potential. It is caused by ionic concentration differences across the cell membrane.

🔄 所有神经纤维的膜内部都有一个约-90毫伏的电位,称为膜电位。它由跨细胞膜离子浓度差造成。(李少如译)

例 5-10 Scientists at Harvard University, collaborating with researchers at Bio-Rad Laboratories, have developed a new platform for rapid single-cell sequencing. The approach combines microfluidics and novel software to scale up single-cell ATAC-seq, which identifies parts of the genome that are open and accessible to regulatory proteins.

🔄 哈佛大学的科学家与Bio-Rad实验室的研究人员合作,开发出一个新的快速单细胞测序平台。该方法结合了微流体和新的软件来放大单细胞ATAC测序法。ATAC-Seq测序法能识别出DNA上开放的(未被组蛋白包裹的)及可被调控蛋白所靠近的部分。

例 5-11 Recently, Bruce Rothschild has developed a technique for scanning dinosaur bones using X-rays and fluoroscopy. The technique is limited to bones less than 28 centimetres in diameter, and for this reason he surveyed large numbers (over 10,000) of dinosaur vertebrae. The vertebrae came from representatives of all the major dinosaur groups from a large number of museum collections.

🔄 最近,布鲁斯·罗思柴尔德开发出利用X射线和荧光透视法扫描恐龙骨骼的技术。该方法限于直径小于28厘米的骨骼，出于这个原因，他测量了大量恐龙脊椎(超过一万个)。这些脊椎来自数目众多的博物馆收藏标本，代表了所有主要的恐龙类群。(史立群译)

(二)重复关键词

关键词重复可以是同一词汇、同义词或近义词或范畴词、代词等的重复。

例5-12 Scientific method is the only effective way of strengthening the love of truth. It develops the intellectual courage to face difficulties and to overcome illusion that are pleasant temporarily but destructive ultimately. It settles differences without any external force by appealing to our common rational nature.

译 科学方法是增强人们对真理的热爱的唯一有效途径。它培养人们敢于面对困难的无畏精神，使之克服那些眼下表面上不错但从长远看来却是有害的幻想。它通过诉诸我们共同的理性特点，而不是利用任何外部力量来解决分歧。(严忠志译)

例5-13 One of most powerful meaning-of-life questions without an upbeat solution is known as tragedy. Of all artistic forms, tragedy is the one that confronts the meaning-of-life question most searchingly and unswervingly, intrepidly prepared as it is to entertain the most horrific of responses to it. Tragedy at its finest is a courageous reflection on the fundamental nature of human existence, and has its origin in an ancient Greek culture in which life is fragile, perilous, and sickeningly vulnerable. (位于第一句句尾强调的tragedy，也是后面句子或段落要展开论述的新话题。后面的两句重复tragedy，既是对新话题的展开论述，也是对tragedy的强调。)

译 悲剧乃是诸多无乐观方案的人生意义问题中最有力的之一。在所有的艺术形式中，悲剧最彻底、最坚定地直面人生的意义问题，大胆思考那些最恐怖的答案。最好悲剧是对人类存在之本质的英勇反思，其源流可追溯至古希腊文化，这种文化认为人生脆弱、危险、极易受到打击。(朱新伟译)

例5-14 Of the many problems in the world today, none is as widespread, or as old, as crime. Crime has many forms, including crimes against property, person, and government. There is even a class of crimes called crimes without victims (e.g., prostitution). Crime, in all its forms, penetrates every layer of society and touches every human being.

译 在当今世界的许多问题中，没有任何其他问题像犯罪一样广泛蔓延，像犯罪那样由来已久。犯罪有多种形式，包括侵吞财产、侵犯人权和反政府的罪行等。甚至有一类罪行称为"没有受害者的犯罪（如卖淫）"。犯罪以各种形式渗透于社会的各个阶层，涉及每一个人。（谭卫国译）

例 5-16 Nearly everything we do in the modern world is helped, or even controlled, by <u>computers</u>, the complicated descendants of his simple machine. <u>Computers</u> are being used more and more extensively in the world today, for the simple reason that <u>they</u> are far more efficient than human beings. <u>They</u> have much better memories and can store huge amounts of information, and <u>they</u> can do calculation in a fraction of the time taken by a human mathematician.

译 在当今世界，电脑用途日益广泛，其理由很简单，它们的工作效率远远超过人类。电脑能够存储大量信息，其超强记忆远非人类记忆所及。电脑计算速度极快，只需数学家所需时间的一瞬间。（谭卫国译）

例 5-16 The fame of classical authors is originally made, and it is maintained, by <u>a passionate few</u>. Even when a first-class author has enjoyed immense success during his lifetime, the majority have never appreciated him so sincerely as they have appreciated second-rate men. He has always been reinforced by the ardour of <u>the passionate few</u>. And in the case of an author who has emerged into glory after his death the happy sequel has been due solely to the obstinate perseverance of <u>the few</u>.

译 世上的经典作家，其起初之成名，其日后之经久，其实都只是少数热爱者的功劳。即使一位在其生前即曾享有盛名的一流大家，他能受到多数人赏识的程度也每每逊于不少二流作者。他们能够历久不衰主要是因为得到少数钟爱者的屡屡强调。至于一名直至死后才变得显赫的作者，其幸运之结局更全凭的是那些少数人毫不松劲的顽强坚持。（高健译）

（三）使用过渡词

过渡词不仅在段落内使用，往往在段落开头或结尾使用。有时，段落开头的句子使用某些过渡词，可在前一句指向上一段落内容，后一句指向所在段落论述的内容，或者在复合句中的分句部分指向前文的内容，主句部分指向新段落的内容，这样承上启下来过渡。段落结尾使用某些过渡词，可为后面的段落内容张本。下面举几个使用过渡词实现衔接和连贯的例子，更多的例句参看第六单元。

例 5-17 As already indicated, Freud was a highly civilized man himself, <u>but</u>

nevertheless regard civilization as oppressive, since, in his view, it imposed more restraints upon instinctual fulfillment than most human beings could tolerate without developing at least some neurotic symptoms. It is therefore not surprising that Freud was an eager student of primitive and early man; of man as he might have been before civilization had instigated the iron grip of repression. Unfortunately, Freud was writing in the era of 'armchair' anthropology, characterized by extensive theorizing unsupported by evidence from fieldwork.

🔄 如我们已经提到的，弗洛伊德是一个非常有教养的人，但是他认为文明具有压迫性，因为在他看来，文明加于本能的限制已超过人类能够承受的限度、会导致某些神经官能症症状的出现。因此，弗洛伊德热心于研究原始的、早期的、被文明牢牢约束之前的人类就不足为怪了。遗憾的是，弗洛伊德写作的时候是处于人类学的"扶手椅"时代，其特点是没有实地调查支持的大量理论的出现。（尹莉译）

例 5-18 Liberal pluralism, however, has its limits. For some of the answer proposed to the meaning-of-life question are not only in conflict with each other, but are mutually contradictory. You may hold that the meaning of life lies in caring for the vulnerable, whereas I may maintain that it lies in bullying as many sick, defenseless creatures as I can lay my hands on. Though we might both be wrong, we cannot both be right.

🔄 可是，多元自由主义也有自身的局限。因为，为人生意义问题提出的某些答案不仅互相冲突，甚至完全相悖。你可以认为人生的意义在于关怀弱小，而我则认为人生的意义在于尽量欺凌患病、无助的弱者。我们两人的观点可能都是错的，但不可能都是对的。（朱新伟译）

例 5-19 Sacrificing one's happiness for the sake of someone else is probably the most morally admirable action one can imagine. But it does not therefore follow that it is the most typical or even the most desirable kind of loving. It is not the most desirable because it is a pity that it is necessary in the first place; and it is not the most typical because, as I shall be arguing in a moment, love at its most typical involves the fullest possible reciprocity.

🔄 为他人牺牲自己的幸福，这可能是我们所能想到的道德上最高尚的行为。但这并不意味着，这种行为是最典型的，甚至是人们最希望获得的爱。之所以不是人们最希望获得的爱，因为这种行为一开始便是不得不做的事情；

之所以不是最典型的爱，因为正如我即将论证的，最典型的爱包含着最大限度的互惠互助。（朱新伟译）

例 5-20　The new world of remarketized capitalism provides greater choice and more freedom for the individual but also a less secure life, intensified work pressures, and greater inequality. Whether one considers consumer goods, media channels, holiday destinations, or schools, there is no denying the provision of greater choice. Futures have, however, become less secure, particularly in those critical areas of people's lives — employment, housing, and pensions.

🔵 **译**　重新市场化的资本主义为个人提供了更多的选择和更多自由，但也使得生活变得更不确定，工作压力增大，不平等现象加剧。无论是对于消费品、媒体渠道、假日旅游或者学校，不可否认现在有了更多选择。但是，未来变得更为不确定，尤其是民众生活的关键领域，如就业、住房和养老金。（张罗和陆赟译）

例 5-21　The eventual goal of science is to provide a single theory that describes the whole universe. However, the approach most scientists actually follow is to separate the problem into two parts.

🔵 **译**　科学的最终目标是提供描述整个宇宙的单一理论。然而，大多数科学家实际遵循的方法是将这个问题分成两部分。（谭卫国译）

例 5-22　Although they had many things in common, Beethoven and Lennon belonged to different ages and thus were different in many ways.

🔵 **译**　虽然贝多芬与列侬有许多共同之处，但是由于他们属于不同的时代，因而在许多方面互不相同。（谭卫国译）

例 5-23　Besides care for personal appearance, you should pay particular attention to your manner of speaking and to the quality of your speech.

🔵 **译**　除了要注重个人外表之外，还应该特别注意谈吐风度和讲话质量。（谭卫国译）

例 5-24　Although Africa is the major focus of fieldwork today, it was not that way until well into the 20th century.

🔵 **译**　虽然非洲现在是寻找早期人类化石工作的中心，但在 20 世纪之前，这一工作主要集中在欧洲和亚洲。（冯兴无译）

例 5-25　In addition to analyzing fossils in order to classify them and arrange them in a cladogram and then a phylogeny, palaeoanthropologists also use the fossil record to work out the adaptations of hominin species.

🔵译 古人类学家除了分析化石以便确定它们在进化分支图中的位置和种系发育关系之外，还利用化石记录了解人种的适应特点。（冯兴无译）

例 5-26　<u>While</u> researchers were working on ways to refine the evidence for modern human origins that could be extracted from regional variations in modern human mtDNA, other research groups had set about tackling other parts of the genome.

🔵译 一些研究人员一直在想方设法从现代人类线粒体 DNA 地区差异中找出证据以完善现代人类起源理论，而另一些研究小组则已开始着手探索基因组的其他部分。（冯兴无译）

例 5-27　<u>Although</u> there were a few important predecessors of the formal approach to dreaming described in Chapter 1, most dream theorists preferred to focus on content.

🔵译 如第一章所述，尽管在梦的形式分析方面曾有过一些重要的先驱者，但大多数梦学的理论家们更偏爱关注梦的内容。（韩芳译）

例 5-28　<u>Although</u> a constructive response, the proof of the pudding was found in Arnold's steadfast opposition to revising the classicism of the university canon.

🔵译 虽然这种回应富有启发，但对此的检验却是阿诺德对修正大学标准的古典主义表示坚定的反对。（江怡译）

例 5-29　<u>However</u>, if the concept of Continental philosophy is taken at face value as a geographical category, then other problems arise. There are philosophers from the Continent, such as Frege and Carnap, who are not adjudged continental, and philosophers from outside the Continent who are.

🔵译 然而，如果把欧陆哲学这个概念依其表面看作是一个地理范畴，那么，又会引起其他问题。有些哲学家来自欧洲大陆，比如弗雷格和卡纳普，但他们并不被认为是欧陆哲学家，而有些哲学家在欧洲大陆之外，但却被看作欧陆哲学家。（江怡译）

例 5-30　<u>But</u>, as we shall see, in a world which is increasingly modeled on the procedures of the natural sciences, such a view is not without problems of its own.

🔵译 但我们会看到，在一个越来越多的以自然科学的程式塑造的世界中，

这样一个观点自身也不是毫无问题的。(江怡译)

例 5-31 <u>But</u> there were political implications to this outburst of religious fervour.

㊣ 但是这种宗教狂热的爆发却蕴含着政治意义。(朱刚和麻晓蓉译)

例 5-32 <u>But</u> international conferences could highlight differences and resentments as well as connections.

㊣ 然而,国际会议既能彰显相互联系,也能凸显分歧与怨恨。(朱刚和麻晓蓉译)

例 5-33 The degree to which chronic, low-level pollution constitutes a risk to biodiversity is less clear than for acute exposures, <u>but</u> several facts are worth noting.

㊣ 缓慢的低水平的污染对生物多样性构成的威胁不很明显,但是有几个事实值得人们引起注意。(李铁刚和孙艳华译)

第六单元
过渡词用法

英语造句与汉语造句有很大的区别，即英语句子中词语或分句之间表达语法意义和逻辑关系(如因果、条件、让步关系等)的形式手段(如副词或关联词)必不可少，而汉语造句则主要通过词语或分句的含义来表示，形式手段并非不可忽缺。也就是说，英语采用形合法造句，而汉语主要采用意合法造句。

为保持句与句之间的有机衔接，以及段落内和段落间句子安排的连贯性和逻辑性，英语有多种过渡手段。其中，形式手段或过渡词(如副词或关联词)法是重要的一种。本篇主要对过渡词(也就是带有连接标志的连词和副词)的用法进行举例说明，读者可通过丰富的例证来体会和学习各种过渡词的用法。

一、相似关系

表示相似关系经常用到的过渡词有：similarly, likewise, as, just as, in the same way 等。

(一) similarly

similarly 意思为"类似地，同样，相似地，差不多地"，多位于句首。

例 6-1 Where in primitive religion souls are deemed material, in modern religion they are deemed immaterial and are limited to human beings: …. <u>Similarly</u>, where in primitive religion gods are deemed material, in modern religion they are deemed immaterial.

🔴译 在原始宗教中，灵魂被看作是物质的，而在现代宗教中，灵魂却被看作是非物质的，而且只有人类才有灵魂：……。与此类似，在原始宗教中，神被看作是物质的，而在现代宗教中，神却被看作是非物质的。(刘象愚译)

例 6-2 Yet even in this formal, logical activity (proving a theorem in geometry), there is no set of rules which will tell the student how to construct proofs for any problem. Basic principles must be mastered, and after some practice, it is assumed that intelligence will show the way to a solution. <u>Similarly</u>, in scientific activity there are no rules which one can study and then use to construct good, faithful experiments for every problem.

🔴译 但即使在这种形式逻辑活动(几何学证明定理)中，也没有任何固定的规则指导学生如何进行证明。必须掌握基本原理，有了一些实践后，理智将会指示解决问题的方法。同样，在科学活动中不存在人可以学习，然后用来

进行正确、有效的实验以解决所有问题的规则。(严忠志译)

(二)likewise

likewise 意思为"同样地,类似地,也,还,亦"。

例 6-3　It was succeeded by two further Intergovernmental Conferences (IGCs) that led to the Maastricht and Amsterdam Treaties, likewise strengthening both powers and institutions, and responding to similar combinations of pressures.

🔵译　此后又召开了两次政府间会议,缔结了《马斯特里赫特条约》与《阿姆斯特丹条约》,同样强化了共同体的权力及其机构,并对类似的各种压力做出了回应。(戴炳然译)

例 6-4　The situation is the same as that with any complex machine. An airplane can function if thousands of parts are working together in harmony, but only one defective part, if that part affects a vital system, can bring it down. Likewise, the development and functioning of every trait require a large number of genes working in harmony, but in some cases a single mutant gene can have catastrophic consequences.

🔵译　这种情况与任何复杂的机器都是一样的。如果成千上万个部件协调工作,一架飞机就可以飞行,但如果一个部件有缺陷,这个部件影响到一个重要的系统,它就可以使飞机坠落。同样,每个性状的发育和功能需要大量的基因协调工作,但在某些情况下,一个基因突变就可能产生灾难性后果。

(三)as

as 意思为"同(像)……一样,如同",用于引导非限制性定语从句、过去分词或介词结构。

例 6-5　If the nuclear lamina is defective, then the normally anchored genetically inactive chromatin might stray into a transcriptionally active region of the nucleus and become inappropriately expressed, as happens in some of the diseases called laminopathies, such as Duchenne muscular dystrophy.

🔵译　如果核膜层有缺陷,那么通常锚定的遗传上失活的染色质可能会进入细胞核的转录激活区,并不适当地表达,如一些称为核纤层蛋白病(如杜氏肌营养不良)中发生的那样。

例 6-6　As such, to borrow Rorty's word, the distinction has become tiresome.

译 这样，借用罗蒂的说法，这种区分变得令人厌烦了。（江怡译）

学术英语中，经常用到 as noted above（如上所述）、as noted earlier（如前所述）、as mentioned above（如上所述）、as noted by/ in（如某人/在某文中所称的/指出的/提到的那样）。

例 6-7 As mentioned earlier, the internal volume of eukaryote cells is a thousand times that of a bacterium, so that the eukaryotic cell requires a vast internal membrane system around a hundred times the area of the plasma membrane itself.

译 如前所述，真核细胞的内部体积是细菌的1000倍，因此真核细胞需要一个巨大的内膜系统，这大约是质膜本身面积的100倍。

例 6-8 As noted in Section 3.15, for single crystals of some substances, the physical properties are anisotropic; that is, they are dependent on crystallographic direction.

译 如第3.15节所述，对于某些物质的单晶，其物理性质是各向异性的；也就是说，物理性质取决于其晶体学方向。

此外，as with / as is 的意思是"如同，和……一样，就……而言"。

例 6-9 Algebra is a very complex and complicated form of math. As with other branches of mathematics it has grown beyond the circumstances of its birth.

译 代数是一种非常复杂的数学形式。和其他数学分支一样，它的发展已经超越了其诞生环境。

例 6-10 The removal of border controls within Schengenland is nevertheless a major achievement, as is the transfer of these competences to the Community, with the Court of Justice fulfilling its normal functions — except in the fields of internal security and law and order, which remain under the control of the member states.

译 然而，在申根国家间取消边境控制仍然是一个重大的成就。同样，将这些权限移交至共同体并让法院行使其正常职能——但内部安全和法治仍受成员国控制——也是一个重大成就。（戴炳然译）

例 6-11 As with / As is the case with so many things, paying attention to the basics is vital.

译 正如是很多事情那样，关注基础是至关重要的。

二、增补或递进关系

表示增补或递进关系经常用到的过渡词有：furthermore, moreover, besides, in addition, also, so, nor, again, and, and then, as well as that, on top of that, what's more 等。

（一）furthermore

furthermore 意思为"此外，而且，再者"，正式用词。furthermore 的使用是为了在前述原因或事项之外再增加一个类似的原因或事项。

例 6-12 However, while we are enjoying the remarkable wonders of the new century, we may be suffering from environmental pollution, green house effect, etc. Therefore, we must overcome these troubles by further advancing science and technology. Furthermore, although life in the new era will become simplified and more convenient, yet there will surely be more strains and pressures, for the new century will be more keenly competitive and challenging.

译 然而，我们在享受新世纪的非凡奇迹时，我们可能遭受环境污染、温室效应等之苦。因此，我们必须通过进一步发展科学技术来克服这些问题。此外，虽然新时代的生活会简单化并更加方便，但肯定会有更多的紧张和压力，因为新世纪将是一个竞争更加激烈、更富于挑战的时代。（谭卫国译）

例 6-13 As the state of the brain changes continuously, it only gradually changes its mode. It does not suddenly switch from one stat to another. Furthermore, the continuous and gradual modulatory changes do not affect every singe neuron of the brain identically or even simultaneously.

译 因为大脑状态的改变是持续性的，所以其模式的改变也只会是渐进性的，它不会突然从一种转变为另一种，更进一步讲，这种持续而渐进的调节变化不会以相同的方式或同时去影响每一个神经元。（韩芳译）

例 6-14 X-rays capture only a slice of the body's three dimensional structure. Furthermore, each X-ray exposes a person to potentially harmful radiation, although today's minute doses are almost completely safe.

译 X射线仅能获得身体某一部分的三维构造。而且，每一X射线都将人体暴露在具有潜在危害的辐射中，尽管今天的微小剂量几乎是十分安全的。（李铁刚和孙艳华译）

(二) moreover

moreover 意思为"此外,而且,也",正式用词。moreover 的使用是为了在前述原因或事项之外再增加一个不同类型的原因或事项。

例 6-15 Freud attacked philosophy on the grounds that, unlike science, it attempted to present a picture of the universe which was too coherent, too lacking in gaps. Moreover, he affirmed philosophy was of interest only to a few intellectuals, and was scarcely intelligible to anyone else.

🔴 他攻击哲学的原因是他认为哲学不同于科学,哲学试图展现一个过于连贯、没有空白的宇宙图景。而且,他还宣称,哲学只能引起为数不多的知识分子的兴趣,其他人几乎都无法理解。(尹莉译)

例 6-16 In reality, the story is not so simple. The preformationists were as careful and accurate in their empirical observations as the epigeneticist. Moreover, if heroes we must have, that honor might as well fall to the preformationists who upheld, against the epigeneticists, a view of science quite congenial with our own.

🔴 其实故事不是那么简单。预成论者和渐成论者一样,在基于经验的观察中谨慎而又准确。况且,如果我们非要有英雄的话,那份荣誉倒不如归于预成论者,因为他们反对渐成论者主张的是完全与我们的观点相吻合的一种科学观点。(杨自伍译)

例 6-17 In an overcrowded country, very few people own enough to make them financially independent, very few are in a position to accumulate purchasing power, and there is no free land. Moreover, in any country where population presses hard upon natural resources, the general economic situation is apt to be so precarious that government control of capital and labor, production and consumption becomes inevitable.

🔴 在一个人口过于拥挤的国家,拥有足够的财富以致财经上独立的人寥寥无几,能够积累购买力者也为数极少,而且也没有空闲的土地。此外,在任何人口对自然资源压力很大的国家里,总的经济状况往往很不稳定,以致政府对资本和劳力、生产和消费的控制就变得不可避免了。(谭卫国译)

例 6-18 This conclusion was dramatically supported by chemical microstimulation experiments, which showed, unequivocally, that REM sleep could be induced by injecting very small amounts of a cholinergic drug into the area of the brain stem known as the pons. Moreover, the pattern and timing of the REM sleep-enhancing effect depended on what part of the pontine brain stem was chemically altered.

译 这一结论得到了化学微刺激实验的有力支持，因为后者明确显示向脑干的特定区域——桥脑注射极微量的胆碱药物即可诱导快动眼睡眠。而且，快动眼睡眠增强效应的模式和时程取决于脑干桥脑的哪一部分被化学性选择激活。（韩芳译）

例 6-19 Changes in how the land is used are probably the principal contributor to the current decline in biodiversity. The pressures on terrestrial resources and land depend very much on population growth and the demands of early stages of economic development. <u>Moreover</u>, land acquisition, especially for agriculture and forestry, focuses initially on those areas with the most fertile soils and equable climates, which are often the areas of greatest biological diversity.

译 土地利用方式的变化，可能是目前生物多样性下降的主要原因。陆地资源和土地承受了压力，主要是因为人口增长和经济发展早期的需要。再者，土地的需求，尤其是为了农业和林业，最初集中在土壤最肥沃和气候温和的地区，而这些地方经常是生物种类最丰富的地方。（李铁刚和孙艳华译）

（三）besides

besides 意思为"此外，另外，况且，再说，以及"，非正式用词。该词可作副词，放在句首，后面跟逗号；也可作介词，接名词、动名词、不带 to 的动词不定式或 that 引导的从句。使用 besides 时，是为了在前述原因、理由或事项之外再增加一个新的原因、理由或事项来加以强化。

例 6-20 Constancy makes success a certainty. On the other hand, inconstancy often results in failure. If we study day after day, there is nothing that cannot be achieved. We should remember a worthy proverb 'Constant dropping of water wears away a stone'. <u>Besides</u>, there is another rule that contributes to one's accomplishments, that is, punctuality.

译 持之以恒是成功的保证。反之，缺乏恒心常常导致失败。如果我们日复一日地坚持学习，就没有达不到的目的。我们应当记住一条值得重视的谚语"滴水穿石"。此外，还有一条帮助人们取得成就的规则，即准时。

例 6-21 <u>Besides</u>, to be conscious of our limits, which death throws into unforgiving relief, is <u>also</u> to be conscious of the way we are dependent on and constrained by others.

译 另外，意识到自身的局限，也即意识到我们与其他人互相依赖、互相束缚的方式。死亡把局限丢给我们，给我们带来无情的宽慰。（朱新伟译）

例 6-22 <u>Besides</u> the questions of origin, function, and subject matter, questions often asked about myth include: is myth universal? is myth true?

译 除了起源、功能和主题之外，关于神话人们常常提出的问题还有：神话是普遍存在的吗？神话是真实的吗？（刘象愚译）

例 6-23 <u>Besides</u> its role in protein synthesis, the ER is a versatile organelle which can both receive and transmit signals and act as a cellular store for calcium, and is also responsible for the synthesis of lipids.

译 除了在蛋白质合成中的作用外，内质网还是一种多功能的细胞器，既能接收和传输信号，又能作为钙的细胞储存处，还负责脂质合成。

例 6-24 <u>Besides</u> causing insomnia, which is unpleasant, these conditions also induce sleep deprivation or, at least, sleep curtailment.

译 除引起令人不快的失眠外，它们还能导致睡眠剥夺，或至少是睡眠减少。（韩芳译）

例 6-25 The hypothesis of REM sleep correspondence across species was greatly strengthened by the subsequent finding that all but the most primitive mammals had periodic brain activation during sleep. If they had eyes, they also had REMs in their activated sleep phases. <u>Besides</u> shoring up the homology hypothesis, this surprising fact suggested that REM was biologically important to all mammalian life, whatever its relationship to human dreaming. <u>Conversely</u>, it suggested that the correlation of REM and dreaming was a very limiting way of thinking about the functional significance of brain activation in sleep.

译 快动眼睡眠的特种一致性假说得到后续研究发现的强有力支持，所有最原始的哺乳动物在睡眠期间都有周期性的大脑激活。如果他们有眼睛的话，在激活的睡眠时相也会有快速眼动。除了能支持同源性假说之外，这一惊人发现还表明快动眼睡眠对所有哺乳动物都具有生物学重要性。另一方面，有证据表明在考虑睡眠期间大脑激活功能的重要性时，研究快动眼睡眠和梦境的关系意义不大。（韩芳译）

（四）also, so, nor

also 表示"而且，此外，也"，与前面的词相比，相对不那么正式。so + be/情态动词/助动词，以倒装句的形式，置于肯定句之后，表示"也是，也如此"。nor + be/情态动词/助动词,以倒装句的形式,置于否定句之后,表示"也不是,也非如此"。nor 常与 neither 连用时,为"既不……,也不……"。

例 6-26 Now scientists and archeologists agree that women invented agriculture. Before it was invented, men were hunters and life was difficult and dangerous. It's women who happened to find that seeds can grow into crops and then they began to live a stable life. Also, scientists believe it's women who kept the first domestic animals: Dogs, sheep, goats and so on. People began to stay at home and civilization began.

🔵 现在科学家和考古学家们一致认为是女人发明了农业。在农业被发明之前,男人是猎手,生活困苦而危险,是女人偶然发现种子可以长成庄稼,然后人类过上了稳定的生活。而且,科学家们也认为是女人饲养了第一批家畜:狗、绵羊、山羊等。人们待在家里,文明由此开始。(谭卫国译)

例 6-27 They also drew a distinction between how they manage money and the approach of public-sector groups whose low returns are often augmented by taxpayers.

🔵 他们还要对自己管钱的方式和公共部门常因纳税人而增加的低回报管钱方式做出区别。(何凯文译)

例 6-28 Thus, conflict within the mind, conflict between competing stimuli like sex and hunger, or conflict between parts of the mind like ego and super-ego, are essential aspects of psychoanalytic thinking. So is the notion of the ego using 'defence mechanisms' like repression, projection, denial, and sublimation as ways of coping with the pressures upon it.

🔵 因此,心灵内部的冲突、互相竞争的刺激如性欲和饥饿之间的冲突,或者心灵不同部分之间如自我和超我的冲突,都是精神分析思想的重要方面。使用压抑、投射、否认和升华等"防范机制"来对付压力的自我概念同样是精神分析的重要方面。(尹莉译)

例 6-29 To recognize this fact, however, is not to counsel inaction, indecision, or despair. Nor is it to fall back on the comfortable but wholly fallacious assumption that since no one has all the answers, everyone's opinion is equally valid.

🔵 然而,承认这一事实并不是要人无所作为、犹豫不决,或者陷入绝望;也不是要人求助那种使人感到安慰但却是虚妄的假定:既然没人可以提供全

部答案，那么每个人的意见同样有效。(严忠志译)

例 6-30　When my house is on fire, I must act quickly and promptly — I cannot stop to consider the possible causes, <u>nor</u> even to estimate the exact probabilities involved in the various alternative ways of reacting.

🔵 当我的房子着火时，我必须立刻行动——我不能停下来考虑造成火灾的可能原因，甚至不能就各种可供选择的反应方式所涉及的确切可能性进行估计。(严忠志译)

例 6-31　That is, goodness is an objective quality in the world which does not alter with each new regime; <u>nor</u> does it depend on the changing character of human opinion.

🔵 这就是说，善是世界的客观性质，既不因为当权者的更迭而变化，也不取决于人们意见变动不居的特点。(严忠志译)

例 6-32　There is no historical record which indicates what kind of relationship Leonardo may have had with his mother or his stepmother, or which tells us what kind of people they were. <u>Nor</u> is known at what age Leonardo was removed from his mother to be brought up by his stepmother and father; although it is recorded that he was part of that household by the time he was five years old.

🔵 没有历史记载显示列奥纳多与他的母亲或继母之间是怎样一种关系，或者她们是什么样的人。也无从知道列奥纳多何时离开母亲转由父亲和继母抚养；尽管有记录表明他在 5 岁的时候已经是父亲家里的一名成员。(尹莉译)

(五) in addition, in addition to

in addition 和 in addition to 意思是"另外，此外，除……之外，加之"。in addition 用作副词短语，常位于句首，后面为逗号，接完整的句子；而 in addition to 则相当于一个介词，后面要接名词或名词结构。

例 6-33　This garden has the best collection of native plants. <u>In addition</u>, it contains numerous trees and flowers from overseas.

🔵 这座花园很好地收集了本地植物。此外，它还有无数来自海外的花草树木。

例 6-34　<u>In addition to</u> the important conclusions reached by pioneer geologists about the history of the earth, several other factors influenced 17th- and 18th-century scientists to consider alternatives to the *Genesis* account of human origins.

◉ 译 除了地质学开创者得出的关于地球历史的重要结论，还有其他几个因素也影响着 17 和 18 世纪的科学家，促使他们在《创世记》外寻求关于人类起源的其他解释。（冯兴无译）

例 6-35 Developments in biochemistry during the first half of the 20th century meant that, <u>in addition to</u> this traditional morphological evidence, scientists could use evidence about the physical characteristics of molecules.

◉ 译 在 20 世纪前半段，生物化学的发展表明，科学家除了利用传统的形态学证据之外，还可以利用分子的物理特征来确定生物间的亲缘关系。（冯兴无译）

三、例证关系

表示例证关系经常用到的过渡词有：for example, for instance, to illustrate, such as, like, including, namely specifically, or, or rather, rather, still, that is, yet 等。

（一）for example, for instance, to illustrate

for example 和 for instance 的意思都是"例如"，可用作插入语，位置不固定，可置于句首、句中或句末，举例时，一般只以同类事物或人中的一个为例。for example 和 for instance 之间没有实质的区别，但 for example 比 for instance 略为正式，在学术英语写作中也更为常用。顺便提一下，e. g. 为拉丁语 *exempli gratia* 缩写，意思是"for example"（字面意思是"for the sake of example"），但同样也可以代替"for instance"。而另一个缩略词 i. e. 意思是"即"，与"that is"同义。两者不要混淆。to illustrate 也可用来举例说明。

例 6-36 However, despite the importance of DNA in our lives, fossilization quickly causes nucleic acids to degrade. <u>For example</u>, after 50,000 years, only small amounts of DNA survive, and even this is broken into short fragments.

◉ 译 然而，尽管 DNA 在我们生命中具有重要性，石化作用会很快使核酸降解。比如，5 万年后只有少量 DNA 存留下来，而且剩下的只是 DNA 片段。（冯兴无译）

例 6-37 Response times for white cell production are staggering. <u>For example</u>, if we catch flu, our white cell production can be tripled within hours of the infection.

◉ 译 白细胞产生的响应时间之短是令人吃惊的。例如，如果我们感染了流感，我们的白细胞产量在感染后的几个小时内会增加两倍。

例 6-38 Brain activation, which must be powerful, and highly selective, can account for some aspects — the hallucinatory imagery and the associated movements, for example.

[译] 强烈和高度选择性的大脑激活可以解释其中的某些方面，例如幻觉性的意象和相关的运作。(韩芳译)

例 6-39 Numerous practical applications have resulted from scientific investigation into the structure, reproduction, metabolism and environmental adaptation of microorganisms. Cheese making, for instance, has been revolutionized by the knowledge and techniques that allow microbiologists to isolate and mass-produce the particular strains of bacteria responsible for the textures and flavors of different types of cheese.

[译] 无数的科学实践应用源自对微生物的结构、繁殖、代谢和环境适应等方面的科学研究。举例来说，微生物学家能够分离并大量生产决定奶酪质地和风味的特定细菌菌株，正是这些知识和技术革新了奶酪制作。

例 6-40 Writing in the disciplines, on the other hand, refers to writing assignments tailored to the genres of a specific discipline or field. For instance, a science course might require students to write a lab report, while a sociology course might assign a case study.

[译] 另一方面，专业写作指的是根据某一特定学科或领域量身定制的写作作业。例如，理科课程可能要求学生写一份实验报告，而社会学课程可能布置一个案例研究。

例 6-41 To illustrate, first grade pupils afraid of policemen will probably alter their attitude after a classroom chat with the neighborhood officer in which he explains how he protects them.

[译] 比如说，害怕警察的一年级小学生可以进行一次与邻里警官的课堂座谈，让他来讲述他是如何保护他们的，那么，孩子们就有可能改变对警察的看法。(马锦儒等译)

(二) such as

such as 意思是“如，比如，例如，诸如，像，象……这样”。such as 后面并非罗列全部对象，但会列举同类人或事物中的几个例子，一般也不在列举对象后加 etc. (等)；such as 后可接名词和名词结构，也可接状语从句和介词结构。

例 6-42 Direct trauma such as mechanical damage, or extreme heat or cold, produces instant and indirect effects such as rupture of the cell membrane, or instant destruction of proteins.

❂ 直接创伤，如机械损伤，或极热或极冷，会产生瞬间和间接的影响，如细胞膜破裂，或蛋白质的瞬间破坏。

例 6-43 Apoptosis is routine in developmental processes such as the removal of webbing between fingers in humans, the loss of tadpole tails in amphibians, and insect metamorphosis.

❂ 细胞凋亡是发育过程中的常规现象，如人类手指间蹼的去除、两栖动物蝌蚪尾巴的丧失和昆虫的变形。

(三) like

like 的意思是"如，诸如"，用于举例时，不必列举全部对象。

例 6-44 You may not realize how all-encompassing and debilitating a vitamin B_{12} deficiency can be until symptoms like fatigue, nausea, vision problems and others morph into more serious disorders and diseases.

❂ 在疲劳、恶心、视力问题和其他症状演变成更严重的疾病之前，你可能不会意识到维生素 B_{12} 缺乏是如何使人全身无力的。

例 6-45 When you experience symptoms like fatigue, numbness, faint nausea, foggy vision or an increased tendency toward forgetfulness, you might entertain many different scenarios.

❂ 当你出现疲劳、麻木、轻微恶心、视力模糊或越来越容易健忘等症状时，你可能会遇到许多不同的情况。

(四) including

including 意思是"包括……在内"，后面也无须(也不能)罗列全部对象。

例 6-46 Some eminent authorities, including Einstein, have pointed out that there is a danger of the extinction of all life on this planet.

❂ 包括爱因斯坦在内的一些著名的权威，曾指出地球上生命有全部灭绝的危险。

例 6-47 These include memory loss, psychosis including hallucinations and delusions, fatigue, irritability, depression and personality changes.

㋐ 这些包括失忆、包括幻觉和妄想在内的精神病、疲劳、易怒、抑郁和人格变化。

（五）namely

namely 意思是"即，也就是"，后面需要罗列全部对象。

例 6-48　Like most vitamins, B_{12} is not manufactured by your body, so it must come from another source — namely food and supplements

㋐ 像大多数维生素一样，B_{12}不是由身体制造的，所以它必须来自另一个来源——即食物和补充剂。

需要注意的是，与例证关系相关的两个表示省略后面罗列项目的词 etc. 和 and so on（等等，诸如此类，以及其他）由于其非正式性和不清晰性，因此，尽可能不要在学术英语写作中使用。

四、强调关系

表示强调关系经常用到的过渡词有：in fact, indeed, certainly, of course, surely, especially, in particular, actually, in practice, in effect, anyway, anyhow, at any rate, in any case, above all, as a matter of fact, what's more 等。

（一）in fact

in fact 意思为"事实上，其实，准确地说，确切地说"，用于强调对前述看法的修正，或引出相反意见。as a matter of fact 的用法与之类似，也是强调对前述观点的修正或反驳。

例 6-49　This sounds merely silly; but in fact it has some fairly momentous implications.

㋐ 这听起来愚蠢，实际上却有一些相当重要暗示。（朱新伟译）

例 6-50　In fact, Aristotle's 'great-souled' moral prototype is much like this: A prosperous Athenian gentleman who is a stranger to failure, loss, and tragedy — interestingly, for the author of one of the world's great treatises on the latter topic.

㋐ 实际上，亚里士多德脑中拥有"高尚灵魂"的道德原型大致是这样的：一位富有的雅典绅士，他没有接触过失败、损失和悲剧——有趣的是，亚里士多德却创作了世界上最伟大的悲剧论著之一。（朱新伟译）

（二）indeed

indeed 意思是"实际上，真正地，其实，确切说来"，用于强调肯定的陈述或断言。

例 6-51 Although the Greeks were comfortable with the idea that the behaviour of an animal could change, they did not accept that the structure of animals, including humans, had been modified since they were spontaneously generated. Indeed Plato championed the idea that living things were unchanging, or immutable, and his opinions influenced philosophers and scientists until the middle of the 19th century.

[译] 虽然希腊人较容易接受动物的行为可以改变，但他们不接受动物(包括人类)的身体结构在自发产生以来会改变的事实。事实上，柏拉图支持，生物是不变的或永恒的。他的观点直到 19 世纪中期还影响着哲学家和科学家们。(冯兴无译)

例 6-52 We are not saying that dream content is unimportant, uninformative, or even uninterpretable. Indeed, we believe that dreaming is all three of these things, but it is already crystal clear that many aspects of dreaming previously thought to be meaningful, privileged, and interpretable psychologically are the simple reflection of the sleep-related changes in brain state that we start to detail in Charpter 3.

[译] 这里并不是说梦的内容不重要，不能提供什么信息，甚至无法解析。实际上，我们认为梦在上述三个方面都是对的，但我们已经清楚地知道，先前认为有意义的、保密的、心理学上可以解释的梦的许多方面，都不过是与睡眠相关的大脑活动状态改变的简单反映而已，具体内容将在第三章详加讨论。(韩芳译)

(三) certainly

certainly 意思是“无疑，当然，确定，肯定”，用于强调所说内容属实。

例 6-53 Certainly, dreaming is a hyperassociative state (i. e. a state in which many, many associations are made), as Freud could have quickly determined had he examined dream reports before rushing to interpret them.

[译] 当然，梦是一种超联想状态(亦即一个各种联想大量产生的状态)，如果弗洛伊德能在急于释梦之前先审查一下梦例，他也能很快得出上述结论。(韩芳译)

例 6-54 Animals certainly can't report dreams even if they do have them.

[译] 动物即便真的能做梦，也无法报告出来。(韩芳译)

(四) of course

of course 意思是"当然，自然"，用于强调表示应该了解的事实或众所周知的事实。

例 6-55　This is not of course to suggest that all questions are answerable. We tend to assume that where there is a problem there must be a solution, just as we tend rather oddly to imagine that things which are in fragments should always be put back together again. But there are plenty of problems to which we will probably never discover solutions, along with questions which will go eternally unanswered.

🔵 这当然不是说所有的问题都能解答。我们习惯于有问必答，就像我们总觉得一堆碎片应该拼成原貌。但是世界上总归会有大量问题我们可能一直无法解决，还有许多问题永远不会有人去解答。（朱新伟译）

例 6-56　By 'the world', of course, one means both the processes of nature and activities of human beings.

🔵 当然，说到"世界"，是同时指自然的过程与人类的活动。（颜元叔译）

例 6-57　This, of course, implies activation of generators of motor patterns in the brain, for which there is now abundant evidence.

🔵 当然，这意味着大脑中各种运动模式发生器的激活，现在已有很多证据支持这一点。（韩芳译）

例 6-58　What we can say unequivocally at this point is that, of course, since dreaming is a brain function, brain damage will affect it. How could it be otherwise?

🔵 不过此刻我们可以肯定，鉴于梦是大脑功能的一种，脑损伤当然会对梦有影响。若非如此，那又能如何呢？（韩芳译）

(五) surely

surely 用于肯定句时，表示对自己的话很有把握，希望他人同意，意思是"想必"；用于否定句时，表示难以置信，意思是"无疑，必定"。

例 6-59　Advances in technology and science are transforming our world at an incredible pace, and our children's future will surely be filled with leaps in technology we can only imagine.

🔵 技术和科学的进步正在以令人难以置信的速度改变我们的世界，我们孩子的未来肯定会充满我们所能想象到的技术飞跃。

例 6-60　But it is surely not irrelevant to the arguments of Heidegger's *Being and Time* that the book was written in just such a period of historical tumult, appearing as it did in the wake of the First World War.

🌐 但是,海德格尔的《存在与时间》的写作时间恰好是历史动乱时期,问世是在一战之后,这与该书的观点无疑存在关联。(朱新伟译)

(六) especially

especially 意思是"尤其,特别,格外"。

例 6-61　For anyone to observe REM sleep behaviour directly, it can be done with bed partners, especially in the wee hours of the morning, most conveniently on vacation, in the summer time when the hillock of the cornea can be seen in the early dawn light to glide to and fro under the closed — or perhaps half-open — eyelids.

🌐 任何想要直接观察快动眼睡眠行为的人,都可以通过观察同床而眠者达到目的,尤其是利用凌晨一两点钟的时间。最方便的莫属夏季度假的时候,在黎明的微光中,可以看见角膜凸起部在紧闭或半开的眼睑下来回滑动。(韩芳译)

例 6-62　Modern religion has surrendered the physical world to science and has retreated to the immaterial world, especially to the realm of life after death — that is, of the life of the soul after the death of the body.

🌐 现代宗教将物质世界完全让给了科学,自己撤退到非物质世界之中,特别是躯体死亡之后灵魂的生活中。(刘象愚译)

(七) in particular

in particular 意思是"尤其,特别"。

例 6-63　In particular, two of the chemical systems necessary to waking consciousness are completely shut off when the brain self-activates in sleep.

🌐 特别是清醒意识必需的两个化学系统在睡眠中大脑自我激活时被完全关闭。(韩芳译)

五、重复关系

表示重复关系经常用到的过渡词有:or, in other words, put another way,

to put it the other way round, that is, that is to say, namely, i. e., or rather, to repeat, as stated previously, as we have seen before, in simpler terms 等。

(一) or

or 在肯定句中连接两个或两个以上的成分时,意思为"或,或者";连接两个句子时,意思为"或者,或者说"。

例 6-64　Freud set out by believing that the meaning of life was desire, or the ruses of the unconscious in our waking lives, and came to believe that meaning of life was death.

🀄 弗洛伊德一开始相信人生的意义是欲望,或者是我们清醒时的无意识的诡计,后来觉得人生的意是死亡。(朱新伟译)

例 6-65　Or it can suggest that live in an awareness of our mortality is to live with realism, irony, truthfulness, and a chastening sense of our finitude and fragility.

🀄 或者可以表示,怀着人必有一死的意识生活,就是怀着现实主义、反讽、诚实以及对自我有限性和脆弱性怀着磨炼意识而生活。(朱新伟译)

(二) in other words

in other words 置于句首或作为插入成分置于句中,意思为"换言之,换句话说,也就是说"。

例 6-66　Language, in other words, allows us not only to get a fix on ourselves, but to conceive of our situation as a whole.

🀄 换句话说,语言不仅使得我们把握自身,也帮助我们从整体上思考自身的状况。(朱新伟译)

例 6-67　Just before the middle of the last century, two classic sensorimotor physiologists, Giuseppe Moruzzi and Horace Magoun, working at Northwestern Medical School in Chicago, discovered that the experimental stimulation of the brain stem of cats could cause a shift in the EEG pattern from that of sleep to that of waking. In other words, they established an experimental basis for brain activation in sleep.

🀄 就在20世纪中叶前,芝加哥西北大学医学院两位著名的感觉运动生理学家——看朱塞佩·莫鲁齐和霍勒斯·马古恩发现:给猫的脑干予以实验性刺激,可使脑电图模式从睡眠转换到觉醒。换言之,他们建立了睡眠期间大

脑激活的实验基础。(韩芳译)

(三) put another way, to put it the other way round

put another way, to put it the other way round 意思为"换言之,换句话说"。

例 6-68　So we sleep, perchance to dream. And we dream, perforce to reactivate the brain basis of self-hood that is embedded in our built-in capacity to generate movement. <u>Put another way</u>, our dreams — so constantly and elaborately animated — remind us that we were born with an already huge talent for movement and for the sensorimotor perceptions of movement that become the centre of our sense of self as agents.

🔖 我们睡觉时可能会做梦,而做梦必然会重新激活与人类固有运动能力直接相关的自我意识的大脑基础。换句话说,我们的梦是如此连续而精巧、栩栩如生,提醒我们自己在出生时就拥有运动和感知运动的巨大天赋,而后者最终成为我们自我存在感的核心。(韩芳译)

例 6-69　Since the treaty can be amended only by unanimity, the other governments had to accept the opting-out if these items were to be included in it; and this led to growing interest in the idea of 'flexibility', enabling those states wanting further integration in a given field to proceed within the Community institutions or, <u>to put it the other way round</u>, letting a minority opt out.

🔖 鉴定条约只能经全体一致同意才能修改,如果要将这些条款写入条约,其他国家政府就不得不接受英国与丹麦的退出。这使得人产对"灵活性"观念越来越感兴趣:让那些希望在一特定领域加深一体化的国家,能在共同体机构内继续推行其计划,或者换句话说,让少数国家选择不参加。(戴炳然译)

(四) that is, that is to say, i.e.

that is, that is to say 意思是"即,就是说",后面跟逗号。i.e. 的全称是 id est,表示解释,没有举例的意思,意思是"即,那就是说,换句话说",与"that is"同义。

例 6-70　Although psychoanalysis is not a science in the same category as the 'hard' sciences of physics and chemistry, the history of ideas demonstrates that, in so far as our understanding of ourselves and the world can be said to increase, it progresses in the way that Popper claims for science; <u>that is</u>, by refutation of existing hypotheses.

译 尽管精神分析不属于物理和化学那样的"硬"科学类别，但是思想发展的历史表明，只要可以说我们对自身和世界的理解增强了，那么它就按照波普宣称的科学发展的方式前进，即通过对现存假说的证伪来取得进步。（尹莉 译）

例 6-71　That is, there is a cultural distinction, some would say a divide — perhaps even an abyss — between the 'Continental' and whatever opposes it, what Baroness Thatcher, in tones deliberately reminiscent of Winston Churchill, calls 'the English-speaking world'.

译 这就是说，有一种文化差异，某些人会说是分歧——或许甚至是一个深渊——存在于"欧洲大陆"与其对立者之间，而这个对立者，撒切尔夫人有意用使人回想起温斯顿·丘吉尔的口吻把它称作"英语世界"。（江怡 译）

例 6-72　It is therefore impossible that in the same respect and in the same way a thing should be both mover and moved, i. e., that it should move itself.

译 因此，一个事物不可能在同一个方面、以同样的方式既是推动者且又被推动；换言之，事物不可能自我推动。（严忠志 译）

例 6-73　The largest step in the evolution of living things on earth was the switch from prokaryotic to eukaryotic cell organization, i. e. the acquisition of a nucleus containing genetic material inside an isolating membrane.

译 地球上生物进化的最大一步是从原核细胞向真核细胞组织的转变，即获得在隔离膜内含有遗传物质的细胞核。

（五）namely

namely 意思为"即，也就是"。该词后面一般跟逗号，后面引出同位语。

例 6-74　Other animals may be anxious about, say, escaping predators or feeding their young, but they do not give the appearance of being troubled by what has been called "ontological anxiety": Namely, the feeling (sometimes accompanied by a particularly intense hangover) that one is a pointless, superfluous being — a 'useless passion', as Jean-Paul Sartre put it.

译 其他动物会为躲避追捕、喂养幼雏这样的事感到焦虑，但它们不会产生我们所说的"本体论的焦虑"：感到自己是一个没有意义的、多余的存在（有时伴随着极为强烈的惆怅）——如萨特所言，是一股"无用的激情"。（朱新伟 译）

例 6-75　For logical positivists like Carnap, meaning is rooted in the principle of verification, namely that a word or sentence is meaningful only if it is in principle verifiable.

译 对卡纳普这样的逻辑实证主义者来说，意义根植于证实原则，就是说，一个词或句子，只有当它原则上是可以证实的，才是有意义的。（江怡译）

六、转折或对比关系

表示转折关系经常用到的过渡词有：however, but, although, though, whereas, while, in contrast (to), on the contrary, on the other hand, despite, in spite of, yet, conversely, rather, instead, nevertheless, otherwise, even if, even though, save that, apart from, far from, unfortunately, surprisingly, still, as a matter of fact, at the same time, for all that, in fact, to a certain degree, clearly, after all, of course 等。

（一）however/but

however 和 but 都是表达转折的连词，意思是"然而，但，但是，而是"。however 比较正式，尤其是在书面语中，使用得非常多。however 经常连接两个较长的句子，而 but 则可以连接短句子、短语甚至是单词。

至少一百年来，语法专家一直告诫作者"不要用 however 作为句子开头"，如果这样用，就用 nevertheless 来代替 however. 但是很多作家还是在句子开头使用 however. 句首使用连接词 however 是否合适，有两种意见，保守派的观点认为 however/ but 置于句首是错误的，甚至避免使用不正式的 but 来代替 however. 例如，小威廉·斯特伦克（William Strunk Jr.）在《风格的要素》（*The Elements of Style*）中写道：however 表示"然而（nevertheless）"的意思，就不要放在句首。但几乎所有现代风格写作指南都认为这些传统的建议是不合理的。现代风格的写作指南并不认为 however/ but 置于句首是错误的。如《芝加哥风格手册》（*The Chicago Manual of Style*），《加纳的现代美国用法》（*Garner's Modern American Usage*）等认为，句子用 however 开头没有错。however 放在句首，它提示从前一句话到下一句话发生句意转折，其意思是"nevertheless"（然而）。甚至认为句子用 but 开头一般来说更好一些，因为使用简单的单词 but 更有效。我们注意到，保守派写作风格（大多为人文学科）的文章中，几乎很少使用 but，即使使用 however，也很少置于句首。相反，在现代风格的学术文章中，尤其是自然科学文章中，however 和 but 经常不加区别换用，句首也经常使用 however/ but.

需要注意的是，当 however 放在句首，后面插入逗号时才表示句意转折。如果将 however 放在句首，修饰后面形容词，不插入逗号，则用作副词，并不起连接词的作用。表示"不论以可种方法（in whatever manner）""不论到何种程度（to whatever extent）"或"无论如何（no matter how）"。

例 6-76 <u>However</u> inhuman the facilities of the port might seem in scale, it is in the end only our own personal and prosaic appetites that have created them.

🔵 译 不论这些建在港口的庞大厂房看上去多么不符合人性，毕竟它们也是受人类自己平淡无奇的爱好驱动才建立起来。（袁洪庚译）

例 6-77 But <u>however</u> great the economic advantages of segmenting the elements of an afternoon's work into a range of forty-year-long carreers, there was reason to wonder about the unintended side effects of doing so.

🔵 译 然而，不论将一下午的工作当作长达 40 年的职业生涯来仔细分割会带来多大的经济效益，人们仍有理由怀疑这样做会带来何种意想不到的副作用。（袁洪庚译）

即使不在句首，however 后面为形容词，不插入逗号时也是一样。

例 6-78 Six countries in the middle of Western Europe, <u>however</u> important, could hardly be called Europe.

🔵 译 位于西欧中部的 6 个国家，不论它们多么重要，也很难被称为欧洲。（戴炳然译）

把 however 放在一个分号（不是句号）后面的句子的前面是没有问题的。此外，为了避免放在句首被人认为不正确，或者为了句子节奏的关系，however 也可作为一个插入语，置于句中。同样表示与前面的内容形成对比，表示接下来的句子部分是重点。

例 6-79 Any animal dying on land is likely, of course, to have its soft, fleshy remains scavenged and recycled; <u>however</u>, for such a creature to be preserved as a fossil it would need to be subject to some form of burial.

🔵 译 当然，任何在陆地上死亡的动物的软组织和肌肉都很可能被吃掉并进入再循环；然而，要使这样的动物成为化石，它们就必须经过某种形式的埋藏。（史立群译）

例 6-80 Dinosaurs were anatomically reptiles (that is to say, members of the general group of egg-laying, cold-blooded, scaly vertebrates); <u>however</u>, the reptiles living today were a degenerate group of creatures when compared to Owen's magnificent dinosaurs that had lived during Mesozoic times.

🔵 恐龙在解剖学上属于爬行动物(换句话说就是产卵、冷血且有鳞的脊椎动物类群的成员);然而,与欧文提出的曾经生活在中生代的健壮恐龙相比,生活在今天的爬行类是一个退化的动物类群。(史立群译)

例 6-81 American hegemony in defence will, however, remain unchallenged for as long ahead as can be contemplated.

🔵 然而在可以预见的很长一段时期,美国的防务霸权仍将不可撼动。(戴炳然译)

例 6-82 These reports do, however, have corresponding deficiencies, which need to be overcome if dream science is to be universally valid.

🔵 不过,这些报告确实有其相应的缺陷,梦的科学要想具有普遍适用性就必须克服这些缺陷。(韩芳译)

例 6-83 The reflex doctrine could not, however, help the pioneer sleep and dream scientist very much, because no link could be established between the activity of circuits of neurons (neuronal ciruits) and the EEG.

🔵 但反射学说对研究睡眠和梦的先驱科学家们帮助有限,因为在神经元回路活动(神经回路)和脑电图之间无法建立任何联系。(韩芳译)

例 6-84 The present arrangements may, however, become a step towards further reforms that will surely be required to make the system effective.

🔵 不过现时的安排,或许可以成为走向进一步改革的步骤,而这正是使此体制有效所必不要少的。(戴炳然译)

例 6-85 There is, however, a danger that a legitimate worry about scientism can develop into an anti-scientific attitude.

🔵 然而,有一种危险在于,对于科学主义的合理性担忧会发展成为反科学的态度。(江怡译)

例 6-86 Each cell usually has one nucleus. However, some cells have no nucleus, such as red blood cells, and a few types of cells have multiple nuclei, such as skeletal muscle cells.

🔵 通常一个细胞只有一个细胞核。但是有些细胞却没有细胞核,如红细胞;而少数细胞类型有多个细胞核,如骨骼肌细胞。(李少如译)

例 6-87 Many philosophers have been intuitionists believing that the ultimate test for the morality of an action is moral vision — an immediate intuition of the rightness or wrongness of the act. However, it should be pointed out that this does not eliminate the role of reason.

    译 许多哲学家是直观主义者，相信行为道德的最终检测是道德洞察——一种对该行为正误的直感。但是应该提出，这并不排除理性的作用。（严忠志译）

例 6-88 However, historians have suggested that there was a gradual reduction in the scope of their concerns; by the 1680s, they were confining themselves to 'womanly' matters.

    译 然而，历史学家们认为她们关注的范围在逐渐缩小。到了17世纪80年代，她们将自己局限于"女人的"问题。（朱刚和麻晓蓉译）

例 6-89 This arrangement is only found in muscle cells, so for many years the possibility that actin and myosin could interact to produce contraction in non-muscle cells seemed unlikely. However, in 1973, Tom Pollard showed that there was more than one type of myosin in non-muscle cells.

    译 这种排列只在肌肉细胞中发现，因此多年来非肌肉细胞中肌动蛋白和肌球蛋白相互作用产生收缩的可能性似乎不大。然而，在1973年，汤姆·波拉德发现非肌肉细胞中存在不止一种类型的肌球蛋白。

例 6-90 The distinction between muscles that are under voluntary control and those that are not is not a hard and fast one, however.

    译 然而，可以自主控制的肌肉和无法自主控制的肌肉之间并没有严格的区分。（石林译）

例 6-91 The computer can provide a correct number, but it may be an irrelevant number until judgment is pronounced.

    译 电脑能提供一个正确有的数字，但在未被作价值判断之前它可能是个缺乏相关性的数字。（颜元叔译）

例 6-92 They introduce thoughts, feelings, and percepts related to the laboratory situation, but this has no effect on dream hallucinations, delusions, or bizarreness.

    译 它们带入了与实验室条件相关的想法、感情和感知，但这对梦境的幻想、错觉和怪诞没有影响。（韩芳译）

例 6-93 What Wittgenstein probably means is not that the meaning of life is a pseudo-question, but that it is a pseudo-question as far as philosophy is concerned.

🔵 维特根斯坦的意思大概不是说人生的意义是一个伪问题，而是说，在哲学范围内这是一个伪问题。（朱新伟译）

例 6-94 The key to the universe turns out to be not some shattering revelation, but something which a lot of decent people do anyway, with scarcely a thought. Eternity lies not in a grain of sand but in a glass of water.

🔵 宇宙的关键原来不是什么令人震惊的启示，而是许多正直的人都能做到的事，根本不用多想。永恒并不存一粒沙当中，面是在于一杯水之中。（朱新伟译）

例 6-95 The meaning of life is not a solution to problem, but a matter of living in a certain way. It is not metaphysical, but ethical. It is not something separate from life, but what makes it worth living — which is to say, a certain quality, depth, abundance, and intensity of life. In this sense, the meaning of life is life itself, seen in a certain way.

🔵 人生的意义不是对某个问题的解答，而是关乎以某种方式生活。它不是形而上的，而是伦理性的。它并不脱离生活，相反，它使生命值得度过——也就是说，它使人生具有一种品质、深度、丰富性和强度。在这个意义上，从某种角度看人生的意义便是人生本身。（朱新伟译）

例 6-96 It was thought that brown fat was lost by adulthood in most humans, but in small mammals such as rats and mice, where heat loss is greater, brown fat cells are retained throughout life.

🔵 据认为，大多数人成年后会失去棕色脂肪，但在诸如大鼠和小鼠等小型哺乳动物中，热量损失更大，棕色脂肪细胞一生都会保留。

例 6-97 We are inclined to assume that it is the slow progress of technological development that impeded scientific advances in studying dreaming. But this is a face-saving sop for those who were so conceptually blinded that they could not imagine the simple experiments that could have led to the brain activation conclusion.

🔵 我们倾向于认为是技术发展的缓慢阻碍了梦科学研究的进展，而事实上这不过是某些人用来保全面子的幌子而已，因为他们在概念上如此盲目，以至于无法设想本能得出大脑激活结论的实验。（韩芳译）

例 6-98 Theories of myth may be as old as myths themselves. Certainly they go back at least to the Presocratics. But only in the modern era — specifically, only since the second half of the nineteenth century — have those theories purported to be scientific.

㊀ 神话理论与神话一样古老,其出现至少可以追溯到前苏格拉底时代。然而,只是到了现代,特别是19世纪下半叶以来,神话理论才仿佛具有了科学的形态。(刘象愚译)

例 6-99　But it should not be forgotten that although the unexamined life is not worth living, the unlived life is not worth examining, and philosophy for the ancients was not divorced from the practical to and fro of everyday social life. Rather, philosophy as a reflective practice of examining what passes for truth in the name of truth is something that took place in what the ancient Greeks called the *polis*, the public realm of political life.

㊀ 但不应忘记,尽管未经审视的生活是不值得过后,失去了生命的生活则是不值得审视的;在古人看来,哲学并不是对日常生活的实际的背离,相反,哲学是以真理的名义考察何为真理的反思性实践,它正是发生于古希腊人所说的"城邦"之中,这是政治生活的公共领域。(江怡译)

例 6-100　Preformationists and epigeneticists did not disagree about their observations; but, whereas epigeneticists were prepared to take those observations literally, the preformationists insisted on probing "behind appearance."

㊀ 预成论者与渐成论者对于观察结果并未产生分歧;不过,渐成论者乐于就事论事地看待那些观察结果,而预成论者则坚持"透过表象"去探究。(杨自伍译)

例 6-101　Currently the earliest good fossil evidence of hominins beyond Africa comes from the site of Dmanisi in the Caucasus. There are no absolute dates for the sediments from the site, but the radioisotope age of the lava beneath the sediments and the fossil animals found with the hominins suggest an age of around 1.7–1.8 MY. The hominins found there have yet to be studied in detail, but they appear to belong to a relatively primitive *H. ergaster*-like creature. However, what is intriguing is that the stone tools recovered from the same horizon as the Dmanisi hominins are like the earliest African stone tools that archaeologists refer to as belonging to the Oldowan culture.

㊀ 迄今为止,非洲以外保存良好的最早人类化石出自高加索德马尼西的

一处遗址。虽然没有遗址沉积物的绝对测年数据，沉积物之下的熔岩的放射性同位素和与人类化石一起也发现的动物化石的测年数据表明，年代大约距今 180 万到 170 万年。虽然尚未对那里发现的人类化石详加研究，大致可以看出该化石人类属于一个相对原始的、类似匠人的类群。然而令人非常感兴趣的是，在德马尼西人类化石层位发现的石器却与非洲最早的石器相似，考古学家认为后者属于奥杜威文化。（冯兴无译）

(二) although, though

although 和 though 意思是"虽然，尽管，即使，不过，然而"。引导让步状语从句，可置于主句前后，有时还可作为插入语置于句中。相对而言，although 更为正式。although 和 though 引导的从句都不能与 but/however 连用，但可与 yet/still/nevertheless 连用。

although 和 though 一般可相互换用，但它们之间也有区别。though 可指假设的情况，这时从句用虚拟语气；although 不这样使用。另外，though 引导的从句可用倒装语序；although 则否。though 从句如果是系表结构时，可省略从句主语和 be 动词。

例 6-102 Although World War Two is receding into a more distant past, the motive of peace and security that was fundamental to the foundation of the Community remains a powerful influence on governments and politicians in the six founder states.

译 尽管第二次世界大战正日渐淡出历史，成为一个更为遥远的过去，但作为创建共同体的基石，谋求和平与安全的动机仍然对 6 个创始国的政府和政治家具有重大的影响。（戴炳然译）

例 6-103 Although artists and poets have long championed this approach and have appropriately celebrated the differences between conscious states, scientists have shied away from their study because they had no objective measures of subjective experience and because subjective experience was considered to be hard to trust or deal with.

译 尽管艺术家和诗人们长久以来对这一领域倾注了极大的热情，对意识状态之间的差别也给予了适当的评价，但科学家们却避开了这一研究课题，因为他们没有客观方法去测量主观的体验，而主观的体验又被认为是不可靠且难以处理的。（韩芳译）

例 6-104 Although electron microscopy has produced vast amounts of information on the workings of the cytoplasm, it has been relatively less successful for the nucleus.

🌐 尽管电子显微镜已经产生了大量有关细胞质工作的信息，但对于细胞核来说，它的成功率相对较低。

例 6-105 Although cell biology is generally in agreement about the origin of mitochondria and chloroplasts by engulfment, no such consensus exists for the origin of the nucleus.

🌐 虽然细胞生物学普遍认同线粒体和叶绿体是通过吞噬作用起源的，但对于细胞核的起源却没有这样的共识。

例 6-106 Although the nucleus is the largest and most obvious organelle within the cell, the processes within it have proved rather more difficult to study than those in the surrounding cytoplasm.

🌐 尽管细胞核是细胞内最大和最明显的细胞器，但其内部的过程比周围细胞质中的过程更难研究。

例 6-107 Although the mechanics of transcription are understood, how genes are selected for transcription is less clear.

🌐 虽然转录的机制已经被理解，但是还不太清楚基因是如何被选择转录的。

例 6-108 Although the nuclear envelope clearly separates nucleus and cytoplasm, it also physically links them.

🌐 尽管核膜清楚地将细胞核和细胞质分开，但它也在物理上将它们联系起来。

例 6-109 Thus, although insufficient as a criterion, to identify the distinction between traditions in terms of a superficial difference between proper names and problems leads on to deeper questions of tradition and history, and the centrality of the latter for the Continental tradition.

🌐 因此，尽管这并不足以作为一个标准，但用专名与问题之间的表面差异去确定这两个传统之间的差异，就导致了更为深层的传统与历史问题，以及历史在欧陆传统中的核心性的问题。（江怡译）

例 6-110 The grandiosity and fearless elation of mania are shared with dream psychosis, although these features are also found in organic delirium, especially in its chronic, post-intoxication phase.

译 梦中的精神失常具有躁狂症夸张而无畏的情感高涨特征，但这些特征也见于器质性谵妄，尤其是在其慢性、宿醉期后。（韩芳译）

例 6-111 An organized cytoskeleton is a property restricted to eukaryotes, although similar proteins do exist in a rudimentary form in some bacteria.

译 有组织的细胞骨架仅限于真核生物，尽管在某些细菌中类似的蛋白质确实以初级形式存在。

例 6-112 Because organisms in the same species share the same developmental plan, organisms that are members of the same species usually resemble one another, although some notable exceptions usually are differences between males and females.

译 由于同一物种的生物具有相同的发育蓝图，因此属于同一物种的生物通常彼此相似，尽管雌雄之间的差异是明显的例外情况。

例 6-113 The vast majority of the cells lining the small intestine are called enterocytes, although there are other cell types with important functions.

译 小肠内绝大多数细胞称为肠细胞，尽管还有其他具有重要功能的细胞类型。

例 6-114 Though the pleasure which works of art give us must not be confused with other pleasures that we enjoy, it is related to all of them simply by being our pleasure and not someone else's.

译 虽然艺术作品给我们的乐趣决不能和我们所享受的其他乐趣相混淆，但它和它们全有关系，因为那是我们的乐趣而不是任何别人的乐趣。（朱树飏译）

例 6-115 Though antioxidants from foods confer sun protection to skin, consuming them in supplement form poses risk.

译 尽管食物中的抗氧化剂能使皮肤防护日晒，但以补充剂的形式摄入会带来风险。

（三）whereas, while

whereas 和 while 意思是"虽然……但是……，尽管，但是，然而，而"。引导的从句可在主句前，也可在主句后，用以比较或对比两个事实，但 whereas 更为正式。whereas 强调的是从句与主句在意义上对立和相反，从句和主句可以互换，句意不变；while 则强调的是对比和不同，但不一定是相反或对立。

例 6-116　Whereas its common tariff had made the Community a trading power equivalent to the USA, before the euro it had no monetary instrument that could become the equal of the dollar in the international monetary system.

㊌ 虽然共同关税使共同体成为可与美国匹敌的贸易伙伴，但在欧元出现之前，它在国际贸易货币体系中并没有可与美元抗衡的货币手段。（戴炳然译）

例 6-117　Whereas previously students of dreaming had invariably asked 'What does the dream mean?', we asked what the mental characteristics of dreaming are the distinguish it from waking mental activity.

㊌ 以前那些梦的研究者总是千篇一律地重复着同样一个问题：这个梦意味着什么？而我们现在要问的却是：做梦时大脑的活动与清醒时有什么不同？（韩芳译）

例 6-118　In its frenzied hedonism, it pays homage to the death it tries to disavow. For all its bravura, it is a pessimistic view, whereas the acceptance of death is a realistic one.

㊌ 这种策略通过狂热的享乐主义向它所蔑视的死亡低下了头。它虽然使尽浑身解数，但仍是一种悲观的观念，而接受死亡则是实事求是的态度。（朱新伟译）

例 6-119　What distinguishes the Russian context from the German one is that in the German version nihilism is largely a metaphysical or epistemological issue, whereas in the Russian it has a more obviously socio-political dimension.

㊌ 德语语境和俄语语境的区别之处在于，在德语语境中，虚无主义主要是形而上学的或认识论的问题，而在俄语的语境中，它具有更为明显的社会政治特性。（江怡译）

例 6-120　Further evidence for the importance of chromosomes was provided by the observation that, whereas the number of chromosomes in each cell may differ among biological species, the number of chromosomes is nearly always constant within the cells of any particular species.

㊌ 尽管不同生物物种中每个细胞中的染色体数量可能不同，但任何特定物种的细胞内染色体数量几乎总是恒定不变的，这种观察对染色体的重要性提供了进一步的证据。

例 6-121　Interestingly, China appears to have made the most progress in p53

-based treatments, with a drug called Gendicine have been approved for head and neck cancer in 2003, whereas the US Food and Drug Administration by 2010 had not approved any p53-based treatments.

🔹译 有意思的是,看起来中国在基于 p53 的治疗方面取得了最大的进展,2003 年一种叫称为金雀花碱的药物被批准用于头颈癌,而美国食品和药物管理局到 2010 年还没有批准任何基于 p53 的治疗。

例 6-122 The common gut bacterium *Escherichia coli* has 4300 genes, whereas the smallest flu virus has but 11 genes.

🔹译 普通肠道细菌大肠杆菌有 4300 个基因,而最小的流感病毒只有 11 个基因。

例 6-123 While moving closer together on agriculture, the Community and the USA have been diverging over environmental, cultural, and consumer protection issues, with the Europeans favouring standards which lead to restriction of their imports from the USA and which the Americans regard as protectionist.

🔹译 共同体与美国在农业上趋于接近,但在环保、文化与消费者保护问题上一直存在分歧:欧洲实行的标准限制了来自美国的进口,美国则认为那是贸易保护主义。(戴炳然译)

例 6-124 While skin provides a remarkably efficient watertight and mechanical barrier to the external environment, these parameters are exactly the opposite of the requirements of gut epithelium, where we need to optimize our uptake of nutrients, while at the same time inhibiting the uptake of anything potentially harmful.

🔹译 虽然皮肤对外部环境提供了一个非常有效的防水和机械屏障,但这些参数与肠道上皮的要求正好相反,后者需要优化摄取营养物质,同时抑制摄取任何潜在有害物质。

例 6-125 While the economic impact of the agreements, preferences, and aid can hardly be measured and may not have been very great, the Union has gained political credit which may be of help in the future development of its relationships with countries of the Third World.

🔹译 尽管这些协定、优惠和援助对经济的影响难以衡量,甚至可能成效并不太显著,但欧盟在政治上赢得了认可,这可能有助于今后与第三世界国家关系的发展。(戴炳然译)

例 6-126 While such reforms are likely to introduce more federal elements into the institutional structure responsible for the Union's defence operations, they should not be confused with the creation of a federal state.

㊣ 虽然这种改革很可能会在负责欧盟防务行动的体制结构中引入更多的联邦因素，它们不应与创建一个联邦国家混为一谈。（戴炳然译）

例 6-127 Sexuality was packaged as a profitable commodity in the marketplace, <u>while</u> culture meant for the most part profit-hungry mass media.

㊣ 性被包装成了市场上贩卖的牟利商品，文化则成为逐利的大众媒体的主角。（朱新伟译）

（四）by / in contrast, on the contrary

by / in contrast 意思是"相比之下，与之相对照的是，相反"，on the contrary 意思是"恰恰相反，正相反，相反地"。in/by contrast 强调比较，凸显不同；而 on the contrary 强调完全相反；in/by contrast 在前后相反或截然不同的事实论述对比时使用，而 on the contrary 在第二句反驳或否定第一句观点时使用。in contrast to 意思是"与……（截然）不同，与……或鲜明对比，相比之下，与…相反"。

例 6-128 The very first recognizably human members of our species lived about 500,000 years ago. <u>By contrast</u>, the very last dinosaurs trod our planet approximately 65 million years ago and probably perished, along with many other creatures, in a cataclysm following a giant meteorite impact with Earth at that time.

㊣ 可鉴定出的最早的与我们同种的人类成员生活在大约 50 万年前。相反，最后在地球上漫步的恐龙存在于大约 6500 万年前，之后它们很可能在一场因一颗巨大的陨星撞击地球而引发的灾变中与许多其他动物一起灭绝了。（史立群译）

例 6-129 <u>By contrast</u>, twentieth-century theories have tended to see myth as almost anything but an outdated counterpart to science, either in subject matter or in function. <u>Consequently</u>, moderns are not obliged to abandon myth for science.

㊣ 相反，20 世纪的理论则倾向于认为，不论就其主题还是功能而言，神话绝不是科学的过时对应物。因此，现代人无需为科学而丢弃神话。（刘象愚译）

例 6-130 Fibroblasts grown in culture are long and flattened, and move around the surface of the culture dish with a broad leading edge and a narrow trailing edge. In contrast, cells from epithelia stay flattened and many-sided in culture.

译 培养中生长的成纤维细胞长而扁平，在培养皿表面移动，前缘宽，后缘窄。相反，上皮细胞在培养过程中保持扁平和多面。

例 6-131 In contrast to mammals, where the body plan is final at birth, the formation of new root branches ensures that the root system keeps growing throughout a plant's life.

译 与哺乳动物不同的是，在哺乳动物出生时，身体蓝图是最终的形式（后面是不会改变的），而新的根分支的形成确保了根系在植物的整个生命周期中保持生长。

例 6-132 On the contrary, its diversity was the quality which Romantic artists and writers prized most highly as the expression of their individuality, and which has defeated every attempt to define it.

译 相反，它的多样化正是浪漫主义艺术家和作家最最珍视的品质，认为这是他们的个别性的表现，是无法一言以蔽之的。（董乐山译）

例 6-133 This does not mean that Wittgenstein dismissed such talk as nonsense, as the logical positivists did. On the contrary, he thought it far more important than talk about factual states of affairs.

译 这不是说维特根斯坦把这些讨论当做无意义的话丢在一边，那是逻辑实证主义者的做法。相反，他认为，这些讨论要比讨论实际的事态更加重要。（朱新伟译）

例 6-134 On freezing the general tendency of matter is to contract. On the contrary, water anomalously expands on freezing especially below 4℃, and the ice thus formed floats in water.

译 在受冷时，物体总的趋势是体积变小。水恰恰相反，尤其是水温降至4℃时体积膨胀，因此冰漂浮在水面上。（李铁刚和孙艳华译）

（五）on the other hand

on the other hand 表示"另一方面"，叙述某一事物或事件另一面，或者增加入一个不同的事实或观点，或者换一个不同角度或切入点论述某一事物或事件。on the other hand 可单独使用，也可与 on the one hand 连用，与 while 和 whereas 类似，用来比较两个形成对比但并不相互矛盾的事实或看法。与此不同，by contrast, in contrast（对照之下，形成对比的是）用来对比截然不同、相互对立或差异的事物，对比的两个事物不见得互有优劣。on the contrary(恰恰相反、相反地)表示与前述看法或观点相反，更强调后者的正确性或真实性，而之前的说法是错误的或不真实的。

例 6-135 Since bones show up clearly as white objects against a darker background, Roentgen's rays proved particularly suited for examining fractures and breaks, but they could also spot cancer tumors, respiratory diseases such as tuberculosis or black lung, and a variety of other tissue abnormalities. <u>On the other hand</u>, X-rays do not distinguish well between tissues of similar densities. As a result, some body features are unclear.

译 由于当白色的物体对着深色的背景时骨骼显现得很清楚，伦琴射线被证明尤其适合于检查骨折和骨裂，但是它们也可以发现癌症、肿瘤、肺结核或黑肺等呼吸道病症以及一系列其他组织异常。另一方面在密度相似的组织之间 X 射线不能很好地区分。结果，一些体内特征并不明确。(李铁刚和孙艳华译)

例 6-136 Perfluorochemicals are made into fine emulsions for use as oxygen carriers. Their biggest advantage is that they are synthetic materials and so can be produced in large amounts; also, their purity can be more easily controlled. <u>On the other hand</u>, perfluorochemicals have a much lower capacity for carrying oxygen than does hemoglobin, so the patient must breathe an oxygen-rich air mixture.

译 全氟化合物能制成很好的乳剂作为氧载体。它们最大的优点是属于合成材料，因此可大规模生产，而且它们的纯度也很容易控制。但另一方面，全氟化合物与血红蛋白比起来运载氧的能力低得多，因此患者必须呼吸富氧空气。(李铁刚和孙艳华译)

例 6-137 On the one hand, if the body doesn't have enough cholesterol, we would not be able to survive. <u>On the other hand</u>, if the body has too much cholesterol, the excess begins to harden the arteries.

译 一方面，如果身体没有足够的胆固醇，人就不能生存。另一方面，如果身体有太多的胆固醇，多余的胆固醇又会使血管硬化。

(六)despite, in spite of

despite 和 in spite of 意思是"虽然；尽管"。两者后面都是接名词或动名词结构。但 despite 比 in spite of 正式、严谨，为书面用词，但语气轻于 in spite of. 如果要使用 despite / in spite of the fact that 从句结构，最好换作 although。

例 6-138　<u>Despite</u> the introduction of the euro, the EU does not yet show signs of playing a similar part in the international monetary system.

🔹 虽已采用欧元，但欧盟在国际货币体系中尚无扮演重要角色的迹象。（戴炳然译）

例 6-139　<u>Despite</u> the rapid rate, replication is extremely accurate, with enzymes that proofread and correct any mismatched nucleotide, usually leaving only one error in every billion nucleotides.

🔹 尽管复制的速度很快，但复制是非常准确的，因为有酶可以校对和纠正任何配对错误的核苷酸，通常每十亿个核苷酸只有一个错误。

例 6-140　We are sure we are awake and believe our senses — and the associated emotions — <u>despite</u> the incongruities and discontinuities of dream bizarreness, which, were they to occur in waking, would immediately tip us off.

🔹 我们坚信自己是清醒的，笃信自己的感觉以及与之相关的情感，罔顾梦的稀奇古怪及不协调性和不连续性，而这一切倘若出现在清醒状态时，马上就会被识破。（韩芳译）

例 6-141　<u>Despite</u> these conflicts between the intergovernmental and the federal conceptions, the customs union was completed by July 1968, earlier than the treaty required.

🔹 尽管政府间主义与联邦主义之间存在这些分歧，关税同盟还是于1968年7月在条约规定的日期之前建立。（戴炳然译）

例 6-142　<u>Despite</u> the discovery of a relatively large number of crania from Java, China, and elsewhere in the last century, relatively little was known about the limbs of *H. erectus*.

🔹 尽管上世纪在爪哇、中国以及世界其他地区发现了相当数量的头骨化石，但是我们对于直立人的四肢进化还是了解甚少。（冯兴无译）

例 6-143　<u>In spite of</u> their shared interests, their relationship was by no means easy.

🔹 虽然二人志趣相投，但是她们的关系却根本谈不上融洽。（朱刚和麻晓蓉译）

例 6-144　<u>In spite of</u> changes in the teeth and base of the skull in *Ar. ramidus* that link it with archaic hominins, in overall appearance *Ar. ramidus* would have been more like a chimpanzee than like a modern human.

译 尽管牙齿和头盖骨的底部有些变化，类似早期猿人，但地猿始祖种的整个外形更像黑猩猩，而不像现代人类。（冯兴无译）

（七）yet

yet 用作连词时，意思是"但是，然而，可是，不过"。yet 与 but、however 意思相似，都表示转折关系，但 yet 位置不如后两者灵活，通常位于句首，后面不加逗号。此外，yet 还传达一种"意外"之义。

例 6-145 Like microwave ovens, food irradiation has aroused apprehension and misunderstanding. <u>Yet</u> it has been scrutinized more thoroughly than other methods of food treatment that we have come to regard as safe, and it appears to be a method whose time has come.

译 像微波炉一样，食品放射处理也引起了忧虑和误解，但是，人们已经对它进行了比其他被认为安全的食品处理方法更加细致的研究，并且这一处理方法似乎成了一种时尚的方法。（马锦儒等译）

例 6-146 In general, they depict people as basically rational, other-regarding, sincere, and capable of overcoming impulses which are contrary to these traits. <u>Yet</u> one of the most popular moral theories does not accept this picture of human psychology.

译 一般来说，它们认为人在根本上是理性的、关心他人的、真诚的、能够克服与这些特点相悖的种种冲动。然而，最流行的道理理论之一并不接受对人们心理的这种描绘。（严忠志译）

例 6-147 Much of the literature of resistance grows out of the State's potential for evil. <u>Yet</u> the State also has a potential for good.

译 许多关于抵制国家的文献的出发点是国家所具有的作恶潜能。但是，国家也有行善的潜能。（严忠志译）

例 6-148 <u>Yet</u> the idea that the meaning of life consists in pondering the meaning of life seems curiously tail-chasing. It also assumes that the meaning of life is some kind of proposition, such as 'The ego is an illusion' or 'Everything is made out of semolina'.

译 可是，认为人生的意义在于思考人生的意义，这听上去有点同义反复。这种观点预设了人生的意义是某种命题，比如"自我是一种幻觉"或"万物皆由粗面粉构成"。（朱新伟译）

(八) conversely

conversely 一般位于句首,表示从相反的角度思考问题,提出另一种意见或想法,意思是"相反地,反过来"。

例 6-149 If the total number of organisms on the planet is equated with success, then bacteria come out on top. Conversely, in terms of biological complexity, they are also the most simple and consequently 'primitive' organisms on the planet.

❀ 如果地球上的生物总数最多就等于成功,那么细菌就会排在首位。相反,在生物复杂性方面,它们也是地球上最简单的生物,因而也是最原始的生物。

例 6-150 The hypothesis of REM sleep correspondence across species was greatly strengthened by the subsequent finding that all but the most primitive mammals had periodic brain activation during sleep. If they had eyes, they also had REMs in their activated sleep phases. Besides shoring up the homology hypothesis, this surprising fact suggested that REM was biologically important to all mammalian life, whatever its relationship to human dreaming. Conversely, it suggested that the correlation of REM and dreaming was a very limiting way of thinking about the functional significance of brain activation in sleep.

❀ 快动眼睡眠的特种一致性假说得到后续研究发现的强有力支持,所有最原始的哺乳动物在睡眠期间都有周期性的大脑激活。如果他们有眼睛的话,在激活的睡眠时相也会有快速眼动。除了能支持同源性假说之外,这一惊人发现还表明快动眼睡眠对所有哺乳动物都具有生物学重要性。另一方面,有证据表明在考虑睡眠期间大脑激活功能的重要性时,研究快动眼睡眠和梦境的关系意义不大。(韩芳译)

(九) rather, rather than

rather 或 but rather 与前面的否定句一起,用于纠正前面的论述或提供更确切论述,意思是"而是,更确切地讲,更准确地说"。rather than 作并列连词使用时(不与情态动词 would, should, will 等连用时),相等于 and not,意义为"而不是"。后面连接的并列成分可以是名词、动名词、代词、动词、不定式、形容词、介词(短语)、分句等。

例 6-151 For all pre-modern analysts of dream content, the dream as it is experienced by the dreamer is not what it appears to be; rather, it is the distorted read-out of a sick body (Greek *Onirodiagnosis*), or an encoded message about the future from the gods (whether pagan as with Artemidorus or Judaeo-Christian as in the *Bible*).

[译] 对所有前现代梦境内容分析家来讲，梦者所经历的梦境并非它表面看起来的那样，而是有机体生病后一种异常的信息输出(古希腊的析梦诊断)，或是上帝关于未来的神谕(阿尔米多鲁斯所谓的异教徒或《圣经》中的犹太—基督)。(韩芳译)

例 6-152 The Earth's mantle is not composed of a single mineral, with a sharp melting/freezing point. Rather, it is a mixture of a large number of different substances, each with a different melting temperature.

[译] 地球的地幔并不是由具有明显熔点或冰点的单一矿物组成。相反它是一个很多不同物质的混合物，每种物质都具有不同的熔点。(李铁刚和孙艳华译)

例 6-153 Now, this would seem to be more or less right insofar as Continental philosophy is habitually presented by people like me as a roughly chronological sequence of proper names beginning with Kant, rather than the problem—orientated approach that one tends to associate with the tradition of analytic philosophy.

[译] 现在看来，这可能或多或少是对的，因为欧陆哲学通常表现为是由我这样的人提出的开始于康德的大致依编年顺序的一系列专名，而不是人们通常与分析哲学传统相联系在一起的以问题为主导的方法。(江怡译)

例 6-154 Two organelles in the cytoplasm — mitochondria and, in plants, chloroplasts — have double, rather than single membranes.

[译] 细胞质中的两个细胞器——线粒体和植物中的叶绿体——具有双层膜，而不是单层膜。

(十)instead, instead of

instead 可在句首、句尾或句中，意思是“反而，相反地”。instead of 作为短语介词，后面可跟名词、代词、动名词、形容词、副词、动词、不定式、介词短语和从句等多种成分，意思是“代替……，而不是……”。

例 6-155 Neurophysiologists were every bit as slow as psychologists to move dream science forwards. They knew about reflexes but they didn't know about spontaneous activation. Instead they assumed that the brain was as dependent on stimulation for all of its activated states as was the mind in sleep.

[译] 和心理学家一样，神经生理学家推动梦科学向前发展的速度也很缓慢。他们知道反射但不懂得自发的激活，与此相反，他们认为大脑和睡眠中的思想一样，其所有的激活状态都依赖于外界刺激。(韩芳译)

例 6-156 They encourage doctors to prescribe cheaper generic drugs instead of more expensive brand names.

[译] 他们鼓励医生给患者开便宜的普通药(或仿制药、非专利药)，而不是价格昂贵的品牌药。

例 6-157 They raised prices and cut production, instead of cutting costs

[译] 他们不是降低成本，而是抬高价格并削减产量。

(十一) **nevertheless**

nevertheless 对前面所提到的信息的让步，可以出现在句首、句中或者句末，位于句首时后面跟逗号，意思是“尽管如此，不过，仍然，然而”。该词用于正式文体，和 however 类似，强调后者与前者形成对比。

例 6-158 Freud claimed to be a scientist, and was certainly not a philosopher in the technical sense, not particular interested in the subject, although, as a young man, he had translated a book by John Stuart Mill. Nevertheless, he resembled some philosophers in being a system-builder.

[译] 弗洛伊德声称自己是一名科学家，在专业意义上他显然不是一名哲学家，他对哲学没有特别的兴趣，尽管在年轻的时候他曾翻译过约翰·斯图亚特·密尔的一部著作。不过，在创建思想体系方面，他与一些哲学家们有类似之处。(尹莉译)

例 6-159 When we are dreaming, even without the help of the chemical unification conferred by noradrenaline and serotonin, and even without the focus and control of thought and action conferred by the part of the brain called the dorsolateral prefrontal cortex, our experience is nevertheless convincingly integral and convincingly real.

[译] 即便没有去甲肾上腺素和 5-羟色胺帮助进行化学整合，甚至没有前额叶背外侧皮质对思维和动作实施控制和集中，我们在做梦时的体验仍然是完整、真实且有说服力的。(韩芳译)

例 6-160 While his parents have yearned for a child and decide to sacrifice him only to save the father, they nevertheless do decide to sacrifice him.

[译] 尽管他的双亲渴望有一个孩子，只是因为要保全父亲才决定牺牲他的性命，但是不管怎么说，他们确实是决心要把他当作牺牲品的。(刘象愚译)

（十二）otherwise

otherwise 用作连词的意思是“否则，要不然”，相当于 or，or else 或 if not….

例 6-161 The theory was that life in the workhouse had to be worse than life outside the workhouse, otherwise it would be overrun with the poor.

[译] 理论上，济贫院的生活必须比济贫院外的生活更糟，否则济贫院就会满是穷人。

例 6-162 It is also important to make sure that the name of an existing taxon is not inadvertently used for a new taxon, otherwise they will be confused.

[译] 同样重要的是，现有的分类名称不能随意用于新分类，避免产生混淆。(冯兴无译)

（十三）even if，even though

even if 引导的从句是往往是非事实的、推测性的或假设性的，还可用虚拟语气，意思是“即使、纵然就算、哪怕”。与之相近的 even though 引导的从句则往往是真实的，主要用于引出不利用于主句情况，意思是“尽管，虽然”。

例 6-163 Even if you are able to accomplish it, there would not be sufficient time.

[译] 即使你能够完成它，也没有足够的时间。

例 6-164 Following certain rules has been shown to promote the most long-term overall happiness, even if not in particular circumstances.

[译] 即使不是在特殊情况下，遵循某些规则也表明能促进最长期的整体幸福感。

例 6-165 The single market legislation provides a framework for economic strength and prosperity, even if it remains incomplete in a few sectors and will need further development to cater for the new economy of e-commerce and information technology; and the single currency completes the single market in the monetary domain, though without, so far, the participation of all member states.

[译] 尽管单一市场立法在一些领域并不完善，而且还需要进一步的发展以适应电子商务与信息技术带来的新经济，但它为经济发展与繁荣提供了一种

架构。单一货币则在货币领域中完善了单一市场，尽管目前它并不应用于所有成员国。(戴炳然译)

例 6-166　Even though decades of these experiments on primates have failed to produce effective vaccines for humans, monkeys are still infected with HIV-like diseases that cause them to suffer acute weight loss, major organ failure, breathing problems, and neurological disorders before they die excruciatingly painful deaths or are killed.

🔑 译　尽管几十年来对灵长类动物的实验未能为人类生产出有效的疫苗，但猴子仍然感染了类似艾滋病的疾病，这些疾病导致它们在极度疼痛中死亡或被杀前遭受严重的体重减轻、主要器官衰竭、呼吸问题和神经紊乱。

(十四) save/except/but that

save/except/but that 意思是"只不过，只是，不同的是，除了，除……之外"。它们为复合从属连词，不是"介词 + that"结构，用来引导排除状语从句，以排除主句中所述情况。

例 6-167　The council for its part would be akin to a house of the states, save that the unanimity procedure still applies to one-fifth of the legislation, its legislative sessions are not held in public, and it has retained executive powers that ill accord with its legislative role.

🔑 译　理事会则有些像一个参议院，只不过五分之一的立法需要全体一致议决，其立法会议不对公众开放，而且它还保留了与其立法功能不相称的执行功能。(戴炳然译)

例 6-168　The system is similar to that to the United States, save that the Joint Economic Policy Committee of the Congress has over the years become a powerful body disposing of a big budget to provide it with the necessary economic analysis and advice.

🔑 译　此制度与美国的类似，不同的是多年来美国国会的联合经济政策小组委员会已成为一个强有力的机构，拥有巨额预算来为国会作出必要的经济分析和提供建议。(戴炳然译)

例 6-169　Active transport is similar to facilitated diffusion except that it can transport a substance even when the concentration of the substance is higher on the side of the membrane toward which it is being transported, which is called 'uphill transport'.

> 主动运输与协助扩散类似，而唯一不同之处是，它可以朝着浓度比较高的一侧进行该物质的运输，称为"上坡运输"。（李少如译）

（十五）apart from

一般词典认为，apart from 既可在包含（including）关系中使用，意思是"除此之外，还有……"，相当于 besides, in addition of；又可在排除（excluding）关系中使用，表示"除了……之外，除此之外，不考虑……"，相当于 except (for), not considering. 但据英语专家 David W. Ferguson 的观点，apart from 在包含（including）关系中使用是错误的，尤其是在正式书面语中；如果要表达包含（including）关系，最好使用 in addition to 和 together with 代替。

例 6-170 <u>Apart from</u> Germany which, as a rich country gaining much from the Community, willingly accepted for many years its role as the largest net contributor, the other states were until the 1990s all net recipients.

> 作为共同体获益甚多的富有国家，德国多年来心甘情愿地接受了作为最大净贡献国的角色。除此之外的其他国家直到 20 世纪 90 年代都是净收益国。（戴炳然译）

例 6-171 The British government has indicated it intends to participate fully in the *Schengen aguis*, <u>apart from</u> the aspects relating to border controls, for which it awaits evidence that the external border controls and internal co-operation are sufficiently effective.

> 英国政府已表态，它有意加入除边境控制方面之外的整个《申根协定》，但将视外部边境控制的情况和内部合作是否充分有效来决定。（戴炳然译）

例 6-172 Parliaments do not usually play much part in relation to trade negotiations, <u>apart from</u> formally approving the results.

> 除了正式批准达成的结果，议会通常不大过问贸易谈判。（戴炳然译）

例 6-173 Both the nuclear membrane and the lamina below it are pierced by nuclear pore complexes, which control the flow of everything into and out of the nucleus, <u>apart from</u> very small molecules which can pass directly through the nuclear envelope.

> 核膜及其下面的薄层都被核孔复合物穿透，除能直接穿过核膜的非常小的分子不受控制以外，核孔复合物控制着所有物质进出细胞核。

(十六) far from

far from 意思是"根本不,远远不"。

例 6-174 The Germans, far from opposing this, saw it as part of the design for a Europe united on federal lines.

译 德国不仅没有反对,还将此看作是按联邦方向构造统一欧洲的组成部分。(戴炳然译)

例 6-175 From relatively recent research, it has become apparent that far from being a mere repository for DNA, the nucleus is just as varied and dynamic as the cytoplasm in terms of content and activity.

译 从最近的研究来看,细胞核很明显不是单纯地储存 DNA,而是在内容和活性方面与细胞质一样变动不居。

七、时间关系

表示时间关系经常用到的过渡词有：now, later, since then, after that, at present, at this point, earlier, finally, former, immediately, while, as, meanwhile, simultaneously, soon, in the meanwhile, prior to, recently, so far, then, until now 等。

(一) when, while, as, meanwhile

当作连词引导时间状语从句时,when 意思是"在……时候,当……时,在……期间",while 的意思是"在……(过程)中,在……期间",as 的意思是"当……时"。这三个词引导的从句和主句的动作都发生在同一时间段内,但 when 引导的从句行为状态持续时间可以是瞬时的,也可以短于或等于主句的行为状态的持续时间；while 引导从句往往为进行时态,行为状态持续时间较长,长于或等于主句的行为状态的持续时间；而 as 引导的从句中的动作与主句中的动作同时发生,通常持续一段时间。meanwhile 意思是"同时,与此同时"。但要注意 meanwhile 是两个不同的主体在同一时间内做某事,或两件不同的事件同时发生,如果表示同一个主体在同一时间内做两件不同的事情,要使用 at the same time.

例 6-176 When those who manage a dominant currency have to choose between dealing with a domestic problem and taking account of the impact on other economies that are influenced by their choice, they naturally choose their domestic interests.

[译] 当掌握着优势货币的人们，面临着应付本国问题或是考虑其选择对他国经济影响抉择时，他们自然而然地选择本国的利益。(戴炳然译)

例 6-177 When DNA replication is required, it takes place in around 100 'replication factories' distributed throughout the nucleus.

[译] 当 DNA 需要复制时，它就在分布于整个细胞核的大约 100 个"复制工厂"中进行。

例 6-178 In the first half of the twentieth century, while sleep and dream science were being prepared at the more global level of the electroencephalograph (EEG), neurobiologists were learning more about neurons than had even been imagined in anyone's speculative philosophy — and that anyone includes Sigmund Freud, Charles Sherrington, and Ivan Pavlov.

[译] 在 20 世纪前半叶，当睡眠与梦的科学还只停留在宽泛的脑电图层面上时，神经生物学家们正在对神经元进行深入了解，而且已经超出了任何思辨哲学者所能想象的范围——这里说的任何人也包括弗洛伊德、谢灵顿、巴甫洛夫这样的大家。(韩芳译)

例 6-179 As radio waves travel along the surface of the earth, part of its energy will be lost.

[译] 当无线电波沿地球表面传播时，要损耗掉一部分能量(秦荻辉译)。

例 6-180 Meanwhile, the more religion loomed up as an alternative to the steady haemorrhaging of public meaning, the more it was driven into various ugly forms of fundamentalism.

[译] 同时，宗教越是充当公共意义不断流失后的替代选择，它就越是被灌输为各种糟糕的宗教激进主义。(朱新伟译)

例 6-181 Meanwhile, even as the dream debate grew fractious and became sterile, the sleep lab was unearthing a treasure trove of physiological findings of great interest to dream science, as well as to behavioural biology generally. The Aserinsky-Kleitman discovery was made in 1953, the same year that Watson and Crick published their epochal double-helix model for DNA. There are two important implications of this coincidence. One is that biology came of molecular age at the same moment that dream science came of physiological age. In the subsequent half-century, biology has changed beyond recognition — in fact, it is now in danger of becoming nothing but the molecular biology of the gene.

正当梦的辩论进入白热化阶段，变得缺乏新意时，睡眠实验室揭开了一系列宝贵的生理学发现，对梦科学和行为生物都意义重大。阿瑟林斯基-克莱特曼的发现是在1953年，同年沃森和克里克发表了划时代意义的DNA双螺旋模型。这一巧合有两个重要的意义，即生物学进入了分子时代，而梦科学同时进入了生理学时代。在接下来的半个世纪里，生物学已经变得让我们无法辨识，事实上，现在的生物学面临着完成变成基因分子生物学的危险。（韩芳译）

（二）before, after, until, since

before 的意思是"之前，以前"，主句的动作发生在从句动作之前。after 意思是"之后，后"，主句的动作发生在从句动作之后。until 或 till 的意思是"直到…为止"，主句的动作持续到从句动作发生时为止，常与表示延续性动作的动词连用。其否定句形式(not…until…)常与表示瞬间性动作的动词连用，表示"到…为止，直到…才"。since 的意思是"以前"，表示主句动作从从句动作发生的某个时间算起。

例 6-182 Before the newly transcribed RNA passes out of the nucleus, the leading end is capped, and a tail is fixed to the trailing end.

译 在新转录的 RNA 输出细胞核之前，前端加帽，后端加尾。

例 6-183 They engulf cellular debris and pathogens and swallow them whole before breaking their components down for further use.

译 它们吞噬细胞碎片和病原体，并将其囫囵吞下，之后分解其成分以供进一步使用。

例 6-184 After the study has been completed, the researchers should inform the participants of its purpose and the methods they used.

译 研究完成后，研究人员应告知参与者研究目的和使用的方法。

例 6-185 Publication may occur at any time during the course of the clinical trial life cycle, although it most often occurs after study completion.

译 尽管最常在研究完成后发表，但可在临床试验生命周期过程中的任何时间发表。

例 6-186 The brighter the student, the more he is asked to read, until he develops prodigious skill in reading quickly and cleverly, for purpose of taking examinations and talking in discussions.

㊋ 学生愈聪明，被要求读的东西愈多，直到他有了读得又快又精明的惊人技巧，以便应试及在讨论中发言。

例 6-187 Until recent times, pestilence almost invariably proved far more fatal than enemy action.

㊋ 直至晚近，瘟疫之能致人命几乎总是远胜敌人的行动。（颜元叔译）

例 6-188 Science is not finished until it's communicated.

㊋ 科学只有在交流之后才算完成。

例 6-189 Now, nearly a dozen years since the wolves returned, the recovery of that system to its natural balance is well underway, say ecologists William Ripple and Robert Beschta of Oregon State University.

㊋ 俄勒冈州立大学的生态学家威廉·里普特和罗伯特·贝斯赫塔说，自从狼回来将近十多年后，这个系统目前正在向到自然平衡的恢复过程中。

例 6-190 The names of the disciplines of science have changed since Thomas Edison's time.

㊋ 自从托马斯·爱迪生时代以来，科学学科的名称已经改变。

例 6-191 The first iPhone appeared in 2007, and since then it has steadily become more sophisticated.

㊋ 第一部 iPhone 出现在 2007 年，从那时起，它逐渐变得更加复杂

八、顺序关系

表示先后顺序关系经常用到的过渡词有：first, second, third, then, next, last, finally, first of all, to begin with, above all, eventually 等。

例 6-192 Bioethics is important for many reasons. First, it provides medical workers with an increased awareness of medical practices that allow for the best results. Second, bioethics allows medical personnel learn how to best treat the personal and medical needs of each specific patient.

㊋ 生物伦理学是很重要的，这有很多原因。首先，它使医务工作者对医疗实践的认识提高，从而获得最佳效果。其次，生物伦理学允许医务人员学习如何最好地满足每个特定患者的个人和医疗需求。

例 6-193 In the 1950s and 1960s, a series of observations accumulated that supported Wegener's views. Firstly, very detailed models of all the major continents showed that they did indeed fit together remarkably neatly and with a correspondence that could not be accounted for by chance. Secondly, major geological features on separate continents became continuous when continents were reassembled jigsaw-like. And finally, palaeomagnetic evidence demonstrated the phenomenon of sea-floor spreading — that the ocean floors were moving like huge conveyor belts carrying the continents — and the historical remnants of magnetism in continental rocks confirmed that the continents had moved over time.

译 在20世纪50年代和60年代，一系列的观察资料积累起来，支持了魏格纳的观点。首先，所有主要大陆的详细模型显示，它们的确可以非常完美地组合在一起，其一致性无法以偶然来进行解释。第二，当各个大陆像拼板玩具一样重新组合在一起时，不同大陆的主要地质特征是连续的。最后，古地磁极的证据证明了海底扩张现象——即大洋底像巨大的传送带一样承载着各个大陆移动，大陆岩石地磁的历史遗迹亦证实，各个大陆确实在时间的长河中发生了移动。（史立群译）

例 6-194　First a long glass tube is taken. The tube is closed at the top and is then completely filled with water. Next it is placed vertically in a large barrel half-full of water.

译 首先取一支长玻璃管。封闭管子顶部，然后完全注满水。接着将其垂直放置在半桶水的大桶中。

九、目的关系

表示目的关系经常用到的过渡词有：so that, in order that, for this purpose 等。

（一）so that, in order that

so that 和 in order that 意思为"为了，以便，目的在于"。但 so that 更为常用，而 in order that 更为正式。

例 6-195　The patient had to ask the doctor to increase the dosage of her pain-killer so that she could get some sleep.

译 病人必须要求医生增加止痛药的剂量，以便她能入睡。

例 6-196　The native people have asked the museum to return to them the bones of their ancestors so that they may be returned to their original burial place.

译 当地人要求博物馆把他们祖先的骨头还给他们，以便可以放回到原来的埋葬地。

例 6-197　As mentioned earlier, the internal volume of eukaryote cells is a thousand times that of a bacterium, so that the eukaryotic cell requires a vast internal membrane system around a hundred times the area of the plasma membrane itself.

🔁 如前所述，真核细胞的内部体积是细菌的 1000 倍，因此真核细胞需要一个巨大的内膜系统，这大约是质膜本身面积的 100 倍。

例 6-198　In order that the family may prosper, the individual members are often sacrificed to it.

🔁 为了使家族繁荣，个体成员常常被牺牲。

例 6-199　They worked hard in order that they might succeed.

🔁 他们努力工作，以便能够获得成功。

（二）for this purpose

for this purpose 意思是"为此，因此"。

例 6-200　For this purpose, an effective drug supply and management system is essential.

🔁 为此，保证有效的药物供应和管理制度至关重要。

例 6-201　For this purpose the study of globular clusters is most instructive.

🔁 因此，研究球状星团最富有启发意义。

十、结果关系

表示结果关系经常用到的过渡词有：therefore, thereby, thus, hence, consequently, accordingly, so, as a result, as a consequence, then, it follows that, indeed 等。

（一）therefore, thereby, thus, hence

therefore, thereby, thus 和 hence 这些词都有"因此"的意思，但 therefore 强调"因此原因（for this reason, because of this or that）"，引导一种逻辑推理的结果。thereby 强调"因此行动（by that means, as a result of that）"，引导一种动作或行动的实际结果。thus 强调"因此方式（in this/that way）"，与发生的方式有关。hence 强调"因此位置或时间点（from this/that）"。

另外，需要注意的是，therefore 是引导结果或结论的副词，不能误作连词用，意思是"因此，为此，所以"。也就是说，therefore 可引出独立句，却不能用来连接两个句子，如果要在并列分句间使用 therefore，须在 therefore 前使用连词 and 或分号。此外，如果要在并列分句间使用 hence，须在 hence 前使用连词 and；hence 还可引导省略后的句子成分。

例 6-202　The word 'isomorphism' means similarity of form or shape, and brain-mind isomorphism that every form of mental activity has a similar form of brain activity. Therefore, if we detect a dream form, we can seek a corresponding brain form.

❂译　"相形论"这个词意为形式或形状的相似，大脑－精神相形意味着精神活动的每种形式都有类似形式的大脑活动。因此，如果我们监测到一个梦境，就能够找到一种对应的大脑活动。（韩芳译）

例 6-203　A special feature of the lipid bilayer is that it is fluid and not a solid. Therefore, portions of the membrane can literally flow from one point to another in the membrane.

❂译　脂质双层的一个特点是，它是液体而不是固体。因此，膜的一些部分可由一点流动至膜的另一点。（李少如译）

例 6-204　So, all logical propositions are reducible to either tautologies or contradictions, which are either necessarily true or necessarily false, but all such propositions are verifiable and therefore meaningful.

❂译　所以，所有的逻辑命题都可以还原为重言式或矛盾式，它们或者必然为真，或者必然为假，但所有这些命题都是可以得到证实的，因而都是有意义的。（江怡译）

例 6-205　When antioxidants stop free radicals in their tracks, they also prevent DNA damage, thereby decreasing mutations and reducing the risk of skin cancer, Katta explained.

❂译　卡塔解释道，当抗氧化剂在阻止自由基活动时，还能防止 DNA 受损，从而降低基因突变及患皮肤癌的风险。

例 6-206　I choose this myth, first, because it is extant in such varying versions, thereby showing the malleability of myth.

❂译　我之所以选择这则神话，首先是因为它拥有相互之间差别甚大的各种版本，由此体现了神话的可塑性。（刘象愚译）

例 6-207　Under these circumstances, myth provides the ideal kind of fulfillment. True, the outer layers of the myth hide its true meaning and thereby block fulfillment, but they simultaneously reveal that true meaning and thereby provide fulfillment.

> 译 在这种情况下，神话提供了实现这一情结的最理想形式。诚然，神话外在的那些层面掩盖了它的真实意义，因而妨碍了这一情结的实现，但它们又同时透露了这一真实意义，因而提供了实现这一情结的可能。(刘象愚译)

例 6-208　When a neuron was sufficiently excited, its membrane potential could suddenly reverse its sign and the resultant differential in voltage, or action potential, could spread from the cell body over the entire surface of the neuron, including its endings, which were thereby induced to secrete their own brand of chemical neurotransmitter.

> 译 当神经元兴奋到一定程度时，其膜电位会骤然逆转极性，生成的电位差又称为动作电位，可从胞体扩散至神经元的整个表面，包括末梢，进而诱导其分泌其特有的化学神经递质。(韩芳译)

例 6-209　Some environments are more likely to lead to fossilization and subsequent discovery than others. Thus, we cannot assume that more fossil evidence from a particular period or place means that more individuals were present at that time, or in that place.

> 译 某些环境更利于形成化石，也更容易发现化石。因此我们不能说，某一特定时期或特定地方的化石多就意味着出现在那个时候或那个地方的人类个体就多(冯兴无译)

例 6-210　The other is to obtain comparable reports from two states of waking by beeping the same participants with a home pager during the daytime. Thus, the same participants who give us dream reports also give us reports of their waking consciousness.

> 译 另一个则是可以在白天给受试者配备家庭传呼器，动态监测他们在两种醒觉状态下的信息。这样的话，同一个受试者既然可给我们梦的报告，又可给我们意识清醒时的报告。(韩芳译)

例 6-211　The Roman philosopher Lucretius, writing in the 1th century BCE, proposed that the earliest humans were unlike contemporary Romans. He suggested that human ancestors were animal-like cave dwellers, with neither tools nor language. Both classical Greek and Roman thinkers viewed tool and fire making and the use of verbal language as crucial components of humanity. Thus, the notion that modern humans had evolved from an earlier, primitive form was established early on in Western thought.

🔵 译 公元前 1 世纪，罗马哲学家卢克莱修在他的著述中指出，最早的人类与现代的罗马人不同，他们像动物一样过着穴居的生活，既不会制造工具也不会使用语言。古希腊和古罗马的思想家都把制造工具、用火和使用语言看作人类的重要特征，因此，西方人的思想里很早就萌生了现代人起源于早期某种原始形态生物的观念。（冯兴无译）

例 6-212 These results show that a very tight regulation of cell size impacts the position of cell divisions, and <u>thus</u> the location and growth of new root branches.

🔵 译 这些结果表明，细胞大小的严格调控影响细胞分裂的位置，从而影响新根分支的位置和生长。

例 6-213 This is possible in spite of the fact that we only have 23,600 genes because the genetic message can be modified inside the nucleus after transcription, and outside the nucleus, <u>thus</u> increasing the overall number of possible protein products.

🔵 译 尽管我们只有 23,600 个基因，但这是可能的，因为转录后的遗传信息可以在细胞核内和细胞核外进行修饰，从而增加了可能的蛋白质产物的总数。

例 6-214 The nuclear lamina was originally visualized in the electron microscope as a fibrous matrix on the inside of the inner nuclear membrane. These protein filaments resist stretching and form the 'high-tensile cables', closely related to the intermediate filaments of the cytoskeleton. <u>Thus</u>, the nuclear lamina protects the nuclear contents from mechanical stress, and also anchors the position of the nucleus in the cell, providing sites for attachment to the cytoskeleton in the cytoplasm.

🔵 译 核纤层最初在电子显微镜下被视为核内膜内部的纤维基质。这些蛋白丝抗拉伸，形成"高强度缆绳"，与细胞骨架的中间丝密切相关。因此，核纤层不仅保护核内容物不受机械应力的影响，也把细胞核固定在细胞中的某个位置，为细胞质中的细胞骨架提供附着部位。

例 6-215 This means that our brains never turn off completely, and <u>hence</u> they are always capable of some level of mental activity, even if waking and dream consciousness both depend on a robust level of brain activation.

> **译** 这意味着我们的大脑从来不会彻底关闭，因而大脑总能维持一定水平的精神活动，即使清醒或睡梦时的意识都有赖于一定活跃程度的大脑激活。（韩芳译）

例 6-216 Economics and politics were also both involved in the substance and outcomes of the projects, because the integration of modern economies requires a framework of law, and <u>hence</u> common political and judicial institutions.

> **译** 这些计划的实施与结果也涉及政治与经济，这是因为，现代经济的一体化需要一个法律体制，从而需要共同的政治和法律制度。（戴炳然译）

例 6-217 The most potent instrument is the offer of accession, <u>hence</u> of participation in the Union's institutions and powers as a whole, to other European states.

> **译** 最强有力的手段是接纳其他欧洲国家加入，从而使之整个参与欧盟的机构和分享权力。（戴炳然译）

（二）consequently, accordingly, so

consequently 意思是"因此，所以"，正式用词，表示符合逻辑的结果或推论，或表示由前面提到的事项引起或发生，具有结果的必然性，但未必是因果必然性。可作插入语使用，也可置于句首，后跟逗号。accordingly 意思是"相应地，因此，所以"，正式用词，但使用位置灵活，可在句前（一般后跟逗号）、句中或句尾，强调根据某种原因自然地或一般地得出某种结果，但并非结果上的必然性或不可避免性。so 意思是"这样，如此，因此"，为非正式用词，表示推论。

例 6-218 If the total number of organisms on the planet is equated with success, then bacteria come out on top. Conversely, in terms of biological complexity, they are also the most simple and <u>consequently</u> 'primitive' organisms on the planet.

> **译** 如果地球上的生物总数最多就等于成功，那么细菌就会排在首位。相反，在生物复杂性方面，它们也是地球上最简单的生物，因而也是最原始的生物。

例 6-219 It had long been assumed that the EEG was the register of voltage changes in the brain (i.e. cerebral action potentials), although this could not explain the patterns of the EEG seen in sleep (e.g. spindles and slow waves), unless neuronal activity was continuous, i.e. spontaneous, as well as reflexive. <u>Conse-</u>

quently, work at the cellular and EEG levels proceeded along entirely separate but parallel tracks, similar to those that Descartes thougt God had used to set mind and body in perfect but independent motion.

☯ 长久以来,人们一直认为脑电图是大脑活动电压改变(即动作电位)的反映,除非大脑的神经活动是连续的,即自发、自反射的,否则这还不能解释睡眠期间所见的脑电图模式(如纺锤波和慢波)。因此,细胞学和脑电图层面的研究独立开展,并行不悖,就像笛卡尔思想中上帝为人类的思想和身体设立了完美而又独立的运动方式那样。(韩芳译)

例 6-220 We have a different background, a different history. Accordingly, we will have different futures

☯ 我们有不同的背景和不同的历史。因此,我们将有不同的未来。

例 6-221 They should be adjusted accordingly on the basis of clinical effectiveness and laboratory assessment.

☯ 应根据临床疗效和实验室评估对其进行相应调整。

例 6-222 As the economy develops, the living conditions of the people have been improved accordingly.

☯ 经济发展了,人民的生活水平也相应地提高了。

例 6-223 Despite the richness of the cranial evidence for *P. boisei*, no postcranial remains have been found in association with cranial remains that we can be sure belong to *P. boisei*. So, we have no good evidence, only guesswork, about its posture or locomotion.

☯ 虽然发现的傍人包氏种的颅骨化石很多,但没有发现过我们确信属于它的颅下骨。由于没有确切的证据,我们只能猜测其体态和行为模式(冯兴无译)

例 6-224 So the invention of photography has made the painter and the patron lose interest in the likeness and transfer it to some more formal pattern.

☯ 摄影术的发明同样使得画家和赞助者的兴趣不再关注于惟妙惟肖,而把兴趣转向某种比较注重形式的格调。(杨自伍译)

例 6-225 This arrangement is only found in muscle cells, so for many years the possibility that actin and myosin could interact to produce contraction in non-muscle cells seemed unlikely.

☯ 这种排列只在肌肉细胞中发现,因此多年来非肌肉细胞中肌动蛋白和肌球蛋白相互作用产生收缩的可能性似乎不大。

（三）as a result, as a consequence

as a result 和 as a consequence 意思是"因此，结果"，一般置于句首，后面用逗号隔开，表示最终产生的某种结果。as a result of 后面跟名词或动名词结构，意思是"由于"。

例 6-226　The more culture, religion, and sexuality were forced to act as substitutes for fading public value, the less they were able to do so. The more meaning was concentrated in the symbolic realm, the more that realm was twisted out of true by the pressures that this exerted on it. As a result, all three areas of symbolic life began to exhibit pathological symptoms.

🔴 文化、宗教和性越是被迫充当衰落的公共价值的替身，它们就越无力扮演这种角色。意义越是集中在象征领域，这一领域就越是被意义施加的压力所扭曲。结果，生命的这三个象征领域都开始显出病症。（朱新伟译）

例 6-227　The now privatized domain of symbolic life had been hassled into delivering more than it decently could. As a result, it was becoming harder to find meaning even in the private sphere

🔴 现已私人化的象征生活领域不堪烦扰，开始提供自己无力恰当提供的东西。结果，甚至在私人领域，寻找意义也变得愈发困难。（朱新伟译）

例 6-228　As a consequence, the whole field of palaeobiology became more dynamic, questioning, and also outward-looking; it was also prepared to integrate its work more broadly with other fields of science.

🔴 结果是，整个古生物学领域变得更有活力、更引人探寻，而且视野更开阔；人们还准备将这个领域的工作与其他科学领域更广泛地结合在一起。（史立群译）

例 6-229　As a result of the conceptual and political split between psychiatry and neurology caused first by the mind-body problem and deeply aggravated by Sigmund Freud's inadvertent dualism, it took dream science an inordinately long time to notice that cerebrovascular accidents (better known as strokes) and epileptic seizures (better known as fits) could cause decreases and increases in the formal features of dreams, respectively.

🔴 先是心身问题造成了精神病学和神经病学之间观念和政治上的裂痕，随后弗洛伊德不慎的二元论又使这一裂痕变得更深，结果梦科学花费了相当

长的时间才认识到脑血管意义（俗称中风）和癫痫发作可分别导致梦的形式特征减少和增加。（韩芳译）

（四）then

then 意思是"因此，那么"。

例 6-230　Our problem is <u>then</u> to explain how both the sun and the planets were formed out of this mixture of materials.

🔵 译　因此，我们的问题是解释太阳和行星是如何由这种混合物质形成的。

例 6-231　If the main formal features of dreaming can be shown to be physiologically determined, <u>then</u> content analysis does not have to account for them.

🔵 译　如果能证明梦的主要形式特征由生理学确定，那么内容分析就不需要为此作也解析。（韩芳译）

十一、原因关系

表示原因关系经常用到的过渡词有：because, as, since, for, insofar as, because of, owing to, due to, on account of, thanks to, for the reason, inasmuch as 等。

（一）because, as, since, for, insofar as

上述词都可译为"因为，由于"，但其间有细微的区别。because 引导原因状语从句语气最强，也最常用，可对 why 提出问题进行回答，表示一种直接的因果关系。because 引导的从句可置于主句前，也可置于主句后。as 引导原因状语从句时语气较轻，说明比较明显的原因，一般置于主句前。可译为"由于，鉴于"。since 表示显然的或已知的理由，或者引导交流双方都知道的原因，可译为"既然，因为"。for 引导的原因状语从句不放在句首，表示附带解释或说明主句的理由。insofar as 的意思是"在…的情况下，就…一点上（来说），在…范围（限度）内"，但仍有表示原因的意思在里面。

例 6-232　The electroencephalograph (or EGG) revolutionized sleep and dream science as much as it altered clinical neurology <u>because</u> it provided an objective tool for assessing dynamic brain activity in normal individuals as well as in patients with epilepsy.

🔵 译　正如其改变临床神经病学一样，脑电图也让睡眠和梦科学发生了彻底变革，因为它为评估癫痫患者和正常个体大脑动态活动提供了客观工具。（韩

芳译)

例 6-233 This is possible in spite of the fact that we only have 23,600 genes because the genetic message can be modified inside the nucleus after transcription, and outside the nucleus, thus increasing the overall number of possible protein products.

㊙ 尽管我们只有23600个基因,但这是可能的,因为转录后的遗传信息可以在细胞核内和细胞核外进行修饰,从而增加了可能的蛋白质产物的总数。

例 6-234 Genetic differences between species were impossible to define, because organisms of different species usually do not mate, or they produce hybrid progeny that die or sterile.

㊙ 不可能确定物种间的遗传差异,因为不同物种的生物通常不交配,或者它们交配产生的杂种后代死亡或不育。

例 6-235 Language, because it inevitably has a degree of uniformity about it, tends to make different kinds of utterance look pretty much the same.

㊙ 由于语言必然具有一定程度的规整性,它很容易使不同类型的话语显得极为同一。(朱新伟译)

例 6-236 Because our skin is warm and moist, it provides an attractive surface that is constantly colonized by bacteria and fungi.

㊙ 因为我们的皮肤温暖、湿润,它为细菌和真菌不断繁殖生长提供了一个有吸引力的表面。

例 6-237 Because you inherit the vast majority of your mtDNA from your mother, the evolutionary history of mtDNA is effectively a history of maternal inheritance.

㊙ 人类的绝大多数的线粒体DNA是从母亲那里继承的,因此,线粒体DNA的进化史实际上是一部母系遗传历史。(冯兴无译)

例 6-238 Because organisms in the same species share the same developmental plan, organisms that are members of the same species usually resemble one another, although some notable exceptions usually are differences between males and females.

㊙ 由于同一物种的生物具有相同的发育蓝图,因此属于同一物种的生物通常彼此相似,尽管雌雄之间的差异是明显的例外情况。

例 6-239 As dreaming is so vivid, so complex, and so emotional, it has inspired religious movements, artistic representations, and introspective scientific theories.

译 梦是如此生动复杂而又富于情感,它启发了无数的宗教运动、艺术表象及内省的科学理论。(韩芳译)

例 6-240 As he was so close to us in time and spirit, and because our brain-based theory is so different from his, in this chapter we focus on Freud's psychoanalytic model as it was developed in his *Project for a Scientific Psychology* (1895) and *The Interpretation of Dreams* (1900).

译 鉴于弗洛伊德生活的时代和时代精神与我们如此相近,而我们以大脑为基础的理论和他的又如此不同,本章将着重讨论他在《科学心理学方略》(1895 年)和《梦的解析》(1900 年)中建立起来的精神分析模型。(韩芳译)

例 6-241 As it seems unlikely that the cell should go to the trouble of replicating more than nine-tenths of its DNA each time it divides for no reason, we would do best to consider this vast majority of our DNA to have an unknown rather than no function.

译 由于细胞似乎不太可能在无缘无故地每次分裂时复制超过十分之九的 DNA,所以最好认为我们绝大多数的 DNA 都有未知的功能,而不是没有功能的。

例 6-242 Since scholarship implies a relation between one who knows more and one who knows less, it may be temporary; in relation to the public, every review is, temporarily, a scholar because he has read the book he is reviewing and the public have not.

译 既然学问涉及一个懂得多一些的人和懂得少一些的人之间的关系,这种关系就可能是一时的。对公众来说,每一个评论者都是一时的学者,因为他读过他正在评论的那本书,而公众却还没有读过。(朱树飚译)

例 6-243 The environment can also be seen as a vital aspect of security, since global warming and destruction of the ozone layer are among the gravest threats to the welfare, and perhaps the lives, of the world's people.

译 环境也可以被看成安全的一个重要方面,因为全球变暖和臭氧层的破坏是对世界人民的福祉乃至生命的最严重的危胁之一。(戴炳然译)

例 6-244 Since our grammar allow us to construct nouns, which represent distinct entities, then it also makes it seem plausible that there can be a kind of

Noun of nouns, a mega-entity known as God, without which all the little entities around us might simply collapse.

🔾 既然语法允许我们建构一系列名词，而名词代表独特的实体，那么，似乎也可以建构一个位于一切名词之上的名词，一个被称作"上帝"的元实体，若没有它，我们身边所有的小实体都将崩溃。（朱新伟译）

例 6-245　To read is to translate, for no two persons' experiences are the same.

🔾 读书就是翻译，因为从来不会有两个人的体验是相同的。（朱树飏译）

例 6-246　There are no theories of myth itself, for there is no discipline of myth in itself.

🔾 神话理论本身并不存在，因为神话这一学科本身就不存在。（刘象愚译）

例 6-247　Modern warfare, so far, has not been more destructive of life than the warfare of less scientific ages, for the increased deadliness of weapons has been offset by the improvement in medicine and hygiene.

🔾 到目前为止，近代战争并未比较不科学化时代的作战更具毁灭力，因为武器的增强的杀伤力已经被医药与卫生的改进所抵消。（颜元叔译）

例 6-248　The pervasiveness of classical, or pagan, mythology is even more of a feat than that of biblical mythology, for classical mythology has survived the demise of the religion of which, two thousand years ago, it was originally a part.

🔾 古典神话——或者说异教神话——的流行相比《圣经》神话是一件更加了不起的事，因为它 2000 年前原属的宗教在随后的历史中已经消失了，而古典神话却留存了下来。（刘象愚译）

例 6-249　In the twentieth century Tylor's and Frazer's theories have been spurned exactly for pitting myth against science and thereby precluding traditional myths, for subsuming myth under religion and thereby precluding secular myths, for deeming the subject matter of myth the physical world, for deeming the function of myth explanatory, and for deeming myth false.

🔾 到了 20 世纪，人们摒弃了泰勒和弗雷泽的理论，原因正是因为它们将神话与科学置于相互敌对的立场，因而排除了传统神话；又因为它们将神话归于宗教之下，因而排除了世俗神话；还因为它们认定神话的主题是物质世界，神话的功能是解释性的，神话是虚假的。（刘象愚译）

例 6-250 However, the appeal to tradition need not at all be traditional, insofar as what the notion of tradition is attempting to recover is something missing, forgotten, or repressed in contemporary life.

🔵 然而,对传统的诉求并不一定是传统的,因为传统这个概念所要揭示的正是某些在当代生活中缺失的、被遗忘的或受到压抑的东西。(江怡译)

例 6-251 Now, this would seem to be more or less right insofar as Continental philosophy is habitually presented by people like me as a roughly chronological sequence of proper names beginning with Kant, rather than the problem-orientated approach that one tends to associate with the tradition of analytic philosophy.

🔵 现在看来,这可能或多或少是对的,因为欧陆哲学通常表现为是由我这样的人提出的开始于康德的大致依编年顺序的一系列专名,而不是人们通常与分析哲学传统相联系在一起的以问题为主导的方法。(江怡译)

(二)because of, owing to, due to, on account of, thanks to

这些词意思均为"由于,因为",后接名词,但 because of, owing to, on account of, thanks to 结构多用作状语,现代英语中也有人将 due to 结构用作状语,但在传统语法中 due to 用来引导表语(也就是 due to 在 to be 之后作形容词成分,相当于 a result of). thanks to 除具有随意或讽刺的语气外,与别的词没有真正的区别。

例 6-252 We can see this even today in the attitudes of minority groups who, because of a feeling of insecurity, still preserve cohesive family ties.

🔵 甚至今天,我们从少数民族团体的态度也可以看出这一点。由于缺乏安全感,他们仍然保持着富有凝聚力的家庭纽带。(谭卫国译)

例 6-253 Fossils from different sites, and even fossils from different parts of same site, show different degrees of fossilization because of small-scale differences in their chemical environment.

🔵 由于周围环境的小差别,不同地点、甚至同一地点不同部位的化石所表现出来的石化程度都不尽相同。(冯兴无译)

例 6-254 Whereas scientists, because of random fluctuations in the weather, cannot determine the transition from one season to the next by monitoring temperatures on a daily basis, so they cannot determine the onset of global warming by monitoring average annual temperatures.

🔵 然而,由于天气随机波动,科学家无法通过每天监测温度来确定从一个季节到下一个季节的转变，因此他们无法通过监测年平均温度来确定全球变暖的开始。

例 6-255 Owing to the psychological changes experienced by adolescents, which of the following would improve learning in a middle school environment?

🀄 由于青少年所经历的心理变化，以下哪一项将改善中学环境中的学习？

例 6-256 Global warming owing to emissions is called the 'temperature effect'.

🀄 由于排放引起的全球变暖被称为"温度效应"。

例 6-257 Threatened species face extinction owing to 'God clause', scientists say.

🀄 科学家说，由于"上帝条款"，濒危物种面临灭绝。

例 6-258 The difficulty arises on account of the fact that all business units do not keep a record of the changing inventories, and even those who do maintain the record not in physical units but in terms of value.

🀄 困难的产生是因为所有的业务部门都没有记录不断变化的库存，甚至那些业务部门不以实物单位记录，而是以价值的形式记录。

例 6-259 The is due to the intense packaging and fibrous nature of the nuclear contents, which make it virtually impossible to follow a length of chromatin over any distance in the thin sections required for transmission electron microscopy.

🀄 这是由于细胞核内容物具有的高强度包装和纤维性质，因而几乎不可能在透射电子显微镜所需的薄切片中跟踪染色质的纵长。

例 6-260 Although the nucleus is the largest and most obvious organelle within the cell, the processes within it have proved rather more difficult to study than those in the surrounding cytoplasm This may have been due to the difficulty of biochemical separation of its constituents.

🀄 尽管细胞核是细胞内最大和最明显的细胞器，但其内部的过程比周围细胞质中的过程更难研究。这可能是因为难以对其成分进行生化分离的缘故。

例 6-261 The longevity of bone is due to the deposition of minerals such as calcium phosphate into the bone matrix by cells called osteoblasts, creating the structural rigidity.

🀄 骨的持久性是由于矿物质（如磷酸钙）被成骨细胞沉积到骨基质中，形成结构刚性。

例 6-262　Global warming refers to the increase in the average temperature of the earth, particularly at the lower atmosphere, <u>due to</u> the abundant increase of greenhouse gases. This is primarily <u>due to</u> the human's intervention and the lifestyle they have adopted in recent years.

🔹 全球变暖是指由于温室气体的大量增加，地球平均温度上升，特别是在低层大气中平均温度上升。这主要是由于人类的干预和他们近年来所采取的生活方式所致。

例 6-263　<u>Thanks to</u> science, you can soon wipe out your worst memories.

🔹 多亏了/由于科学，你很快就能抹去最糟糕的记忆。

例 6-264　<u>Thanks to</u> science, we can hear the voices of icebergs.

🔹 多亏了/由于科学，我们能听到冰山的声音。

十二、结论关系

表示结论关系经常用到的过渡词有：in conclusion, in summary, on the whole, to sum up, in short, in brief, in a/one word, in a nutshell, broadly speaking, collectively, in general, in all/most/many/some cases, by and large, to a great extent, to some extent, finally, therefore, at last 等。

in conclusion/to conclude/to draw a conclusion(总而言之，最后)、in summary(总之，概括起来)、on the whole(大体上说，总的说来)、to sum up(总之，总而言之，概括地说)等一般作为独立成分，置于句首，后用逗号与其他句子成分隔开。in short(简言之，总之)、in brief(简言之，简短地，总之)、in a/one word(简言之，总之)和 in a nutshell(简言之，概括起来说)的用法与上述词类似。

例 6-265　<u>In conclusion</u>, our results showed that the herbicide Roundup© leads to glutamatergic excitotoxicity and energy deficit in hippocampal cells from immature rats.

🔹 总之，我们的研究结果表明，除草剂农达©会导致未成熟大鼠海马细胞产生谷氨酸兴奋毒性和能量不足。

例 6-266　<u>In summary</u>, I have made two historical claims for Continental philosophy: it is a professional self-description and it is a cultural feature.

🔹 综上所述，我对欧陆哲学作出了两种历史断言：它是一种专业的自我描述，也是一种文化特征。（江怡译）

例 6-267　To summarize, the information revolution is making obsolete old institutions and old modes of operation, requiring the individual, the firm, and the nation to change.

㊣ 现在我来总结一下以上所讲的话，信息革命正使旧体制和旧的运作方式变得过时了，从而要求个人、公司和国家做出相应的变化。（谭卫国译）

例 6-268　To summarize this story, the serotonin and noradrenaline cells that modulate the brain during waking reduce their output by half during non–REM sleep but are shut off completely during REM sleep.

㊣ 概括而言，那些在清醒状态下调节大脑的去甲肾上腺素和5-羟色胺细胞，在非快动眼睡眠时将自身的输出下调一半，而在快动眼睡眠时则彻底关闭。（韩芳译）

例 6-269　On the whole, scientist do their most creative work before age of forty, a tendency that has been taken to show that ages carries with it a loss of creative capacity.

㊣ 总的来说，科学家在四十岁之前就完成了他们最具创造性的工作，这一趋势被用来说明，随着年龄的增长，创造性的能力也随之丧失。

例 6-270　To sum up, for a healthy heart you must take regular exercise and stop smoking.

㊣ 综上所述，为了有颗健康的心脏，你必须经常锻炼并戒烟。

例 6-271　In short, the name of the game these days, in both internal and external affairs, is integrity and accountability.

㊣ 总之，当今的根本要点，不分内政外交，都是要诚实负责。（颜元叔译）

例 6-272　In brief, an intellectual property policy must be integrated into other policies and programs.

㊣ 简而言之，必须将知识产权政策纳入其他政策与计划中去。

例 6-273　In a word, the social heritage does not ensure the future of culture with the same probability with which it provides the conditions of civilization.

㊣ 总而言之，社会遗产为文明进步提供环境条件时给了相当成功把握，却不能以同样的把握担保文化的未来。（颜元叔译）

例 6-274　Darwin's other related contribution was the idea of natural selection. In a nutshell, natural selection suggests that, because resources are finite, and because of random variation, some individuals will be better than other at accessing those resources. That variant will then gain enough of an advantage that it will produce more surviving offspring than other individuals belonging to the same species.

🔵 译 达尔文的另一个相关贡献是他提出了自然选择的观点。简言之，自然选择理论认为，由于资源有限，由于偶发的变异，一些个体比其他个体更利于获取资源。这样，获取资源多的个体就有足够的优势，其后代就比同种其他个体的后代有更强的生存能力。（冯兴无译）

学术写作中另外四个常用的过渡词是 broadly speaking, overall, collectively 和 taken together。broadly speaking 意思是"一般来说、大体上说、概括地说、总起来讲、泛泛地说"。overall, collectively 和 taken together 意思是"总之、总起来说、总体来讲"。

例 6-275 Broadly speaking, there are two different ways of thinking about modern art, or two different versions of the story.

🔵 译 大体上讲，现代艺术有两种不同的思考方式，或者说有两种不同的故事版本。

例 6-276 Science, broadly speaking, deals with the study and understanding of natural phenomena, and is concerned with empirically (i. e., either observationally or experimentally) testable hypotheses advanced to account for those phenomena.

🔵 译 概括地说，科学涉及对自然现象的研究和理解，并涉及为解释这些现象而提出的、在经验上（即通过观察或实验）可检验的假说。

例 6-277 Overall, these results indicate that heparin-DOCA may have potentials as therapeutic agent that prevents tumor metastasis and progression.

🔵 译 总之，这些结果显示肝素-乙酸脱氧皮质酮有可能成为阻止肿瘤转移和发展的治疗药物。（洪班信译）

例 6-278 Collectively, these findings demonstrate that constitutive and LPS-induced type I IFN play significant roles in regulating the differences in phenotype and function between BMM and GM-BMM

🔵 译 总之，这些发现表明组成型和脂多糖诱导的Ⅰ型干扰素在调控 BMM 和 GM-BMM 之间的表型和功能差异方面发挥重要作用。

例 6-279 Collectively, these forms of health research have led to significant discoveries, the development of new therapies, and a remarkable improvement in health care and public health.

[译] 总的来说，这些形式的健康研究已导致重大发现和新疗法产生，并使卫生保健和公共卫生方面取得显著改善。

例 6-280 Taken together, our results suggest that RTN3 could bind with Bcl-2 and mediate its accumulation in mitochondria, which modulate the anti-apoptotic activity of Bcl-2.

[译] 总之，我们的结果表明 RTN3 能与 Bcl-2 结合，介导其在线粒体的聚积，从而调节 Bcl-2 的抗凋亡活性。(洪班信译)

第七单元

常用的修辞

修辞或修辞学(rhetoric)定义较为宽泛，按照 Nichols(1971)的观点，修辞(学)可定义为"对演讲听众或文章读者产生某种效果的语篇组织手段(a means of so ordering discourse as to produce an effect on the listener or reader)". 简单来说，修辞就是在演讲或写作过程中，根据题旨情境，利用多种语言手段和表现手法，以收到良好的表达效果。事实上，rhetoric 在美国英语中可泛指"写作"。英语修辞格(figures of speech 或 rhetorical devices)或修辞手段可分为音韵修辞格、语义修辞格和句法修辞格三类。音韵修辞格包括拟声、头韵和脚韵等；语义修辞格包括明喻、暗喻、拟人、转喻、提喻、类比、夸张、对仗、反语、双关、委婉、移就、仿拟、矛盾修饰、轭式搭配等；句法修辞格包括重复、倒装、对比、平行等。除前文论述过的句法修辞格外，学术英语最常用的修辞手段为比喻和类比。此外，学术英语还常常需要对专业术语或概念进行定义说明，进行逻辑推理以得出结论。因此，以下就比喻、类比、定义和推理这四个方面加以举例说明。

一、比喻

学术英语中，比喻利用日常生活中的常见的事物和现象来帮助理解抽象的学术思想和观念，可激发读者的想象力，使表达更为生动、形象。比喻大体分为明喻(simile)和暗喻(metaphor)两种。

(一)明喻

明喻是在两个类别完全不同但又在某方面具有共性或相似性的事物间进行比较，通常是用熟悉的事物来与具有某种主观共性但不熟悉的事物进行比较，使读者能形象地理解所描述的事物。常用介词 like 或 as 等比喻词将本体和喻体相连接。

例 7-1 Within this constant motion of the lipids, groups of membrane proteins float around freely in the lipid bilayer rather <u>like</u> ice floes in the polar seas.

🔘 译 在脂质不断运动的过程中，一组组膜蛋白在脂质双层中自由漂浮，就像极地海洋中的浮冰。

例 7-2 The rocket engine, with its steady roar <u>like</u> that of waterfall or thunderstorm, is an impressive symbol of the new space age.

🔘 译 发出像瀑布或雷暴那样持续的轰鸣声，火箭发动机成为新太空时代令人印象深刻的象征。

例 7-3 Cells in the body are wired like computer chips to direct signals that instruct how they function, research suggests.

[译] 研究表明，人体内的细胞就像电脑芯片一样，被连接起来，以引导信号如何工作。

例 7-4 Each protein cargo is ‘tagged’ by an amino acid sequence that acts like a luggage label to ensure that they finish on the correct side of the nuclear membrane.

[译] 每一种蛋白货物都被一个氨基酸序列(像一个行李标签)“标记”，以确保它们最终到达核膜的正确一侧。

例 7-5 Beauty is as summer fruits, which are easy to corrupt and cannot last.

[译] 美貌如同夏日水果，易腐难存。

除利用介词 like 或 as 表示比喻关系外，还可用 as…as…, as…so…, (no) more than, as if/as though, may/might as well …as, something of, (a) kind of, the way 结构, and 结构, with 结构, what 结构等，此外，还可直接利用 resemble, seem, compare to, remind of, be likened to, be similar to, consider/respect/describes/hounour/treat … as 等动词或动词结构表示比喻关系。

例 7-6 Whatever the Europeans may actually think of artists, they have killed enough of them off by now to know that they are as real — and as persistent — as rain, snow, taxes or businessman.

[译] 不论欧洲人对待艺术家的实际态度如何，他们毁掉的艺术家已经够多的了，而现在他们终于认识到艺术家就像雨、雪、税收和商人一样是真实存在，并且永远会存在。(王晓军等译)

例 7-7 The brain controls all the activities of cells through its network of nerves much the way telephose office maintains normal scrve through its network of wires.

[译] 大脑通过它的神经网络来控制细胞的一切活动，很像电话局通过它的电话线网来维持正常业务一样。(何远秀译)

例 7-8 What sculpture is to a black of marble, (that) education is to the soul.

[译] 教育之于心灵犹如雕刻之于大理石。(何远秀译)

例 7-9 Marx did for the development of society what Darwinn did for the development of the biology.

> 译 马克思对社会发展的贡献和达尔文对生物学发展的贡献一样。(周瑞英译)

例 7-10 The greatness of a people is <u>no more</u> determined by their number <u>than</u> the greatness of man is determined by his height.

> 译 一个民族的伟大并不取决于它人口的多少,正如一个人的伟大不能取决于他的身高一样。(周瑞英译)

(二)暗喻

暗喻也称隐喻,根据喻体具有本体的共同特点或性质,将喻体直接代替或说成本体,而本体和比喻词(like 或 as)都不出现的修辞方法。暗喻比明喻在语气上更为肯定、有力。

例 7-11 It was thought that the various organs and structures inside a cell float around in <u>an open sea</u> called the cytoplasm

> 译 人们认为,细胞内的各种器官和结构漂浮在一个叫作细胞质的开阔海域。

例 7-12 Many of the important advances made by biologists in the past 150 years can be reduced to a single metaphor. All living, or extant, organisms, that is, animals, plants, fungi, bacteria, viruses, and all the types of organisms that lived in the past, are situated somewhere on <u>the branches and twigs of an arborvitae or Tree of Life.</u>

> 译 生物学家在过去150年里所取得的许多重大进展可以简化作一个比喻,即包括动物、植物、真菌、细菌、病毒等在内的所有现生生物,和所有曾经存在的生物体都可以在一棵"生命树"的大枝小杈上找到位置。(冯兴无译)

例 7-13 The discovery of archaea in the late 1970s led scientists to propose that <u>the tree of life</u> diverged long ago into three main <u>trunks</u>, or 'domains'. One <u>trunk</u> gave rise to modern bacteria; one to archaea.

> 译 20世纪70年代末,考古学的发现促使科学家们提出,生命之树在很久以前就已经分叉为三个树干或"域"。一个树干产生现代细菌;一个树干产生古细菌。

例 7-14 One of the oldest intellectual defenses of theism is the cosmological argument, also known as the argument from the first cause… The argument is nonetheless <u>a weak reed</u> on which to rest the theistic thesis.

🔄 有神论最老的理性辩护之一是宇宙成因论,也称第一推动力论。……但是,它是一根脆弱的芦苇,难以给有神论提供什么支撑。(严忠志译)

例 7-15 Some books are to be tasted, others swallowed, and some few to be chewed and digested.

🔄 一些书可以浅尝辄止,一些书可以囫囵吞下,而少数书则需要细嚼慢咽,好好消化。

毛荣贵教授在《英译汉技巧新编》中引用美国语言学家 Peterr Newmark 的话"By metaphor, I mean any figurative expression: the transferred sense of a physical work; the personification of an abstraction; the application of word or collocation to what it does not literally denote, i. e., to describe one thing in terms of another"(我的意思是,隐喻是任何形象化的表达:有形物体可移用的意义;抽象事物的拟人化;将词语或搭配应用到字面含义上不同的事物,即用某一事物来描述另一个事物。),说明英语 metaphor(比喻)的广义性。"metaphor (比喻)是英语的最大优势。""这个并非狭隘意义上的把 A 比作 B 的不使用喻词(如 as, like, as if 等)的"隐/暗喻",而是广义上的英语词汇的 figurative sense / metaphorical meaning(比喻义),换言之,也可以说是英语词汇 denotation(本义)之外的 connotation(转义)。"他以《英汉大词典》中 trigger(本义为"扳机",引申为引发、引起)和 gnaw(本义为"咬、啃、啮"引申为"侵蚀、腐蚀、消耗,使苦恼、折磨")的词条为例,说明"英语使用词的转义,简直到了不遗余力的地步。"从这个意义上讲,英语词汇中有大量这样的词汇,尽管我们在使用中已不再关注其本义。

二、类比

所谓类比(analogy),就是由两个有相同或相似的性质的对象在几个共同特征或相似点之间进行平行比较,既可以用熟悉的对象或关系来解释不熟悉的对象或关系,也可以利用熟悉的对象或关系来帮助推理或论证不熟悉的对象或关系。与着重于通过形象化的方法提高表达效果的比喻相比,类比的作用主是要通过平行比较来说明某个观念、关系或过程,让人理解或信服。

例 7-16 It is as transparent as an old-fashioned melodrama: Truth (as we perceive it today) is the only arbiter and the world of past scientists is divided into good guys who were right and bad guys who were wrong.

🔄 这就犹如一出旧式传奇剧中那么容易识破:真理(就我们今日把握的

程度而论)是唯一的仲裁者,以往科学家的世界被分割为两部分:正确的便是好汉,错误的便是罪人。(杨自伍译)

例 7-17　A scaled-up analogy of pore traffic activity would involve a short length of drainpipe (as the pore channel) through which a mixture of tennis balls, golf balls, and marbles would pass in both directions at a rate of 1000 journeys per second.

　　译 将核孔运输活动按比例放大,孔隙通道就像一小段排水管,网球、高尔夫球和大理石的混合物以每秒1000次的速度双向通过。

例 7-18　The optical system of the eye, like that of a camera, has a lens, a muscular mechanism for focusing the lens, and a diaphragm (the pupil), which controls the amount of light entering through the lens.

　　译 眼的光学系统与照相机相似,有一个透镜,也就是一个晶状体聚焦的肌肉机制,和一个光圈(瞳孔),瞳孔控制进入通过晶状体的光量。(李少如译)

例 7-19　Each DNA strand has a polarity, or directionality, like a chain of circus elephants linked trunk to tail. In this analogy, each elephant corresponds to one nucleotide along the DNA strand. The polarity is determined by the direction in which the nucleotides are pointing. The 'trunk' end of the strand is called the 3′ end of the end, and the 'tail' end is called the 5′ end.

　　译 每一条DNA链都有极性,或者说方向性,就像马戏团象鼻象尾连在一起的大象链。在这个类比中,每头大象对应于DNA链上的一个核苷酸。极性方向由核苷酸指向决定。链上的"象鼻"端称为3′端,而"象尾"端称为5′端。

例 7-20　The situation is the same as that with any complex machine. An airplane can function if thousands of parts are working together in harmony, but only one defective part, if that part affects a vital system, can bring it down. Likewise, the development and functioning of every trait require a large number of genes working in harmony, but in some cases a single mutant gene can have catastrophic consequences.

　　译 这种情况与任何复杂的机器都是一样的。如果成千上万个部件协调工作,一架飞机就可以飞行,但如果一个部件有缺陷,这个部件影响到一个重要的系统,它就可能使飞机坠落。同样,每个性状的发育和功能需要大量的基因协调工作,但在某些情况下,一个基因突变就可能产生灾难性后果。

例 7-21　Intellectual assimilation takes time. The mind is not to be enriched as a coal barge is loaded. Whatever is precious in a cargo is carefully taken on board and carefully placed. Whatever is delicate and fine must be received delicately, and its place in the mind thoughtfully assigned.

🔵 吸收知识需要时间。头脑的充实不能像驳船装煤那样。正如珍贵的货物必须小心翼翼地搬运上船，并小心翼翼地安放好，知识的精华必须灵敏巧妙地吸入头脑中，并加以缜密的安排。（李定坤译）

例 7-22　Classification schemes try to group similar things together in increasingly broad, or inclusive, categories. Think or the following example of a classification of automobiles. It has seven levels, or categories; it begins with the most inclusive category and ends with a small group. The levels are 'Vehicles', 'Powered Vehicles'. 'Automobile', 'Luxury Car', 'Rolls-Royce', 'Silver Shadow', and '1970 Silver Shadow II'. The Linnaean classification system also recognizes seven basic levels. The most inclusive category, the equivalent of 'Vehicles' in our example, is the kingdom, followed by the phylum, class, order, family, genus, with the species being the smallest, least inclusive, formal category.

🔵 分类方案尽可能把相似的生物归入广泛性和包容性递增的类别。以汽车分类为例。汽车可划分为 7 个级别或类别，第一级别最具包容性，最后级别是个小类；即依次为"车辆""机动车""汽车""豪华汽车""劳斯莱斯""银影"和"1970 年的银影 II". 林奈的分类系统也采用了七个基本级别，相当于"车辆"级别的是"界"，下面依次为"门""纲""目""科""属""种"；"种"是最小的、最不具包容性的正式分类单位。（冯兴无译）

三、定义

定义（definition）是对某一事物的概念或术语进行确定性说明，也就是对事物本质特征的内涵和外延加以明确而简要的描述。下定义既需要揭示概念的本质，也需要能呈现该概念与其他概念区分开来的特征。因此，一个专业术语或名词的定义格式（pattern of definition）至少包括范畴或类别（category）及区别性特征（distinguishing features）两个部分。一个概念可以从形式与形态、材料与来源、成因与目的等几个方面加以界定。通常可借助冒号、系动词 is、defined as、delimited as、refers to 等来进行定义。

例 7-23　Gene: The hereditary unit containing genetic information transcribed into an RNA molecule that is processed and either functions directly or is translated into a polypeptide chain

🔸 基因：包含遗传信息的遗传单位，转录成一个 RNA 分子，RNA 分子经过加工，可以直接发挥作用，也可以翻译成一个多肽链。

在这个定义中，The hereditary unit（遗传单位）就属于范畴，而后面的修饰部分都属于区别性特征。

例 7-24　Hydrogeology is a science dealing with the properties, distribution, and circulation water on the surface of the land, in the soil and underlying rocks, and in the atmosphere.

🔸 水文地质学是研究地表、土壤和地下岩石以及大气中的水的性质、分布和循环的科学。（吴中东和宫玉波译）

例 7-25　Epilepsy is an abnormal condition in which the normal activity of affected brain regions may be enhanced as well as impaired, and so constitutes an experiment of nature that is the opposite of stroke.

🔸 癫痫是受到影响的大脑区域的正常活动被强化和损伤后的一种异常状态，它提供了一个与中风完全相反的天然实验模型。（韩芳译）

例 7-26　Consciousness may be simply — and unarguably — defined as our awareness of the world, our bodies, and ourselves.

🔸 意识可简单而无可争辩地定义为人们对外部世界、自己身体和自我的察觉。（韩芳译）

例 7-27　Psychosis is, by definition, a mental state characterized by hallucinations and/or delusions.

🔸 精神病被定义为一种以幻觉和/或妄想为特征的精神状态。（韩芳译）

例 7-28　In response to the disorientation, which is caused by the recent memory deficit, the patient with organic delirium makes up stories that are not lies but false beliefs, sincerely — and often fatuously — advanced to cover the huge holes in memory. We call this trait 'confabulation'.

🔸 为了应对短时记忆丢失带来的定向障碍，器质性谵妄病人会编造故事，这些故事不是谎言而是错误的信念，它们被真诚地——通常是愚蠢地——提出，以俺盖记忆的巨大黑洞，我们把这一特质称为"虚构"。（韩芳译）

例 7-29　Diagenesis is the word scientists use to describe all the changes that occur to bones and teeth during fossilization.

🀄 成岩作用是科学家用来描述骨骼和牙齿在石化地中发生的所有变化的词语。(冯兴无译)

例 7-30　The synthesis of a polypeptide under the direction of an mRNA molecule is known as translation.

🀄 在信使核糖核酸(mRNA)分子指导下合成多肽过程被称为翻译。

例 7-31　The term mutation refers to any heritable change in a gene or to the process by which such a change takes place.

🀄 突变一词是指基因中任何可遗传的变化或指这种变化发生的过程。

四、推理

推理是从已知的判断(前提、条件)推出新判断(结论)的过程。演绎推理中的一种简单推理判断是三段论推理(syllogism),它包括一个大前提、一个小前提以及结论三个部分。在学术英语中,可以使用 therefore, consequently 等连词来描述推理,但常用的推理和逻辑结构句式为 if...then....。其中大前提可能是前面的句子,也可能是自明而不必写出来的(即三段论的省略形式)。引导条件状语的 if 也可用 once, in case that (in the case of), in the event that (in the event of), provided that, when, where, should 等代替。推理在哲学与法律英语中最为常用。

例 7-32　Each molecule blindly runs. The human body is a collection of molecules. Therefore, the human body blindly runs, and therefore there can be no individual responsibility for the actions of the body. <u>If</u> you once accept that the molecule is definitely determined to be what it is, independently of any determination by reason of the total organism of the body, and it you further admit that the blind run is settled by the general mechanical laws, <u>there can be no escape from this conclusion</u>.

🀄 每个分子盲目地运动。人体是分子的积聚之处。因此,人体盲目地运动,因此对于身体的行动也根本无所谓个人的责任可言。要是一旦接受分子是确切地注定成为它本来的面目,不依傍于身体整个有机体的任何决定,要是进一步承认盲目运动是由一般力学规律所确定的,那就无法逃避这个结论。(杨自伍译)

例 7-33　<u>Provided that</u> the entombing sediment compacted sufficiently to retain their shape, prior to the inevitable rotting and disappearance of the dinosaur's organic tissue, then (as with simple clay moulds) an impression of the texture of the skin surface would have been preserved in the sediment.

译 如果埋藏恐龙的沉积物足够结实，就能在恐龙的有机组织不可避免地腐烂和消失之前保留它们的形态，那么（就像简单的陶器模子一样）皮肤表面结构的印痕就会保存在沉积物中。（史立群译）

例 7-34 If science is simply a method or an attitude, so that anyone whose thought-processes are sufficiently rational can in some sense be described as a scientist — what then becomes of the enormous prestige now enjoyed by the chemist, the physicist, etc. and his claim to be somehow wiser than the rest of us?

译 因为如果科学仅仅是一个方法或是一种态度，任何一个思维过程足够理性化的人就都是某种意义上的科学家——那么，化学家、物理学家等现在享有的巨大声誉将会如何，他们又怎么自诩比其他人高明？（吴简清译）

例 7-35 If the total number of organisms on the planet is equated with success, then bacteria come out on top.

译 如果地球上的生物总数最多就等于成功，那么细菌就会排在首位。

例 7-36 If the mass of newly divided cells stay put, then the resulting tumour is benign and can usually be successfully removed by surgery or killed by radiation therapy.

译 如果新分裂细胞的群体保持在原位，那么产生的肿瘤是良性的，通常可以通过手术成功地切除，或者通过放射疗法杀死。

例 7-37 In general, if a primitive organism has a particular gene, then organisms of increasing complexity will contain a number of related genes in proportion to their position on the evolutionary scale.

译 总的来说，如果一个原始生物有一个特定的基因，那么，复杂度增加的生物将根据其在进化尺度上的位置，包含相应数量的相关基因。

例 7-38 If the total number of organisms on the planet is equated with success, then bacteria come out on top. Conversely, in terms of biological complexity, they are also the most simple and consequently 'primitive' organisms on the planet.

译 如果地球上的生物总数最多就等于成功，那么细菌就会排在首位。相反，在生物复杂性方面，它们也是地球上最简单的生物，因而也是最原始的生物。

例 7-39 If white fat cells could be converted to brown fat cells (as has been achieved in tissue culture), then we could have a useful tool in the battle against obesity, literally 'burning of' fat.

🅣 如果可以将白色脂肪细胞转化为棕色脂肪细胞（如在组织培养中已经实现的那样），然后我们就可以拥有一个对抗肥胖斗争的有用工具，真正地"燃烧"多余的脂肪。

例 7-40 If you think that you are in love with wisdom, then philosophy is presumably the subject to study.

🅣 如果你认为自己爱上了智慧，那么，哲学大概就是你要研究的对象。（江怡译）

例 7-41 If these simple or elementary propositions reflected the facts, then they could be verified against the facts.

🅣 如果这些简单的或者说基本的命题反映了事实，那么它们就是可以相对于事实加以证实的。（江怡译）

例 7-42 This is, if philosophy does not deal with — not necessarily answer, but at least tackle — the question of the meaning of life, then philosophers cannot be said to be doing their job properly.

🅣 也就是说，如果哲学并不讨论（不必要回答，但至少要处理）生活意义的问题，那么，我们无法说哲学家们的工作做的妥当。（江怡译）

例 7-43 If things and events are caused, then it is possible to specify a set of conditions which, when present, produce the effect without exception.

🅣 如果事物是有成因的，那就有可能确定一组条件。那些条件如果出现，就会毫无例外地产生特定的结果。（严忠志译）

例 7-44 The most natural position to adopt is that a deterministic universe rules out free will. If this assumption is correct, then one is forced to choose between free will and determinism.

🅣 可供采取的最自然的立场是，决定论的宇宙排除了自由意志。如果这一设想是正确的，那么，人们将被迫在自由意义与决定论之间做出选择。（严忠志译）

例 7-45 If I say, 'Jesus Christ is the redeemer of humankind', and offer no empirical proof, then whether I accept the claim or not is wholly a matter a faith. But if I say that the substance of water is characterized by having at all times two parts hydrogen to one part oxygen, then I can show this in an experiment to prove the result.

　　🔹 如果我说"耶稣基督是人类的拯救者",但没有提供任何经验证明,那么,我是否接受这个说法就完全是一个信仰问题。但如果我说,水这种物质可以描绘为在任何时候都具有两个氢原子和一个氧原子的东西,那么,我就可以用实验去证明这个结果。(江怡译)

　　例 **7-46**　If that is so, then the problem for us moderns is clear: In the face of the disenchantment of nature brought about by the scientific revolution, we experience a gap between knowledge and wisdom that has the consequence of divesting our lives of meaning.

　　🔹 如果是这样的话,那么我们现代人的问题就很清楚了:面对科学革命带来的对自然的去魅,我们体验到了知识与智慧之间的鸿沟,这个鸿沟结果会迫使我们放弃有意义的生活。(江怡译)

　　例 **7-47**　If one focuses on the First Critique, then one is usually concerned with the success of the argument of the transcendental deduction: Here Kant tries to show that in order to experience objects at all we have to presuppose the operations what he calls the 'categories of the understanding' and hence a human subject who understands, that is, who unifies the blooming, buzzing confusion of perceptual experience under concepts.

　　🔹 如果我们关注的是第一批判,那么我们通常关心的是先验演绎论证的成功:康德在这里试图表明,为了体验对象,我们就必须预设他所谓的"知性范畴"的运作,由此才有对之加以理解的人类主体,即后者把大量的、杂乱无章的感觉经验统一到概念之下。(江怡译)

　　例 **7-48**　If free will did exist, it would be possible for a person to choose a course of action against all forces of heredity and training which have been building in the opposite direction.

　　🔹 假如自由意志存在,一个人就有可能选择一种行为方式,对抗所有正在朝反方向发展的遗传和训练力量。(严忠志译)

　　例 **7-49**　If the world is deterministic, then the future is conditioned to be what it is by the past.

　　如果世间万物是先定的话,那么过去已决定未来的样子。(严忠志译)

　　例 **7-50**　But if that is true — if reason can criticize all things — then surely it must also criticize itself. Therefore, there has to be a *meta-critique* of critique if the critique is to be truly effective.

🌐 但是，如果这是真的，就是说，如果理性可以批判一切事物，那么，它也一定可以批判自身。因此，如果这种批判的确有效，这里就一定有一种对批判的元批判。（江怡译）

例 7-51 So, if reason must criticize all things, there must also be a meta-critique of reason. But if that is so, then what prevents this meta-critique from becoming scepticism, radical and total scepticism?

🌐 所以，如果理性一定要批判一切事物，也就一定有一种对理性的元批判。但如果是这样的话，那么什么东西可以防止这种元批判变成一种激进彻底的怀疑论呢？（江怡译）

例 7-52 That is, as he puts it in his diaries, once human beings have lifted themselves above the level of cattle, then the 'basic', 'loftiest', and most 'sublime' idea of human existence becomes absolutely essential: belief in the immortality of the soul. Once this belief breaks down, as Dostoevsky saw in the nihilism or indifferentism of the Russian educated classes of the 1860s, then suicide is the only logical conclusion.

🌐 他在日记中这样写道，一旦人类把自己提升到牲畜之上的程度，那么，关于人类存在的"基本的""最高的"和最为"崇高的"观念就变成了绝对是完全必要的：相信灵魂的不朽。一旦这个信念坍塌了，就像陀思妥耶夫斯基在19世纪60年代的俄罗斯知识分子阶层的虚无主义或麻木不仁中看到的那样，自杀就成了唯一的逻辑结果。（江怡译）

第八单元

标点的使用

英语标点常用的有句号(.)、问号(?)、感叹号(!)、连字符(-)、破折号(—)、省略号(…)、括号(圆括号( )，方括号[ ]，大括号{ })、双引号(" ")、单引号(' ')、斜号(/)、逗号(,)、分号(;)、冒号(:)等多种，大体上与中文标点符号用法类似，但要注意英语中没有中文的顿号(、)和书名号(《》)，英语中用逗号来代替顿号，用引号(或斜体字或黑体大写)来代替书名号。专有名称通常首字母大写(冠词与介词首字母除非位于最前面，否则一般不必大写)或下划线表示。英语中的拉丁语通常用斜体，表示强调的词语常用斜体或黑体字表示(非汉语的双引号表示)。圆括号内不能再使用圆括号；圆括号内为单个词语时，圆括号内不用标点符号；圆括号内为完整句子时，句号放在括号内，但是当圆括号内的句子包含在前面句子中时(如括号内容作为前面句子词语的注解)，那么句号要放在圆括号之外。使用双引号时，原直接引文或摘录内容中的双引号要变为单引号；直接引用或摘录文字(不论是词语还是句子)，逗号或句号要放在右引号之内，但语言学、哲学和神学等学科用单引号来分隔的词语除外，逗号和句号要放在单引号之后；此外，问号或感叹号除非是直接引文或摘录文字中原有的，否则要放在右引号之后；分号或冒号则总是放在右引号之后。详细句例可参阅《芝加哥大学论文写作指南》和《美国心理协会写作手册》。

学术英语中最常用、也最易出错的标点符号是逗号、分号、冒号、破折号，而且这四种标点符号与句法关系甚大。所以，本单元主要介绍这四种标点符号的用法。

一、逗号的用法

(一)引导性成分

一般而言，短的引导性成分无须用逗号将其与后面的句子主语分隔，长的引导性成分可用逗号与后面的句子主语分隔。但位于句首的引导性副词表达对后面句子的总体评论性意见(如 absurdly, actually, allegedly, ambiguously, amazingly, briefly, certainly, clearly, evidently, fortunately, frankly, generally, incongruously, incredibly, ironically, paradoxically, specifically, strangely, surprisingly, typically, undoubtedly, unfortuantley 等)时，或者起到承上启下的过渡作用(accordingly, also, besides, consequently, conversely, equqlly, furthermore, hence, however, instead, likewise, meanwhile, moreover, nevertheless, rather, similarly, still, therefore, thus 等)时，可用逗号将引导性词语与后面的句子分隔。引导性成分看起来容易与句子主语混淆时，可用逗号将引导性成分与句子主语分隔。当一个短语或从句同时修饰后面的两个主句时，可用逗号将前面的短语或从句与后面的主句分隔，但后面的两个主句不能用逗号分隔。

例 8-1　At first the patient felt numbness in the legs and then a pricking sensation.

🔴 译　最初，病人觉得两腿麻木，继之有刺痛感觉。（洪班信译）

例 8-2　From such evocative beginnings public interest in dinosaurs has been nurtured and maintained ever since.

🔴 译　从这些令人记忆深刻的开端起，公众对恐龙的兴趣就被培养起来，并一直接保持下去。（史立群译）

例 8-3　During the early part of the 19th century it was becoming recognized (though not without dispute) that the rocks of the Earth, and the fossils that they contained, could be divided into qualitatively different types.

🔴 译　在 19 世纪早期，人们逐渐认识到（尽管不地争议），地球上的岩石以及其中包含的化石可以从性质上分为不同的类型。（史立群译）

例 8-4　Not surprisingly, given the requirement of unanimous agreement among the fifteen governments before a decision could be taken, there had not been much progress by the time the *Amsterdam Treaty* was negotiated.

🔴 译　鉴于需要取得 15 国全体一致同意后才能作出决定，到进行《阿约》谈判时还没有取得多少成果就不足为奇了。（戴炳然译）

例 8-5　Politically, the single market has enjoyed a remarkable degree of approval across the spectrum from federalists to eurosceptics.

🔴 译　政治上，单一市场深得从联邦主义者到欧洲怀疑论者的各个派别的嘉许。（戴炳然译）

例 8-6　Strictly, theories of myth are theories of some much larger domain, with myth a mere subset.

🔴 译　严格来说，关于神话的理论是某种涵盖了更广阔领域的理论，而神话只是其中的一个子集。（刘象愚译）

例 8-7　Unfortunately, this fertile intellectual ground was not so obviously available to palaeontologists.

译 遗憾的是，这片丰饶的知识沃土并没有为古生物学家带来明显的益处。（史立群译）

例 8-8 <u>Self-evidently</u>, genetic mechanisms could not be studied in fossil creatures, so it seemed that they could offer no material evidence to the intellectual thrust of evolutionary studies during much of the remainder of the 20th century.

　　译 人们无法研究化石生物的遗传机制，这是不言而喻的，因此，在 20 世纪余下的大部分时间里，它们似乎没有给进化研究的学术突破提供实质性的证据。（史立群译）

例 8-9 <u>More positively</u>, the euro could, although the Union's monetary policies have initially been inward-looking, become the basis for an exchange-rate policy that favours international monetary stability.

　　译 更为积极的是，虽说欧盟的货币政策最初是向内的，欧元却可以成为有利于国际货币稳定的汇率政策的基础。（戴炳然译）

例 8-10 <u>Rather disconcertingly</u>, these earliest remains are not rare, solitary examples of one type of creature: the common ancestor of all later dinosaurs.

　　译 非常棘手的是，这些最早的化石并不是同一种动物罕见的、个别的标本：即所有后来出现的恐龙的共同祖先之标本。（史立群译）

例 8-11 <u>Ironically</u>, many compact digital cameras have more megapixels than digital SLRs and picture quality is still compromised.

　　译 讽刺的是，许多袖珍数码相机比数码单反相机高出百万像素，但图像质量并不怎么样。

例 8-12 <u>Generally</u>, the part-timers work in low-status, low-wage occupations.

　　译 一般说来，做兼职工作的人从事的都是地位低下、工资微薄的职业。（闫文培译）

例 8-13 <u>Briefly</u>, these substances can be identified analytically.

　　译 简而言之，这些物质可以用分析方法加以鉴定。（闫文培译）

例 8-14 <u>Furthermore</u>, through the work of science's helpmeet, technology, our lives have been transformed and improved to an extent unimaginable to someone from the ancient world, or even indeed to our great-grandparents.

　　译 而且，通过科学的合作者（即技术）的工作，我们的生活已经发生的转变和提高是古人难以想象的，甚至我们的祖辈也是难以想象的。（江怡译）

例 8-15 However, he underestimates the scale of the problem

译 然而,他低估了问题的严重性。

例 8-16 To appreciate this, it is necessary first to consider the case of a shelled creature living in the sea, such an oyster.

译 为了理解这一点,我们有必要首先考虑一下生活在海里的贝壳类动物的情况,例如牡蛎。(史立群译)

例 8-17 Once buried, the shell has the potential to become a fossil as it becomes trapped under an increasingly thick layer of sediment.

译 一旦被埋葬,随着它陷入越来越厚的沉积层之下,贝壳就有可能变成化石。(史立群译)

例 8-18 As regards security, the fight against cross-border crime remains mainly in the intergovernmental third pillar, whose designation, since competence regarding free movement has been transferred to the Community, has been reduced to 'Police and Judicial Co-operation in Criminal Matters'.

译 至于安全,打击边境犯罪仍主要属于政府间第三支柱的职责。鉴于有关人员自由流动的权限已经移交至共同体,第三支柱的名称已经缩小至"刑事事务上的警察与司法合作"。(戴炳然译)

例 8-19 As previously mentioned, patients differ in their tissue sensitivity.

译 如前所述,机体组织的敏感程度因病人而异。(洪班信译)

例 8-20 As far as the patient's liver is concerned, there is nothing to worry about.

译 就病人的肝脏来说,没有什么可以担心的。(洪班信译)

例 8-21 In line with ever-growing concern about crime, the *Amsterdam Treaty* extended the list to include trafficking in persons, offences against children, and corruption; and money-laundering, forging money, and 'cyber-crime' have been added since.

译 针对人们对跨界犯罪的日益关注,《阿约》在犯罪形式的清单中增加了人口走私、伤害儿童和腐败,而后又增加了洗钱、制造假币与"网络犯罪"。(戴炳然译)

例 8-22 Because of the volume of work, the Commission has recently sought to return some of these responsibilities to the member states' competition authorities.

㊎ 由于工作量太大，委员会最近在寻求将某些职责交还成员国的竞争管理当局。（戴炳然译）

例 8-23　Along with the subsidies, non-tariff barriers proliferated in those years, becoming the main obstacle to trade between member states.

㊎ 除补贴外，非关税壁垒也在那些年蔓延滋生，成为成员国间贸易的主要障碍。（戴炳然译）

例 8-24　With the intense relationship engendered by their economic integration, the member states have a special need for such cooperation.

㊎ 随着成员国间有关系因经济一体化而强化，它们对这种合作有着特别的需求。（戴炳然译）

例 8-25　To allay fears that widening would result in weakening, there was also the condition that the Union should have 'the capacity to absorb new members while maintaining the momentum of integration'.

㊎ 为缓解成员国对"扩大将导致弱化"的担忧，条件中还包括欧盟应该具有"在吸纳新成员的同时保持一体化势头的能力"。（戴炳然译）

例 8-26　To illustrate a few of the trials and tribulations inherent in any such programme of palaeontological investigation, we will examine a rather familiar and well-studied dinosaur: Iguanodon.

㊎ 为了展示所有这些古生物学研究项目必然经历的艰难困苦，我们将分析一种大家非常熟悉而且研究透彻的恐龙：禽龙。（史立群译）

例 8-27　If pre-modern cultures were generally less bothered by the meaning of life than Franz Kafka, the same would seem to be true of postmodern ones.

㊎ 如果说前现代文化大体上不像弗兰兹·卡夫卡那般为人生的意义所烦排扰，后现代文化似乎也是如此。（朱新伟译）

（二）插入语和修饰成分

句中的插入语、分词结构、同位语或非限制性定语从句放在两个逗号之间；句末的非限制性定语从句与被修饰词或中心词之间要用逗号分隔；限制性定语从句无须逗号分隔。

插入语虽然会打断读者的注意力，影响句子的通顺性。但插入语有多种语言效果，如表达从属和修饰关系、举例、评论、引用、增加题外话，或者扩展一个概念。对事件叙述和情况描述起到一定的缓和或复杂化的效果，插入语能增加文章的空间信息容量，在信息密集推送时给读者以一定的喘息空间。

例 8-28　Dreaming, like any other mental state, is subject to pathological deformation.

🔘 梦和其他任何精神状态一样可能出现病理性异常。（韩芳译）

例 8-29　But the three structural funds, though at first small, grew steadily and were available to respond to the demand for a major expansion in the 1980s when the Community was enlarged to the south.

🔘 这 3 个结构性基金尽管起初规模很小，但都得到稳定的增长，并足以满足 20 世纪 80 年代共同体一次重大发展——向南扩大——的要求。（戴炳然译）

例 8-30　The EEC was also, thanks to French insistence on surrounding the common market with a common external tariff, able to enter trade negotiations on level terms with the United States.

🔘 由于法国的坚持，欧洲经济共同体实行统一的对外关税，从而能够以平等的地位与美国进行贸易谈判。（戴炳然译）

例 8-31　Most politicians as well as business organizations, having experienced the benefits of stable exchange rates, favoured the single currency.

🔘 尝到了汇率稳定的甜头，大多数政治家和商业机构都赞成单一货币。

例 8-32　The cost of exchange-rate transactions, estimated at ecu 13~19 billion a year, which bear particularly hard on individuals and small firms, would be eliminated.

🔘 有了汇率机制，汇率兑换的成本将可省去，而这笔费用估计每年高达 130 亿到 190 亿埃居，对个人与小企业是格外沉重的负担。（戴炳然译）

例 8-33　The other four founder states, Belgium, Italy, Luxembourg, and the Netherlands, also saw the new Community as a means to ensure peace by binding Germany within strong European institutions.

🔘 其他 4 个创始国——比利时、意大利、卢森堡与荷兰——也认为，新的共同体能将德国约束于强有力的欧洲机构内，不失为保障和平的手段。（戴炳然译）

例 8-34　This kind of proposal, which Robert McCarley and I made in our original 1977 papers about the activation-synthesis hypothesis, has never been popular.

🔄 我和罗伯特·麦卡利在1977年关于激活—整合假说的原创论文里就已提出这种观点，但从未获得广泛认同。（韩芳译）

例 8-35　This story, which seems so crazy to my waking mind, seemed so normal to me in the dream.

🔄 这个对清醒而言如此疯狂的故事，在梦中的我看来却是如此正常。（韩芳译）

例 8-36　The basic hypothesis, for which evidence was previously consistent and positive but not impressively robust, is that rapid eye movement (REM) sleep subserves consolidation of memory.

🔄 最基本的假说是快动眼睡眠有助于巩固记忆，这一假说以前一直有许多正面的证据支持，但均不够分量。（韩芳译）

例 8-37　We can see, then, that nightmares, however unpleasant, are normal events in sleep, suggestion that the maintenance of these emotional systems of the brain, which ensure our survival, may be one of the functions of brain activation in sleep.

🔄 到时可以发现，无论多么不愉快的噩梦，都是睡眠中的正常事件，这意味着维系这些保证人类生存的大脑情感系统，可能是睡眠中大脑激活的功能之一。（韩芳译）

例 8-38　This suggests that serotonin, which is known to be a potent inhibitor of REM, may interact with brain dopamine systems and upset the balance between inhibition and excitation of the motor systems in sleep.

🔄 这表明5-羟色胺作为已知的快动眼睡眠强效抵制剂，可能与大脑多巴胺系统产生交互作用，从而扰乱睡眠时运动系统的抑制—兴奋平衡。（韩芳译）

例 8-39　These generalizations, which all flow from neurobiological work on the state control systems of the brain stem, have far-reaching implications for a general theory of mind as well as for a specific theory of dreaming.

🔄 这种研究脑干状态控制系统的神经生物学工作成果，对于精神的一般理论和梦的特殊理论都有着深远的意义。（韩芳译）

例 8-40　The removal of non-tariff barriers was already implicit in the *Rome Treaty*, which prohibited 'all measures having equivalent effect' to import quotas.

🔄《罗马条约》中禁止与进口配额"具有同等作用的一切措施"，其实已包

含消除非关税壁垒的目标。(戴炳然译)

注意下面句中的限制性定语从句前后无须逗号分隔。

例 8-41　In fact, dreams from which we spontaneously awaken are characteristically dominated by anxiety, fear, and anger.

🔵译 事实上，那些能让人自发觉醒的梦通常都被焦虑、恐惧和愤怒所主宰。(韩芳译)

例 8-42　The system that has provided a framework for half a century of peace is regarded as a guarantee of future stability.

🔵译 半个世纪以来，这一体系为保持和平提供了一种架构，被看作是未来稳定的一种保证。(戴炳然译)

例 8-43　The focus on the economic aspects of integration that has been common among British politicians has diverted attention away from this underlying motive and restricted their ability to play an influential and constructive part in such development.

🔵译 而在英国，政治家们普遍关注的是经济一体化，这便使他们的注意力转离了这一体系的根本动机，并阻碍其在此类发展上产生重大与建设性的作用。(戴炳然译)

例 8-44　A theory which contends that myth arises and functions to explain physical processes will likely restrict myth to societies supposedly bereft of science. By contrast, a theory which contends that myth arises and functions to unify society may well deem myth acceptable and perhaps even indispensable to all societies.

🔵译 认为神话的产生和功能是要解释物质过程的那种理论很可能会把神话限定在尚出现科学的社会中。相反，认为神话的产生和功能是为了统合社会的那种理论则会把神话看作是一切社会形态来说均可接受的，甚至是必不可少的。(刘象愚译)

例 8-45　The feeling that the Union should provide more effective military backing for its common policy in former Yugoslavia spurred governments to strengthen its capacity in the field of defence.

🔵译 欧盟应该为其对前南斯拉夫的共同政策提供更为有效的军事支持的想法，促使各国政府加强欧盟在防务领域的能力。(戴炳然译)

例 8-46　The chances that an early hominin skeleton would have been preserved in the fossil record are very small.

🔄 早期人类骨骼保存下来成为化石记录的概率非常小。(冯兴无译)

(三)两个独立分句的连接

两个独立分句之间不能用逗号直接连接;用逗号连接时,要在第二个独立分句前加连词(如 and, but, yet, for, so, or, nor 等),且逗号置于连词前。

例 8-47 His knowledge of the brain was so incomplete that he was forced to abandon his famous 'Project for a Scientific Psychology', and he turned to dreaming for insights about what he construed to be the dynamic unconscious.

🔄 他(指西格蒙德·弗洛伊德,Sigmund Freud)对大脑的了解是如此不充分,以至于他不得不抛弃自己著名的"科学心理学方略",转而向梦寻求灵感,即后来所谓的动态潜意识。(韩芳译)

例 8-48 The killing is definitely intentional, and the cause is not revenge but sexual frustration.

🔄 这弑父无疑是蓄意的,其原因也不是出于报复,而是出于性挫折。(刘象愚译)

例 8-49 Masculine gallantry and flattery are seen simply as attempts to keep woman in their places, and the most 'feminine' woman is the one who best fulfils male fantasies.

🔄 男性的殷勤和奉承被看作只是企图给女人画地为牢,最"有女人味"的女人是最能满足男性幻想的女人。(朱刚和麻晓蓉译)

例 8-50 The drive for originality usually entails a very negative attitude toward one's predecessors, and the history of philosophy inevitably loses its interest.

🔄 这种追求独创性的驱动往往需要对其先行者持一种完全否定的态度,所以哲学的历史难免会丧失其重要性。(孙喆译)

例 8-51 Happiness for Aristotle is attained by virtue, and virtue is above all a social practice rather than an attitude of mind.

🔄 在亚里士多德看来,幸福是通过美德实现的,美德道德首先是一种社会实践,而不是一种心灵态度。(朱新伟译)

例 8-52 On the contrary, virtuous people for him (Aristotle) are those who reap pleasure from doing good, and those who do the decent thing without enjoying it are not in his view truly virtuous.

🔄 相反,在他(指亚里士多德)看来,具有美德的人就是那些从好事当中获得快乐的人,那些没有从做正派的事当中感到快乐的人不是真正具有美德

的人。(朱新伟译)

例 8-53 Academic philosophy in England has for some time been largely limited to logic and theory of knowledge, and there is a tendency to confine philosophy to this sense and to regard its traditional association with general moral and intellectual systems as an error.

[译] 有一个时期，英国的学院派哲学大多都只是讨论逻辑和知识论，倾向于把哲学限定在这一范围，而将其传统上与一般道德体系和思想体系之间的联系看作一种错误。(江怡译)

例 8-54 The purpose of this short book is to explain why this has happened, why that fact is important, and what it might entail for the activity of philosophy now and in the future.

[译] 这本小书的目的就是要解释，为什么会发生这种情况，为什么这个事实很是重要，以及它对现在和未来的哲学活动意味着什么。(江怡译)

例 8-55 Descartes spoke of a tree of knowledge and the quest for method sought a new systematic integration of the different sciences, but philosophy became progressively more isolated from the natural sciences and mathematics.

[译] 笛卡尔描述了一种知识树结构，方法性地探索寻求一种不同学科的新的有机整合，但哲学却进而更加脱离了自然科学和数学。(孙喆译)

(四)排比成分

三个或三个以上的项目(单词、短语或句子)并列时，一般在最后一项前使用连词，其余各项用逗号隔开。但当排比或并列成分内部有逗号时，用分号而不是逗号隔开排比或并列成分(参阅第二单元的对称句与平行句)。

例 8-56 Futures have, however, become less secure, particularly in those critical areas of people's lives — employment, housing, and pensions.

[译] 但是，未来变得更为不确定，尤其是民众生活的关键领域，如就业、住房和养老金。(张罗和陆赟译)

例 8-57 It was a way of life dedicated to power, profit, and the business of material survival, rather than to fostering the values of human sharing and solidarity.

[译] 这是一种生活方式，追求权力、利润和物质生存条件，而不是培育人类共享和团结等各种价值。(朱新伟译)

例 8-58 Some discriminatory regulations still, in 2000, remained in a few important sectors of the economy, including air transport, electric power, telecommunications, and financial services.

译 在 2000 年，在一些重要的经济领域，包括空运、电力、电信与金融服务等，仍然存在某些歧视性法规。（戴炳然译）

例 8-59 With the challenging of almost every traditional value, belief, and institution, the conditions were now ripe for art to pose the most searching questions about the fate of Western culture as such, and be yond that the destiny of humanity itself.

译 几乎每一种传统价值、信念和制度都发出了挑战，时机已然成熟，艺术可以提出关于西方文化本身之命运的最根本问题，并进而提出关于人性本身的命运问题。（朱新伟译）

例 8-60 What marks modernist thought from one end to another is the belief that human existence is *contingent* — that it has no ground, goal, direction, or necessity, and that our species might quite easily never have emerged on the planet.

译 现代主义思想的标志性特征是一种信念，认为人的存在是偶然的——没有根基、没有目标、没有方向、没有必然性，人类本来很有可能从未出现在这颗星球上。（朱新伟译）

例 8-61 It is a question of the way we talk about things, not a feature of things themselves, like texture, weight, or colour.

译 这是我们谈论事情的某种方式，而非像纹理、重量、颜色那样，是事物本身的属性。（朱新伟译）

例 8-62 Sport involves tribal loyalties and rivalries, symbolic rituals, fabulous legends, iconic heroes, epic battles, aesthetic beauty, physical fulfillment, intellectual satisfaction, sublime spectaculars, and a profound sense of belonging.

译 体育包含不同团体间的忠诚与敌对、象征性的仪式、炫目的传奇故事、偶像般的英雄、史诗般的战斗、华丽的美感、身体上的实现、精神上的满足、壮丽的奇观和强烈的归属感。（朱新伟译）

例 8-63 Interpretation has always been the main goal of content analysis, whether for medical diagnosis (in the hands of the early Greeks), fortune telling (in the work of Artemidorus), religious prophecy (in the *Bible*), or psychological divinations (in the proto-scientific schema of Sigmund Freud).

译 无论是为了医学论断（古希腊人）、算命（阿尔米多鲁斯的著作）、宗教

预言(《圣经》)，还是进行心理占卜(西格蒙德·弗洛伊德的原始科学架构)，释梦从来都是内容分析的主要目的。(韩芳译)

例 8-64 One might attempt a *wertfrei* account of the terrain, giving a narrative of what philosophers are doing here and there, staying above the battle, and accepting the by now mandatory distain for philosophy's past.

🌐 有人可能会尝试对这个领域做纯客观的描述，叙述哲学家们在各个方面的所作所为，那么他将置身于风口浪尖，承受现在人们对哲学历史的蔑视。(孙喆译)

例 8-65 Under these circumstances, Christianity offered itself to the world, armed with the strength of the *Mosaic Law*, and delivered from the weight of its fetters.

🌐 正当此际，基督教乃横空出世，彼恃摩西律法之强护其身，复能脱于其教条底负荷。(刘怡译)

例 8-66 For tragedy, there is often enough no answer to why individual lives are crushed and mutilated beyond endurance, why injustice and oppression appear to reign sovereign in human affairs, or why men are deceived into chewing the roasted flesh of their own slaughtered children.

🌐 悲剧经常会展现没有答案的事件：为何个体生命会被碾碎或伤害到无法忍受的程度？为何不公正与压迫似乎主宰着人类事务？为何父亲会受到欺骗，去咀嚼自己遇害的孩子那烤焦的肉？(朱新伟译)

(五)句子中任何需要停顿的地方

出于分隔、强调或节奏的需要，在句子中任何需要停顿的地方，都可使用逗号。

例 8-67 In solids, very few, if any, of the molecules are free to move from one point to another.

🌐 在固体中，没有分子可以自由地从一个点移动到另一个点。

例 8-68 The hero's revenge, if the parricide is even committed knowingly, is, then, understandable: who would not consider killing one's would-be killer?

🌐 由此，即便这位英雄的弑父是有意为之，他的报复也是可以理解的：谁不曾想过要杀死那个想谋害自己的人呢？(刘象愚译)

例 8-69 Myth resolves or, more precisely, tempers a contradiction 'dialectically', by providing either a mediating middle term or an analogous, but more easily resolved, contradiction.

> 神话化解，或者更确切地说，是"辩证地"调和矛盾；它的方式有两种，或是提供一个折中的调解条件，或者提供一个类似的、但更易化解的矛盾。（刘象愚译）

例 8-70 Perhaps, then, pre-modern peoples in general, despite Heidegger's very general claims, were less plagued by the meaning-of-life question than we moderns are.

> 因此，尽管有海德格尔极为普遍的主张，前现代的人也许不像我们现代人那么受人生的意义问题困扰。（朱新伟译）

例 8-71 What interests me is that in all three of his Critiques, Kant's focus, like Rousseau's, is on man, not on the transcendental, nor on the natural world, but on human experience, and the creative powers of the human mind and the human imagination.

> 使我感兴趣的是，在他所有的三大批判中，康德的焦点，像卢梭一样，集中于人，不是超验的或自然的世界，而是人的经验，人的思考和人的想象的创造性力量。（董乐山译）

例 8-72 But removal of the longer term risks of exchange-rate instability would be the main economic benefit, definitively eliminating the exchange-rate risk, not just from trade but also, most significantly, from cross-border investments and from those that depend on reliable access to the Union-wide market: Both of growing importance for a dynamic European economy.

> 不过汇率机制给经济带来的主要好处在于消除汇率波动的较长时期的风险：它将决然地消除汇率风险，不仅是贸易方面的汇率风险，而且最重要的是在跨国投资方面，以及那些有赖于能毫无风险地进入整个欧盟市场的企业的汇率风险；而这两方面对欧盟经济的活力有着愈来愈重要的作用。（戴炳然译）

例 8-73 For Hamann, in another uncanny prediction of later philosophical developments, namely the linguistic turn, the separation between reason and experience, or form and content, is impossible because thought depends on language, which is, of course, a mixture of both.

> 在哈曼看来，理性与经验，或者说形式与内容之间的分离是不可能的，因为思想依赖于语言，它当然是两者的混合；这是对之后的哲学发展，即向

语言学方面转向的另一个不可思议的预言。(江怡译)

例 8-74 These hopes were qualified by reservations, particularly about the price of progress; but progress, they believed, was possible, if not certain, and the possibility of its rested, not in an inscrutable Divine Grace, or the capricious hands of Fortune, but in man's own hands.

🔵 译 有人对这些希望是抱保留态度的,特别是在进步的代价上。但是他们相信,进步还是可能的,即使不是肯定的,而进步的可能性不在莫测高深的天意,也不在无法捉摸的命运,而在人自己的手中。(董乐山译)

二、分号的用法

分号可以无须用 and/or/but 而直接连接两个语义相关的独立句子。这种情况下,使用分号比句号更能显示两个句子之间的紧密联系。分号之后经常紧跟连接副词 however, instead, therefore 和 thus 等,并且这些词语之后跟逗号,但分号之后的连词 but 和 and 一般后面不跟逗号。例如:

例 8-75 There is no reason for us to think that development stops once we have acquired language; we go on throughout our lives needing to reconstruct our brains and our minds.

🔵 译 没有理由认为一旦掌握了语言,发育就会停止,其实我们终生都需要重建大脑和思想。(韩芳译)

例 8-76 We begin with logic, so we will recognize good arguments when we meet them; we go next to mathematics, because even children can learn it.

🔵 译 我们从学习逻辑开始,这样我们能认识到所遇到的好论点;接着学习数学,因为即便是孩童也能学会数学。(孙喆译)

例 8-77 In any case, the search for truth no longer has any positive interest in theism; furthermore, it must be seen as in a polemical relation to Christianity.

🔵 译 无论如何,探索真理不再对有神论有任何积极的兴趣,而且它必须被看成关于基督教的论战。(孙喆译)

例 8-78 For allegory, things do not carry their meanings on their faces; instead, they must be grasped as signs of some underlying 'text' or latent truth, usually of a moral or religious kind.

🔵 译 在寓言中,事物的意义并未直接呈现于表面;相反,它们必须被理解为某种"文本"或潜在真理的符号,通常是道德或宗教的符号。(朱新伟译)

例 8-79　Religion, art, and sexuality may have been more central to public affairs than they are today; but they could also act as the obedient handmaidens of political power, and for much the same reasons.

🔄 过去的宗教、艺术和性在公共事务中的作用也许比现在更加重要；但是，出于同样的原因，它们也可能成为政治权力的忠诚侍女。（朱新伟译）

例 8-80　By the industry and zeal of the Europeans, it has been widely diffused to the most distant shores of Asia and Africa; and by the means of their colonies has been firmly established from Canada to Chili, in a world unknown to the ancients.

🔄 懒此辈欧洲人之勤劳热忱，基督教已惠及亚细亚与阿非利加远海之滨；凭此辈欧洲人之殖民地，是教固已傲立于加拿大直至智利——此方域实非古人所能知。（刘怡译）

例 8-81　Power and wealth belong fairly obviously to the instrumental category; and anything which is instrumental cannot have the fundamental quality which the meaning of life seems to demand, since it exists for the sake of something more fundamental than itself.

🔄 权力和财富明显属于工具性的范畴；而任何工具性的事物都不具有人生的意义看起来所要求的那种根本特质，因为这些事物之所以存在，是为了比它更为根本的东西。（朱新伟译）

例 8-82　'Will to Power' in Nietzsche's thought means the tendency of all things to realize, expand, and augment themselves; and it is reasonable to see this as an end in itself, just as Aristotle regards human flourishing as an end in itself.

🔄 在尼采的思想中，"权力意志"表示所有事物都倾向于实现、扩张和增殖自我；我们有理由把这种倾向本身当做目的，就像亚里士多德把人的发展本身当成目的一样。（朱新伟译）

三、冒号的使用

使用冒号要注意在完整的句子之后，也就是冒号前面的是一个有主语和谓语的完整句子。冒号后面可以是单词、短语或句子，在内容上起解释、例证和引用等作用。如：

例 8-83　A bad reader is like a bad translator: He interprets literally when he ought to paraphrase and paraphrases when he ought to interpret literally.

译 一个拙劣的读者就好比一个拙劣的译者:他会在应该意译的时候直译,而需要他直译的时候意译。(朱树飏译)

例 8-84 These findings were a blow to two major theories of the moon's origin: ①That it had fissioned from the earth and ② that it was a sort of uncooked supermeteorite. The findings supported a less popular theory: That the moon was a separate planet, captured by the earth.

译 这些发现对于月球起源的两大理论是一个打击,这二学说即:①月球自地球分裂出来,②月球是某种未至成熟的超级陨石。探测的发现却支持一个赞同者较少的理论:月球是一独立的行星,被地球牵引。(颜元叔译)

例 8-85 There were both economic and political motives for each of the three projects: The benefits of economic rationality; and the consolidation of the Community system as a framework for peaceful relations among the member states.

译 这三项计划各有其经济与政治动机:发挥经济合理性的好处,强化共同体制度以巩固成员国间的和平关系。(戴炳然译)

例 8-86 Cross-border criminal activity grows for reasons similar to those that drive cross-border economic activity: Advancing technology, particularly in transport and communications.

译 跨境犯罪活动增加与跨境经济活动增加的原因相似,即技术的进步,特别是交通与通信技术的进步。(戴炳然译)

例 8-87 In this area, a woman's supposed passivity, her receptivity to outside influence, could, ironically, be claimed as an advantage: She might prove more receptive, more open, to becoming a channel for the voice of God.

译 具有讽刺意味的是,在这个领域,女性被认为应有的被动性和对外界影响的接受性,倒可以说是优势了:她可能会更容易、更乐于成为神的传声筒。(朱刚和麻晓蓉译)

例 8-88 The group initiated more organized campaigns around issues that had already been clearly defined: Women's urgent need for better education and for increased possibilities of employment, as well as the improvement of the legal position of married women.

译 该团体围绕业已明确的问题——妇女迫切需要更好的教育、更多的工作机会以及提高已婚妇女的法律地位——发起了更多有组织的活动。(朱刚和麻晓蓉译)

例 8-89 The West find itself faced with a full-blooded metaphysical onslaught at just the historical point that it has, so to speak, philosophically disarmed. As far as belief goes, postmodernism prefers to travel light: It has beliefs, to be sure, but it does not have faith.

译 西方世界发现自己正遭受一种狂热的形而上学层面的攻击,而自己却处于可以说是哲学上被解除了武装的历史时刻。关涉信念之处,后现代主义宁愿轻装上路:后现代主义诚然有各种各样的信念,但没有信仰。(朱新伟译)

例 8-90 Let's begin our analytical odyssey by accepting the most broad, general, and indisputable definition of dreaming: Mental activity occurring in sleep.

译 对梦的分析之旅始于对梦最宽泛、全面且无可争辩的定义:梦即睡眠时大脑的活动。(韩芳译)

例 8-91 With regard to mental state, we need to note two important points: One phenomenological, the other methodological.

译 关于精神状态,我们需要注意两个重要的方面:一个是现象学的,一个是方法论的。(韩芳译)

例 8-92 The mechanics of meiosis are relatively simple: Two rounds of chromosome division are completed without a round of DNA replication in between.

译 减数分裂的机制相对简单:染色体两次分裂后,两次分裂中间DNA不再进行复制。

例 8-93 For phenomenology, the term 'mental state' implies global features: Every aspect of mental activity changes when the mental state changes.

译 在现象学方面,"精神状态"意味着整体性,当精神状态改变时,精神活动的每一个方面都会发生改变。(韩芳译)

例 8-94 The distinction is made with ease in other fields: Consider linguistics, where grammar and syntax are complementary; consider poetry, where meter and verse enhance one another; and consider the visual arts, where genre and subject matter interact for strong effect.

译 其他领域,两者的区别显而易见:就语言学来说,语法和句法互为补充;拿诗歌来讲,韵律和诗体相辅相成;而在视觉艺术领域,形式和题材相

得益彰。(韩芳译)

例 8-95　Aristotle goes on to argue that it is indeed the case that every change involves three factors: A subject and contrary states of that subject.

🔘 亚里士多德继而论述道：确实，每种变化都涉及三个因素：主体与主体的相反状态。(孙喆译)

例 8-96　It is typical of the modern era that what one might call the symbolic dimension of human life is pushed steadily to the margins. Within this dimension, three areas have traditionally been vital: Religion, culture, and sexuality.

🔘 现代时期的一个典型特征是，人类生命的所谓"象征维度"被一直挤到了边缘。在这一维度之内，有三个领域在传统上至关重要：宗教、文化和性。(朱新伟译)

例 8-97　For me, the meaning of the dream is transparent: I am anxious about my property and about entrusting it to people who are careless about their own houses.

🔘 对我而言，该梦的意义是显而易见的：我为自己的财产感到焦虑，担心它所托非人，因为这些人对自己的房子都毫不在意。(韩芳译)

例 8-98　In relation to this scientific conception of the world, the propositions of metaphysics are not so much false as simply meaningless: They have no cognitive content.

🔘 与这种科学的世界观相关，形而上学的命题之所以为假，并不仅仅是由于它们没有意义：它们没有认识内容。(江怡译)

例 8-99　In summary, I have made two historical claims for Continental philosophy: It is a professional self-description and it is a cultural feature.

🔘 综上所述，我对欧陆哲学作出了两种历史断言：它是一种专业的自我描述，也是一种文化特征。(江怡译)

例 8-100　These are the cardinal cognitive features of dreaming: Loss of awareness of self (self-reflective awareness); loss of orientational stability) loss of directed thought; reduction in logical reasoning; and, last but not least, poor memory both within and after the dream.

🔘 梦的主要认知特点如下：自觉意识丧失、定向稳定感丧失、定向思维能力消失、逻辑推理能力下降，最后但同样重要的是，梦中和梦后记忆均出现缺失。(韩芳译)

例 8-101　And we have already noted that dreaming can be so unpleasantly exciting as to provoke awakening, leading to another erroneous assumption: That all dreams are unpleasantly exciting, i. e. all dreams are characterized by negative emotions such as anger, anxiety, or fear.

译　并且我们还注意到梦的刺激可以令人不快以至于引起觉醒，这就引出了另一个错误观念，即所有的梦都是不愉快的，即都以负性情绪如愤怒、焦虑、恐惧等为特征。（韩芳译）

例 8-102　Membrane are also crucially important inside cells for two reasons: First, to provide surfaces on which chemical reactions can proceed, and secondly to provide separate areas inside the cell, allowing chemical reactions to proceed which might otherwise interfere with each other.

译　膜在细胞内也非常重要，原因有两个：第一，提供进行化学反应的表面，第二，在细胞内提供分别的区域，使得化学反应能够进行，否则可能相互干扰。

例 8-103　This buried root system is essential for the plant: It provides stability, water, and food.

译　这种埋在地下的根系对植物来说是必不可少的：它提供稳定性、水分和营养。

例 8-104　The basic orientation of the Vienna Circle can be expressed in the formula of Otto Neurath, a prominent member of the Circle: 'science free from metaphysics'.

译　维也纳学派的基本倾向可以表达为其主要成员奥托·诺伊拉特的说法："摆脱了形而上学的科学"。（江怡译）

四、破折号的使用

可在句中插入成分的前后用逗号、括号或破折号分隔。逗号比括号或破折号更正式，括号分隔较少用，而破折号分隔更醒目，并可作语气上的停顿，因此强调的程度上要比逗号强。尤其是当插入成分中也有逗号的情况下，用破折号分隔可清楚地表明插入成分的范围。两个破折号连用时，其间的插入成分可长可短，通常作为对插入成分的分隔，但更多是一种突出强调。单个破折号可引导较长的同位语，解释性、例证性或总结性的成分或语句。

例 8-105　They met it by constructing a category of 'feminine art' whose hallmarks were — of course — sentimentality, domesticity, and charm.

🔄 批评家们的应对是建立一个"女性艺术"领域,其特点当然是多愁善感、家庭生活和妇性魅力。(朱扬明译)

例 8-106 Not only in that the creativity that is licensed as artistic is awarded that licence by a system of professionalization, whose gatekeepers are art schools (recognized artists who did not go to art school are rare indeed) and galleries, each of which are governed by strict, if tacit, protocols and criteria set — ultimately — by modern art's dominant institutions.

🔄 一方面因为这种创造性必须经过专业化体系的裁定才能被认为是富有艺术性的,该体系的看门人是艺术院校(被承认的没有经过艺术学校训练的艺术家毕竟很少)和画廊,而它们又受到严格的(即使是默而不宣的)规矩和标准的统治,最终受命于现代艺术的主要学术机构。(朱扬明译)

例 8-107 The difficulties — indeed, the outspoken scorn — confronting any woman who actually dared to publish her writings are clearly indicated by the experiences of Margaret Cavendish, Duchess of Newcastle.

🔄 任何胆敢发表作品的女性所面临的困境——其实就是公开的嘲讽——在纽卡斯尔公爵夫人玛格丽特·卡文迪什的遭遇中体现得淋漓尽致。(朱刚和麻晓蓉译)

例 8-108 Consciousness-raising was never intended — as its detractors sometimes claimed — merely as 'group therapy'.

🔄 提高觉悟从来都不是仅仅意在——像诋毁者有时声称的那样——进行什么"集体治疗"。(朱刚和麻晓蓉译)

例 8-109 Our senses are instrumental — we call them organs, after all — and their most obvious role is in helping us live our lives.

🔄 我们的感觉具有工具性的作用——我们毕竟称它们为器官——因而它们最明显的作用是帮助我们生活。(孙喆译)

例 8-110 Most importantly, Darwin suggested a mechanism — natural selection — by which such transmutations might occur and how new species appear on Earth.

🔄 最重要的是,达尔文提出了一个演变有可能发生的机制——自然选择,以及新的物种如何在地球上出现。(史立群译)

例 8-111 The battle for legal, civil, and educational equality has been —

and to some extent still is — a central element in feminism.

[译] 为法律平等、公民平等和教育平等而奋斗过去一直是——从某种程度上说现在依然是——女权主义的核心内容。(朱刚和麻晓蓉译)

例 8-112 Big business — as opposed to the churches — was responsible for the founding of most of the new research universities.

[译] 一些大的工商企业——而不是教会——创建了多数新的研究型大学。

例 8-113 What this means is that our sense of psychological reality — whether normal dreaming or a psychotic symptom — is set by the strength of percepts and feelings as well as by our thoughts about them.

[译] 这意味着我们的心理现实感，无论是正常做梦还是精神病症状，都是基于感知和感情的力量及我们对感知和感情的看法。(韩芳译)

例 8-114 Now, strangely perhaps, it is this model that most people *outside* philosophy — that is, outside the academic study of philosophy — think that most people *inside* philosophy are in the grip of.

[译] 现在，或许有些奇怪的是，哲学之外(就是说在作为学术研究的哲学之外)的大多数人认为，哲学之内的大多数人都陷入这种研究，无法摆脱。(江怡译)

例 8-115 One of the most interesting — and in the long run, most significant — episodes in the early 20th century concerned a subject that had rarely been publicly discussed, and which could still arouse bitter opposition: contraception.

[译] 20 世纪早期最有意思——从长期来看影响也最为深远——的事件之一便是避孕。这个话题当时很少被公开讨论过，而且时至今日仍然能激起强烈的反对。(朱刚和麻晓蓉译)

例 8-116 The idea of so-called 'metanarratives', that is, overarching explanations of the human condition, or of the dynamic of history — such as those offered by Christianity, or Marxism, or the notion of the inevitable progress of civilizations — was rejected along with the absolute certainties on which they rested, since all had been built on (what were now seen as) the shifting sands of individualism.

[译] 所谓"宏大叙事"的思想，即对人类状况或历史动力的全面性解释，如基督教、马克思主义或关于文明必然进步的观念，连同其所依附的那些绝对确定的事物一起被拒斥了，因为所有这一切都是建立在(按时下的看法)个人

主义的流动沙丘之上的。(朱扬明译)

例 8-117　The effect of this revelation — the existence of an unexpectedly gigantic fossil lizard of a former time in Earth history — was truly profound.

🔄 这一新发现揭示了在地球历史的更早时期生存过一种异常巨大的蜥蜴，影响极为深远。(史立群译)

例 8-118　It is often said, and my observation leads me to believe it true, that our seemingly great growth in social morality has oddly enough taken place in a world where private morality — a sense of the supreme importance of purely personal honor, honesty, and integrity — seems to be declining.

🔄 当有人说，我自己的观察也使我相信这是事实，我们这看似伟大的社会道德成长相当奇怪地发生在一个私人道德——认为纯粹个人的荣誉、诚实、正当有极度重要性的意识——似乎日渐衰微的世界之中。(颜元叔译)

例 8-119　Heidegger is convinced that philosophical questions — and the question of being is, for him, the philosophical question — cannot be reduced to scientific enquiry.

🔄 海德格尔相信，哲学问题——在他看来，存在问题就是唯一的哲学问题——无法简化为科学的探究。(江怡译)

例 8-120　Two organelles in the cytoplasm — mitochondria and, in plants, chloroplasts — have double, rather than single membranes.

🔄 细胞质中的两个细胞器——线粒体和植物中的叶绿体——具有双层膜，而不是单层膜。

例 8-121　Within two to three years — a surprisingly short time — these organisms are capable of removing most traces of any large mammal.

🔄 在令人惊异的两至三年之短的时间内细菌就能把任何一个大型哺乳动物分解得几乎不留痕迹。(冯兴无译)

例 8-122　With that almost complete institutionalization — and its corollary, the expansion of the field of art practice to the point where anything can count as art as long as it has been consecrated as such by art institutions — what remains as particular to the artist, as her or his unique attribute, is creativity.

🔄 当艺术几乎完全体制化时——其必然结果是，艺术实践领域扩张到了什么都可以当作艺术的地步，只要艺术机构将其作为艺术品奉献给大家——剩下的归艺术家所特有的，属于他或她的独特属性，就只有创造性。(朱扬明

译）

例 8-123 The Revolution was the outcome of a combination of factors — economic, financial, political; state bankruptcy, aristocratic revolt, the peasants' grievances, and demand for land.

🔵 革命是许多因素结合的结果，有经济上的、财政上的、政治上的因素；还有国有破产、贵族造反、农民不满及对土地的需求等。（董乐山译）

例 8-124 When Plato observed that philosophy begins in wonder, he was thinking of two senses of wonder — the wonder that is awe and the wonder that comes from not yet knowing why.

🔵 当柏拉图评说哲学起于好奇时，他想到的是两种好奇——敬畏的好奇和尚不知所以然的未知的好奇。（孙喆译）

例 8-125 For if science is simply a method or an attitude, so that anyone whose thought-processes are sufficiently rational can in some sense be described as a scientist — what then becomes of the enormous prestige now enjoyed by the chemist, the physicist, etc. and his claim to be somehow wiser than the rest of us?

🔵 因为如果科学仅仅是一个方法或是一种态度，任何一个思维过程足够理性化的人就都是某种意义上的科学家——那么，化学家、物理学家等现在享有的巨大声誉将会如何，他们又怎么自诩比其他人高明？（吴简清译）

例 8-126 The 19th century saw an increasingly widespread and articulate statement of women's claims — perhaps in reaction to the emergence of an image of true 'femininity' that seemed to become more constricted as the century wore on: A class-based ideal of gentility and refinement.

🔵 19世纪，女性的诉求得到越来越广泛、越来越清晰地表达——或许这是对当时出现的真正"女子气质"形象作出的反应，随着世纪时光的流逝，这种"女子气质"似乎变得愈加狭隘：成了一种建立在阶级基础之上的有关教养和优雅的理想。（朱刚和麻晓蓉译）

例 8-127 It is true that he is concerned not with being successful as this or that kind of person — a businessman, for example, or a politician — but with being successful at being human.

🔵 诚然，他（亚里士多德）关心的不是作为这种人或那种人——例如商人或政治家——而成功，而是要作为人而成功。（朱新伟译）

例 8-128 At a deeper level, all schemes that analyse content are essentially two-pronged: There are always two agencies — us and them, the body and the spirit, the ego and the id, the brain and the mind.

🔵 **译** 从更深的层次来说，所有的内容分析体系在本质上都是两极分化的，即总存在两股力量——我们和他们、身体和灵魂、自我和本我、大脑和精神。（韩芳译）

例 8-129 To identify novel factors involved in governing root branching, we explored which genes are expressed during the early stages of the process. This led to the identification of a cell wall modifying enzyme — a molecule that regulates chemical reactions — that controls the cell divisions leading to the growth of a new root.

🔵 **译** 为了鉴定控制根分支的新因素，我们探索了在这个过程早期阶段表达的哪些基因。这导致一种控制着细胞分裂，使新根生长的细胞壁修饰酶(酶是一种调节化学反应的分子)。

例 8-130 All eukaryotic cells have the ability to make lipids, which produce all the naturally occurring oils and fats — from rapeseed and olive oil in plant cells to milk fats, lanolin, and lard in animal cells.

🔵 **译** 所有真核细胞都有能力制造脂类，这些脂类形成所有的天然油脂——从植物细胞中的菜籽油和橄榄油，到动物细胞中的乳脂、羊毛脂和猪油。

第九单元

易错的句子

英语是综合语，也就是利用形态变化、相对固定的语序及大量虚词来表示语法关系。尤其是，英语名词有具体与抽象、可数与不可数、单数与复数、加不加（定）冠词等区别，而动词有语态（主动与被动）、时态（过去、进行、完成、将来等）、虚拟动词和非谓语动词等多种变化形态，而在句中主语和谓语之间、代词与其先行词之间的数、形上应当保持一致，主从复合句在时态上也应保持一致。同样，修饰语（分词短语、不定式与介词结构等）应与句子主语之间存在逻辑关系，平行结构与比较结构中的各成分应当一致。违反这些一致性原则就会导致错误。此外，初学者还容易出现中式英语问题，如汉语中某些主谓搭配可以说通，英语中则不妥当；汉语中可以使用无主句，英语则不行。

以下就初学者最容易犯错几个问题进行介绍，这几个问题包括单复数问题、垂悬修饰语问题和平行结构错误问题。

一、单复数问题

（一）谓语动词的单复数与定语从句动词的单复数

主语的单复数决定谓语动词的单复数，中心词或被修饰词的单复数决定定语从句动词的单复数。

例 9-1 One in four scientists have experienced harassment or discrimination. （主语是复数的 scientists，因此谓语动词为复数形式 have）

译 四分之一的科学家经历过骚扰或歧视。

例 9-2 A quarter of people working in science have experienced sexual harassment, bullying and discrimination over issues ranging from disabilities to diet. （主语是复数的 scientists，因此谓语动词为复数形式 have）

译 四分之一的科学工作者在诸如从残疾到饮食等问题上经历过性骚扰、欺凌和歧视。

例 9-3 A survey of nearly 3700 scientists across Europe and North America suggests that harassment, bullying and discrimination are widespread. （主语是单数的 a survey，因此谓语动词为单数形式 suggests）

译 一项对欧洲和北美近 3700 名科学家的调查表明，骚扰、欺凌和歧视现象普遍存在。

例 9-4 The contingent and largely arbitrary nature of disciplinary boundaries has unfortunately been reinforced, and even made to seem 'natural' by our drive to construct dichotomies — with science versus art as perhaps the most widely accepted of all. (主语是单数的 nature, 因此谓语动词为单数形式 has)

[译] 不幸的是，学科界限的偶然性和很大程度上的武断性已经得到加强，甚至被我们构建二分法的驱动变得"自然"——科学与艺术可能是最广泛接受的两分模式。

例 9-5 He's one of those writers who have won the Booker prize. (中心词或被修饰词为复数的 writers, 故其定语从句动词为复数的 have)

[译] 他是那些获得布克奖的作家之一。

例 9-6 As part of our Forensics Hall of Fame, we have collected 10 forensic scientists who have made history and are organized by earliest to most recent. (中心词或被修饰词为复数的 forensic scientists, 故其定语从句动词为复数的 have 和 are)

[译] 作为我们法医名人堂的一部分，我们收集了 10 位曾经创造历史、从最早到最近出现的法医科学家。

例 9-7 These are scientists who have invented the Internet and fiber optics, challenged AIDS and cancer, developed new drugs, and in general made crucial advances in medicine, genetics, astronomy, ecology, physics, and computer programming. (中心词或被修饰词为复数的 scientists, 故其定语从句动词为复数的 have)

[译] 这些科学家发明了互联网和光纤，挑战了艾滋病和癌症，开发了新药物，并在医学、遗传学、天文学、生态学、物理学和计算机编程方面取得了重要进展。

例 9-8 In petals, the first visable signs of senescence are often wilting, changes in coloration, and rolling, which are closely coordinated with the sexual maturation of the flower and the production of scent to attract pollinators. (中心词或被修饰词为复数的 the first visable signs, 而非最后一个并列动名词 rolling, 故其定语从句动词为复数的 are)

[译] 花瓣最早见到的衰老迹象往往是花瓣枯萎、颜色变化和弯卷，这与花的性成熟及能吸引传粉昆虫的气味产生密切相关。

(二) 非 and 连接的名词或名词结构作主语

当一个单数主语后面或前面有 with, as well as, coupled with, together

with, along with, in addition to, except, no less than 相连的名词或名词结构时，谓语动词仍用单数形式。

例 9-9 Apart from the question of rights, the system for governing the Union, with its complex mix of intergovernmental and federal elements, makes decision-making difficult and a satisfactory relationship between the institutions and the citizens hard to achieve.

[译] 除了基本权利的问题，由于政府间因素与联邦因素间关系错综复杂，欧盟的管理体制使得决策困难，并使欧盟机构与公民间难以建立和谐的关系。（戴炳然译）

例 9-10 The steady improvement in technological resources, as well as their potential to be used to answer palaeobiological questions, has manifested in a number of distinct areas in recent years.

[译] 近年来，技术手段的平稳进步，以及利用它们解决古生物学问题的可能性在许多不同领域中已崭露头角。（史立群译）

例 9-11 All this frenzied metabolic activity, as well as exposure to the continual threat of bacterial invasion, has resulted in the life of an enterocyte being a short time, with each cell lasting no more than two or three days before replacement.

[译] 所有这种激烈的代谢活动，以及暴露在细菌入侵的持续威胁下，导致肠细胞的寿命很短，每一个细胞在替换前不超过两到三天。

例 9-12 This fact, coupled with the findings of post-traumatic stress disorder in veterans of military combat, suggests that, just as waking thought tends to be dominated by preoccupations with these unpleasant experiences, so does sleep mental activity tend to be dominated by them.

[译] 这一事实与战后退伍军人中出现的创伤后应激障碍共同说明，正如清醒时的思维易被这些不愉快体验的担忧主宰那样，睡眠时的思想活动也易被它们所左右。（韩芳译）

例 9-13 Thus the EU, together with its member states, has become by far the world's largest source of aid.

[译] 这样，欧盟及其成员国成了目前世界上最大的援助来源。（戴炳然译）

例 9-14 Along with this influence in the world trading system, the Union has used its environmental powers to play a leading part in international negotiations to protect the ozone layer and curb global warming.

译 除了在国际贸易体系中发挥影响，欧盟还利用其在环保方面的力量，在保护臭氧层和控制全球变暖的国际谈判中起到了主导作用。（戴炳然译）

（三）抽象名词、不可数名词、代表不可数名词的代词、动名词与动词不定式作主语

抽象名词作主语，谓语动词用单数形式。不可数名词如 advice, evidence, information, proof, research 等（只有单数形式）及代表不可数名词的代词如 much 和 little 作主语，谓语动词用单数形式。动名词与动词不定式作主语，谓语动词用单数形式。

例 9-15 The recognition of fallibility is simply an acknowledgment of our humanity.

译 承认人皆有错不过是正视人性而已。（严忠志译）

例 9-16 The basic assumption of philosophical inquiry is that the most intractable puzzles of life — no matter how large — will ultimately give way to rational analysis.

译 哲学探讨的基本假设是：即便是人生最对对付的问题——无论它们有多大——最终也可采用理性分析的方法来解决。（严忠志译）

例 9-17 The sufficiency of this kind of explanation becomes apparent, however, when the importance of novelty, surprise, complexity, incongruity, ambiguity, and uncertainty is considered.

译 然而，当考虑到新奇、吃惊、复杂、不适、含混及无常等情况时，这种解释显然是不充分的。（马锦儒等译）

例 9-18 The search for hidden assumptions and fundamental premises is actually part of a larger enterprise.

译 这种对隐藏假设和基本前提的探讨实际上是一个宏大探索的组成部分。（严忠志译）

例 9-19 The pursuit of private interests with as little interference as possible from government was seen as the road to human happiness and progress rather than the public obligations and involvement in the collective community that were emphasized by the Greeks.

译 在尽可能少的政府干预之下，追求个人利益被视为人类幸福和进步之路，而不是希腊人所强调的公共责任和对集体社区的参与。（马锦儒等译）

例 9-20　The amount of pressure required to stop the osmosis completely is called the osmotic pressure.

　🔘 完全阻止渗透所需要的压力就称为渗透压。（李少如译）

例 9-21　Freedom was to be realized by limiting the scope of governmental activity and political obligation and not through immersion in the collective life of the polis.

　🔘 自由应当通过限制政府行为及政治责任的范围来实现，而不是沉浸在古希腊城邦的集体生活中来实现。（马锦儒等译）

例 9-22　Lived experience is the testing ground for these partial insights.

　🔘 人们的亲身经验是检验偏见的基础。（严忠志译）

例 9-23　Active transport of a substance through the cell membrane, which is an entirely different transport mechanism from diffusion, means movement of the substance through the cell membrane by a specific membrane chemical mechanism.

　🔘 通过细胞膜主动运输某物质是与扩散完全不同的一种运输机制。它是指该物质凭借某种特殊膜化学机制通过细胞膜的一种运动。（李少如译）

例 9-24　Evidence is given in research work, or is quoted in essays and thesis statements, but is paraphrased by the writer.

　🔘 证据是由研究工作中提供，或是在论文和论文陈述中加以引用，但由作者阐释的材料。

例 9-25　Much has been written about the diversity of terrestrial organisms, particularly the exceptionally rich life associated with tropical rain-forest habitats.

　🔘 有关陆地生物体，特别是与热带雨林栖息地相关的异常丰富的生物已有诸多的论述。（马锦儒等译）

例 9-26　Little is known of Hippocrates who lived around 400 B. C., not even whether he actually authored the collection of books that bears his name.

　🔘 希波克拉底出生于大约公元前 400 年，人们对他了解极少，甚至不知道署其姓名的著作是否真的出于他的笔下。（马锦儒等译）

例 9-27　Relatively little has been said, however, about diversity of life in the sea even though coral reef systems are comparable to rain forests in terms of richness of life.

　🔘 但是对于热带海洋中的生命多样化相对提及较少，尽管就生物的丰富性而言，珊瑚礁系统可直比雨林。（马锦儒等译）

例 9-28 Enabling such a patient to recover the memory of the experience, to go through it in detail, and to discharge or 'abstract' the emotions of fear and horror which accompanied the existence does indeed have beneficial results, as those who treated wartime neuroses have repeatedly demonstrated.

㊟ 就像那些治疗战后神经官能征的医师反复证明的那样，帮助病人重现这些记忆、回忆当时的细节、释放或发泄伴随这些经历的担忧和恐惧，确实取得了有益的效果。（尹莉译）

例 9-29 To recognize this fact, however, is not to counsel inaction, indecision, or despair.

㊟ 承认这一事实并不是要人无所作为，犹豫不决，或者陷入绝望。（严忠志译）

二、垂悬修饰语问题

一般而言，修饰语的逻辑主语应与句子的主语一致，如果不一致，或者说当句首的修饰语与后面句子的主语没有修饰关系时，就会形成悬垂修饰语（dangling modificr）。造成悬垂修饰语问题可以是分词结构（现在分词和过去分词）、不定式结构，还可以是"介词+动名词"结构或"介词+名词"结构，甚至还可以是单个的形容词结构；而且位置也不一定局限于句首（虽然多数情况下在句首），还可以位于句尾。修饰语的逻辑主语与句子的主语一致的正确句子如下：

例 9-30 Using data from many magnetic observations, geophysicists can make mathematical representations of the field and how it is changing.

㊟ 利用许多磁观测站的资料，地球物理学家对磁场及其变化方式进行数学描述。（李铁刚和孙艳华译）

例 9-31 Wielding the common instrument of the external tariff, the Community was becoming, inn the field of trade, a power comparable to the United States.

㊟ 凭借共同对外关税这一手段，共同体正在成为贸易领域可与美国并驾齐驱的"强国"。（戴炳然译）

例 9-32 Using these admittedly simple proxies, he suggested that dinosaurs (or at least the predators) must have had metabolic requirements more similar to mammals.

译 利用这些相当简单的替代研究，他提出，恐龙（或至少是食肉恐龙）一定具有哺乳动物更相似的代谢需要。

例 9-33 Combining all these lines of argument, Bakker was able to propose that far from being slow and dull, dinosaurs were intelligent, highly active creatures that had stolen the world from the traditionally superior mammals for the remaining 160 million years of the Mesozoic.

译 将这连串的论证结合起来，巴克指出，恐龙远非缓慢而迟钝，它们是有智慧而且高度活跃的动物，在中生代余下的1.6亿年里从传统上被认为是更高级的哺乳动物那里窃取了世界的统治权。（史立群译）

例 9-34 <u>Seen in this way</u>, the distinction between analytic and Continental philosophy is not geographical distinction between different places, like Britain and the Continent, but is rather a difference that is internal to what might be called 'the English philosophical mind'.

译 这样看来，分析哲学与欧陆哲学之间的差别就不是不同地方的地理上的差别，比如英国与欧陆的差别，而是一种所谓的"英国人的哲学心灵"内在的差异。（江怡译）

例 9-35 <u>Rightly understood</u>, the myth depicts not Oedipus' failure to circumvent his ineluctable destiny but his success in fulfilling his fondest desires.

译 对这则神话正确的理解应该是，它描述的不是俄狄浦斯如何未能避免那不可抗拒的宿命，而是他如何成功地实现了自己最热切的欲望。（刘象愚译）

例 9-36 <u>Not satisfied with this</u>, France proposed a 'European judicial area' to work towards harmonization of member states' laws regarding cross-border litigation and enforcement of judgments, together with common minimum standards in citizens' access to courts.

译 不满于现状的法国提议建立一个"欧洲司法区"，以推进成员国间有关跨界诉讼和执行裁决的法律协调，以及建立公民诉诸法院的最低共同标准。（戴炳然译）

例 9-37 <u>Properly managed as a tool to serve society</u>, technology is the best hope for overcoming economic and social problems facing people everywhere.

译 技术作为服务社会的工具得到妥善管理，就是解决各地人民面临的经济和社会问题的最大的希望所在。（吴中东和宫玉波译）

例 9-38 Armed with more recent discoveries of dinosaurs around the world, Ostrom was able to show that a number of dinosaurs did actually possess small clavicles, removing at a stroke Heilmann's big stumbling block to a dinosaurian ancestry for birds.

译 在掌握了世界各地更新的恐龙发现之后，奥斯特罗姆指出，许多恐龙确实都具有小的锁骨，这一举搬开了海尔曼在恐龙是鸟类祖先问题上所搁置的大绊脚石。（史立群译）

例 9-39 To protect people and the environment, most developed nations have placed limits on the amount and type of pollution that can be released into the environment.

译 为了保护人类和环境，许多发达国家都对排放到环境中的污染物进行了类型和数量的限制。（李铁刚和孙艳华译）

例 9-40 To try to investigate the degree of relatedness of creatures (in this particular case fossil creatures), palaeosytematists are most interested in identifying as wide a range of anatomical features as are preserved in the hard parts of their fossils.

译 为了研究动物（在这里是化石生物）的亲缘关系，古生物系统分类学家最感兴趣的是在保存下来的化石硬体部分识别出尽可能多的解剖特征。（史立群译）

例 9-41 To eliminate any possibility of a mistaken identity, analysts use several different probes to look at several different DNA fragment patterns in a sample.

译 为了排除出现任何错误鉴定的可能性，分析者在一个样品上利用几种不同的探针来观察若干不同的 DNA 片段带型。（李铁钢和孙艳华译）

例 9-42 To determine the strength and location of earthquakes, scientists use a recording instrument known as a seismograph.

译 为了测定地震的强度和位置，科学家使用一个被称为地震仪的记录仪器。（李铁钢和孙艳华译）

例 9-43 Alongside the ups and downs of Community politics, the Court of justice made steady progress in establishing the rule of law.

译 共同体政治起起伏伏的同时，法院在确立政治上却稳步发展。（戴炳然译）

例 9-44 With the success of the internal tariff disarmament in the 1960s in mind, some business leaders and members of the Commission's staff worked on the idea of a programme to remove the non-tariff barriers.

[译] 考虑到 20 世纪 60 年代消除内部关税获得了成功，一些企业界领袖与委员会委员就消除非关税壁垒计划作出了构想。(戴炳然译)

下面的句子中，不定式的逻辑主语与句子的主语是一致的，也就是说，句子前面不定式短语动词的动作是句子的主语发出的，因此句子语法是正确的：

例 9-45 To test this hypothesis, we divided the participants into two groups.

[译] 为了检验这项假说，我们将参与者分成两组(陈玉玲和王明杰译)。

例 9-46 To examine whether more widespread changes in genome methylation occur during the progression from green to red fruit, the authors use a whole-genome bisulfite sequencing method to produce the first base pair - resolution methylome maps of the tomato epigenome.

[译] 为了检查番茄果实从绿色到红色发育过程中基因组甲基化是否发生更广泛的变化，作者使用全基因组亚硫酸氢盐测序方法来产生番茄表观基因组的首个碱基对分辨率甲基化组图谱。

但下面句子中不定式的逻辑主语与句子的主语是不一致的，句子前面不定式动词的动作不是句子的主语发出的，造成句首的不定式短语与后面句子的逻辑关系混乱，或者说使使句首的不定式短语成为悬垂修饰语，因此句子语法是错误的：

例 9-47 To test this hypothesis, the participants were divided into two groups. (to test this hypothesis 的主语不是 the participants)

例 9-48 To enhance the annotation of sequenced genomes, NGS has also been applied to small non-coding RNA (ncRNA) discovery and profiling. (to enhance the annotation of sequenced genomes 的主语不是 NGS)

[译] 为了促进测序基因组的注释，下一代测序(NGS)也被应用于小的非编码 RNA(ncRNA)的发现和分析。

同样，下面的句子中过去分词的逻辑主语与句子的主语是一致的，也就是说，过去分词结构的动词动作是由句子主语发出的，因此句子语法是正确的：

例 9-49 Based on the assumption that criminal behavior is caused by biological or psychological conditions that require treatment, a model of corrections was developed by Herbert Packer in 1978.

🔄 基于犯罪行为是由需要治疗的生物或心理疾病引起的假设，赫伯特·帕克在1978年提出了一种矫正模式。

例 9-50 A model of corrections based on the assumption that criminal behavior is caused by biological or psychological conditions that require treatment was developed by Herbert Packer in 1978.

下面句子中过去分词的逻辑主语与句子的主语是不一致的，也就是说，过去分词结构的动词动作不是由句子主语发出的，造成句首的过去分词与后面句子的逻辑关系混乱，或者说使使句首的过去分词短语成为悬垂修饰语，因此句子语法是错误的：

例 9-51 Based on the assumption that criminal behavior is caused by biological or psychological conditions that require treatment, Herbert Packer developed a model of corrections in 1978. (based on 结构不能修饰主语 Herbert Packer)

但如果将 based on 分词结构换作介词结构 on the basis of(介词短语用来修饰句子的谓语动词)，则没有问题。

例 9-52 On the basis of this assumption that criminal behavior is caused by biological or psychological conditions that require treatment, Herbert Packer developed a model of corrections in 1978. (on the basis of 结构修饰动词 develop)

下面的句子中现在分词的逻辑主语与句子的主语是一致的，也就是说，现在分词结构的动词动作是由句子主语发出的，因此句子语法是正确的：

例 9-53 Using CRISPR, researchers have expanded chromatin immunoprecipitation (ChIP) to allow purification of any genomic sequence specified by a particular gRNA

🔄 使用 CRISPR 基因组编辑技术，研究人员已经将染色质免疫沉淀(ChIP)推广应用于对特定 gRNA 指定的任何基因组序列进行纯化。

但下面这一句现在分词的逻辑主语与句子的主语是不一致的，也就是说，现在分词结构的动词动作不是由句子主语发出的，造成悬垂修饰语问题，尽管它出现在权威出版物中：

例 9-54 Following the biochemical isolation of numerous miRNAs in nematodes, fruit flies, and humans, four groups of miRNAs were cloned from *Arabi-*

dopsis using similar techniques. (four groups of miRNAs 不能作现在分词结构 using similar techniques 的主语)

🔄 在对线虫、果蝇和人类中的许多 miRNAs 进行生化分离后，利用类似的技术从拟南芥中克隆了四组 miRNAs。

"by + 动名词"（表示方式、手段）这样的介词结构如果动名词的逻辑主语与句子的主语不一致时，同样会造成悬垂修饰语问题。

下面这一句动名词的逻辑主语与句子的主语是一致的，也就是说，动名词的动作是由句子主语发出的，因此是正确的：

例 9-55　<u>By comparing modern communities of endotherms (cats) and ectotherms (predatory lizards)</u>, he estimated that endotherms consume, on average, ten times the volume of prey during the same time interval.

🔄 通过比较现代内温动物（猫）和外温动物（捕食性蜥蜴）群落，他估计，在相同的时间间隔里，内温动物平均消耗的猎物是外温动物的 10 倍。（史立群译）

但下面这两句虽然是正式发表文章中摘出的，但动名词的逻辑主语与句子的主语是不一致的，也就是说，动名词的动词动作不是由句子主语发出的，因此存在垂修饰语问题：

例 9-56　<u>By dividing a diploid cell twice</u>, four haploid gametes are produced.

🔄 通过将二倍体细胞分裂两次，产生四个单倍体配子。

例 9-57　Here, <u>by using parallel analysis of RNA ends (PARE) for global identification of miRNA targets and comparing four different stages of tomato fruit development</u>, a total of 119 target genes of miRNAs were identified.

🔄 利用 RNA 末端平行分析（PARE）对 miRNA 靶点（或靶序列）进行全局鉴定，并对番茄果实发育的 4 个不同阶段进行比较，共鉴定出 119 个 miRNA 靶基因。

事实上，由于科技文体具有客观性的特点，人称主语使用较少或不突出，而被动语态使用较多，因此，在科技文体中垂悬修饰语并不鲜见。因此，有专家指出，在科技英语中，当阐述客观科学事实或一般性真理时，悬垂修饰语的逻辑主语是泛指而非特指时，或者句子以 it 为形式主语，或者是 there be 句型时，垂悬修饰语问题很多时候并不认为是错误的。如：

例 9-58　<u>Using this theory</u>, black holes are fascinating objects where space and time become so warped that time practically stops in the vicinity of black hole.

㊋ 利用该理论，黑洞被描述成使人非常迷惑的物体，那里的时空变得扭曲不堪，在黑洞附近时间实际上都停止了。（李铁刚和孙艳华译）

例 9-59 Remembering that the nucleotide base A always pairs with T and C with G, if one strand has a sequence ATCG then the new strand will have a sequence TAGC.

㊋ 记住碱基 A 总是与碱基 T 配对，碱基 C 总是与碱基 G 配对，如果一条链的序列为 ATCG，那么新链的序列将为 TAGC.

例 9-60 Judging from previous analyses, this new star cluster is likely to have a high carbon content.

㊋ 从先前分析来看，这个新星群可能碳含量高。（束金星和徐玉娟译）

例 9-61 All objects, neglecting friction, fall at the same rate to the g round.

㊋ 如果不计空气摩擦，一切物体都以同样速度落向地面。（束金星和徐玉娟译）

例 9-62 To give one an idea of the timing of these processes, when a glandular cell is bathed in radioactive amino acids, newly formed radioactive protein molecules can be detected in the granular endoplasmic reticulum within 3 to 5 minutes.

㊋ 为了让人们对上述过程有一个时间概念，当腺细胞被浸浴在有放射性氨基酸的浴液中时，仅 3-5 分钟内在颗粒性内质网中就可检测到新形成的放射性蛋白质分子。（李少如译）

例 9-63 To develop software, the application to be implemented is broken down into a set of smaller tasks, which are then implemented as modules within a program.

㊋ 大型软件制作过程中，通常将任务分成一系列小型任务，然后以模块的形式分别执行。（李铁刚和孙艳华译）

例 9-64 Tracing the general evolutionary history of ornithopods across the Mesozoic Era, it became clear that these types of dinosaur became increasingly diverse and abundant in time.

㊋ 追溯鸟脚次目在整个中生代的总体进化史，很明显这些恐龙类型最终变得越来越多样和丰富。（史立群译）

例 9-65 And using this information it is possible to construct what is, in effect, a sort of genealogy or phylogeny representing a model of the evolutionary history of the group as a whole.

🕮 利用这些资料可以有效地建立一种系谱或系统发育关系，以代表该类群总体进化历史的模型。（史立群译）

例 9-66 Armed with this battery of prevailing opinion and Ostrom's observations and interpretations based on *Deinonychus*, it is easier to appreciate how this creature must have been challenging his mind.

🕮 考虑到这一串流行观点的存在以及奥斯特罗姆基于恐爪龙的观察和解释，我们就更能想象得到这种动物一定给他的思想带来莫大的挑战。（史立群译）

例 9-67 To avoid drowning during sleep, it is crucial that marine mammals retain control of their blowhole.

🕮 为避免在睡眠时溺水，海洋哺乳动物保持对呼吸孔的控制至关重要。（李铁钢和孙艳华译）

例 9-68 To explain the development of the membrane potential, it is necessary to understand that the resting axon membrane is very impermeable to sodium ions but very permeable to potassium ions.

🕮 要解释膜电位的发生，就必须了解静息轴突膜对钠离子很不易通透，但对钾离子则通透性很高。（李少如译）

例 9-69 To put dinosaurs as a whole into some sort of perspective, it will be necessary to outline the techniques used to do this, and our current understanding of dinosaurian evolutionary history.

🕮 为了对恐龙作为一个整体有正确的认识，就必要简要说明用于进行这项工作的方法，以及当前我们对恐龙进化历史的了解。（史立群译）

例 9-70 To meet the expanding needs and demands of the visually impaired person, there is a sequence of instruction that begins during the preschool years and may continue after high school.

🕮 为了满足视觉障碍者不断增长的需求，在学龄前设有一系列的教育课程，这些课程在中学以后还可能开设。（马锦儒等译）

例 9-71 By studying the DNA fingerprints of relatives who have a history of some particular disorder, or by comparing large groups with or without the disorder, it is possible to identify DNA patterns associated with the disease in question.

译 通过研究某种特定疾病史的亲属的 DNA 指纹，或者通过对具有或不具有某种疾病的大批人群的对比，是有可能鉴定与这种疾病相关的 DNA 图谱的。（李铁钢和孙艳华译）

例 9-72 By separating the embryo and making one baby into two, it is possible to make perfectly identical twins.

译 通过分离胚胎，使一个婴儿变成两个，这就有可能产生完全相同的孪生子。（李铁刚和孙艳华译）

例 9-73 By using this technology (making clones by nuclear transplantation), unlike the way to make clones from separating the embryo, it is possible to make many lifeforms that have the exact same DNA safely.

译 使用该项技术（即通过核移植制备克隆）与通过分离胚胎制备克隆的方法不同，核转移植技术可以安全地获得许多具有相同 DNA 的生命形式。（李铁刚和孙艳华译）

例 9-74 By collecting and analyzing these signals, it is possible to compute a three-dimensional image, which, like a CT image, is normally displayed in two-dimensional slices.

译 通过收集和分析这些信号，就能计算一个三维图像。这种三维图像与计算机 X 射线断层摄影技术图像一样，通常显示在二维切面上。（李铁刚和孙艳华译）

此外，科技英语中实际上已经大量使用一些充当插入语的悬垂分词或悬垂不定式，如 generally/broadly/strictly speaking, considerng, judging by/from…, putting it simply / briefly, taken as a whole, to sum up, to tell the truth, to be frank；以及充当介词或连词的悬垂分词，如：concerning/regarding…, providing/provided (that)…, owing to …, given (that)…, assuming/presuming/supposing…等。

例 9-75 Considering the health consequences of being overweight, it is surprising that fat at the cellular level has received relatively little attention, with lipid droplets thought of as no more than simple storage depots.

译 考虑到超重对健康的影响，令人惊讶的是，细胞水平的脂肪受到的关注相对较少，脂滴被认为只是简单的储存库。

三、平行结构错误

平行结构是指句子中并列有几个结构相同或相似的词汇、短语和子句。

有些是用关联词 and, or, both...and..., not...but..., not only...but also..., neither...nor..., either...or...、first, second, third 等连接的成分，两边应呈现对等的结构。不同层次的平行结构，一般要求意思上要平行，形式结构（属同一语法范畴）上要平行。单词不能与从句平行，即使是单词平行，也要词性相同（名词对名词，形容词对形容词），类型相同（抽象名词对抽象名词，实体名词对实体名词，现在分词对现在分词，过去分词对过去分词，不定式对不定式）。短语平行时，结构要类似。句子与句子平行时，句子的级别要一致（主句对主句，从句对从句），结构最好也一致。如果排比的成分要在语法结构上不相同或不相似，就会产生平行结构错误，使读者的对平行结构的心理期待落空。

例 9-76 The names were both difficult to pronounce and to spell. (不能写成 The names were both difficult to pronounce and spell.)

💬 这些名字很难发音，也很难拼写。(陈玉玲和王明杰译)

例 9-77 We recorded the difference between the performance of subjects that completed the first task and the performance of subjects that completed the second task. (不能写成 We recorded the difference between the performance of subjects that completed the first task and the second task.)

💬 我们记录完成第一次工作受试者的表现和第二次工作受试者的表现之间的差异。(陈玉玲和王明杰译)

例 9-78 The following activities can be done at the mall: buying groceries, eating lunch, and paying bills. (注意 paying bills 不能用 bill payment 代替)

💬 购物中心可以进行以下活动：买杂货、吃午饭和付账单。

例 9-79 The patient's symptoms were weakness, fatigue, fever, dizziness, and headache. (注意不能将个别名词更换为形容词，如 weakness, dizziness 不能更换为 weak, dizzy)

💬 患者的症状是体虚、疲倦、发烧、头晕和头痛。

例 9-80 The influence of the mother on the offspring, statistics, is represented by counting, measuring, describing, tabulating, ordering, and the taking of censuses – all of which led to modern descriptive statistics. (注意不能将个别动名词更换为名词，如 counting, measuring, describing 不能更换为 count, measurement, description)

💬 母亲（上文提到的政府机关的有序记录）对其后代（统计学）的影响表现

为记数、测量、描述、列表、排序及人口普查，所有这些都导致了现代描述统计学的产生。(马锦儒等译)

例 9-81 Formerly, science was taught by the textbook method; now it is taught by the laboratory method. (注意后半句不能更换为 while now the laboratory method is employed)

[译] 以前，科学是用教科书方法教的，现在则是用实验室方法教的。

例 9-82 Comfortably fixed Americans were going without, making things last longer, sharing things with others, learning to do thing for themselves and so on. (并列的个别动名词不能换作动词不定式，如 making things last longer 不能改为 to make things last longer)

[译] 舒适安逸的美国人将就度日，延用旧物，与他人合用物品，学着自己做事等等。(马锦儒等译)

例 9-83 That is why women remain children their whole life long; never seeing anything but what is quite close to them, sticking fast to the present moment, taking appearance for reality, and preferring trifles to matters of the first importance. (并列的个别动名词不能换作动词不定式，如 taking appearance for reality 不能改为 to take appearance for reality)

[译] 这就是为什么女人一生都不成熟，只看到身边的事物，固守眼前事物，把表面现象视为本质，宁捡西瓜不要西瓜。(马锦儒等译)

例 9-84 The participants were told to make themselves comfortable, to read the instructions, and to ask about anything they did not understand. (不定式不能换成从句，如 to ask about anything they did not understand 不能改为 that they should ask about anything they did not understand.)

[译] 研究者告诉参与者可以放松地作答，先阅读指导语，然后有斜体不懂的地方都可以发问。(陈玉玲和王明杰译)

但是，how 引导的从句可与名词并列。

例 9-85 We will attempt to delineate the problems of education in developing nations and how coordinated efforts can address them in economical ways.

[译] 我们将试图描述发展中国家的教育问题，以及如何协调行动以经济方式来解决这些问题。

英语与汉语不同，英语造句主要采用形合法，多使用关联词或过渡词。句子之间不能仅靠意思前后排列，多数情况下需要用连接词编织或组织起来，使段落和篇章的意思通顺、连贯。连接词反映前后句子或主从句之间的逻辑关系，是句子之间逻辑关系的信号或线索，对于读者对文章的理解至关重要。如果省略必要的关联词或过渡词会使逻辑不明、行文不畅。同样值得注意的是，连接词不能滥用（如有的人满篇满纸都是 however 和 moreover），也不能乱用（如表示并列或增补关系的连词 and 与表示转折关系的连词 but 和 however 的混淆使用；此外，while 除表示 during the time that 引导时间状语从句外，与表示对比关系的连词 whereas，but，by contrast 用法类似，但通常不要代替 and 使用）。

　　语言啰唆、结构臃肿固然不好，但造句过于简略也会影响表达。要避免为了句子精练简洁而过度删除表明句法结构的词语如 that/which/who、am/is/are、the 等。上下文的关键词或中心词可适当重复或用代词指代，但如果缺少必要的重复或者代词指代就会影响连贯性，而使用代词过多过滥则会产生指代不明问题。利用 when 和 if 等引导的从句主语如果与主句主语相同时，从句中的主语可省略；但如果从句主语与主句主语不相同时，则不能省略从句主语。

　　此外，英语中还有歧义问题（意义不明确，可以有几种不同的解释或理解）需要引起重视。在"形容词+形容词+名词"、"形容词+名词+名词"、"形容词+名词所有格+名词"或"名词+名词+名词"结构中，因修饰关系不明或层次不清而引起歧义。在存在多个并列的被修饰语的情况下，前修饰语和后修饰语的修饰范围如果不加以明确限定，则会引起歧义。介词和介词短语、副词和副词短语在英语句子中的位置前面有一个以上的被修饰词，也会引起歧义。一般修饰语应紧邻中心词，而独立成分（修饰整个句子的成分）应位于句首，否则会引起歧义。在一个包含从句（如 because 引导的原因状语从句、when 引导的时间状语从句等）的否定句里，会因否定范围（否定从句或否定主句）难以确定而引起歧义。采取以下措施可以减少写作中出现的歧义现象：避免中心词与修饰它的从句或短语分隔，同时应将无关的短词分开，或者使用标点符号切分句子成分（尤其是并列成分和修饰语的范围）。歧义在一般的学术英语中尚不会产生太大问题，但在法律英语中，歧义则会引发诉讼。相关句子歧义内容可参阅威廉·斯特伦克（William Strunk）著《英语写作手册：风格的要素》、史蒂芬·平克（Steven Pinker）著、王烁和王佩译的《风格感觉：21世纪写作指南》与陶博（Preston M. Torbert）著，罗国强（Steel Rometius）编的《法律英语：中英双语法律文书中的句法歧义》，这里不再赘述。

中国作者写作易受汉语影响,会产生中式英语问题。琼·平卡姆(Joan Pinkham)在《中式英语之鉴(The Translator's Guide to Chinglish)》中提到中式英语最重要两个方面:一个方面是词语冗余,如不必要的名词和动词,不必要的修饰语,冗余的成对词语,同样的意思说两遍,用同样的名词多次重复提及同一件事等;另一个是中式英语的句子结构问题,如抽象名词泛滥成灾(noun plague),代词前面没有先行词或找不到对应的先行词,或者代词前面不只一个先行词,修饰短语或从句与被修饰的中心词相阻隔,修饰关系易被误解,由分词结构、不定式结构、动名词等造成悬垂修饰语问题,平行结构的形式错误,逻辑连接词的错误使用等。

第十单元
论文的写法

研究性论文的写作不仅仅是文稿的写作，实际上前期的论文选题、设计、构思也应考虑在内。以下就这3个方面进行介绍。

一、论文选题与设计

粗略来讲，论文的选题可能是来源于文献中遇到的理论问题，也可能是生产实践中遇到的技术及其原理问题；可能是前人已经研究过的问题，也可能是自我总结出来的问题。

问题可以粗略地分为新与旧，解决问题的技术和方法（或者所用的新材料包含在内）同样也可粗略地分为新与旧。论文选题在问题和技术方面可大致分为：①新技术解决新问题；②新技术解决老问题；③老技术解决新问题；④老技术解决老问题4类。其中以①和②最容易得出可发表的成果，③次之，④则难取得新成果。陈寅恪先生在《敦煌劫余录序》中说："一时代之学术，必有其新材料与新问题。取用此材料，以研求问题，则为此时代学术之新潮流。治学之士得预于此潮流者，谓之预流。其未得预者，谓之未入流。"他的话强调了学术研究中"新材料（我们这里说的新技术）"和"新问题"的重要性，只有利用新技术解决新问题（某种程度上是指学科前沿问题），才能跟上学术发展潮流，甚至引领学术发展潮流。除了新问题，如果你有新技术和好思路，那么选择经典的老问题（已解决或未完全解决的）也是很好的选题。如果解决得当，那也是可以写入教科书的成果。

不论问题新旧，选取一个重要的科学问题都是非常重要的，因为在很多情况下，取得成果的意义与解决的问题的重要性成正比。当然重要的科学问题往往也是学术研究中较难啃的"骨头"，解决的难度也比较大。爱因斯坦说："提出问题比解决问题更重要。"海森堡说："提出正确的问题，往往等于解决了问题的大半。"巴尔扎克说："打开一切科学的钥匙毫无异议的是问号。"陶行知也说："创造始于问题，有了问题才会思考，有了思考，才有解决问题的方法，才有找到独立思路的可能。"这些都说明提出问题的重要性。但是怎样才能提出问题呢？这就需要学者有足够的批判意识和问题意识。除了在生产实践中观察、调查获得问题外，在批判性地大量阅读文献的基础上才能提出别人想不到的问题。那什么是好问题呢？第一它是重要的，值得研究；第二它是可以用现有手段加以解决的，如果你的问题在现有的条件下无法解决，那也难以研究并产出可发表的成果。

此外，好的科学家要对新技术足够敏感，经常关注领域内外相关技术的发展，善于找到学科内或跨学科解决问题的新技术和新方法，这对科研选题也是至关重要的。多数情况下，解决一个问题，既需要传统的方法，也需要新出现的技术。因此，在实验设计上，就需要精读文献，借鉴前人的设计理念和考虑的因素，以期所得结果能与前人的结果进行比较分析。具体实验设计需要符合统计学分析的要求，如设置重复和对照，这对于结果可靠性的检验是至关重要的。

有了好的问题，还需要有具体的、可验证的科学假设，以及能够从多角度、多方法证实你提出的科学假设的实验步骤。好的问题只是一流成果的一半，另一半需要你的方法和证据能保证你的结果是靠得住的，是可以信服的。

二、论文构思

开展实验和论文写作实质上是生产知识的过程。这个过程就像拼图一样，将缺失的版图拼起来，或者像在断开的知识链条上补上缺失的一环。论文的构思就是要找到版图中缺失的部分或知识链条中缺失的那一环，然后提出自己的假说、猜想或主张，然后通过实验获得足够支持自己假说、猜想或主张的数据，从而将数据转化为知识，镶嵌到人类知识版图中，或接入人类知识的链条上。

有重要的问题，也有好的主张，还要有好的数据。所谓好的数据就是指能充分论证你主张的数据。通常获得的数据不可能全部应用于论文中，需要根据主张对数据进行整理，过滤无关的和无效的数据，然后选择有效数据整理成几组，每组数据作为一个模块，足以得出一个特定的论断。同时，要考虑这些模块之间的逻辑关系，如何在论文中恰当安排，使得这些模块得到的论断根据逻辑最终能证明所提出的主张或中心论点。

人们常说一篇好的论文就是能讲一个好的"故事（story）"。好的"故事"要求：第一要完整，有问题、有猜想、有数据，也有结论。这些要素一个不少。此外，数据是充分的，能够完全支持所提主张，足以获得一个确定的或相对确定的知识。如果实验数据太少，不足以得出一个确定性的结论，那就不是一个好的"故事"。第二要合理，就是故事合理，能自圆其说。整个论文的逻辑是自洽的，逻辑链条是坚实的，经得起检验和批判。第三要有亮点，科研贵在创新，故事需要高潮，论文需要亮点。不论是编辑，还是审稿人，对一篇平铺直叙、没有亮点的论文是打不起精神来的。初学者和写作高手之间的一个很大区别，就在于能否深入挖掘数据结果的亮点，并发现其对相关领域发展的意义。很多初学者在获得数据后，并不一定能识别出自己结果的亮点所在，主要原因是论文读得太少，对自己的数据把握不够。论文构思阶段就是要在熟读论文的基础上，知己知彼，找出自己数据的创新点，然后提炼成论文的亮点。亮点可能是提出了一个创新的概念，或者是开发出一种创新的技术。这个亮点需要在论文写作的不同部分（摘要、前言、结果、讨论与结论）加以突出和强调。

虽然说论文的选题与设计也可看作论文写作的一个要素，但真正写作时，论文却可能与原先设计的那种情况有所不同。因为实验结果不一定像当初设想的那样。如果实验结果与预期是一致的，那就根据论文的选题与设计思路来写作。如果获得的数据与设想不同甚至根本相反（数据是真实可靠的），那么就需要根据结果，量体裁衣，修改主张，重新查阅文献，重新选择问题和新的论述角度。通常在论文选题阶段需要根据问题进行查阅和综述文献，在获得数据之后也需要根据结果再进行论文查阅和阅读，以便更深入理解和把握获得的结果。之后根据结果进行构思论文的写作，考虑如何在导言切入研究问题和意义，如何组织数据，如何加以讨论等。

写作过程往往因人而异，有的人喜欢先写方法和结果（这些部分可以随着实验进程而及时总结和写作）后写其他部分，也有的人在对结果和结论胸有成竹的情况下，先写导言，然后是材料与方法、结果、讨论，最后再归纳结论和写作摘要。

三、论文写作

论文的写作语言要在精确性、逻辑性和清晰性上下功夫。这需要平时大量阅读专业领域的论文和专著，以及常年的写作训练才能做到。

好论文与差论文的区别在于批判性分析（critical analysis）。不能简单地说前人做过什么样的工作，而应比较你自己的工作与前人的工作，以及与前人工作之间的异同、强弱和高下。如果不能对前人工作进行批判性分析，就无法显示出你自己工作的创新性，编辑和审稿人可能会认为你的工作并不先进。

学术写作的一个重要衡量指标是能清楚地传达信息，让读者容易理解。一篇论文应该围绕中心贡献这一条逻辑线，所有的句子、段落和部分都应该串在或编织在这条线上，与此无关的句子、段落和部分都应该删除。在描述自己的工作时，不要简单地说做了什么，结果是什么，而应先交代你的目的是什么，采用什么手段，有时还需要说明为什么采用某种手段或方法。每一个段落只论述一个主题。句子尽可能直接、简短、结构简单。尽量减少从句、复合句和过渡词的使用，以便读者将注意力集中在主要信息上。

好的论文写作不仅仅是详细地提供所有信息，还应该强调重要的或创新的科研结果。同时，编辑和审稿人也希望明确地看到你的工作具有创新性。因此，作者要明确论文要传达的中心贡献和创新成果，并且围绕这一点来写作。这在论文写作之前的构思立意时就应该胸有成竹。同时，需要在摘要、前言(最后一段)、结果、讨论和结论中多次明确强调。如果不明确说明，他们可能就意识不到，或者认为不存在。

要注意平衡(balance)。重要的工作要分配更多的精力和时间来写，并在论文中占足够多的空间。同时，注意论述结果的正面和反面，以及方法的优点和缺点。

(一)标题

论文标题(title)一般采用名词结构(后有现在分词、过去分词或介词短语修饰)、动名词结构或介词结构，也有采用陈述句或疑问句作标题的。但不论是短语还是句子，标题都应表述简洁、清楚和完整。标题要避免使用不必要的词语，如 studies on, research on, investigation on, observation on, a study of, report on 等。标题 10~12 个字最好，这样概括性更强，给读者的印象更深，并容易被读者理解和记忆，而长的标题不易使读者抓住重点。

论文标题多用名词短语表示，但带动词的陈述句显得更为明确，有时采用疑问句作为标题(最常见于讨论最新进展的综述文章)则可提高下载量和被引量，如这样的标题"Binding or Hydrolysis? How Does the Strigolactone Receptor Work?"。要在标题中点出研究主题，最好能反映论文的重点发现或中心贡献。标题最好出现能检索到论文常用的关键词，这对于通过浏览器或搜索引擎寻找相关论文的潜在读者至关重要。标题还应突显论文的创新性，在表述上能保证在本领域与其他同类文章相区别，或能在同类文章标题中脱颖而出。论文标题最好能吸引更广泛的读者，尽可能不用公式、化学式、缩略语(除非已经为学界所熟知)和意义太狭窄或罕为人知的专业用语。尽可能避免使用系列论文标题，因为系列标题给人以零散和不完整的印象。

有些综述性论文既有主标题，也有副标题。一般主标题笼统概括，但具有共鸣性；副标题更具描述性和切合主题性。如这样的标题："Molecular Recognition: How Photosynthesis Anchors the Mobile Antenna？""Tuning the Orchestra: miRNAs in Plant Immunity" "Feeling the Heat: Searching for Plant Thermosensors"。

（二）摘要

摘要(abstract/summary)作为论文主要内容的概括，是独立于正文的一个部分。因此，研究性论文的摘要需尽可能概括论文各个要素(研究背景、或研究的问题、目的意义，主要研究方法，重要结果、结论)。背景部分用一两句概括论文涉及的研究领域及存在的问题和不足，然后是论文的研究目的及重要意义。方法部分可概括主要的或创新的方法，并且可以与结果一起论述。结果部分不宜赘述细节，而应主要阐述重要结果。最后是概括论文的结论，及对领域的意义。

由于摘要与标题都可以作为检索内容，并且是主编、审稿人和读者最先阅读的部分，所以要在摘要中包括标题中的关键词，还要做到行文简要，突出亮点，尽可能吸引读者。摘要中第一次出现的缩写要给出全称，物种要给出拉丁学名。避免出现公式、图表和参考文献(但也有一些期刊允许论文在摘要中征引参考文献的情况)。

已完成的观察、调查和研究用过去式，描述实验结果也可用过去式。陈述事实，以及对于不受时间影响的结论可用现在时。

关键词(keywords)应由论文正文内容选取，应为能够反映论文主要技术和中心内容的具有实质意义的词汇，可以是单词，也可以是词组，但不要使用缩略语和太过狭义的专业术语。

（三）前言

前言或引言(introduction)，有的期刊论文也称背景(background)。其作用是提供研究背景，使读者了解研究的领域、问题及前人所做的相关研究工作。一般在前言末尾还要对论文内容及研究意义进行概述。这部分内容要考虑吸引读者的阅读兴趣，要提供读者最关心的问题和背景信息。例如，为什么本文研究的问题很重要？研究解决了什么问题？使用了何种主要技术和方法？实验得到了哪些有意思的结果？研究结果对知识积累有什么推进？

前言一般遵循"漏斗形""倒三角形"或"倒金字塔"结构，也就是先从广泛的专业背景及研究领域介绍开始，通过批判性地综述相关研究进展，聚焦或收缩到本文所研究的问题及本文所提出的可检验假设上来。前言的目的：一是提供足够的背景信息，使读者理解论文选题的来源和意义，二是吸引读者来阅读全文。前言中提供的背景或领域过于狭窄，将会降低研究的意义，也会使更多读者失去阅读兴趣。此外，前言的各个层次要条理清楚，对研究领域由宽到窄进行介绍，然后对前人相关研究工作进行回顾和综述，最后识别出知识链条上缺失的那一环，也就是引出自己要解决的科学问题，再次是介绍论文对解决这个问题提出的假设和猜想。前言末尾可简要说明所采用的研究方法、所得出的结果和结论，以及本研究的意义和重要性。这样可使读者在前言中就能预先了解本文的主要结果和内容，既是对自己所做工作的第一次强调，也符合多数读者的阅读预期。

前言切忌对前人的研究工作和论著不加过滤，写成全面的综述，这样读者就不清楚与本文研究课题相关的重点背景内容。但是也不能过于简短，对前人的研究工作批判性论述不够，或引用文献不够，这样就对本文研究问题的选择难以给出坚实的理据。前言中"漏斗形"或"倒三角形"结构的顶点，或前言的中心点，是本文所研究的问题或目的。前言所有的语句都应与之有关，或为之服务。

前言对于研究背景目的和意义的一般性描述可用现在时，对于过去已完成工作的描述可用过去时。

(四) 材料与方法

材料与方法（materials and methods）部分主要描述具体的实验材料、方法和技术流程，使审稿人和编辑判断获得的结果是否合理、可靠、充分。这部分内容要提供足够的材料与技术细节，使其他研究者能够重复试验来验证本论文的实验结果，或借用于别的研究。如果方法为自己独创，前人未报道，要详细描述实验细节和实验条件，确保别人可以重复。如果使用别人的方法，只需提供方法出处即可。如果对前人的方法进行了改进，则需详细说明改进之处。关键的仪器和实验用品需要提供详尽的商标名称、型号、制造商、产地等信息。复杂的方法可利用详细的图表辅助说明。

材料与方法和结果之间通常存在一定的对应关系，因为一般一种方法会产生一组结果。这部分通常需要根据所用的不同方法分为几个小节来进行写作，每个小节设置一个标题。小节按实验前后顺序进行安排。每个小节按照实验步骤写作。每节前面要说明具体的实验目的和为获得何种结果，采用了何种方法。

材料和方法部分主要采用被动语态进行描述，描述的重点是材料与方法，而不是实验者。对已完成动作用过去时，对一般的方法和原理的描述采用现在时。

(五)结果

结果(results)部分主要用于描述论文所得的结果。结果部分通常利用图表结合文字描述来详细说明实验取得的结果。文字表述要清晰、简洁、适当,再配合精美醒目的图表,才能引起读者的兴趣。不是所有实验结果都放在论文中,只有那些对中心结论有直接支持作用的数据呈现在结果中,而非直接支持的数据或大量原始数据放入附件,上传到特定网站或数据库(论文需要提供链接)。

结果部分根据达到中心结论的逻辑步骤或获得的不同阶段或不同方面的实验结论而划分成小节,每一节叙述一组相关的实验结果。每一段以简短地介绍实验目的或实验背景开始,然后介绍结果。具体数据或结果宜采用图表顺序呈现,文字部分应提及主要结果,简要解释其变化趋势和数据意义。结果不应提及详细的实验方法(这部分应放在材料与方法),也不应进行冗长的解释、推测和与前人结果的比较(这部分应该放在讨论中)。

图表应根据呈现目的和要求来选择。当突出精确的数字结果时,可采用表的形式,表一般采用三线表格;散点图可用以表示变量之间的关联;饼状图可用以比较不同部分的数量和比例。当反映不同处理的对比情况及动态化趋势时,可分别采用柱状图和线状图,因为柱状图(条形图)着重于独立项目或处理之间的对照,线状图或折线图突出趋势,通常是随时间推移出现的趋势。如果呈现直观的形态、结构和位置,那就用不同精度的照片来呈现。为了说明某种原理或流程,可采用示意图来呈现。图表可直观地呈现论文结果,是读者和审稿人极看重的部分,因此,很大程度上,图表的制作水平和精美程度决定文章能否被接受发表。

图表应具有自明性,也就是说可不依赖正文而独立存在,或者说读者只看图表,不看正文,即可获得比较完整的信息。图表的标题和注解要详细而完整。目前,一般采用一组图表呈现一个结果,图表标题虽然简洁,但注释必须详细。数据的统计信息应包含图表中,并在文字部分中解释统计结果。显微图要提供标尺,并用箭头标出关键位置或部位;示意图要借助文字,形象地展示主要特征、动作或过程;坐标图要给出坐标轴恰当的单位和图示。图表注解中要详细说明各项目处理名称、表中采用的缩写和统计分析符号等。

由于结果为过去的实验获得或观察所得,因此结果报道一般采用过去式。也就是说,观察结果、已完成的行为及过去特定结论的描述采用过去时;普遍认可的概念和观点、不受时间限制的结论和一般性信息描述采用现在时。

(六)讨论

讨论(discussion)主要引用参考文献，对结果进行解释、比较、分析和评价，回应是否解决前言所设定的问题，总结和归纳出论文的结论，并指出其理论和实践重要性。如果有意外的发现或研究存在局限性，也应一并指出。

这一部分的总体结构与前言相反。前言为"倒三角形"或"倒金字塔"结构，从总体到特殊；而讨论则采用"三角形"或"金字塔"结构，由特殊到一般。也就是说，讨论通过对具体问题的解答，解释研究结果对未知方面或相关领域的适用性，得出一般性的结论，并指出该结论对领域总体的重要性。

如果内容包含多个方面，可分节讨论，每节设置相应的标题。讨论部分不需要重复前言和结果内容和语句，但要在开始用一两句话简述研究目的或背景，再简述主要研究结果和关键发现点。讨论首先要回答是否解答了前言中设定的问题，然后对主要结果进行解释和分析，与前人的发现比较异同及分析其原因。讨论部分要使读者明确哪些工作是作者的工作，哪些工作是别人的工作，不要令自己的工作埋没在一大堆参考文献之中，要重点突出自己的创新发现，同时也要对论文提供的支持性证据进行解释说明。如果自己的发现与前人发现存在分歧，要客观公正地讨论支持或反驳的意见。讨论要针对主要结果进行，不需要针对所有结果进行讨论，更不要对结果部分未提到过的任何数据进行讨论。对于归纳得出的复杂结论或在证据基础上提出的假说模型，可用示意图加以辅助说明。

需要指出的是，讨论应该指出本研究的局限性和未解决的问题，对于一些阴性结果、非预期结果、结果的不可靠性也不应予以回避。实事求是地去论述和评价自己的结果和发现是对学术共同体的一种负责任的态度，这些不足的地方既可能是作者未来努力的方向，也可能孕育其他研究者更好的实验设计和新的研究主题。

讨论的最后一段应提出一般性的结论及其对本领域的意义。但结论不是罗列结果，而是论文的主张或总论点，也就是根据论文结果得出了什么普遍性观点。结论部分要说明揭示了何种原理或规律，或者适用于什么样的生产、实践或实验，论文成果具有哪些的理论价值或应用意义。如果有尚未解决的问题或有待深入研究的方面也可在这部分加以说明。

在语态上可采用 we 和 our 等来突出自己的主张和发现。过去完成的行为采用过去时，不受时间限制的一般性陈述(结论和意义等)可采用现在时。

(七)参考文献

学术文章需要参考和引用文献（references/literature），其原因在于：第一，自己的研究不可能前所未有，总是在前人研究工作的基础上开展的，因此，参考和引用文献，表示对前人工作的认可；第二，对论文中提到的事实、信息、资料和观点要提供其来源，提高论文陈述的可靠性和准确性；第三，引述文献进行讨论和论述，不管是支持和拓展，还是反对和纠正，都可将自己的研究置于整个研究系统中，使自己的成果融入整个知识系统和知识链条中去；第四，便于论文读者追踪研究的前因和后果、历史和进展。由于文献浩繁，可以使用 EndNote、RefWorks、Zotero 等软件对文献进行搜集和管理。

除公知公认的常识无须注明出处外，引用他人的任何概念、思想、数据、资料、结果和结论都应注明出处。直接引用原话要加引号，总结或改写相关内容不加引号，但要标出相应的参考文献。在主题概述方面，可引用第二次文献或第三次文献(综述论文和专著等)，但在关键结果介绍、评价、论证(证实或反驳)方面最好引用最重要的、最新的和最高水平的第一次文献(研究性论文)。引用参考文献应确保引用的文献准确无误，要避免模糊引用，务必读过所有引用的文献。正文中引用文献不一定都置于句尾，而是根据不同文献的内容而置于相应的句中或句尾位置。文献征引和参考文献的排列格式要根据期刊格式进行设定和调整。

一般而言，应避免将网上信息作为参考文献。原因是：网络信息很多没有可确定的作者、出版方或提供方，不具有足够的权威性和可靠性；有时，多个网站都有类似内容，无法辨识那个网站的内容具有原创性和可靠性。此外，网络内容随时可修改和变动，而且网上信息是通过 URL 来定位，而 URL 随时都可能消失或屏蔽，因此，无法提供长久有效的参考。

参考文献著录方法有顺序编码制和著者—出版年制两种。顺序编码制是将参考文献按照其在正文中出现的先后顺序，以阿拉伯数字连续编码。某一文献如果被多次反复引用，在正文中仍用同一序号标注。著者—出版年制是指在参考文献按照作者姓氏的英文字母顺序排列，第一个字母相同的，按第二个字母顺序排列，第二个字母也相同的，按第三个字母顺序排列，以此类推。正文征引时在标注位置用"(著者姓氏，出版年)"标出。需要注意的是，两种著录体制不能混用，且不同期刊即便采用同一种著录体制，仍然会有很多不同，需要作者参照期刊最新格式加以调整。有的期刊需要将参考文献中的作者全部列出，有的则要求只列前三位名前五位或前十位，后面省略的作者名用"et al."代替。

四、论文修改与写作水平的提高

"好论文是改出来的",这句话千真万确。所谓"玉不琢不成器",一篇论文如果不精心修改,很难达到文从字顺、妥帖自然、精确晓畅。在取得一批实验数据后,应根据结果来确定论文写作的思路,也就是确定从哪种角度来写才能凸显实验结果的创新性和重要性。有时,在写出论文初稿后,经权衡比较,确定当下的写作思路不是最优,就需要推倒重来。同时,论文要保证逻辑性强,清晰易懂,这就需要在段落安排、语句组织、图表设计等方面推敲修改。如果有足够的时间,最好在论文初稿完成后,放置一段时间,然后再回头细细修改。修改时,首先利用 Word 软件自带的检查拼写功能,纠正单词拼写错误,然后修改语法错误(如名词的单复数、定冠词和不定冠词的使用错误,主谓语之间的照应错误,句子不完整,句子的标点符号和连词错用等),再看简洁、清晰和逻辑问题(存在冗词冗句,句子过渡不自然,句子前后安排不合逻辑等)。修改完后,最好朗读两遍,检查句子是否通顺及用词是否妥贴。有些错误和不足自己可能一下子看不出来。如果有条件的话,也可请其他人帮助审读并提出修改意见。在论文投稿之前,还要保证论文符合所投期刊格式。

论文的写作水平取决于论文的阅读和范围。不会读论文,或者论文读得少,就写不出好的论文。论文的阅读和写作是输入和输出之间的关系。平时多阅读好的论文,从写作的角度分析论文各部分的结构,琢磨其写作方法,领会作者措词、造句、绘图、行文的用意,日积月累,写作水平自然就会提高。初学者应该在精读和泛读论文的基础上,归纳总结论文各个部分(如摘要、前言、结果、讨论和结论)和各种功能(如描述研究的背景、目的和主题,提出假说,引证观点,列举证据,陈述结果,分析结果,描述研究结果与前人一致或不一致,指出研究的创新与不足,给出原因和建议,总结结论,描述成果应用前景和意义等)常用的高频词汇和句型模式,以便在写作中加以模仿使用。例如,表示研究目的常用表达词汇和句型有:To / In order to assay / evaluate / measure / test / examine / investigate / address / characterize / determine ⋯, This analysis / study / research / investigation / paper / article attempts to/aims to (at) ⋯, The purpose / objective / goal / aim of the article / paper / study / research is to ⋯;表示研究结果的常用表达词汇和句型有:We describe

/ compare / emphasize / present / provide / report / introduce / demonstrate / reveal / establish / characterize / define / determine / recognize / prove …, The study / research /analysis of … shows / suggests / indicates / reveals / demonstrates / establishes / proves that …；报道前人做出的工作或提出的观点经常用到的表达有：Author reported / found / noted / suggested / revealed / proved / concluded / proposed / claimed / presumed / argued / assumed that …。

  论文写作是一项技能。凡是技能，都需要在不断的实践中提高。对于作文而言，苏轼在《孙莘老识欧阳文忠公》(又名《记六一语》)曾提到欧阳修对于如何写好文章的建议。欧阳修说："无它术，唯勤读书而多为之，自工。"又说："疵病不必待人指摘，多作自能见之"。也就是说，只有多读论文，并且勤于写作，才能写好论文。只有写的多了，文章的毛病自己就能看出来。

  还需要指出，论文能否发表在顶级期刊，能否产生巨大影响，写作水平只是一个方面，更重要的是文章的内容，也就是文章是否解决了重要的理论或生产问题，是否推进了人类的认识进程，是否对人类知识增量有所贡献。萧统在《文选序》中说文章应"以立意为宗"，王夫之《姜斋诗话》有言"无论诗歌与长行文字，俱以意为主。意犹帅也，无帅之兵，谓之乌合。"这些都说明文章内容比写作技巧还要重要。

参考文献

阿兰·德波顿, 2010. 工作颂歌[M]. 袁洪庚, 译. 上海: 上海译文出版社.

阿兰·德波顿, 2014. 写给无神论者[M]. 梅俊杰, 译. 上海: 上海译文出版社.

埃里克·阿约, 2017. 人文学科学术写作指南[M]. 陈鑫, 译. 北京: 新华出版社.

爱德华·古本, 2012. 企鹅口袋书系列·伟大的思想: 基督徒与罗马之陷落(第3辑)(英汉双语)[M]. 刘怡, 译. 北京: 中国对外翻译出版有限公司.

安东尼·斯托尔, 2008. 弗洛伊德与精神分析[M]. 尹莉, 译. 北京: 外语教学与研究出版社.

安吉利卡·H·霍夫曼, 2012. 科技写作与交流: 期刊论文、基金申请书及会议讲演[M]. 任胜利、莫京、安瑞、刘徽, 译. 北京: 科学出版社.

包惠南, 2001. 文化语境与语言翻译[M]. 北京: 中国对外翻译出版公司.

波玲·理查德森, 2018. 英语常见错误辨析: 理查德森帮中国人学英语[M]. 徐冬梅译. 北京: 商务印书馆.

伯纳德·伍德, 2016. 人类进化简史[M]. 冯兴无, 译. 北京: 外语教学与研究出版社.

陈全根, 2015. 英文复合句——开启阅读和写作的钥匙[M]. 北京: 中国书籍出版社.

《读者文摘》编辑部, 2013. 读《读者文摘》学英文·智者的话(英汉对照)[M]. 高瑞武, 等译. 南京: 译林出版社.

达子, 2011. 读懂天下事——环球周刊[M]. 哈尔滨: 黑龙江科学技术出版社.

戴维·科廷顿, 2008. 走近现代艺术[M]. 朱扬明, 译. 北京: 外语教学与研究出版社.

戴维·诺曼, 2008. 恐龙探秘[M]. 史立群, 译. 北京: 外语教学与研究出版社.

迪伦·埃文斯,2007. 解读情感[M]. 石林,译. 北京:外语教学与研究出版社.

范武邱,2011. 科技翻译能力拓展研究[M]. 北京:国防工业出版社.

冯志杰,1998. 汉英科技翻译指要[M]. 北京:中国对外翻译出版公司.

傅敬民,张顺梅,薛清,2005. 英汉翻译辨析[M]. 北京:中国对外翻译出版公司.

高健,2012. 枕边书与床头灯——英美随笔译粹[M]. 上海:上海译文出版社.

何凯文,2012. 考研英语阅读同源外刊时文精析[M]. 北京:中国时代经济出版社.

何远秀,2011. 英汉常用修辞格对比研究[M]. 成都:西南交通大学出版社.

亨利·塞德尔·坎比,2019. 耶鲁写作课[M]. 范斌珍,祝欣,译. 南京:江苏凤凰科学技术出版社.

洪班信,2008. 英语医学论文及摘要写作[M]. 北京:北京大学医学出版社.

胡曙中,2011. 现代英语修辞学[M]. 上海:上海外语教育出版社.

黄任,1996. 英语修辞与写作[M]. 上海:上海外语教育出版社.

黄闯,2008. 英汉妙语佳句赏析[M]. 北京:中国城市出版社.

凯特·L·杜拉宾,2015. 芝加哥大学论文写作指南[M]. 雷蕾,译. 北京:新华出版社.

康妮娜,2007. 试论悬垂分词的逻辑主语[J]. 浙江万里学院学报,20(3):68−71.

拉尔夫·M. 麦克伦尼,D. G. 哈特,2015. 学科入门指南:哲学·宗教学[M]. 孙喆,译. 杭州:浙江大学出版社.

蓝纯,2010. 修辞学:理论与实践[M]. 北京:外语教学与研究出版社.

李定坤,1994. 汉英辞格对比与翻译[M]. 武汉:华中师范大学出版社.

李继燕,李杰,庄会彬,2018. 英文写作的要素与实践[M]. 汕头:汕头大学出版社.

李旻,2019. 英文论文核心写作精讲[M]. 长沙:中南大学出版社.

李少如,1992. 英汉对照医学读物:生理学[M]. 上海:上海科学技术出版社.

李铁刚,孙艳华,2001. 读点科技[M]. 上海:上海科技教育出版社.

刘进平，2018. 英语阅读理解科技英语翻译和 SCI 论文写作技巧[M]. 北京：中国林业出版社.

刘宓庆，2019. 新编当代翻译理论[M]. 北京：中译出版社.

刘园丽，2018. 大学学术英语写作研究[M]. 北京：中国水利水电出版社.

龙璐，金晓琳，王霞，2016. 悦读英语看世界——科技趣闻篇[M]. 杭州：浙江大学出版社.

罗伯特·A·西格尔，2008. 神话理论[M]. 刘象愚，译. 北京：外语教学与研究出版社.

罗伊·彼得·克拉克，2018. 精简写作[M]. 黄筠，译. 北京：中国华侨出版社.

马丁，2015. 科技论文成功发表的技巧[M]. 北京：清华大学出版社.

马锦儒，范淑芹，张现彬，2003. 高级百科读物英汉对照 50 篇[M]. 上海：上海外语教育出版社.

玛格丽特·沃特斯著、朱刚和麻晓蓉译，2015. 女权主义简史[M]. 朱刚，麻晓蓉，译. 北京：外语教学与研究出版社.

毛荣贵，2000. 每天多"活"一小时：英汉对照 50 篇短文[M]. 上海：上海交通大学出版社.

毛荣贵，2003. 英译汉技巧新编[M]. 北京：外文出版社.

毛荣贵，1998. 英语写作纵横谈[M]. 上海：上海外语教育出版社.

美国心理协会，2008. 美国心理协会写作手册[M]. 陈玉玲，王明杰，译. 重庆：重庆大学出版社.

彭发胜，2016. 每天 5 分钟，忙里偷闲读英语散文[M]. 北京：外语教学与研究出版社.

琼·平卡姆（Joan Pinkham），2000. 中式英语之鉴（The Translator's Guide to Chinglish）[M]. 北京：外语教学与研究出版社.

乔治·奥威尔，2008. 我为什么写作[M]. 刘沁秋，赵勇，译. 南京：南京大学出版社.

秦荻辉，李滔，2016. 学术论文写作英语惯用法[M]. 西安：西安电子科技大学出版社.

秦荻辉，2001. 实用科技英语写作技巧[M]. 上海：上海外语教育出版社.

任怀平，李玉军，1995. 英语写作能力提高[M]. 上海：上海交通大学出版社.

沈国威, 2019. 一名之立 旬月踟蹰：严复译词研究[M]. 北京：社会科学文献出版社.

史蒂芬·平克, 2018. 风格感觉：21世纪写作指南[M]. 王烁, 王佩, 译. 北京：机械工业出版社.

束金星, 徐玉娟, 2000. 英语"悬垂结构"刍议[J]. 江苏理工大学学报, （社会科学版）, （6）：66-69.

斯旺, 2010. 牛津英语用法指南[M]. 严维明, 等译. 北京：外语教学与研究出版社.

孙骊, 1997. 英语写作[M]. 上海：上海外语教育出版社.

谭美云, 2008. 从句法角度看英语歧义结构[J]. 管理观察, 12：184-185.

谭卫国, 2004. 英语背诵范文精华[M]. 2版. 上海：华东理工大学出版社.

陶博（Preston M. Torbert）著, 罗国强（Steel Rometius）编, 2008. 法律英语：中英双语法律文书中的句法歧义[M]. 上海：复旦大学出版社.

特里·伊格尔顿, 2012. 牛津通识读本：人生的意义[M]. 朱新伟, 译. 北京：凤凰出版传媒股份有限公司, 译林出版社.

托马斯·赫胥黎, 2011. 天演论[M]. 严复, 译. 南京：译林出版社.

王蓝, 1997. 英译汉误差辨析[M]. 合肥：安徽科学技术出版社.

王晓军, 孟凡艳, 孟庆梅, 庄冬文, 2014. 英语修辞学[M]. 济南：山东人民出版社.

王炤, 2011. 英语名篇诵读与赏析[M]. 北京：北京大学出版社.

威廉·斯特伦克, 2016. 英语写作手册：风格的要素[M]. 北京：外语教学与研究出版社.

吴中东, 宫玉波, 2014. 记录人类文明的那些美文：英文[M]. 北京：中国人民大学出版社.

西蒙·克里奇利, 2005. 解读欧陆哲学[M]. 江怡, 译. 上海：上海译文出版社.

闫文培, 2008. 实用科技英语翻译要义[M]. 北京：科学出版社.

严忠志, 2001. 读点哲学[M]. 上海：上海科技教育出版社.

颜元叔, 2001. 现代经典英文散文选[M]. 广州：广东人民出版社出版.

杨自伍, 1995. 英国散文名篇欣赏[M]. 上海：上海外语教育出版社.

杨自伍, 1996. 英国文化选本（上、下）[M]. 上海：华东师范大学出版社.

杨自伍, 2017. 英语诵读菁华（大学卷）[M]. 上海：上海外语教育出版社.

杨自伍，1998. 英语诵读菁华（研究生卷）[M]. 上海：上海外语教育出版社.
余莉，陈洁，梁永刚，2015. 学术英语写作[M]. 上海：清华大学出版社.
约翰·平德，2009. 欧盟概览[M]. 戴炳然，译. 北京：外语教学与研究出版社.
詹姆斯·富尔彻，2013. 资本主义/牛津通识读本[M]. 张罗，陆赟，译. 南京：凤凰出版传媒股份有限公司，译林出版社.
张俊东，杨亲正，国防，2016. SCI 论文写作和发表：You Can Do It[M]. 2版. 北京：化学工业出版社.
张梅岗，1998. 科技英语修辞[M]. 长沙：湖南科学技术出版社.
张培成，2016. 汉英对比与英语学习[M]. 北京：北京大学出版社.
周华，李慧杰，秦怡，2016. 英语名篇诵读与赏析[M]. 北京：经济科学出版社
周瑞英，2012. 高级英语常用修辞格赏析[M]. 北京：中国农业科学技术出版社.
卓言英语工作室，2014. 读新闻学科技生活英语[M]. 北京：中国水利水电出版社.
Ferguson D W, 2018. 我可能学的是假英语：英语、中式英语和偏误英语[M]. 周雅芳，译. 北京：石油工业出版社.
Hartl D L, Jones E W, 2001. Genetics：Analysis of Genes and Genomes[M]. 5th ed. Jones and Bartlett Publishers, Inc.
J. 艾伦·霍布森，2008. 梦的新解[M]. 韩芳，译. 北京：外语教学与研究出版社.
Nelson G, Greenbaum S, 2016. An Introduction to English Grammar[M]. 4th ed. London and New York：Routledge.
Terence, Graham, 2011. The Cell：A Very Short Introduction[M]. Oxford：Oxford University Press.
Williams J M, Bizup J, 2014. Style lessons in clarity and grace[M]. 11th ed. Pearson.